# Singing in the Saddle

# Singing
# in the Saddle

## The History
## of the Singing Cowboy

*Douglas B. Green*

*The Country Music Foundation Press*
*& Vanderbilt University Press*

NASHVILLE

Published by Vanderbilt University Press and the
Country Music Foundation Press.

This book is printed on acid-free paper.
Manufactured in the United States of America
Text design by Dariel Mayer

Library of Congress Cataloging-in-Publication Data

Green, Douglas B.
Singing in the saddle : the history of the singing cowboy /
Douglas B. Green.— 1st ed.
    p. cm.
Includes bibliographical references (p.    ) and index.
    ISBN 0-8265-1412-X (alk. paper)
    1.  Country musicians—United States—Biography.
2. Motion picture actors and actresses—United States—Biography.
3. Cowboys—Songs and music—History and criticism.  I. Title.

ML400 .G73 2002
781.642'0973—dc21

                                    2002006639

*Frontispiece:* The Sons of the Pioneers sing "Blue Shadows on the Trail"
in Walt Disney's *Melody Time* (1948). *From left:* Tim Spencer, Lloyd
Perryman, Hugh Farr, Bob Nolan, and Pat Brady. (Author's collection)

*For James D. Green Jr.*

# Contents

# Illustrations

# Acknowledgments

The first thing I must acknowledge is that in my day job, I am Ranger Doug, singer, guitarist, yodeler, actor, and songwriter with Riders In The Sky. I can only promise that I have done my best to be objective in presenting this history; I await the judgment of future historians as to whether I have succeeded.

Like any history, this work owes an enormous amount to a number of people who contributed greatly to my research, many of whom worked tirelessly in my behalf. First, of course, the Vanderbilt University Press and the Country Music Foundation Press deserve my deepest thanks for believing in this project from the start, in particular, Chris Dickinson at the CMF Press and the elegant and enthusiastic copy editing of Bobbe Needham.

Several others on the staff of the Country Music Foundation Library and Media Center were also very generous with their time and encouragement, including Kent Henderson, Paul Kingsbury, Bob Pinson, Ronnie Pugh, John Rumble, and Alan Stoker. Likewise, the archival staff at the Autry Museum of Western History was extremely gracious: Leah Arroyo and Kevin Mulroy. Gene Autry's office, in the persons of Karla Buhlman, Alex Gordon, and Maxine Hansen, was also very generous with time, advice, information, encouragement, and photographs. Anne Bower's careful and creative indexing has greatly enhanced the usefulness of the text. And in this book's darkest hour, Betsy Phillips, Erin McVay, Dariel Mayer, and Polly Law Rembert at the Vanderbilt University Press rode in on silver stallions to save the day. I truly cannot be more grateful!

A number of music and film scholars, and some friends, worked very hard on my behalf as well, providing great information as well as correcting errors in fact and interpretation, and giving encouragement. These include Sherry Bond, Dave Bourne, B. Jerry Campbell, Bobby Copeland, Don Cusic,

Ann Marie Flores, Les Gilliam, Fred Goodwin, Larry Hopper, Rick Huff, Bill and Mary Jacobson, Guy Logsdon, Elizabeth MacDonald, O. J. Sikes, Hal Spencer, Lillian Turner, and Johnny Western. Bobby Copeland and Larry Hopper were particularly diligent in fact checking, and my gratitude to them knows no bounds.

The conscientious historian realizes full well that he simply builds upon the foundation prepared by others. This work is a compilation of information from widely disparate sources, but it could not exist without the careful earlier work of a number of fine amateur and professional historians, some of whom are dear friends, some complete strangers. I cannot offer enough thanks to the inspiration and diligent research and often excellent writing of Jonathan Guyot Smith, Jon Tuska, Guy Logsdon, Bill C. Malone, Laurence Zwisohn, Ken Griffis, Bobby Copeland, Boyd Magers, O. J. Sikes, Charlie Seemann, David Rothel, Charles K. Wolfe, Buck Rainey, and many others. Their knowledge, their hard work, and their passion for music and film were a constant source of inspiration.

And it is impossible to contemplate acknowledgments without thanking the singing cowboys themselves. Without their inspiration there would be no book of this sort, no wide-eyed kid who grew to adulthood still enthralled with the music and the vision of the West. Gene and Roy and Tex were my heroes, of course, this goes without saying, and the Sons of the Pioneers were my first—and remained the greatest—musical influence; "Cool Water" is the first piece of recorded music I remember from my childhood. To know these men seemed an impossible dream, yet I discovered as an adult that they were gracious, intelligent, thoughtful people who were quite conscious and proud of the tradition they had created, and who were more than happy to see it carried on. Many took considerable time to answer questions from this wide-eyed kid: Fred Scott, Jimmy Wakely, Eddie and Dearest Dean, Bob and Clara "P-Nuts" Nolan, Buck Page, Lloyd and Violet Perryman, Red River Dave, Merle Travis, Patsy Montana, Rex Allen, Foy Willing. Some—Ray and Kay Whitley, Johnny and Dorothy Bond, Wesley and Marilyn Tuttle, Ken and Gretchen Carson—became, despite a generation's difference in age, real friends. Thank you all.

Finally, in a work of such length and breadth mistakes are bound to occur, despite my finest efforts. I take full responsibility for all errors of fact, and indeed I welcome any comments or corrections, which may be addressed to me personally at 1921 Broadway, Nashville, TN, 37203.

# Introduction

If there can be said to be a defining moment in the long history of the singing cowboy, it may well be during the 1948 Walt Disney feature-length cartoon *Melody Time,* a collection of short segments. The bulk of one of these segments related the wholly fabricated legend of Pecos Bill, portrayed as a lanky cowpoke long on brawn and short on brains, and featured his horse, Widow Maker, "the horse that couldn't be rode" (as Bill was "the cowboy who couldn't be thrown"), fiercely loyal to Bill and savage to the rest of civilization. Rounding out the trio was Slew Foot Sue, blonde and lovely in buttons, bows, and bustles, the only living thing that Bill came to love more than Widow Maker.

As the action unfolds to the rousing Johnny Lange–Eliott Daniel song "(There'll Never Be Another) Pecos Bill," a quiet moment occurs near the end of the segment in which real life intrudes on cartoon mayhem. As the adorable cartoon beasts of the forest and desert look on in curiosity and rapture, and the sun sets in brilliant magentas, purples, and indigos rarely found in nature, a handsome, squint-eyed cowboy sits with a group of trail hands around a flickering campfire. Roy Rogers is dressed less vividly than in some of his films, but he still wears beautifully tailored and embroidered western clothes, replete with short fringe. The Sons of the Pioneers gather close to add their impeccable harmony, dressed with less élan but still well tailored in clothing more suitable for a square dance than for a night serenading the coyotes under the stars.

Roy sings a couple of introductory lines extolling the beauty of the gathering night, then is joined in lush four-part harmony in "Blue Shadows on the Trail," gorgeous and immaculate in its tight phrasing and beautifully controlled dynamics, both melody and lyrics (again by Lange and Daniel), a hymn to the timeless beauty of the western landscape. It is a romantic scene, and the lover is the West itself. A moving set piece, it features a group of friends, untouched by worldly concern, singing about their loves: the desert, the sunset, and the West.

And at the same time it is as insubstantial as moonbeams, straight from Hollywood, that land of dreams and illusions, and cuts straight to our deepest fantasies, heedless of reality and fact. This should not be and is not surprising. Documentaries excluded, the film industry has from the first been dedicated to touching hearts, entertaining, and manipulating feelings. This indeed is ultimately why we plunk our money down at the box office, to escape reality and journey to a place and time that we cannot go to in our daily lives.

Why Hollywood and we placed such a peculiar burden of unreality on the cowboy is an interesting, even compelling, question, for along the way its answer encompasses much of the history of American entertainment, and indeed the way in which Americans view themselves. It is a colorful story, full of strong characters, gifted people, historical figures, twists of fate, colossal egos, and talented men and women with a little luck and a gift for creating or entertaining who have achieved recognition for awhile, leaving us with beautiful memories and music. It is the story ultimately not of individuals, of corporate politics, of stars and bands, of the commercialization of the cowboy and the plunder of the West, though all these things and many more will figure in. It is ultimately the story of the power of music in our lives, a power every gathering of humankind has acknowledged and reckoned with and celebrated.

For awhile, part of our civilization attached this enormous power of music to the myth of the cowboy, a perhaps unlikely but ultimately unforgettable union. How it happened is the journey that unfolds on the following pages.

# 1

# The Lure of the West

From the moment more than four hundred years ago that salt-sprayed and weary travelers arrived at the thin crescent of settlement on North America's shores, there was a West beyond the hills, beyond the sunset, a frontier that teased and excited and inflamed the imagination. For a century that West lay just beyond the raw and rugged Appalachians, tantalizing in its promise, unknown in its expanse, frightening in its prospect of cruel and semi-mythical savage man and beast.

The new nation, once consolidation was achieved, turned its eyes to expansion, and the hero-making process of the bold young United States, still tottering on unsteady legs like a newborn colt, turned from the military heroes of the Revolution to the bold and daring men of the frontier. The new Americans looked to the real and imagined exploits of Daniel Boone forging through the Cumberland Gap, and to the wholly fictional and largely implausible exploits of the first hero of what we might call western fiction, Natty Bumppo—the frontiersman, the deer slayer, the far larger-than-life emblem of the wilderness, the creation of James Fenimore Cooper.

From the earliest colonial times the settlers had brought with them their music, their books, their love of entertainment. Plays and concerts were common in colonial cities, while on the frontier the fiddle and the human voice were always portable companions for lonely nights. It was inevitable that all these arts, high and low, would eventually reflect the great obsession of the expanding nation: the western frontier.

Cooper's hero is not unlike many of the fictional westerners we'll meet in the coming pages in that he is slow to anger, wise in the ways of the land, a sure shot, and a peaceable man who rises to moments of great heroism only after extreme provocation, or to help those who cannot help themselves in the environment in which he is master.

Cooper's ponderous writing style and his ignorance of or willful violation of the laws of man and nature have been deservedly and mercilessly lampooned by Mark Twain and others through the years, but the public, eager to feed its hungry fantasy, willingly forgave errors in writing style, historical accuracy, and physics. It is a willingness the consumer of fiction shares to this day. The popularity of the singing cowboy has waxed and waned, it is true, but it could never have blossomed without this universal urge for novelty, for the romance of the frontier, for heroics beyond the pale of our diurnal lives, for heroes unfettered by the chains of historical accuracy or even of physical possibility.

Our young nation's insatiable demand for novelty, for fact and fiction portraying the frontier, was responsible for the success of the 1822 stage creation of Noah Ludlow, who wore buckskin and fur cap to sing Samuel Woodworth's song "The Hunters of Kentucky," celebrating the sharp-shooting frontiersmen who helped Andrew Jackson defeat the British in the Battle of New Orleans. Kentucky was, of course, the Wild West of that time, and for a time Daniel Boone and his exploits in opening Kentucky became a focal point of this growing national fascination with the West and its heroes. Historian Henry Nash Smith estimated that Timothy Flint's 1833 biography of Boone was "perhaps the most widely read book about a Western character during the first half of the nineteenth century."[1]

The frontier was again portrayed notably on stage in the 1831 James Kirke Paulding play titled *The Lion of the West*. Although the buckskin-clad hero was called Nimrod Wildfire (played to great acclaim by actor James Hackett), it was a clear and obvious portrayal, in sweeping and nearly wholly and wonderfully imaginary details, of the early life of David Crockett, member of the U.S. House of Representatives from the new state of Tennessee. A former scout and half-successful farmer, Crockett had succeeded in politics partly by creating this legend himself, boosting himself as "half-horse, half alligator, and a touch of snapping turtle," as able to "grin the bark off a hickory" as to outtalk and outsmart any opponent, bully, Indian, or politician.

As a member of Congress, Crockett eventually distanced himself from this hyperbole, but he did come to at least one District of Columbia performance of the play in 1833, where Hackett on the stage and Crockett in the audience bowed to each other to wild applause. Hackett went on to a long career performing the part; it never failed to rouse an audience, especially after Crockett died heroically defending the Alamo in 1836. Crockett's legend only continued to grow after his death, and in 1872 Frank Burdock and Frank Mayo exploited the frontier hero with a play called *Davy Crockett; or, Be Sure You're Right, Then Go Ahead,* with Mayo in the title role. The play ran for twenty-four years in America and Europe and ceased its run only with Mayo's death in 1896. Indeed, Crockett mania did not end there—some four films, the last a silent version of Burdock and Mayo's play, were released between 1909 and 1916.

The *Davy Crockett Almanac* (fictional to the heights of absurdity), volumes of which appeared both before and after Crockett's death, likewise was symptomatic of the eagerness of the public to devour any morsel describing the new frontier. The Louisiana Purchase of 1803 and Lewis and Clark's celebrated journey of 1805–1807 had already inflamed public interest in the West. The exploits of Jim Bridger and his fellow mountain men were yet another source of great curiosity.

The public's fascination with the West and the westerner did not focus only on white trailblazers. While the Native American was treated in famously shameful and shabby fashion by the swelling nation, the notion of the "noble savage" emerged as well, and Longfellow's *Hiawatha* and Alexander Pope's "An Essay on Man," with the lines "Lo, the poor Indian! whose untutor'd mind/Sees God in clouds, or hears him in the wind," were accepted as gospel by a generation of easterners and Europeans, while heartily mocked and scorned in the expanding West. A happier portrayal of the idylls of native life appeared in what we have come to think of as the first popular song written about the West—Marion Dix Sullivan's "Waters of the Blue Juniata," published in 1844:

> Wild roved an Indian maid,
> Bright Alfarata
> Where sweep the waters of
> The Blue Juniata.

This rollicking tune tells the tale of a happy Indian warrior stoutly plying his canoe "down the rapid river" on his journey to meet his love, the beautiful and bright Alfarata. There is no conflict, no tragedy, no struggle; it is a wilderness portrait of a young man in love, and a beautiful maiden who waits for him at the end of his journey. A love song, pure and simple.

The Juniata is a lovely stream in western Pennsylvania, which was the West of the time. More important is the song's romanticizing of the West, of life in the West, portraying a land of abundance far from the mad haste of crowded, unhealthy civilization. It is this ideal of the West, couched in song, that meshed so perfectly with the image of the bold frontier hero at home in this land, and that gave us the singing cowboy four score and seven years after "The Blue Juniata."

The mid-nineteenth-century gold rush to California, Nevada, Colorado, and the Dakota Territory gave enormous fuel to the fires of popular imagination, as thousands pulled up stakes and headed to the land of untold wealth. So did the opening of the Oregon Territory and the tiny caravans of settlers who crossed the enormous emptiness in wagon trains, heading for a land of plenty. Several of the early songs we think of as cowboy, or at least western, came from this period, and some of them have such power that more than a hundred years later they are sung and taught as folklore in our schools: "Betsy from Pike," "Clementine," and "Dreary Black Hills."

With America's growing population, the rise of high-speed printing (which facilitated sheet music production), and a growing circuit of urban theaters linked by improved roads and railroads, it is not surprising that a burgeoning cadre of songwriters stepped in to fill the need for popular songs. After several years of slavishly imitating British and European models, American songwriters came into their own in the 1840s. Many a love song the cowboys would later sing came from this fertile period, including "Lorena," "Aura Lee," and "Listen to the Mocking Bird."

America's first fully professional songwriter, Stephen Collins Foster, came of age in that era. He began writing what he called "Ethiopian songs" for minstrel shows, which had come into vogue in the 1840s, though their roots stretched back to a couple of entertainers who appeared on stage in blackface in the 1820s, and to the overwhelming success of Thomas D. Rice, who was a stage sensation with the character and song "Jim Crow." By the early 1850s, Foster had produced many of his most memorable songs: "Old Folks at Home" (1851), "My Old Kentucky Home" (1853), "Old Dog Tray" (1853), "Jeannie with the Light Brown Hair" (1854), and "Hard Times Come Again No More" (1855). Another masterpiece, "Beautiful Dreamer," was published only after his death in 1864.

It seems bizarre at best and repugnant at least to modern sensibilities to have northern white men, who knew little to nothing of true African-based music, portray plantation slaves with grotesque accents, degrading humor, and simple, catchy songs. However, to the sensibilities of the age, minstrelsy was a sensation, lauded as the most spontaneous, creative, purely American music ever heard—much as jazz would be lauded eighty years later.

Music also spread to the frontier via tent shows, wagon shows, and showboats, the last a roustabout tradition immortalized by Edna Ferber's 1926 novel *Showboat* and Jerome Kern and Oscar Hammerstein's 1928 Broadway hit of the same title. There were showboats on the Mississippi as early as 1817, though they hit their heyday in the period following the Civil War. Eventually the rise of the talking film and the ravages of the Depression pretty much put an end to this colorful era of entertainment—which ranged from the plays of Shakespeare and Goethe to fiddle contests, vaudeville artists, and aerial acts, as well as minstrel shows—although remnants plied the rivers of the Midwest as late as 1950. The minstrels were, interestingly, sometimes in blackface and sometimes not; the frontier tended to be more democratic.

As with Stephen Foster, there was no western content in the dozens of minstrel songs that became popular standards: "I Wish I Was in Dixie's Land," "Old Dan Tucker," "Jordan Am a Hard Road to Travel," "Jim Crack Corn," "Darling Nelly Gray," and of course Foster's "Uncle Ned," "Nelly

Bly," and "Oh! Susanna." Yet these songs became national favorites and influenced songwriters to come. The first cowboys of the great trail drives, who were born in this era and grew up with these songs, doubtless sang them and began composing their own songs using them as models.

There is plenty of evidence that the cowboys' immediate predecessors did so. The young soldiers during the Civil War were accompanied by music in camps and on marches, music that was often martial, played on fife and drum and brass, but that in the evenings was as likely to be popular or folk. It was Robert E. Lee who said in 1864, "I don't believe we can have an army without music," and while he was probably referring to the stirring music of the regimental bands, he could as well have meant the nightly campfire songs that instilled a sense of camaraderie and solidarity among the foot soldiers.

Pocket-sized songbooks abounded in the war years, with titles like *The Soldier Boy's Songster, Beadle's Dime Songs for the War, Hopkins' New Orleans 5 Cent Song-Book,* and *The Camp Fire Songster.* They contained a mix of the folk and the popular: Scottish ballads like "Annie Laurie" (which had also been a favorite with soldiers half a world away during the Crimean War); songs from Thomas Moore's *Irish Melodies,* such as " 'Tis the Last Rose of Summer" and "Believe Me If All Those Endearing Young Charms"; plenty of the Stephen Foster canon; the ubiquitous "Home Sweet Home"; "Lorena"; and songs we associate with the winning of the West —"Clementine," "The Yellow Rose of Texas," and "Betsy from Pike." As the war dragged on, soldiers' favorites included rousing new songs from the popular songwriters of the day —"The Bonnie Blue Flag" in the Confederate camp and "The Battle Hymn of the Republic" and "When Johnny Comes Marching Home" in the Union camp—and less warlike, more sentimental songs as well, such as "All Quiet along the Potomac," "Tramp! Tramp! Tramp!" and "Just before the Battle, Mother."

At war's end, these were the songs that young men from both sides brought with them as they headed from the exhausted East and ravaged South to the open, beckoning, inviting West. These were the songs the first cowboys and western settlers sang, those young men inured to harsh camp life, used to entertaining themselves with song, familiar with weaponry and skilled in its usage, prepared for hardship and discomfort and danger.

The movement of many of the heartiest young men to the opening West following the war was simply a continuation of the national fascination with the region. It was seen as the land of unlimited opportunity and unlimited abundance, the place of the future. Soon the cowboy, the driver of cattle on immense open ranges who battled rustler and Native American, became an object of intense curiosity, and he increasingly held sway over the American imagination. He took on myriad contradictory and mythical roles: noble knight, warrior hero, half-wild hooligan, peacemaker, laborer, drink- and gun-happy horseman, and more.

This heady mixture of truth and fiction was borne eastward to civilization while the West was still new. By 1872 dime-novel writer and noted cowboy popularizer Ned Buntline was appearing onstage with Buffalo Bill Cody and Texas Jack Omohundro in *The Scouts of the Plains*. The same year, Dr. Brewster Higley of Smith County, Kansas, published a florid poem that began: "O give me a home where the buffalo roam."

In 1878 a novel by Thomas Pilgrim (the pseudonym of Arthur Morecamp) called *The Live Boys; or, Charlie and Nasho in Texas,* was the first to feature the trail drive as a setting. The two juveniles reappeared in a sequel in 1880: *The Live Boys in the Black Hills; or, The Young Texas Gold Hunters.* In 1882 the Beadle people—the publishers of those five-cent pocket songsters so popular during the Civil War—brought out Frederick Whittaker's *Parson Jim, King of the Cowboys; or, The Gentle Shepherd's Big "Clean Out,"* the first dime novel to feature a cowboy as its hero. The same year, Buffalo Bill Cody saw a future in presenting his West onstage to a hungry audience and produced a Fourth of July show in North Platte, Nebraska, replete with cowboys, Indians, and an enactment of the Deadwood stage robbery. The following year he brought his show, now called Buffalo Bill's Rocky Mountain and Prairie Exhibition, to the fairgrounds in Omaha, and in 1885, with Annie Oakley and even Chief Sitting Bull added to the spectacle, he called it "The Wild West, or Life among the Red Men and the Road Agents of the Plains and Prairies; An Equine Dramatic Exposition on Grass or under Canvas of the Advantages of Frontiersmen and Cowboys."

This Wild West exhibition was hugely popular, played all over the world, and toured—in various incarnations with various casts—for some twenty years. Show business had come to, and from, the West while the West was still quite wild, wielding a power over the nation's imagination and pocketbook that continues to this day. There was already the feeling among the public at large that the wild and wonderful western frontier was rapidly disappearing, and that the winning of the West must be lived vicariously through the heroes who tamed it.

While songs and literature had mythologized the scout, the soldier, the adventurer, and the mountain man, the Wild West show may have been the first medium to depict the simple cowboy as hero. In 1884 Buffalo Bill introduced a new character to his show in the person of William Levi "Buck" Taylor (1857–1924), a 6'5" trick-riding Texas cowboy Cody had pulled off his Nebraska ranch. As one revisionist historian has commented: "There was no reason at all for his debut except Cody's desire to find something new with which to entertain eastern audiences. Cody had already exploited virtually every western type in his new but much-traveled show, and it may have been that the cowboy was simply the bottom of the barrel, the last item left to sell."[2] It will come as little surprise that young Buck Taylor was quickly fictionalized. In 1887, Prentiss Ingraham, writing for the omnipresent Beadle folks, ground out *Buck Taylor, King of the Cowboys; or, The Raiders*

*and the Rangers: A Story of the Wild and Thrilling Life of William L. Taylor.*
Suddenly, as historian Richard Slatta wrote, "Thanks to Cody and Taylor the term *cowboy* left behind much of its negative connotations and became a term evoking heroism, courage, and strength."[3]

The influence of Erastus Beadle and his dime novels can hardly be underestimated. A native of Lake Otsego, New York, he moved to New York City in 1858, convinced that the American public was eager for small, mass-produced novels, which advances in printing had made possible. The first of Beadle's orange-backed dime novels appeared in June 1860. His published library, by the time his last book appeared in the early 1900s, came to several thousand volumes, many of them westerns, and his writers virtually defined the term "hack." Prentiss Ingraham alone wrote more than six hundred novels. As literature, the dime novels are formulaic, to put it charitably, but they became immensely popular. Some of the books' heroes were based (extremely loosely) on real people, notably Deadwood Dick and frontier scout Kit Carson, while others glorified fictional characters. More than two hundred written by the inexhaustible Ingraham were still in print in the 1920s.

Surely Edward Z. C. Judson, under the pseudonym Ned Buntline, wrote the most influential series, "Buffalo Bill, King of the Border Men," for the *New York Weekly.* The first story came out in 1869–1870, and, in book form, the series was still in print in 1928. Although it contained a scattering of facts regarding Cody's life, much of the series was laden with glorified heroics. When a play was quickly adapted from the biography, Ned Buntline coaxed Cody and Texas Jack Omohundro into appearing onstage in a play of his own. The prolific Prentiss Ingraham wrote his own Cody play in 1878, followed it with a biography in 1879, and eventually composed a heap of dime novels on the exploits of the frontier scout. A final note on Ingraham: One would scarcely believe he had the time, but he also served as the press agent for Bill Cody's Wild West Show.

For those hungry for truth rather than fiction, Charles Siringo's *A Texas Cowboy; or Fifteen Years on the Hurricane Deck of a Spanish Pony* (which is relatively factual, as far as one can believe Siringo's stoic self-promotion) was published in 1885. Dime novels proliferated in the 1880s, and the tradition was long lasting. This outdoorsy hypermasculine literary genre was carried on in pulp magazines through the middle decades of the twentieth century.

By the 1890s Buffalo Bill's Wild West show had toured Europe and played before Queen Victoria. It should come as no surprise that several other entrepreneurs developed similar Wild West shows, most notably Pawnee Bill (Gordon W. Lillie, 1860–1942).

It was in this era that cowboys and westerners began to write their own songs, usually extremely sentimental tunes about a tragedy on the job, such as D. J. O'Malley's "When the Work's All Done This Fall" in 1893. Three decades later it would become the first "hit" record with a cowboy theme and presentation. The lyrics were typical. They describe "a group of jolly cowboys discussing plans at ease," one of whom, Charlie, tells of his desire to return home at roundup's end, but his plans are dashed by a storm and stampede later that evening. The final stanza is, at the same time, stoic and maudlin:

> Charlie was buried at sunup, no tombstone for his head
> Nothing but a little board, and this is what it said:
> "Charlie died at sunrise, he died from a fall,
> And he'll not see his mother when the work's all done this fall."

"Little Joe, the Wrangler," written by Jack Thorp in 1898, tells a similar story of a little runaway who tags along with the roundup as a horse wrangler and cook's helper. When all hands are called out during the inevitable storm and stampede, Little Joe rides to the fore, only to plunge into an arroyo and be crushed by his horse, Blue Rocket. These are but two of the typical western ballads of the era; there are many more less celebrated but as fine.

The first literary western novel, Owen Wister's *The Virginian,* was published in April 1902, opening the way for serious western fiction such as Willa Cather's *Death Comes for the Archbishop* and *My Antonia,* and Ole Rolvaag's *Giants in the Earth* and *Peder Victorious* in the 1920s, as well as Laura Ingalls Wilder's timeless children's classic *The Little House on the Prairie.* The year 1903 saw the appearance of the first two motion pictures with western themes: Edwin S. Porter's *The Great Train Robbery* in the spring, and American Mutoscope and Biograph's *Kit Carson* in September.

A succession of western-related books and films continued in a steady stream in these dawning years of the twentieth century. In 1908 Jack Thorp's *Songs of the Cowboy* was published, while John Lomax's *Cowboy Songs and Other Frontier Ballads* came out two years later. Broncho Billy Anderson began producing and starring in the first series of western films beginning in 1909, and William S. Hart was onstage as the Virginian in an adaptation of the popular novel. Zane Grey's first novel was published in 1908, and his first popular novel, *Riders of the Purple Sage,* came out in 1912. Vaudeville and Broadway artist Billy Murray ("the Denver Nightingale") recorded "Cheyenne" for Victor in 1906; Charles O'Donnell and Eddie Fields's vaudeville composition "My Pony Boy" became a small sensation on Broadway in 1908 and was recorded in 1909. By 1912 "Ragtime Cowboy Joe" (by Grant Clarke, Lewis Muir, and Maurice Abrahams) was a hit. Neither ragtime nor cowboy, it still struck a national nerve, combining the thrill, danger, and nostalgia of the Old West with the exciting modern music that presaged the jazz age. It was a formula that would work again and again in coming years.

# 2

# *The Cowboy and Song*

While popular culture quickly moved to romanticize and mythologize the western hero on horseback, the real-life figure was quite another story. Some would, by the narrowest of definitions, restrict the use of the term "cowboy" to the young men who drove huge herds of Texas longhorns up the famous cattle trails to railheads in Kansas and beyond, in the period that began at the close of the Civil War and ended a mere twenty or twenty-five years later. By then, such drives were rendered obsolete by the spread of railroads and the constant encroachment of small ranchers, homesteaders, and farmers and their fences on the formerly trackless open prairie. Others apply the term "cowboy" loosely to anyone in jeans and a broad-brimmed hat, up to and including presidents Lyndon Johnson and Ronald Reagan. Some would define it even more loosely still to include anyone with a reckless, heedless, adventurous spirit.

The term itself was used as early as the 1640s in Ireland, to describe young men who tended small herds of cattle. It was applied more than once during the American Revolution to what we'd now call rustlers, young men who pilfered beef on the hoof from the British. Its earliest use in what we'd think of as a modern context is from the 1830s, when the term "cow-boy" was used, not in a flattering way, to describe Texans who raided Mexican cattle.

It was Christopher Columbus himself who, upon returning to the New World, unloaded twenty-four stallions, ten mares, and a number of cattle at what is now Cap Hatien, Haiti, on January 2, 1494. Twenty-five years later the Spanish explorer Hernan Cortes reintroduced the horse to the American continent, where it had long been extinct, landing in Vera Cruz with eleven stallions and five mares; the following year Gregorio de Villalobos, lieutenant governor of New Spain (Mexico), brought cattle to the mainland, landing them near Tampico. The wild herds of cattle and mustangs that were the heart of the practical and romantic views of the West were the descendants of these pioneer stocks, the offspring of strays and runaways through the years. The cattle trade boomed in the lush Mexican midlands, and the herds were tended on horseback by the vaqueros who would become the ancestor, and teacher, of the cowboy. Interestingly, that romantic cowboy legend was never a part of the Spanish Mexican culture, where the vaquero has been looked down upon as a lowly laborer, on the bottom rung of the social order, doing the dirty work the caballeros—the horsemen of the elite classes—did not deign to do. Farther north, the English in Virginia were forced to eat the horses they had brought over in their first difficult winter, but soon both horses and cattle were a fixture of colonial life, and tending cattle (albeit usually on foot, in the colonies) was a fixture of life in colonial and Spanish America throughout the eighteenth century.

With the relentless westward surge following the Louisiana Purchase of 1803, cattlemen welcomed the opening of the sprawling plains to Anglo settlement, and huge herds were developed in the rich, hot areas in the southern part of that section of Mexico that would eventually become the state of Texas. Obtaining wild cattle was a simple thing. After Mexico won its independence from Spain in 1821, it had little interest in and could not effectively govern its vast northern regions; many of the Franciscan padres who effectively controlled the area were loyal to Spain, and they simply departed the area after independence, leaving their cattle to Indian converts or abandoning them to fend for themselves. Thousands of cattle roamed free on these sparsely inhabited ranges in the succeeding years.

Indeed, this is the main reason Davy Crockett ended up at the Alamo. Originally he headed to Texas from Tennessee after being defeated in his attempt to gain a fourth term in Congress. (He famously told voters, having lost that race to a lawyer with a wooden leg, "Since you have chosen to elect a man with a timber toe to succeed me, you may all go to hell and I will go to Texas.") Crockett felt the prospects for developing a thriving business in cattle were excellent in these broad, fecund, empty, and inexpensive acres, and he wrote to his daughter in his last known letter: "I must say as to what I have seen of Texas it is the garden spot of the world. The best land and the best prospects for health I ever saw, and I do believe it is a fortune to any man to come here. There is a world of country here to settle. . . . I am rejoiced in my fate. I had rather be in my present situation than to be elected to a seat in Congress for life. I am in hopes of making a fortune yet for myself and my family, bad as my prospect has been."[1] It was only shortly thereafter, attempting to live up to his own legend, that the forty-nine-year-old Crockett joined William Barret Travis and Jim Bowie and about 170 other independence-minded Texans in that crumbling mission in San Antonio, where a sad doomed battle was fought by Texas settlers against the oppressive regime of Antonio Lopez de Santa Anna.[2] Still, we may take

Crockett's optimism as typical of the breed of sturdy pioneers who moved in a small but steady stream into Texas both before and after it achieved independence in 1836, and statehood in 1845.

All of this expansionism, this desire to fill the empty frontier and make livings and fortunes in the new land, was disrupted during the bloody Civil War, which, after four exhausting years of fighting, left a weakened nation struggling to rebuild. In Texas this meant a return to raising cattle, and the discovery that the huge herds of rangy, half-wild longhorns were in high demand in the East for their stringy beef and hides, if only they could be gotten there. Shipping by sea was impractical due to cost, and the nearest railheads were far to the north, in Kansas. Some hardy pioneering ranchers and cattlemen, with an unerring nose for profit, began driving huge herds northward across the red and rolling sprawl of north Texas and the Indian Territory (later to become Oklahoma) to a series of what came to be called "cow towns": Abilene, Wichita, Newton, and Dodge City.

Even then the cattle business was very much an industry—a profitable one, run by wealthy cattlemen and sometimes owned by eastern investors' syndicates. The young cowboys, however, were merely hired labor, better paid than the farmer or agricultural worker of the era but worse paid than blue-collar factory workers. They were adventurous young men who developed unique, even exquisite, skills that were virtually useless in other trades. Some of them hoped to buy their own spreads some day, some drifted into the trade and drifted out again, some gave no thought to tomorrow. Their work was difficult, dirty, dusty, often monotonous, and though it was not often dangerous, when danger did occur it was extreme. Unpredictable horses and cattle, foul weather, and the violence of human nature were all physical threats to the young drovers.

These cowboys were largely displaced southern farm boys who came home to find their family farms in ruins, their futures in the South bleak. They took their agricultural skills and the use of weaponry they had learned in war and headed west in hopes of better prospects. Young Federals, of course, trekked west as well, and although their influence was more pronounced in the northern plains, a good number wound up in Texas. Many a historian has pointed out that, especially on the Texas ranges and in the state's coastal areas, up to 25 percent of cowboys were black, freedmen and escaped slaves who learned the cattle trade. Another 10 percent were Mexican or Mexican American, and indeed it was from these vaqueros that the bulk of the cowboys learned their unusual and unique skills. The vaqueros were justly famous for their horsemanship and rope work, honed in the three centuries that cattle were raised in Mexico and Spanish America. Like the young ex-rebels, they too had been displaced, first by Texas's hard-wrought battle for independence, and then by the Mexican-American war of 1846–1848.

Not only did the young Anglo cowboys learn many of their skills from these vaqueros, but also much of the most colorful language associated with the cowboy and cowboy life is taken directly from the Spanish, though it is frequently garbled: lariat from *la riata,* mustang from *mesteño,* hackamore from *jaquima,* buckaroo from *vaquero,* dally or dally welt from *dar la vuelta,* hoosegow from *juzgado,* savvy from *sabe,* lasso from *lazo,* and on and on and on. Prejudice and racism were problems then as now, but far more often than not these cowboys put aside their differences to tackle the job at hand: driving the cattle northward. This diversity and cooperation is a reality not often reflected in film, song, or in literature.

Smaller cattle drives existed into the early 1900s, but for the most part by 1890 the slender fingers of railroad lines reached farther and farther into the West, and the open ranges were a thing of the past, replaced by smaller spreads and miles of fences. As early as 1877 "old-time" cowboys were lamenting the passing of the West and of the true cowboy, articulating a nostalgia that extends to the cowboy revival of today. And while the era of the great trail drives lasted but a bit more than two decades, cattle ranching continued to dominate the West and the western experience. Even today, one doesn't have to drive too far off the interstate in any western state to see men and women on horseback, working with cattle. The huge modern agribusiness ranches, which ship cattle in semi-trailers and round up with helicopters, still employ men, often on horseback, to do the hot dirty work of the cattle business: branding, pregnancy checking, dipping, separating mature cattle for market, and castrating calves.

When studying the popular portrayal of the cowboy, it is fascinating to reflect how few of these men are shown actually tending cattle. Folklorist J. Frank Dobie observed that Owen Wister's *The Virginian* is "the classic cowboy novel without cows," and Wister's book is far from alone in this peculiarity.[3] In films this contradiction is exaggerated to the extreme. The cowboy hero is often a lawman or ranger, openly or undercover; he may be a cattleman or ranch foreman; he may be a drifter, a doctor, or a two-fisted newspaperman—but seldom is he portrayed as a bottom-level workaday cowpoke. In a significant number of the singing-cowboy films, he is a radio, stage, or film performer, righting wrongs with fists and guns between performances. What he is, really, is a professional hero, with no need to perform such messy chores as dehorning or branding.

It is plainly that spirit of independence, of owing nothing to any person, of living up to a personal code, that generations have valued in this western hero, investing him with properties real cowboys may or may not have possessed. This is why the cowboy hero is frequently a man from nowhere; why it is convenient to have him come to town or ranch with no past, no baggage, no ties; why it is simple for him, in these morality plays, to right wrongs and clear up injustice with quick decisions, quick draws, quick fists, and occasionally a song or two. In an increasingly industrial and bureaucratic age, the appeal of a lone figure answering only to his own conscience is strong indeed, and popular culture has settled this longing, this need, this fantasy, upon the lowly figure of the cowboy.

So the young, displaced skilled laborers who were the real cowboys have taken on a huge psychic and cultural load. They have become, through the imaginative eyes of writers and singers and songwriters and filmmakers, the repository of our national dreams, transmogrified into heroes and peacemakers. In addition they carry the weight of nostalgia, for they represent for us the wilderness we will never know, an era we can never experience, yet one that we seem to feel is priceless beyond measure. All these conflicting and complementary impulses are inherent in western music as well. This is why the cowboy, whose numbers have always been few, has come to mean so much to us, why the image and sound of his music—no matter how far parted from reality—has continued to fascinate us and move us for more than a century and a quarter.

Popular mythology has cowboys crooning soft lullabies and yodels to the cattle on the open ranges to pacify jittery longhorns, singing old familiar songs and hymns from back home, or creating new songs or new verses to existing songs in the long dark hours of the night. Although this image has long been highly romanticized, the association of music and the cowboy is not purely fictional. Anywhere working men have been isolated for periods of time in particular circumstances, a tradition of song by or about those men and their work develops. Sailors, loggers, railroad workers, boatmen, miners, and others all have musical traditions.

As for cowboys, even witnesses who were there in the days before singing became a profession on record and radio and film can't seem to agree. Journalist John Baumann wrote for the *Fortnightly Review* of April 1, 1887: "The younger hands are whiling away the time 'whittling' and 'plug chawing,' drawling out yarns of love and sport and singing ribald songs, until someone strikes up the favorite wail 'Oh bury me not on the lone prairie, Where the coyotes howl and the wind blows free.'"

Harry Stephens, claiming authorship of "The Night Herding Song," told John Lomax: "Well, we always got night-herd years ago when they didn't have so many fences and corrals, and that was the biggest job for the cowboy. We generally have a two-hour shift, and two to four men on a shift according to the size of the herd. And when I made up this song, why, we always had so many different squawks and yells and hollers a-trying to keep the cattle quiet, I thought I might as well have a kind of a song to it." The highly regarded Texas folklorist and historian J. Frank Dobie remarked that "no human sound that I have ever heard approaches in eeriness or in soothing melody that indescribable whistle of the cowboy," while stockman Joseph McCoy wrote in 1874 that he had "many times sat upon the fence of a shipping yard and sang to an enclosed herd whilst a train would be rushing by. And it is surprising how quiet the herd will be so long as they can hear the human voice. . . . Singing hymns to Texas steers is the peculiar forte of a genuine cow-boy, but the spirit of true piety does not abound in the sentiment."[4]

Other contemporary accounts point to "Sam Bass" or "Red River Valley" as songs frequently sung by cowboys. J. Frank Dobie agreed: "Of course not all the cowboys on all days sang. Many a waddie could no more carry a tune than he could carry a buffalo bull. Often all hands were too busy fighting and 'cussin' them dad-blamed cattle to sing. But in general the cowboys sang."[5] Ramon Adams recalled: "Away back at the beginnin' of the cow business it didn't take the cowman long to savvy that the human voice gave cattle confidence, and kept 'em from junin' around. . . . The practice got to be so common that night herdin' was spoken of as 'singin' to 'em.' "[6] And E. C. Abbott (Teddy Blue) painted the legend in detail in his landmark book *We Pointed Them North:*

> One reason I believe there was so many songs about cowboys was the custom we had of singing to the cattle on night herd. The singing was supposed to soothe them and it did. . . . I know that if you wasn't singing, any little sound in the night—it might be just a horse shaking himself—could make them leave the country; but if you were singing, they wouldn't notice it. The two men on guard would circle around with their horses at a walk, if it was a clear night and the cattle was bedded down and quiet, and one man would sing a verse of a song, and his partner on the other side of the herd would sing another verse; and you'd go through a whole song like "Sam Bass."[7]

Likewise, Charles Siringo, whose *A Texas Cowboy* was one of the very first looks at the life of the cowboy written by a cowboy, unequivocally paints a portrait of cowboys singing, referring to a 1874 trail drive: "The steers showed a disposition to stampede but we handled them easy and sang melodious songs which kept them quieted. But about one o'clock they stampeded in grand shape. . . . I finally about three o'clock got them stopped and after singing a few 'lullaby' songs they all lay down and went to snoring." Later he describes a typical night on the trail: "The nights would be divided up into four equal parts—one man 'on' at a time, unless storming, tormented with mosquitoes, or something of the kind, when every one except the cook would have to be 'out' singing to them."[8]

On the other hand, Jack Thorp, the first collector and one of the first composers of cowboy songs, proclaimed bluntly: "It is generally thought that cowboys did a lot of singing around the herd at night to quiet them on the bed ground. I have been asked about this, and I'll say that I have stood my share of night watches in fifty years, and I seldom heard singing of any kind."[9]

Regardless of how much singing was done on night guard, it is a fairly safe bet that in the days before radio, anytime men were gathered together for long periods of isolation and boredom, any man who could come up with the slightest fragment of entertainment besides poker or some other card game was providing welcome relief from the endless hours not actively spent at work. In lonely bunkhouses, in line camps, and at trail sides some of the more creative of the band of men loosely defined as cowboys doubtless dreamed up the poems that, when put to old familiar melodies, became cowboy songs. Thus D. J. O'Malley's 1893 poem "After the Roundup"—initially printed in the *Stock Grower's Journal*—was popularized by cowpokes who learned the verses and set the lyrics to two very different melodies: the jaunty popular song "Little Old Log Cabin in the Lane," and the tender waltz "After the Ball." Only three decades later, having finally evolved a tune of its own, this plaintive tale became the first recorded cowboy music hit, in Carl T. Sprague's 1925 version on Victor Records, under its now much more commonly known title "When the Work's All Done This Fall."

This sequence is probably pretty illustrative of the way most classic cowboy songs were written. Some were art songs, like Dr. Brewster Higley's 1873 "Home on the Range,"[10] while others were folk songs in the truest sense, a bare skeleton of a tune and no story at all, with endless verses (occasionally exquisitely vulgar) added and subtracted by hundreds of bored or bemused cowhands—for example, "The Old Chisholm Trail," which reputedly is based on an English folk song called "A Dainty Duck." "The Cowboy's Lament," based on "The Unfortunate Rake," dates back to at least 1790, and "Oh Bury Me Not on the Lone Prairie" is based on an 1839 poem called "The Ocean-Buried." Other cowboy songs easily traceable to English and Scottish songs in the folk tradition include many of the most beloved songs of this early period: "Utah Carroll," "Texas Rangers," and others.

Interest in the cowboy and his music, fueled by the dime novel and the Wild West show, began to climb in earnest around the turn of the century. As early as 1901 the *Journal of American Folklore* published the lyrics to "Oh Bury Me Not on the Lone Prairie," and in 1909 it published "Songs of the Western Cowboy," collected by G. F. Will in North Dakota. The most significant publication was N. Howard (Jack) Thorp's booklet *Songs of the Cowboy*, which appeared in 1908, followed in 1910 by John Avery Lomax's landmark *Cowboy Songs and Other Frontier Ballads,* and in 1919 by his *Songs of the Cattle Trail and Cow Camp.* Thorp was an amateur collector (and writer as well; he "collected" his own "Little Joe the Wrangler"), while Lomax was a trained academic who borrowed heavily from Thorp. Lomax became a tireless advocate for folk music in general, and cowboy songs in particular, throughout his long life. Charles Siringo published a companion volume to his *A Lone Star Cowboy* in Santa Fe in 1919 called *The Song Companion of a Lone Star Cowboy,* and Charles Finger published *Sailor Chanteys and Cowboy Songs* in 1923 with a small Kansas publisher; it was expanded and the sailor chanteys dropped when published as *Frontier Ballads* by Doubleday, Page in New York in 1927.

Margaret Larkin was the first to include melodies for the lyrics in her

1931 anthology *Singing Cowboy: A Book of Western Songs* (each song introduced, in the words of folklorist Guy Logsdon, "by a short narrative with much romanticized nonsense"),[11] and cowboy song popularizer, songwriter, and radio star Jules Verne Allen published *Cowboy Lore* in San Antonio in 1933. But by this time the line between cowboy folk songs and songs created for records and movies was blurring.

Owen Wister, in adapting his novel *The Virginian* for the stage, wrote his own cowboy song, "Ten Thousand Cattle Roaming," to replace the minstrel tune the Virginian had sung in the novel. Tin Pan Alley had not been long in discovering the cowboy and his music and between 1905 and 1920 proceeded to churn out clever, cheerful, and wholly inauthentic cowboy songs like "Cheyenne (Shy Ann)" and "San Antonio" (both by Egbert Van Alstyne and Harry H. Williams), "The Pride of the Prairie," "My Pony Boy," "Ragtime Cowboy Joe," "Sierra Sue," "I'd Like to Be in Texas for the Roundup in the Spring" (based on a fragment of a folk song), "Let the Rest of the World Go By," and "The Utah Trail." Many of these songs were recorded (on cylinder, and later on disc) by well-known stage artists of the time such as Len Spencer, Eddie Morton, and Billy Murray. Murray, who had a long vaudeville career and made records from 1903 well into the 1930s, recorded a small but significant number of cowboy songs, though novelty and topical songs made up the bulk of his output.

More than a few of these Tin Pan Alley cowboy songs quickly entered the folk repertoire and were recorded by country and cowboy artists in the 1920s and 1930s, when rural and folk music finally found its way to record, and records and record players became available and affordable to a wider audience. Vernon Dalhart, Patt Patterson, and even Bradley Kincaid recorded "I'd Like to Be in Texas (When They Round Up in the Spring)" in those years; Everett Morgan recorded "Cheyenne" in 1933; and "Pride of the Prairie" was recorded by Aaron Campbell's Mountaineers, Tex Owens, his sister Texas Ruby and her partner Zeke Clements, and Patsy Montana & the Prairie Ramblers, to name a few early examples.

There is a tendency to venerate the folk song and to denigrate the commercially composed in reviewing any traditionally based music, but it is important to remember that even the most unpolished early recording artists were often professionals or semi-professionals who performed music for an audience, and who added to their repertoires as they could—from the Victrolas, traveling medicine shows, or vaudeville troupes. While the Anglo American folk song had hundreds of years to develop, cowboy music was romanticized and popularized in just three decades. Many a performer was first drawn to the world of entertainment by a musician or comedian performing in some long-forgotten tent, schoolhouse, or small-town theater. Some of these songs became virtual folk songs, accepted as age-old with their authors unknown, although the real composer may have been at that moment pounding away at his next composition at a piano in New York or Los Angeles.

By 1930 authentic cowboy songs had been performed on record by concert singers, beginning with Bentley Ball's "Jesse James" and "The Dying Cowboy" in 1919. Carl T. Sprague, Vernon Dalhart, and Jimmie Rodgers had national best-selling records of cowboy songs; Gene Autry was featured on radio as "Oklahoma's Singing Cowboy"; and Warner Baxter, Bob Steele, Ken Maynard, and others had already sung in films, though the singing was central to neither the plot nor the character. The visual and aural image of the cowboy loafing about with a guitar in his idle hours was in no way jarring to the moviegoer. Indeed, it was expected, as much a part of the cowboy's colorful trappings as his sombrero, his rope, his tall boots, and his chaps.

The western was becoming a genre of its own in literature, in song, on radio, on record, in comic strips, and on film. With the coming of sound to film, image and music were united, and a new character—the singing cowboy—was preparing to step into the American consciousness, and with him developed, from these folk and popular sources, what we now think of as western music.

In time, cowboy bands in general used the same instrumentation as the string bands of the Southeast, although the feel was often far different. In the 1940s a smooth, pop-country sound came to exemplify the western music of the era, but the century-long appeal of western music has been, for the most part, the lyrics and the singer. No truly identifiable "sound" has ever developed to set it significantly apart from country music, save its peculiar and subtle loping beat. One can point out a jazz influence here, a mariachi influence there, but the average ear does not hear these fine points—in the public mind, fiddles and guitars have always branded western music as country. Intensifying the association, the records of virtually all cowboy and country singers were targeted toward the same rural audience. Although the purist considers western music a discrete style, it continues to be firmly identified and confused with country music.

And though its influences were quite varied, western music has walked hand-in-hand with country music from the start, though the relationship has shown its strains from time to time. Despite the fact that *Billboard* magazine dropped the catchall "Country-Western" designation from its record charts more than thirty years ago, it is still a commonly used phrase among the public, who usually sees no distinction. Throughout his career Gene Autry easily drifted in and out of popular, country, and western music, as did most of the singing cowboys. But popular music and jazz directly affected the sound of western music in the 1930s. From sophisticated chords and chord progressions to the Django Reinhardt–inspired guitar fills of Karl Farr, the music shaped commercial western music as it matured.

And there is the interesting anomaly of yodeling, which was never associated with the cowboy before Gene Autry brought it to the screen, except in the handful of cowboy songs of Jimmie Rodgers, "the Singing Brakeman," who found yodeling to be obligatory in most of his material. Although yodeling had been established in Autry's repertoire for a number of years—he and many other radio and recording artists learned the trick from the vastly influential Rodgers—there is no evidence at all that traditional cowboys ever yodeled. It is probable that when there was singing, there was the use of the falsetto voice, and a melody hummed in falsetto might generously be termed a yodel, but it is extremely unlikely this ever went beyond the "whoo, whoo" sounds in a song like "The Cattle Call" (composed in the 1930s, though based on an earlier melody). It is conceivable that a kind of proto-yodeling was what Dobie was trying to describe when he referred to "the indescribable whistle of the cowboy," but to the traditional cowboy singer the mournful blue yodels of Jimmie Rodgers or the athletic yodels of the Alps were unknown and unanticipated.

It has long been said that Jimmie Rodgers created the blue yodeling style by combining his own Mississippi music, a rich melange of rural black and white music, with yodeling he had heard from a Swiss or Bavarian troupe appearing at a tent show or vaudeville stage. This may indeed be true, but research by several scholars, including Peter Stanfield, indicates that yodeling may have actually been introduced to the American stage by blackface entertainer Tom Christian in Chicago as early as 1847, and that the yodel moved from minstrelsy to country and cowboy music via medicine shows. It may be significant that Gene Autry appeared in a medicine show as a teenager, but yodeling was apparently not required of him for Dr. Fields' Marvelous Medicine Show, for it was Johnny Marvin who yodeled for Autry on his first recordings in 1929.

The first great popularizer of the blue yodel was well-known blackface vaudeville artist Emmett Miller (February 2, 1900–March 29, 1962), whose career peaked in the 1920s, though he continued to appear well into the 1950s. As Stanfield reports, "In 1924 *Billboard* magazine, reporting on a show at the New York Hippodrome, noted that Miller's 'trick singing stunt' almost stopped the show, and won him 'encore after encore.'"[12] He suggests, though without any hard evidence, that it was from Miller that Jimmie Rodgers learned the blue yodel, and this is certainly a plausible theory. Both men performed and traveled extensively, Rodgers was in and out of entertainment long before he actually recorded, and he could have caught Miller's yodeling act onstage just as easily as that of any troupe of Alpine singers. On quite the other hand, longtime Jimmie Rodgers scholar Nolan Porterfield has posited just the opposite: that Miller may have learned to yodel from Rodgers in the days before either of them recorded. Might not their influences have been mutual?

Regardless, yodeling predated them both. Eminent folk music scholar Norm Cohen has pointed out that one of the Singing Brakeman's most evocative yodels, "Sleep, Baby, Sleep," was recorded, with yodeling, as early as 1897 on a Berliner disc by George P. Watson and was recorded a dozen times between 1897 and 1917 by Watson and several others (Pete La Mar, Frank Wilson, Ward Barton and Frank Carroll, Matt Keefe, and Lucy Gates), on record labels like Edison, Zon-O-Phone, Columbia, and Victor. It was recorded at least five times by hillbilly bands or singers—including Frank Marvin, under the pseudonym Frankie Wallace—and by at least three black quartets before Rodgers's first recording.[13]

Although determining who was first involves a great deal of speculation, what is certain is that yodeling became vastly popular during Jimmie Rodgers's short career, spawning numerous yodelers in emulation of the Singing Brakeman: Johnny Marvin, Ernest Tubb, Ray Whitley, and Gene Autry. Blue yodels were powerfully evocative, expressing loneliness, alienation, dejection, and pain, as well as freedom and joy. They were relatively easy to master by any singer with the ability to break his voice, and the next generation of cowboy singers made yodeling a musical challenge. Although this next generation of yodelers may have lost the sense of profound loneliness and loss, the new crop of singers—including Roy Rogers, Elton Britt, Wilf Carter (Montana Slim), Patsy Montana, and Ray Whitley—brought to the art a fresh sense of excitement and drive. European yodeling had been fast and tricky; it took just a few talented singers to adapt the somewhat formal European approach to the sunbaked music of the cowboy and the West, as did Rogers, Britt, Whitley, and Carter so very quickly in the early 1930s, and as did Autry, who adapted well to the new style.

Did cowboys sing? Did they yodel? It matters to the historian, of course, but in the public mind the image was firmly in place: the cowboy amusing himself, his cattle, and his compadres with songs, yodels, guitar playing, and music making. It is a perception that generations have adopted, and it is just this perception that made possible the movies and the songs that followed.

# 3

# Western Music in the Air

## Records and Radio to 1934

In 1878 Thomas Edison patented the cylinder recording machine and player; within a decade Emile Berliner developed the disc player and gramophone (spring wound, in those long-ago days before most homes had electricity); and by the turn of the century records and record players graced many parlors, despite the fact that they were enormously expensive. A technological wave had crashed ashore, and popular entertainment would never be the same. Opera singers Enrico Caruso, Amelita Galli-Curci, and Alma Gluck could be heard in the family living room. For the first time a performance was no longer an ephemeral thing, as impossible to catch as the wind, but could instead be played repeatedly. This new technology whipped up a scarcely comprehendible national excitement, and records and record players became fixtures of homes both grand and humble all across the country in the early years of the twentieth century.

By 1890 the Columbia Phonograph Company had enough material recorded to print a one-page catalog—chiefly marches by the U. S. Marine Band—and by the turn of the century the technical quality had improved to the point that string music, opera, novelty songs, and popular music could be successfully reproduced.

By today's standards the sound is thin, tinny, insubstantial, and lacking in depth and overtone, but at the time it was a sensation. It is no surprise that in the rush to record everything from opera to vaudeville comedy, a few cowboy songs would eventually get recorded, although it was several years before folk music of any sort was offered to the public. The earliest recorded offerings were skewed heavily to the classics, light opera, and Sousa marches.

The trickle of Tin Pan Alley songs dealing with the cowboy and the West—most of them novelties—were among the mass of popular songs that made it to disc in the dawning years of the century, but it was not until 1919 that any record company saw fit to release a traditional cowboy song, concert singer Bentley Ball's renditions of "The Dying Cowboy" and "Jesse James." Ball was an interesting character, a native Virginian with a full-time career as a typewriter salesman and demonstrator at schools. At the close of his typing presentation he apparently brought out a guitar and gave a concert of American folk music. If these concerts were anything like his fourteen-song recorded repertoire (cut in 1918 and 1919), they were equal parts songs of the mountains, cowboy songs, spirituals, minstrel songs, and Indian-themed story songs. The Columbia catalog of 1919 promoted Ball's offerings as educational material and trumpeted Ball's selections as "probably the most authentic collection of genuine American Folk Songs ever collected." Referring to the two cowboy titles, the catalog continues: "The songs of our border days are less known but even more interesting than the songs of our Indians. 'Jesse James' and 'The Dying Cowboy' are genuinely thrilling 'ballads' of Cowboy life in frontier days."[1] Ball's presentation is very musical and quite listenable, but as one would predict, it is redolent of the concert stage, not the rolling ranges.

A second concert performance recording of cowboy songs was "Cowboy Song—Whoopee Ti Yi Yo," recorded for Victor in 1923 by the Glenn & Shannon Quartet. Apparently, no further western music was attempted by the group.

Country music scholars note that no string band was recorded until 1922—by then record players had become affordable for the middle- and low-income audience for rural music. Perhaps it is no accident that rural-oriented recordings became so popular so quickly. The way had been paved by that other technological instrument of popular culture of the early twentieth century, the radio, which burst on the scene in 1920 after a few years of experimentation. Suddenly a whole new world was opened to people all across America who had never heard a dance band, a newscast, a symphony, a drama, or their president.

Like today's explosive growth in Internet and computer and telecommunications technology, the growth of radio helped fuel the country's economy. Given the overwhelmingly rural character of our nation in the first quarter of the twentieth century, rural programming quickly found its way onto the air, particularly in America's heartland. As with the recording industry, little distinction was made then between cowboy music and other rural-oriented programming, which included not only hillbilly music and string band music, but also often barbershop quartets, gospel quartets, and organists. Rigid categorization meant little then. Whatever a station thought would appeal to its rural and small-town audience was what was broadcast, and many performers, even those with a rural orientation, offered up a potpourri of hillbilly, gospel, cowboy, popular, and dance band songs.

Not just individual performers were allotted radio time, but very early in the game the Saturday night barn dance became a feature of several of the larger stations, most notably WLS's *WLS Barn Dance* from Chicago, which went on the air in 1924, and WSM's Grand Ole Opry, which started up the following year. Both programs (and others that followed them, from such diverse areas as Dallas, Atlanta, New York, Wheeling, Saint Paul, Des Moines, Shreveport, Cincinnati, Tulsa, and Hollywood) were, of course, heavy on the country music of the time, but they frequently featured "old-time" singers and quartets (with an emphasis on Gay Nineties–era sentimental songs), and cowboy songs as well. All these shows used the then ultramodern medium of radio to broadcast a nostalgic, homey image of a gentler time gone by. The radio barn dance offered listeners a return to the simple, down-home days of their parents and grandparents, when life was slow and easy, and the music was homemade. This deliberate appeal to nostalgia was the dominant theme of these shows and was aimed specifically at those hardworking small-town, farm, and ranch folks who felt a little overwhelmed by the fast-paced 1920s and the frenetic jazz music that came to symbolize the era. Middle America, rocked by a world war and the dawn of the Jazz Age, hearkened back (as, for example, Booth Tarkington did in literature) to that gentle period between the Panic of 1873 and World War I, when peace and prosperity and small-town and rural values had dominated the American experience and the American character for some four decades.

Some of this appeal is similar to that of the cowboy: an imaginary escape to a simpler era, the removal from the urgent buzz and hum of urban life to a real or imagined countryside close to nature and the earth. What the cowboy added was the notion of freedom; the small-town farmer or mechanic or shop worker could, in imagination, enjoy an old-fashioned barn dance as an escape from the labors of the day, but the cowboy in the theater of the mind could simply saddle up and ride off into an imaginary sunset. This aspect of his appeal was not as apparent in the Jazz Age, the years between the armistice and the crash on Wall Street in 1929. There was more curiosity about the cowboy's life and work during that decade, and it was reflected in the type of songs cowboy singers sang. It was not until the crushing weight of the Depression began to squeeze hope and confidence out of the American people that the issue and image of the freedom and independence of the cowboy began to mean so very much in music and in film.

In the ensuing years, most of these radio barn dances featured cowboy music, and in fact a great many of the entertainers who played major roles in the singing-cowboy movement first appeared on barn dances. The *National Barn Dance* is the undisputed champion in that regard, having featured at one time or another such cowboy luminaries as Gene Autry, Bob Baker, Rex Allen, Eddie Dean, Louise Massey & the Westerners, Patsy Montana, Bob Atcher, the Girls of the Golden West, and the Prairie Ramblers. The Grand Ole Opry, with its decidedly southeastern and string band orientation—and later its development of a star system—has featured far fewer major cowboys, but it has had its share: Zeke Clements, Pee Wee King & His Golden West Cowboys, the Willis Brothers, and Riders In The Sky, while country superstar Marty Robbins often included western songs in his Grand Ole Opry performances. In the 1930s the *WHN Barn Dance* in New York brought both Tex Ritter and Ray Whitley to prominence before they headed to Hollywood, while the KNX *Hollywood Barn Dance* featured most of the prominent cowboy singers of the 1940s.

It is not difficult to understand the power of these shows for those who found them appealing in the early years of radio. With relatively few stations on the air, the 50,000-watt nighttime signals of WLS and WSM covered dozens of states, bringing the musical mountaineer and the lonely singing cowboy to most of the central and southern United States.

As radio barn dances spread across the nation in the 1930s, the scandalous, scurrilous, and fascinating saga of what has come to be called "border radio" began. The term "border radio" came about because the stations in question were on the very northern border of Mexico, and their monstrously powerful signals, sometimes reaching 500,000 watts, beamed northward across the Rio Grande and into America's heartland. In the infancy of radio, American and Canadian companies and stations were quick to divide up the available frequencies for North American broadcasts, and they settled on a 50,000-watt upper limit at which the most powerful stations could broadcast. Mexico was extremely slow to develop a radio industry, and by the time Mexican stations geared up to do some serious broadcasting, there were no more open frequencies to be had. Not a little resentful, the stations willfully ignored the international protest, as wild-eyed entrepreneurs from the United States like Dr. John R. Brinkley and Norman Baker built giant transmitters along the Rio Grande.

These men needed broadcast facilities away from U. S. supervision, for the flamboyant Baker, who dressed in lavender and purple, sold a cancer cure over his station XENT in Nuevo Laredo, and Brinkley was infamous for an operation wherein he transplanted tissue from goat testicles to humans as a potency cure, which he had pioneered in 1917. Brinkley, whose degree was in eclectic medicine, discovered radio as a profoundly effective way to drum up patients for this operation, and he began attracting customers to his Milford, Kansas, clinic in 1923 by broadcasting over his own KFKB, Kansas's first radio station. He is said to have done more than forty thousand such operations at $750 a pop, and he quickly became a millionaire. Eventually the American Medical Association and the Federal Radio Commission caught up with him, and his license to broadcast was revoked. He responded by moving his entire clinic and radio operation to Del Rio, Texas, where just across the Rio Grande in Villa Acuña, he built a radio transmitter three times more powerful than anything in the United States, via which he invited men with impotence and prostate problems to visit beautiful Del Rio. The 300-foot towers of XER were completed in the fall of 1931, and thus began an era. It should be noted that a station with a less colorful history, XED in Reynosa, was actually the first border station, opening in the fall of 1930. Even the great Jimmie Rodgers played its opening broadcast.

With this kind of power, and the signal directed north, these stations blanketed the central United States and became famous for their endless huckstering of medications such as Pe-ru-na (a cold tonic), prayer shawls, and Dr. Brinkley's Del Rio surgical clinic. Between sales pitches for hair dyes and digestion tonics and prayer cloths, there was music, and plenty of it. By Mexican law some of the content had to be in Spanish and of Mexican origin, and a number of popular singers, mariachi orchestras, and folk divas like Lydia Mendoza and Rosa Dominguez filled the night skies with passionate, romantic songs. But the bulk of the material was cowboy and old-fashioned country and gospel, for the signal was strongest over America's midsection. The country music tended to be homespun (the Carter Family, the Pickard Family, the Delmore Brothers, J. E. Mainer's Mountaineers), but the cowboy image fit the romantic border image like a glove.

Brinkley had used singing cowboy Roy Faulkner back in Kansas, and he became a regular feature of XER programming from the start. Indeed, most of the dozen or so stations that eventually became "border blasters" featured cowboy singers prominently, with monikers like Utah Cowboy, the Lonesome Cowhand, Cowboy Max, the Rio Grande Cowboys, Cowboy Slim Nichols, Cowboy Jack, Tex Ivey & His Original Ranch Boys, Doc Schneider & His Yodeling Texas Cowboys. They included several nationally known western artists, such as Buck Nation, Red River Dave, and even Patsy Montana after she left the Prairie Ramblers in the 1940s.

But the undisputed king of the border radio cowboys was Nolan "Cowboy Slim" Rinehart, born near Gustine, Texas, on March 11, 1911. After working on radio in Texas he was hired at XEPN in Piedras Negras by pitchman Major Kord (Don Baxter), who admired his rough-hewn vocal style and his ability to sell product: "That is the greatest cowboy singer I've ever heard in my life," gushed Kord. "That's how a cowboy would actually sound. I'll put that boy on the air and I'll stake a week's wages that he will pull more mail than everybody on this station put together."[2] Although he never made a commercial record in his brief life, Rinehart became one of the most popular singing cowboys in America on the strength of those border radio broadcasts. Ken Maynard claimed later that he "wanted to use him in my pictures because that man, in my opinion, was the greatest cowboy singer I had ever heard in my life."[3] Rinehart even reportedly took a screen test, but if he did, nothing apparently came of it.

What Slim Rinehart sold was songbooks by the thousands. His solo broadcasts were extremely popular, but he also had a popular transcribed radio show with Patsy Montana, and his career was very much in its prime when, at the age of thirty-seven, he was killed in an auto accident near Detroit on October 28, 1948. By that time the face of border radio was chang-

Cowboy Slim Rinehart, the king of border radio, strikes a casual pose before the microphones of station XEG, Monterrey, Mexico. (Country Music Hall of Fame collections)

ing. The combined efforts of the Mexican and U.S. governments had removed from the air the colorful quacks Brinkley and Baker (a man who famously enjoyed sometimes audible sexual liaisons while announcing and broadcasting). More importantly, times were changing. Many stations began to play records over the radio, a practice that had been resisted by the musicians' union from the very start of commercial radio. These stations had discovered that a smooth-talking disc jockey and a pile of records were far cheaper and lower maintenance than any number of bands, orchestras, soloists, and singers. Recordings, not live or transcribed music, rapidly became the order of the day, and indeed it has remained that way to the present. Although the border stations lasted well into the 1950s and early 1960s (with DJs like Paul Kallinger, Randy Blake, and Wolfman Jack), their truly outrageous era, and the era that included singing cowboys, was over.

Back in the USA, cowboy singers had been quick to come to the air on a local level. As early as 1926 John Crockett, "the Cowboy Singer," had a local program over KMJ in Fresno, while Otto Gray & His Oklahoma Cowboy Band, probably the first touring stars to develop as a result of radio, achieved huge popularity over KFRU in Bristow, Oklahoma, and then over KVOO in Tulsa and KFJF in Kansas City.

Many such singers, although popular regionally, never made it to record or film at all. With no tangible legacy to see or hear, their careers seem evanescent to us today. One such example was Cowboy Loye, born Loye Donald Pack on June 3, 1900, in Nashville, Tennessee. After settling in Nebraska as a young man, he began a radio career in York, Nebraska, in 1929. He became a star over WWVA in Wheeling from 1933 to 1937 (often in conjunction with John Oldham in a duo called Cowboy Loye & Just Plain John) and moved to WMMN in Fairmont, West Virginia. For all his regional popularity, he never made a single recording, and his career was cut short due to complications during a rather routine operation for stomach ulcers; he died at the Cleveland Clinic on March 15, 1941. Another of a great many possible examples is Jerry Smith, "the Yodeling Cowboy" (1910–1986). A star of the *WHO Barn Dance* in Des Moines, he managed to appear in one Ranger Busters film, *West of Pinto Basin* (Monogram, 1940), published two songbooks, and had a long and active career, but he recorded only for tiny regional labels such as Warrior, AD, Blue Star, and Mastertone.

Cowboys and cowboy music came early to network radio, one of the most charming shows also being one of the first, *Death Valley Days,* sponsored by Boraxo and first broadcast on the NBC Blue network in 1930. (In its early years NBC had a Blue network and a Red network; the Red network was eventually spun off and became ABC.) From 1930 to 1936 the part of "the Lonesome Cowboy" was played by John White, a student of authentic cowboy songs. Despite being from the urban East, White conveyed a sincerity and unpretentiousness in his singing, and the sound of cowboy music deftly woven into a radio adventure further solidified the idea of a singing cowboy in the national public mind.

Another of the earliest and most successful programs was *Bobby Benson's Adventures,* which began in 1932 on CBS. A juvenile adventure show, it popularized the weekly exploits of twelve-year-old Bobby, who operated the B-Bar-B Ranch with the help of his B-Bar-B Riders. The ranch foreman, Tex Mason, was played by a number of radio actors, most notably Tex Ritter. Apparently valuing the medium of radio highly, Ritter also appeared with the Lone Star Rangers on WOR in New York, and later on *Cowboy Tom's Roundup,* a daily children's show. In addition, he hosted his own show, *Tex Ritter's Campfire,* on WHN in 1932, and he and Ray Whitley cohosted the *WHN Barn Dance,* New York's attempt to capitalize on the barn dance craze in radio. As for the Bobby Benson show, it lasted well into the 1950s, until the end of network radio. A spin-off, *Songs of the B-Bar-B,* appeared on the Mutual network from 1952 to 1954 and featured New York singing cowboy Tex Fletcher leading campfire sing-alongs.

Recording pioneer Carson Robison, backed by Bill, John, and Pearl Mitchell, broadcast a half-hour show over NBC called *Carson Robison's Bucka-*

John White, who played the part of "the Lonesome Cowboy" on NBC radio's popular western *Death Valley Days* from 1930 to 1936. (Country Music Hall of Fame collections)

*roos* starting in 1938. The same year, future Grand Ole Opry performer the Duke of Paducah (Whitey Ford) began a show on NBC called *Plantation Party.* Primarily a country music and comedy show, it nevertheless featured many western performers, including Dolly and Millie Good (the Girls of the Golden West), Louise Massey & the Westerners, and the Range Riders.

The following year, on the West Coast, action star Johnny Mack Brown launched a CBS network show called *The Johnny Mack Brown Show,* sometimes titled *Under Western Skies.* Though he is not normally associated with singing, music was often a part of his Monogram films, usually when he worked with supporters like Jimmy Wakely, or when he costarred with Tex Ritter. His radio series featured vocalist Isleta Gayle and a band called the Texas Rangers and was for its limited run a musical variety show. Western music on the radio hit a major watershed in 1940, with the advent of the popular Sons of the Pioneers transcriptions and the premier of Gene Autry's hugely successful *Melody Ranch* on CBS.

All this radio exposure had a profound effect on the popularity of western recordings. Although the first country music recordings came out in the early 1920s, it took cowboy music a couple of years longer to make it to disc, Bentley Ball's efforts aside. On August 13, 1924, prolific light-opera tenor Vernon Dalhart stepped to the Victor microphone to sing "Way out West in Kansas," a song he shortly recut for Victor on the milestone session that yielded "Wreck of the Old 97" and "The Prisoner's Song," the 78 release that became country music's first million-seller.

Dalhart was born Marion Try Slaughter in the East Texas city of Jefferson on April 6, 1883. He may, as he claimed, have heard cowboy songs as a youth and have done some ranch work as a teenager, but he studied voice at the Dallas Conservatory of Music and moved to New York upon graduation. Feeling that Marion Slaughter was not a particularly effective professional name, he chose the name of two West Texas towns as his stage name and had a solid, unspectacular career as a concert and recording artist before being among the very first to record folk or country music. Signed by Edison in 1915, he had a good bit of success recording light opera. When that career faded, he began a second successful career recording sentimental and dialect songs like "Can't You Heah Me Callin', Caroline," a 1917 Edison cut that was by far his biggest early record and was the song most associated with him until the second phase of his career cooled. At that point he reinvented himself once again, trying folk and rural music. That experimental session of cowboy and country songs of August 1924 changed his career and the course of country music.

Though Dalhart was a Texan, his style owed far more to the concert stage than to the old corral or barn dance, and though his singing occasionally sounds stiff and mannered by today's standards, he was an enormously popular recording artist of his era. Not only did he sell millions of records, but also he was a nonstop recording machine himself, cutting many sides a week, literally hundreds throughout his career. Exclusive contracts were rare in those days, and he recorded under a variety of pseudonyms for a range of labels, including Victor, Edison, Columbia, and Brunswick.

Had "Way out West in Kansas" become the hit record from that August recording session, Vernon Dalhart might have made a far greater mark on cowboy music, but the unexpected runaway success of "The Prisoner's Song" and "Wreck of the Old 97" pointed to a career in country recording—or at least his version of country. On record he was usually accompanied by a guitar (often played by Carson Robison), his own harmonica, and the mournful violin of Adelyne Hood. Besides standard country songs of the era—many written by Robison, who could write them as fast as Dalhart could record them—he began a fad of commemorating current events in song, and he made dozens of sides for dozens of labels in the middle 1920s with such titles as "Little Mary Phagan," "The Santa Barbara Earthquake," "The Death of Floyd Collins," "The Freight Wreck at Altoona," "The John T.

Vernon Dalhart at the end of his long
career. (Author's collection)

Scopes Trial," "Little Marion Parker," and even "There's a New Star in
Heaven To-Night (Rudolph Valentino)." All were recorded with the homey
guitar, harmonica, and violin accompaniment.

There was a smattering of cowboy songs in this avalanche of material:
"I'd Like to Be in Texas (When They Round Up in the Spring)," "Oh Bury
Me Not on the Lone Prairie," "Jesse James," "Billy the Kid," the first recording of "Home on the Range," "When the Work's All Done This Fall" in
1927 and Robison's "The Little Green Valley" in 1928. Although the collaboration between Dalhart and Robison eventually ended in a rancorous
split over the issue of record royalties, the two men recorded a great many
duets during their professional association. These are some of the best sides
of Dalhart's recorded career; his singing was more intimate, less mannered,
more natural. At times the light-opera or comic hillbilly approaches were
set aside, and Dalhart's voice, both solo and with Robison's harmony, proved
to be quite lovely, unpretentious, and affecting. But time and tastes change
quickly, and though Dalhart recorded hundreds of sides for dozens of labels
between 1925 and 1930, after 1930 months, not days, elapsed between recordings. He cut but twelve songs in 1931, six in 1932, none in 1933, and six
in 1934, and he last recorded as Vernon Dalhart & His Big Cypress Boys in
1939. Of those final six sides, one was western—Everett Cheetham's novelty "Lavender Cowboy," complete with labored hillbilly accent. Dalhart
grew cold as quickly as he'd gotten hot, and he wound up teaching voice,
then eventually working, in total obscurity, as a factory night watchman. He
was a desk clerk at a Bridgeport, Connecticut, hotel at the time of his death
on September 16, 1948.

Although Dalhart holds the honor of having the first cowboy recording released as a rural-oriented record, his achievement was followed within months by the first cowboy songs recorded by a true folk performer. On November 8, 1924, Charles Nabell recorded cowboy and religious songs for OKeh Records in St. Louis, including "The Great Roundup" and "Utah Carl," followed in March 1925 by "The Letter from Home Sweet Home." OKeh may have had big plans for Nabell, for he recorded twelve other songs in subsequent sessions, but none were successful. He, like several others of these early recording artists, has slipped through the cracks of history. No more is known of him except that he cut these sides and then disappeared into the roiling masses of humanity. He was born January 14, 1885, and died in Joplin, Missouri, in January 1977.

Although Dalhart's first cowboy recordings in 1924 caused not much of a ripple, the following year a young Texan named Carl T. Sprague with a real cowboy background recorded the first cowboy hit record. Sprague journeyed to Camden, New Jersey, to record "When the Work's All Done This Fall" on August 5, 1925, along with "Following the Cow Trail," "Cowboy Love Song," and "The Last Great Roundup." He was born on May 10, 1895, on a cattle ranch near Alvin, served in World War I, and graduated from Texas A&M in 1922. He spent the next fifteen years at that college—when not recording—in the athletic department. Sprague's recording career was short, his repertoire pure cowboy. He cut four songs in June 1926, five in 1927, and four in 1929. Like many of his era, a potentially longer career was cut short by the ravaging effects of the Depression, and also by his exhortative singing style, which sounded quite dated as the invention of electrical recording in 1925 ushered in and popularized softer, more intimate singing approaches. Sprague's voice was a rather piercing tenor, and despite the dramatic success of his first record, he apparently had little interest in pursuing a career onstage. He would not record again until 1972, when at the age of seventy-seven he cut an album for a German folk label. Sprague spent most of his life in and around Texas A&M, living in Bryan until his death on February 19, 1979.

The only other recordings related to singing cowboys in 1925 were made in two sessions by Jimmie Wilson's Catfish String Band in Dallas in October. This is the band with which Gene Autry appeared when he got a job at Tulsa radio station KVOO, before he returned to New York to begin a recording career. Overall, the recording repertoire of Wilson's outfit consisted of novelty and old-fashioned pop tunes.

The following April saw the recording debut of Dalhart's singing partner, Carson J. Robison, a great and underrated pioneer in western, popular, and country music. His first appearances on record were as an accompanist, playing guitar or whistling or both, often on records released in the popular series. As a featured artist he did not cut his first true western recording—his own "The Little Green Valley"—until June 1928, for OKeh. Among the dozens and dozens of sides he recorded in the course of his career—for the

Carl T. Sprague, who recorded the first cowboy music "hit," "When the Work's All Done This Fall," in 1925. (Country Music Hall of Fame collections)

Carson J. Robison and Vernon Dalhart, as featured on a piece of sheet music issued in 1927 at the peak of their creative collaboration. (Country Music Hall of Fame collections)

most part popular, hillbilly, or those event songs that he wrote so often and easily—there were many cowboy gems, most of them the popular western songs of that era: "Red River Valley," "The Strawberry Roan," and "When the Work's All Done This Fall." He was also among the first to popularize "Home on the Range."

Carson Jay Robison was born to a musical family (his father was a fiddler and square-dance caller) in Oswego, Kansas, on August 4, 1890. After drifting through a few desultory years of work in railroading and the booming oil business, and after serving in World War I, he decided music was his true calling. Robison moved to Kansas City in about 1920, where besides appearing with jazz bands in the very musical Kansas City jazz scene, he became one of the first cowboy singers on the air, when he began broadcasting over WDAF in 1922. He was first associated with one-hit wonder Wendell Hall (1896–1969), whose "It Ain't Gonna Rain No Mo'" was a national novelty hit in 1923 and 1924.

Robison moved to New York in 1924, where he found immediate work in the heart of the jazz age as a whistler, guitarist, and songwriter. As a singer he had great range and a fine ear for harmony. His vocal style, formed in a pre-microphone era, was at first a tad stiff and overenunciated, yet he eventually learned to sing more gently, becoming intimate with the microphone.

Frank Luther, as depicted on a 1934 songbook. (Country Music Hall of Fame collections)

His guitar playing was similar, a little stiff but highly professional and versatile. Robison's prolific songwriting was remarkable then and now, but it is no wonder that he was first known for his whistling. It is astonishing; he was truly a virtuoso. Within months of his move to New York, he teamed up with Dalhart, with whom he recorded as accompanist and tenor singer, and for whom he wrote songs extensively. By 1924 Dalhart was around forty-one years old; Robison was thirty-four and, though a country boy new to the big city, was a seasoned and experienced professional fluent in styles ranging from pop to jazz to folk to cowboy.

The collaboration between the two men drew on Robison's musical strengths. Dalhart was not a songwriter, and his hectic recording schedule made new material, and a lot of it, a necessity. Robison was there, and any news event or disaster was fodder for a new song. In addition, Robison played guitar, which Dalhart could not, and he was a gifted tenor singer who put his ear for harmony to good use on many a Dalhart session. He also recorded frequently on his own, and his repertoire ran the gamut from topical-event songs to novelties, mountain music, cowboy songs, and light pop. Billing himself as Carson Robison & His Kansas City Jack-Rabbits, he even recorded some early rhythm & blues sides—then known as "race records"—such as "Stuff" and "Nonsense" on Victor. So varied was his recorded output, in fact, that historian Robert Coltman remarked, "A casual listener might be forgiven for believing that a stack of six or eight Robison records was by six or eight different artists."[4]

After the bitter falling out with the contentious Dalhart, Robison found a new recording and songwriting partner in Frank Luther. The duo's first collaboration produced an immediate national novelty hit, "Barnacle Bill the Sailor," in 1929. When national interest in cowboy songs began to perk up in the early 1930s, these two professionals, whose roots were in the West (both were Kansans), were among the avant-garde in writing and recording western material. By 1929 Robison was the subject of a long article and interview in *Collier's* for the success of his songwriting, and by 1930 his song folios trumpeted the national hits he'd written: "Barnacle Bill," "Left My Gal in the Mountains," "Open Up Them Pearly Gates," and "Sleepy Rio Grande."

After recording nearly three hundred songs together, Robison and Frank Luther amicably parted ways in April 1932. Robison then concentrated more and more on a western sound and image similar to what the Sons of the Pioneers were simultaneously developing on the West Coast: a romantic, visual, dreamy approach to western music, as opposed to the cowboy story songs of ranch and range life that were then the staple of the style. More interested in singing harmony than in solo vocals, Robison recorded and appeared on radio and in person with Luther and Zora Layman, then with John and Bill Mitchell and Pearl Pickens Mitchell, first as Carson Robison & His Pioneers, then as Carson Robison & His Buckaroos, adding John Mitchell on tenor banjo and Frank Novak on bass. Despite the western names and image of his several groups, they did not record extensively in the western style. Their repertoire ran heavily to laments for the old Smoky, Cumberland, or Blue Ridge Mountains.

Robison's bands were the first in country or western music to tour overseas. Billed as Carson Robison's Pioneers, the group toured England, Australia, and New Zealand (with Luther and the Mitchells) in 1932, and Robison returned to England with his Buckaroos in 1936 and 1939. He and his Buckaroos concentrated on radio throughout the 1930s and during the war years, and landed a network radio show that emphasized a western setting (it purportedly took place on the CR Ranch) but that musically skipped adroitly from western to contemporary pop to country to popular standards to sentimental songs to novelty—a microcosm of Robison's career from the early 1930s on.

Robison faded into relative obscurity in later years, though he did enjoy an anti-Hitler wartime hit called "1942 Turkey in the Straw" and had a surprise national hit at the age of fifty-eight with the laconic, tongue-in-cheek "Life Gets Tee-jus, Don't It?" in 1948. He died in Poughkeepsie, near his rambling 140-acre Duchess County estate, on March 24, 1957. His death came just as a new craze for folk music was beginning, ironically not unlike

Otto Gray & His Oklahoma Cowboys at station WGY-Schenectady. This pioneering and influential troupe was the first full-time professional cowboy band. (Country Music Hall of Fame collections)

the wave he had ridden—and indeed had helped create—some forty years before.

The year 1926 also saw the recording debut of an extremely influential and often overlooked western-music pioneer, Otto Gray & His Oklahoma Cowboys. Otto Gray (March 2, 1884–November 8, 1967) neither played nor sang; he financed, fronted, and managed—and was a skilled trick roper and a savvy publicist. He began a performing career as Otto & His Rodeo Rubes in 1918 and took over the reins of the Billy McGinty Cowboy Band in 1924, immediately changing the name to Otto Gray & His Oklahoma Cowboys. The group started a career over KFRU in Bristow, Oklahoma (which became KVOO in Tulsa), then moved to KFJF in Oklahoma. Their fame spread rapidly, and from 1928 through 1932 they tirelessly toured and broadcast in the Northeast. Traveling in huge sedans outfitted to look like railroad locomotives, complete with cowcatchers, the group became a success on the theater circuits of the era due to their dramatic showmanship—with whip and rope tricks in addition to music—their flashy costumes, and the visual humor and wide variety of their musical material. Indeed, so great was their nationwide popularity on radio and on the stage that Otto Gray was the first cowboy entertainer ever to grace the cover of *Billboard*.

The band's image may have been pure cowboy, but their recording repertoire was heavily sentimental and hillbilly and featured the sweet vocals of Grace "Mommie" Gray, beginning in St. Louis with their May 1926

OKeh recording of "The Cowboy's Dream," a merry fiddle tune with no relation to the lament of the same title. They lasted until 1936, and although their recorded output left little impression, their enormous success in promoting the romantic cowboy image onstage paved the way for both the singing cowboys and the western-swing dance bands to come. Historian Guy Logsdon sees the Oklahoma Cowboys as pivotal not only to the subsequent popularity of western music, but also to the adoption of western attire by many entertainers: "Their western clothes, combined with their popularity, had an influence on other performers departing from hillbilly attire and using the Western image for costumes."[5] Having left little that is memorable on record, they rank among those influential performers who make mighty waves while active but are quickly forgotten when their particular tide ebbs.

Otto Gray & His Oklahoma Cowboys were influential in fostering careers, as well. Band members through the years included future Grand Ole Opry stars Zeke Clements and Whitey "the Duke of Paducah" Ford and future *National Barn Dance* star Rube Tronson. They made one film, an eponymous 1929 one-reel short, condensing their vaudeville show into a blitz of short skits that captured their manic tomfoolery and top-notch musicianship; it leaves the viewer breathless.

As the decade progressed, record labels afforded more and more opportunity for western performers. Although a few fiddlers had recorded before Vernon Dalhart, his success had opened the floodgates for the recording of folk, blues, hillbilly, and western performers. As the 1920s progressed, more cowboys would sing on record, whether they were genuine cowpokes or simply performers from other styles who took a shot at recording a cowboy song or two. Such was Ewan Hall, who, though billed as the Cowboy Minstrel, had already recorded several sides in Brunswick/ Vocalion's popular series when he cut "The Cowboy's Lament" and "Lavender Cowboy" on March 21, 1927.

A similar case could be made for Frank Marvin (1904–1985), who began his recording career with "Bully of the Town" for the Grey Gull label around July 1927. He was the younger brother of recording and stage star Johnny Marvin (1897–1944), who himself had recorded and yodeled on a few western sides, such as "Little Sweetheart of the Prairie." An adept musician on guitar, ukulele, and steel guitar, Frank was a fine yodeler as well, and much of his early recorded repertoire was blue yodeling in exactly the style of Jimmie Rodgers. In fact, he basically became Brunswick Records's answer to Victor's monumentally popular Rodgers. Much of Frank Marvin's material was released in the popular series as well, though he had several sides released on Supertone as "the Texas Ranger." Who knows where his career might have gone had not fate, in the person of a brash young Oklahoman named Gene Autry, come banging at his and Johnny's door. (We'll take a longer look at the careers of the Marvin brothers in chapter 6, on Gene Autry.)

Johnny Marvin, known in the 1920s on New York radio as "the Lonesome Singer of the Air," later became a trusted friend and colleague of Gene Autry. (Author's collection)

Whatever the success or influence of Otto Gray, Carl T. Sprague, Vernon Dalhart, or Carson Robison, no performer to this point was to have as profound an impact on western music as Jimmie Rodgers, the young vaudeville artist and ex–railroad worker who stood before the Victor microphones in Bristol, Tennessee, to make his first recordings on August 4, 1927. James Charles Rodgers was a tubercular Mississippian who sang popular and sentimental songs in a gentle, soothing voice with a honeyed southern accent. It was his particular genius to integrate the guitar-driven blues music of his black fellow Mississippians with the rural white music of his upbringing—not wholly unlike what Elvis Presley would do thirty years later—and to add to it his trademark "blue yodel."

The result was sensational. The simple but clever twelve-bar blues sung with Rodgers's drawling, likable, thickly accented, slightly adenoidal voice, punctuated by evocative, lonesome yodeling, caught the ear of America's record buyers, and though his appeal was largely in the South it was far from exclusively regional. Those simple blue yodels, and bluesy tales of ramblers and rounders, took much of the nation by storm.

Jimmie Rodgers was not a cowboy and never pretended to be. His general performing attire was a light-colored suit and a straw boater, though he often—and in his only screen appearance—dressed as a railroad brakeman, and indeed was known as the Singing Brakeman. But on at least two photo shoots, and for some live appearances, he decked himself out royally in finest cowboy gear: chaps, vest, leather cuffs, broad-brimmed hat, and rope. Like most Americans at least half in love with the romantic image of the West, he became increasingly enthralled with cowboy songs and the cowboy image, and he relocated to Kerrville, Texas, where he hoped the hot dry climate would slow the advance of his disease. He did not record a cowboy song until his seventh recording session, cutting "Desert Blues" in New York on February 21, 1929, but he then went on to write and record a number of influential songs about the West: "Yodeling Cowboy," "When the Cactus Is in Bloom," "Cowhand's Last Ride," and four other yodeling cowboy songs.

The depth of his influence was partly in the cowboy image he only occasionally projected and partly in the cowboy songs he wrote, which, though not exceptional, were well crafted and vivid and sometimes quite humorous. It was also partly the result of his ubiquity. Virtually every rural home with a record player—and a great many in the city—had several Jimmie Rodgers records. But it was unquestionably his little yodel that made the most lasting mark on western music. Born in Meridian, Mississippi, on September 8, 1897, Rodgers died in New York on May 26, 1933 after finishing up a final recording session at which he was so weak from the progression of his illness that he lay on a cot between takes. He was just thirty-five years old.

Although a kind of yodeling and indeed falsetto singing was not unknown to cowboys, Jimmie Rodgers gave it a shape and a form, and western singers took to it with a passion. Of course, they weren't the only ones. Country and popular singers from far-flung regions also learned to break their voices: Hank Snow and Wilf Carter in Canada, Ernest Tubb in Texas, Grandpa Jones and Bill Monroe in Kentucky, Johnny and Frank Marvin in New York. Two young singers developed the yodel to a stratospheric art, Elton Britt and Ray Whitley. And there was the young Ohioan Len Slye, probably the first to take Rodgers's drawling, bluesy yodels and turn them into astonishing athletic adventures, first as a member of the Sons of the Pioneers, and later when he became known to the world as Roy Rogers. But while these artists owed a strong debt to the Singing Brakeman, none was so clearly influenced at the start of his career as Gene Autry, whose early records feature a voice that is nearly indistinguishable from that of Rodgers.

The year 1928 introduced several more fascinating cowboy singers to the record-buying public. Marc Williams, billed as the Cowboy Crooner and the Singing Texan, began an eight-year recording career March 22–24 when he recorded "Sam Bass," "The Cowboy's Dream, " "When the Work's All Done This Fall," "Jesse James," "Little Joe the Wrangler," "Utah Carroll," and the indescribably haunting "Sioux Indians" for the Brunswick label in Chicago. His repertoire (until his final 1936 sessions, where he cut pop standards like "My Blue Heaven" and "Melancholy Baby") was pure cowboy

Jimmie Rodgers, "the Singing Brakeman," who could certainly spot a strong commercial trend, in full cowboy regalia. (Country Music Hall of Fame collections)

and included many of the finest of the older narrative songs the genre had to offer, songs that focused on the hazardous life of the cowboy, and on the desperadoes who peopled the old Old West. Obviously a trained singer, Williams also brought conviction, authority, and sincerity to his work. His story remains shrouded in mystery; his birth and death have gone undiscovered, and other than a radio stint as Happy Hank over WHO in Des Moines in the 1930s, he rides into the history of the singing cowboy and out again as though in a snowstorm, leaving hardly a trace.

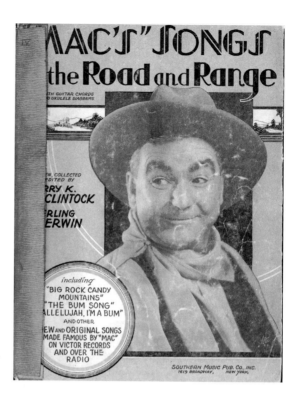

Harry "Haywire Mac" McClintock, as depicted on a 1932 songbook. (Country Music Hall of Fame collections)

March 1928 also saw the recording debut of Haywire Mac, one of singing cowboydom's more colorful characters. Born Harry K. McClintock in Knoxville, Tennessee, on October 8, 1882, he was a forty-five-year-old veteran of the rails and hobo camps, of leftist politics and of radio (KFRC in San Francisco), when he first recorded for Victor in Oakland, California, on March 1. These sessions yielded the historic first recordings of such now familiar cowboy classics as "Get Along, Little Dogies" and "Goodbye Old Paint." He similarly introduced "Billy Venero" and "Sweet Betsy from Pike" on his March 10 sessions; in all, he recorded ten other cowboy classics that month alone. His voice was straightforward and unadorned by vibrato, and his performances were strong and confident. It was with these sessions that Haywire Mac's cowboy recording career begins and ends, for although he recorded a fair bit after March 1928, the majority of his subsequent recordings were hobo and bum songs popular in the difficult times of the Depression. Included among them are his two most famous compositions, "The Big Rock Candy Mountain" and "Hallelujah, I'm a Bum." His career as a musical eccentric and political activist went on for a number of years, ending with his death on April 24, 1957.

Almost as colorful was Jules Verne Allen, born in Waxahatchie, Texas, on April 1, 1883. Although born within the same week as Vernon Dalhart, he studied music not at the Dallas Conservatory but in the cow camps. He became an adequate guitarist and wound up on radio in the 1920s, billing

Jules Verne Allen, the self-styled "Original Singing Cowboy," was a genuine cowboy, though he sang on record only briefly, in 1928 and 1929. (Country Music Hall of Fame collections)

himself as "the Original Singing Cowboy" (and at other times as "Lonesome Luke" and "Shiftless"), and appeared in Los Angeles, Dallas, and San Antonio. He had just turned forty-five when he made his debut recordings in El Paso on April 21, 1928, where he recorded "Little Joe the Wrangler" and "Jack O'Diamonds"; he went on to record five more pure cowboy tunes that month. His only other recordings occurred over three sessions in the spring of 1929, two in Hollywood and one in Culver City, during which he recorded ten other traditional cowboy songs. Allen can be seen as a transitional figure in a way, for his singing (especially on "Longside the Santa Fe Trail") was soft and gentle, far more intimate than the robust, exhortative style of many of his contemporaries who recorded cowboy folk songs.[6] The effects of the Depression on record sales, as well as his old-fashioned repertoire, brought Allen's recording career to a close, though he remained active on radio for a number of years, and he died in 1945. Allen was one of the first to write about the cowboy life and cowboy songs, and his *Cowboy Lore* was published by the Naylor Company of San Antonio in 1933.

Charlie Craver (Arkansas Charlie) also recorded a bit of cowboy material in 1928 and 1929, but his strength, and the bulk of his repertoire, was hobo and hillbilly. The last important figure introduced in 1928 was Luther W. Ossenbrink, known professionally as Arkie, the Arkansas Woodchopper, who first recorded in Dallas on December 6. The label was Columbia, the songs "The Cowboy's Dream" and "The Dying Cowboy." The Arkansas Woodchopper was soon to become a major star of the *WLS Barn Dance,* and though he recorded with relative frequency in the years before the Depression, he was more a radio personality than a record seller. His image, true to his stage name, was that of an outdoorsman rather than a full-fledged cowboy, but he recorded a dozen cowboy songs between 1928 and 1931. That he recorded so many during this time is probably a good indication of the rising interest in the music of the cowboy. In some ways, perhaps, he was paving the way for Gene Autry as a singing cowboy at WLS. Arkie's voice was straightforward and unadorned, featuring, in his early records, the blurring of the letter *r* that so many singers copied from Jimmie Rodgers. The Arkansas Woodchopper proved himself to be quite an adept yodeler, as well, mastering a trickier version of the blue yodel on, for example, "I'm a Texas Cowboy," recorded in November 1931.

Born near Knob Noster, Missouri, on March 2, 1907, Arkie broke into radio on KMBC in Kansas City in 1928 and moved to the *WLS Barn Dance* the following year, staying with the show until its demise in 1960. He died June 23, 1981, in retirement in his native Missouri.

In December 1928 a fine Texas old-time fiddle duo returned to the studio in Dallas. Bernard and Jack, the Cartwright Brothers, had recorded four fiddle tunes for Columbia a year before. According to Jack: "Our first records were instrumentals, later we were expected to sing. There we hit a snag—my voice has such a narrow range, we could sing very few pieces together."[7] In fact, Jack had a haunting voice, and he used it effectively on a number of cowboy standards ("On the Old Chisholm Trail," "Utah Carrol," "When the Work's All Done This Fall") and most unforgettably on the mournful "Texas Rangers," recorded in August 1929 for Victor. The Cartwrights' repertoire was half traditional cowboy, half fiddle tunes, for Bern Cartwright had been one of Texas's most noted fiddlers for years. They both continued musical careers after a final Victor session in October 1929 (again two cowboy songs, two fiddle tunes), playing on WOAI in San Antonio in the 1930s. Bernard eventually gave up music to become postmaster of Boerne, Texas, while Jack played guitar, banjo, and bass with a number of bands until 1954.

The trickle was becoming a steady stream. A dozen new singers of cowboy songs found their way to recording studios in 1929. Many are today merely footnotes, such as Phil Pavey and Dick Devall, the latter a gifted and obviously professional singer who recorded merry cowboy music with guitar and rollicking banjo accompaniment. Others are noteworthy more because they were the first rather than because they demonstrated outstanding musical merit: plaintive and affecting Billie Maxwell (the first woman), and Big Chief Henry's Indians (the first Native Americans). Some are of interest because of who they played with, or who played with them: Len Nash & His Country Boys included both Hugh and Karl Farr, later to gain renown with the Sons of the Pioneers.

Billie Maxwell was an interesting case. Born in Arizona in February

Arkie the Woodchopper, star of WLS's *National Barn Dance*, gets a lesson in strumming technique. (Author's collection)

1906, she trekked to El Paso in July 1929 to record as part of her father Curt's popular string band, the White Mountain Orchestra, which had established a local reputation playing cowboy dances. Almost as an afterthought, legendary Victor producer Ralph Peer asked her if she sang, and she burst forth with a haunting version of "Billy Venero." Peer immediately recorded it at this session, Maxwell's evocative voice accompanied only by her father on fiddle. Suitably impressed, Peer invited her to appear on a second session of her own, and on July 7 she returned to cut, in addition to a couple of older popular tunes, the eerie "Haunted Hunter" and a song from the woman's point of view, "The Cowboy's Wife." The records did not sell well, and these were her only sessions. She had married Chester Warner earlier that year and was four months pregnant when she made these recordings, and although she continued to play in her father's band from time to time, she drifted out of professional music making and concentrated on raising a family until her untimely death in 1954.

Adelyne Hood, long-suffering accompanist of Vernon Dalhart, made her first solo records singing western songs in 1929, and though she was not a cowgirl singer by any means, she deserves a closer look as a fascinating cross-cultural musician, mixing classical, folk, sentimental, and vaudeville comedy strains into her style over a long career. Born in South Carolina in

1897, she moved to New York to formally study piano and violin at Juilliard. In addition to her classical training, she also had a marvelous gift for comedy, and she recorded a number of comic sketches with Dalhart and Carson Robison, and later with John White. Some were western—a song and skits called "Calamity Jane," "The Daughter of Calamity Jane," and "Alaska Ann and Yukon Steve." After Robison and Dalhart's breakup, Hood sang and played popular and concert music all over the United States and Europe, but her gift as a dialect performer landed her the role of Aunt Jemima on radio. Taking the blackface and bonnet to Pittsburgh, she portrayed a similar character, Aunt Caroline, on the air for six years. Marriage to a Pittsburgh food broker in the mid-1940s effectively ended her career, and she died in that city on April 11, 1958. She crossed a great many boundaries in her now largely forgotten career.

Some others who began recording cowboy songs as the Depression dawned, like Bradley Kincaid (1895–1989), are interesting because their willingness, as deeply traditional mountain recording artists, to record such tunes indicates that national interest in western songs was continuing to grow. A couple of them—John White and Stuart Hamblen—deserve a closer look.

Carl Stuart Hamblen was born in Kellyville, Texas, on October 20, 1908; he attended high school in Clarendon, Texas, and college in Lubbock and Abilene, to become a schoolteacher. By 1925 he was already singing on radio in Dallas and Fort Worth, going by the radio moniker Cowboy Joe, and in 1929 he journeyed to Camden, New Jersey, using the $100 proceeds of a talent contest he'd won. His avowed goal was to record for Victor, Jimmie Rodgers's label, and he auditioned and recorded his first sides—all hillbilly—on June 6, 1929. The apocryphal story goes that, having been politely brushed off by the Victor executives and told to come back the next week, he and his dog Shep proceeded to honor what he considered to be his contract by camping out for that week in Victor's lobby. Apparently the dog's ill temper and gamy smell finally wore down the staff and executives, and Victor grudgingly recorded six sides. "I did it, Shep!" he crowed in exultation as they left the studio. The beleaguered receptionist reportedly snapped, "What do you mean you did it? Give all the credit to your dog!"[8]

Hamblen took the proceeds from this first recording session and headed west for California. There, with the brashness and confidence that marked his audition with Victor, he auditioned for KFI, singing and yodeling "The Johnstown Flood"—the tune that had won him the talent contest—and he was hired for the *Saturday Night Jamboree*. It was not until his fourth recording session, in August 1930, that he recorded a western song, "By the Sleepy Rio Grande."

Hamblen briefly joined the Beverly Hillbillies, recorded some more for Victor, formed a band that included the young Patsy Montana, and wrote a great many more songs. On April 18, 1934, he became the first cowboy

Stuart Hamblen, *left,* at the start of his career, with film star Buck Jones.
(Photo courtesy of Lida Rose Maze)

singer to record for Jack Kapp's upstart budget Decca label, and on August 3 he recorded "Poor Unlucky Cowboy" and his classic "Texas Plains" for that label. He and his band, the Lucky Stars, became extremely popular in Southern California at about this time, and a friendly rivalry with the Sons of the Pioneers led to more than a few rather rough practical jokes. Hamblen & the Lucky Stars were the kings of Los Angeles country-western radio for a number of years, on a variety of stations.

Stuart Hamblen did find work in films, but never as a hero. Though an accomplished rider and a large, strapping man, his tough good looks typecast him in roles as bad guy, sheriff, or Indian. Never as popular as the Pioneers on record, he nonetheless recorded frequently for American Record Artists and Four Star, and he concentrated on his limited movie appearances and his very active radio and dance hall career. He signed with A&R (artist and repertoire) man Arthur E. Satherley and Columbia Records in 1949, rather late in his career (he was forty-one), and the association produced several classic nonwestern songs, such as "Remember Me (I'm the One Who Loves You)" and "It Is No Secret," which has been recorded by more than three hundred artists; Jo Stafford's recording alone sold some two million copies. Songwriting had always been one of Hamblen's great strengths; from 1949 it would dominate his career. A conversion after attending a Billy Graham appearance led him to devote the rest of his career to religious pursuits; he even ran for president on the Prohibition Party ticket in 1952.

Hamblen returned to RCA in 1954, where he recorded his biggest hit as a recording artist and songwriter, "This Old House," though Rosemary Clooney's #1 pop version far outsold his. His output for RCA was heavily religious, and with the coming of rock & roll he spent the next couple of decades in genial semi-retirement. The proceeds from his songwriting successes allowed him to purchase Errol Flynn's eight-acre estate and mansion on Mulholland Drive in Hollywood, and from that lofty aerie he picked and chose his appearances, radio shows, and recordings. Hamblen remained active as a rancher and songwriter and was working on an autobiography when he passed away March 6, 1989, at the age of eighty.

John I. White was born in New Jersey on April 12, 1902, and became interested in cowboy songs and music after hearing Romaine Lowdermilk (1890–1970) sing at a dude ranch in Arizona in 1924. On August 9, 1929, he recorded "The Little Old Sod Shanty" and "Great Grand Dad" for producer Arthur Satherley and the American Record Corporation (ARC), probably accompanied by Roy Smeck (who had landed him the contract) on guitar and harmonica; he published a song folio, *The Lonesome Cowboy: Songs of the Plains and Hills,* that same year. From 1930 to 1936 he played the role of the Lonesome Cowboy on the network radio program *Death Valley Days.* The remainder of his recording career consisted, in his words, of "alleged hillbilly numbers written in Tin Pan Alley and songs recorded by that busiest of hillbilly singers, Vernon Dalhart, who for legal reasons could not record for Satherley's company."[9] On his final session in April 1931 he returned to cowboy songs—"Whoopee-Ti-Yi-Yo (Little Doggie)" and "Strawberry Roan." White left show business in 1936 to attend to his mapmaking business— "Radio and recording had both been moonlighting operations"[10]—but when he retired in 1965 he collected information from his lifetime of research into cowboy songs and their origin in a delightful book called *Git Along Little Dogies: Songs and Songmakers of the American West,* published by the University of Illinois Press in 1975. In many ways the publishing of this handsome book was one of the several things that helped spark the revival of interest in western music. White died at his New Jersey home on November 26, 1992, at the age of ninety.

Shortly after Gene Autry began his recording career as a singer of sen-

A 1937 songbook from Powder River Jack and Kitty Lee, who focused on traditional cowboy songs such as "Tying Knots in the Devil's Tail." (Country Music Hall of Fame collections)

timental songs and blue yodels in 1929, a posse of other cowboys were turning up in recording studios. Many, like Jack Webb, J. D. Farley, Bill Simmons, Newton Gaines, Paul Hamblin, and the Two Cow Hands, came and went like drifting tumbleweeds, although Webb's traditional-sounding compositions "The Night Guard" and "The Roving Cowboy" (recorded for Victor in New York in May 1930) are minor masterpieces. Others, like Powder River Jack and Kitty Lee, left a more lasting mark, recording fine old-time cowboy songs, including Gail Gardner's "Tying Knots in the Devil's Tail," which for years Powder River Jack claimed he wrote. His voice was a quavering tenor that picked up well on early microphones and conferred a sort of authenticity, but that quickly sounded rather dated.

Goebel Reeves, "the Texas Drifter," began recording in 1929, as well. Born October 9, 1899, in Sherman, Texas, he had a long career on record and radio—including stints on Rudy Vallee's and Judy Canova's shows, as well as the Grand Ole Opry and the *National Barn Dance*—but he became far better known throughout his long career for his novelty and hobo songs. Although Reeves recorded little western music, reportedly "Little Joe the Wrangler," cut for ARC in 1931, was one of his showstoppers. He too was a yodeler, with a distinctive trill. Increasingly disenchanted with show business, he drifted away from it in the late 1930s and served as a merchant seaman through the war years. He finally settled in Los Angeles and, after a decade of poor health, died of a heart condition January 26, 1959.

ARC producer Art Satherley recorded several sessions with Patt Patterson & His Champion Rep Riders beginning in May 1930. He evidently thought quite highly of Patterson, but nothing in particular came of these releases. Patterson's voice was a strong, forceful, and rough-hewn tenor, with a somewhat exaggerated pronunciation and peculiar drawl. The backing was simple rhythm guitar and somewhat strident Hawaiian guitar, and his 1931 duet with Lois Dexter, "Snow Covered Face," is unsubtle but quite touching in its earnest way. Patterson's sound was unique, his voice surer and stronger than those of many of the folk cowboys recorded at this time, and he even yodeled a bit, though with more energy than precision. One can hear why Satherley thought so well of him, but the crushing effects of the Depression, which cut all record sales tenfold, probably doomed Patterson to a short career.

Gene Autry's sometime supervisor, singing partner, and future uncle-in-law Jimmy Long began an extensive solo recording career in March 1930; in fact, he recorded at least fourteen sessions apart from Autry, somewhat belying Autry's comment that "Jimmy was a very good musician; he could sing harmony, but I don't think he would have ever made it as a solo artist. Never would. But he had that high type of tenor voice in those days, and he could harmonize with me."[11] Although several record companies cut a great many sides on Long, hoping for solo success to strike, history has proved Autry correct: Long's style of singing, high and open throated, was already

A now rare 1932 songbook from Lois Dexter and Patt Patterson. Patterson recorded a dozen songs for the American Record Corporation, including his duets with Lois Dexter, but never achieved lasting fame. (Author's collection)

dated. Autry's more mellow, microphone-friendly approach was the wave of the future.

Long frequently recorded duets with his daughter Beverly, and in at least one instance as the Long Family Trio with Beverly and his niece Ina Mae Spivey just weeks before the latter married Gene Autry. Long's last solo sessions were in 1933, although he continued to record with Autry or as a trio with Autry and Smiley Burnette as late as 1937, after which he returned to the more stable life on the railroad in Springfield, Missouri.

April 1930 also saw the first recordings of the Beverly Hillbillies in Los Angeles, a band that despite its mountain music name had a profound effect on western music, both in the development of the vocal trio, and in the outstanding later careers of many of its members. The band itself was a wholly fictitious invention of three KMPC executives: station owner Raymond MacMillan, station manager Glen Rice, and staff announcer John McIntire. Hoping to boost station ratings, they invented a fictitious scenario and cast of characters, a group of Ozark refugees who lived in a remote hollow in the rugged mountains near Beverly Hills. Completely out of touch with civilization, these displaced mountaineers, according to this fiction, continued to live in the archaic mountain style of the 1850s. Rice was sent to "discover" a band of musicians among these throwbacks, who in reality were musicians recruited from KMPC staff and local talent.

The first was accordionist Leo Mannes, who took the name Zeke Manners in his new identity as leader of the musical mountaineers. Quickly added were local musicians Tom Murray (Pappy) and fiddler Henry Blaeholder (Hank Skillet). Renowned tenor Cyprian Paulette joined the group as Ezra Longnecker, and Aleth Hansen (Lem Giles) on guitar rounded out the aggregation, which recorded cowboy material like "When the Bloom Is on the Sage" and "Red River Valley" for Brunswick on April 25. Though their repertoire was largely of the sentimental mountain variety, there was plenty of western thrown in. By their 1932 recordings in San Francisco (where Charles Crook, professionally known as Charlie Quirk, was the featured vocalist), they were riding the rising boom in cowboy song, recording "The Big Corral," "Whoopi Ti Yi Yo Git Along Little Dogies," "Cowboy Joe," and "Ridge Runnin' Roan," Curly Fletcher's sequel to his own "Strawberry Roan."

Their records reveal a strong, well-rehearsed trio, which, although accurate in pitch, was without the blend the Sons of the Pioneers would later develop. It was on radio, however, that they made their mark. The gimmick dreamed up by the KMPC executives was a smashing success: Crowds in the hundreds and even thousands gathered to visit the Beverly Hillbillies at radio and personal appearances and publicity stunts, such as their discovery of teenage yodeling sensation Elton Britt. Although the Beverly Hillbillies' light shone bright, it was also brief. The novelty wore off for the public, and internal dissension and individual ambition split the group. By 1935 Pappy, Zeke, Ezra, and Elton were based in New York, where all would go on to active careers. Ezra returned to Los Angeles to record as Ezra Paulette & His Beverly Hillbillies in 1937, by which time their once red-hot career had become cold indeed. The San Francisco branch of the group thrived for a time, and then it too faded into obscurity. Manners, Britt, and Stuart Hamblen are the best known of the former members, but several other notable artists spent time among the frequently rotating personnel of the band, including Ken Carson, Curley Bradley, and Jack Ross (who became the Ranch Boys); Wesley Tuttle; and Lloyd Perryman.

The year 1931 was a singularly poor one for new western artists. A plethora of talent who in many cases sounded pretty similar and the effects of the Depression are just two probable reasons. Hank Keene; Ed Crane (alternately spelled Edward L. Crain), an unrelentingly old-fashioned singer of the exhortative nasal tenor stripe; and the popular Southern California radio band the Arizona Wranglers, led by Sheriff Loyal Underwood, all recorded that year without leaving much of an impression.

But 1932 was a different story and began with Everett Cheetham recording "Little Joe the Wrangler" and "The Siree Peaks" in San Francisco.[12]

Born August 19, 1902, he pops up again and again in the saga of the singing cowboy. His genuine cowboy background included years of entertaining dudes, leading trail rides, and competing in rodeos. He is best remembered for composing "Blood on the Saddle" and "The Lavender Cowboy," and for his appearance with Tex Ritter in Lynn Riggs's folk musical *Green Grow the Lilacs* in Boston, New York, and on tour in 1931 and 1932. While appearing in New York as contestants in the annual Madison Square Garden rodeo, he and Hank Worden got the job with Ritter by answering a casting call for cowboy singers, musicians, and yodelers, and Cheetham sang "The Strawberry Roan" and "Red River Valley" in the show. After the play closed, Cheetham worked with Ritter on radio, then gave up on show business to return to Wyoming and the life of singing on dude ranches. It was not a long retirement; he later showed up in Hollywood and appeared in a number of films but never rose to roles of any significance as a singer or actor. He died in Phoenix in January 1977.

Western-swing pioneer Leon Chappelear made his first recordings as a singing cowboy in 1932. Billed as "the Lone Star Cowboy," he cut four sides in Richmond, Indiana, for Gennett on September 13—including "Little Joe the Wrangler," "Cowboy Jack," and "I'd Like to Be in Texas for the Roundup

An early version of the Beverly Hillbillies, the most influential of the early Southern California cowboy string bands. (Country Music Hall of Fame collections)

in the Spring"—but though this session established him on record, it did not establish him as a singing cowboy. He returned to the studio three years later with a swing band and this time left a more lasting mark, recording for Decca as Leon's Lone Star Cowboys and for Capitol, moving smoothly into the emerging honky-tonk style of the 1940s. Born in Tyler, Texas, on August 1, 1909, he died October 22, 1962, by his own hand.

In May, young "Oklahoma Buck" Nation took to the microphones in Grafton, Wisconsin, where he recorded "The Strawberry Roan" and "The Cowboy's Lament." Born in Muskogee, Oklahoma, in 1910, he took off for New York, where he started a recording career cutting hillbilly titles with Ray Whitley on Decca, and later on his own, then with his wife, Texas Ann, sometimes known as TexAnn. The two were instrumental in setting up what he called "amusement ranches" for urban families to experience, in his words, "picnicking, horseback riding, seeing in person famous persons who appear on the stage," and they ran several of these parks in the Northeast beginning in 1934 and continuing until the war years. TexAnn was born in 1916 in Chanute, Kansas, and began on radio with the Girls of the Golden West Trio (unrelated to Dolly and Millie Good, the Girls of the Golden West). She was a champion horsewoman as well, and their act at times featured her derring-do as a rider.

A man of diverse talents, Dwight Butcher recorded "The Lonesome Cowboy" and five other noncowboy sides for Victor on January 9, 1933. His long career wound in and out of western music for decades. Born in Oakdale, Tennessee, on August 6, 1911, he appeared on Knoxville radio in 1929 before he, with the boundless confidence of youth, moved to New York in 1933. That confidence was quickly rewarded. Butcher obtained a radio program on WMCA and teamed with another aspiring singer, Ray Whitley, to form a western band called the Range Ramblers for the radio show. He even obtained a booking at the prestigious Stork Club and got Jimmie Rodgers to record one of his songs ("Old Love Letters") on the Singing Brakeman's final recording session. He worked with all the New York cowboy talent of the day and wrote as well as performed radio programs.

Butcher's style was hard to pigeonhole. On his records his repertoire was of the Jimmie Rodgers–happy vagabond school, with the occasional disaster song and cowboy song thrown in. His look was pure cowboy in those days, but he was at the same time a mainstream country artist. After leaving New York he picked up work hosting, writing, and singing on many of the major radio stations and barn dances around the country—KYW in Philadelphia (1935), WHAM in Rochester (1936–1937), KMBC'S *Brush Creek Follies* in Kansas City (1938–1939), WLW's *Renfro Valley Barn Dance* from Cincinnati (1939–1940), and the *WSB Barn Dance* in Atlanta (1940)—and he was a member and announcer of the Chuck Wagon Gang over WBAP and KGKO in Fort Worth from 1941 to 1942.

He then set his sights on Hollywood, and he both acted in regional theater and grabbed small parts in several films: *Riding High, The Adventures of the Flying Cadets, The Gunmaster,* and *Hollywood Canteen* among them. In addition, two of his songs made it into films: "Goodbye to Old Mexico" in Gene Autry's *The Big Sombrero* (Columbia, 1949) and "Dust on My Saddle" in Tex Ritter's *Sundown on the Prairie* (Monogram, 1939). Not only did he act in several equity plays, but he wrote two as well.

But Butcher struggled with personal problems. As he poignantly put it in a short note dated December 20, 1977: "A question would probably arise . . . as to why a man who had accomplished a reasonable amount of success in many fields of 'show business' suddenly disappears. There is a reason, and the reason can be summed up in one word; alcoholism."[13] Talented but unreliable, he ended up selling real estate and died in Covina, California, November 11, 1978.

On April 11, 1933, the Cumberland Ridge Runners recorded "The Lone Cowboy" for the American Record Corporation. On November 11, 1933, they cut D. J. O'Malley's "The Dying Rustler" for the same firm. They were the most popular string band on the *National Barn Dance* at the time and consisted of Karl Davis (1905–1979) on mandolin and Hartford Connecticut Taylor (1905–1963) on guitar, known later as the old-time duo of Karl & Harty; singer Linda Parker (1912–1935); and bassist and vocalist on this session, Clyde Julian "Red" Foley (1910–1968). Their April 11 session marked the first recording appearance for Foley, whose career in the early years brushed up against western music time and again. Foley recorded another western side for ARC, "Headin' back to Texas," in 1935 and a few more at the dawn of his long association with Decca: "Montana Moon" and "Riding Home" in 1941. Beyond this and a brief foray into films in the early 1940s, he remains a star who shone brightest in other fields.

On November 4, 1932, the thirty-three-year-old singing star Jimmie Davis stepped to the Victor microphones in Camden, New Jersey, to record. He was still several years away from the national success of "You Are My Sunshine," the massive hit that propelled him not only into the movies (where he starred in his own life story, *Louisiana,* in 1947), but twice to the governorship of Louisiana. Born in Beech Springs, Louisiana, on September 11, 1899, he had been recording since 1928 and like many of his contemporaries was heavily influenced by Jimmie Rodgers in content and style.

Although these 1932 sessions show a maturation in style, they are most notable for the presence of his fiddler and harmony singer, the young Rubye Blevins, whom Davis had brought with him from KWKH in Shreveport. After backing him musically and yodeling on several of his sides—"Gambler's Return," "Bury Me in Old Kentucky," "Home in Caroline," and "Jealous Lover"—Blevins was allowed to cut four sides of her own. Billed as Patsy Montana, "Montana's Yodeling Cowgirl," she made her first recordings that afternoon: "When the Flowers of Montana Were Blooming," the Jimmie

Patsy Montana, looking every inch a cowboy's sweetheart in this 1930s publicity photo. (Country Music Hall of Fame collections)

Rodgersesque "Sailor's Sweetheart," "I Love My Daddy Too," and what would become her radio theme song, "Montana Plains," a slight reworking of Stuart Hamblen's "Texas Plains."

There had been singing cowgirls before Blevins, but she was the first to make a national impact. Born Ruby Blevins on October 30, 1908, in Hope, Arkansas, she was one of eleven children in a musical family and finished high school early to pursue a career, moving to California at the age of fifteen or sixteen to enroll as a music student at the University of the West.

She quickly became enchanted with the area's burgeoning cowboy music scene and, adding an *e* to the end of her given name in hopes that it would look more glamorous in print, became Rubye Blevins. By 1930 she had worked on radio with her brother Ken, with Stuart Hamblen, and with a trio called the Montana Cowgirls, where she first took the name Patsy Montana.

A week's booking as a solo artist on KWKH in 1932 proved fortuitous; it was there that she caught the ear of Jimmie Davis, who invited her to appear on his records and opened the door for her own solo recording contract. A similarly fortuitous trip to the Chicago World's Fair the following year got her an audition with the mighty WLS and the *National Barn Dance,* who were looking for a female singer to add to their popular swinging string band, the Kentucky Ramblers. Her talents on fiddle, her yodeling, her personality, and her "million-dollar smile" won her the job, and in mid-1933 she joined, in the words of historians Robert K. Oermann and Mary Bufwack, "one of the finest bands in the history of country music."[14]

Oermann and Bufwack were quite correct in their appraisal of the Ken-

Patsy Montana & the Prairie Ramblers during their 1930s tenure at WLS Chicago. *From left:* Chick Hurt, Patsy Montana, Tex Atchison, Jack Taylor, and Salty Holmes. (Country Music Hall of Fame collections)

tucky Ramblers, but they might have added "most overlooked" to their description. Before returning to the rest of Patsy Montana's career, it is well worth giving the Kentucky Ramblers their due. The band was formed in that musically fertile region of the Blue Grass State that produced, among others, Bill Monroe, Merle Travis, the Everly Brothers, and Grandpa Jones. The band consisted of Floyd "Salty" Holmes (1909–1970) on harmonica and guitar, Charles "Chick" Hurt (1901–1967) on mandola and tenor banjo, Jack Taylor (1901–1962) on bass, and Shelby "Tex" Atchison (1912–1982) on fiddle. They were more gifted as instrumentalists than as singers and brought an eclectic, jazzy approach to string band music that was ahead of its time. Besides Atchison's sizzling left-handed fiddle, the use of the mandola gave their sound distinction; bearing the same relation to the mandolin as the viola does to the violin, it provided a deeper, richer, unique texture.

The Kentucky Ramblers began a professional career over WOC and WHO in 1932, and their exciting blend of string band music and jazz brought them to WLS in 1933. Later that year they not only added Patsy Montana but also—in deference to her cowgirl image, to the growing popularity of cowboy and western songs, and to their new broadcasting home in Illinois, the Prairie State—changed their name to the Prairie Ramblers. Their first recording session, December 6, 1933, was a predictably eclectic mix of country blues ("Go Easy Blues"), fiddle tunes ("Tex's Dance"), novelty ("I Want My Mama," featuring Holmes's "talking harmonica"), and string band classics ("Shady Grove My Darling," "Gonna Have a Feast Here Tonight," which they popularized) and featured Patsy Montana on "Montana Plains."

They spent a couple of years on Victor, but, recalls Atchison: "They didn't sell too much; RCA wasn't pushing them. . . . Then we started doing Gene Autry's backup. Gene got us on Columbia, and then we left Victor, and *then* we started selling records!"[15]

Atchison, recollecting from the distance of forty-five years, vividly recalled how western music and the western image became so dominant so fast among rural audiences in the 1930s, which of course made the singing-cowboy film phenomenon possible. Deciding to change their name and their image from a Kentucky string band to a cowboy band from the prairies was a wise, and probably necessary, career move: "Gene Autry was selling records by the millions and there was a few country people a-buyin' hillbilly music—well, we never did call it that; mountain music, folk music, country music—and we sold a whole lot of records mail order. Sears and Roebuck ran our pictures in their paper. . . . And we looked better in western uniforms instead of overalls. And we wanted something and we went after it. We wanted to become a top act and we did."[16]

An offer to broadcast over WOR brought them to New York from December 1934 through December 1935. In addition to radio work, the Prairie Ramblers became part of the thriving New York folk, country, and western-music scene of the era, befriending and working with Tex Ritter, Ray

Whitley, Rufe Davis, Elton Britt, Carson Robison, Frank Luther, and Tex Fletcher.

More importantly, they made a series of popular records for Art Satherley and the American Record Corporation, including swinging country-pop songs like "Just Because," and plaintive gospel songs like "This World Is Not My Home." As the Sweet Violet Boys, without Patsy Montana, they recorded songs suggestive by the era's standards, primarily for jukebox play. "Of course nobody knew that was us. If we could have booked the Sweet Violet Boys we could have gotten three times as much money!"[17] But nothing they ever recorded with or without Patsy Montana ever approached the whopping success of "I Want to Be a Cowboy's Sweetheart," recorded August 16, 1935, in New York. Oermann and Bufwack beautifully sum up the surprising and enormous success of this cheerful record, though one might quibble with their calling Montana's energetic yodeling "blue," as it was very much in the athletic, rather than the lonesome, yodeling tradition:

> Patsy's own explanation . . . is that it was a musical synthesis, and that its timing was right. Gene Autry's films of the cowboy lost in the modern world were huge box-office draws at the time. Bob Wills had begun recording and popularizing the combination of country and swing that the Prairie Ramblers played so well. The lively fiddling and the blue yodel gave the song a western yet a contemporary sound. Patsy also notes that the song has a polka rhythm, which made it popular with the ethnic groups in the northern cities. Certainly "I Want to Be a Cowboy's Sweetheart" appealed to the dance spirit that was sweeping the country following the 1934 repeal of Prohibition. Patsy also believes the lyrics were important to the song's success. Despite its title, the song is not about a traditional sweetheart. It is expressive of a woman's desire for independence in the rugged outdoor life of a cowhand. . . . This notion of being a cowboy's buddy and lover was repeated over and over in Patsy Montana's recording career.[18]

Patsy and the Prairie Ramblers returned to WLS in December 1935, "and we come back *full* western," recalled Atchison. "We asked Smiley Burnette to write us a theme song, and he wrote 'Riding down the Canyon.'"[19] They may have come back western in dress, but this was not reflected in their recorded output. Though Atchison recalls specifically switching to the long-bow western style of smooth fiddling, their recorded output remained largely country, and increasingly novelty oriented. The records that featured Patsy Montana, on the other hand, remained almost exclusively cowboy and included classics like "The Strawberry Roan," serious modern western songs, proto-feminist songs like "I Want to Be a Real Cowboy Girl" and "The She-Buckaroo," and western novelties like "I'm an Old Cowhand," "I'd Love to Be a Cowboy (But I'm Afraid of Cows)," and "I'm a Wild and Reckless Cowboy."

Not long afterward Patsy Montana made her only film appearance, singing "I Want to Be a Cowboy's Sweetheart" in the Gene Autry film *Colorado Sunset* (Republic, 1939).

As time went on the partnership between members of the Prairie Ramblers began to unravel, despite their success. The most ambitious of the lot, Atchison was eager to try his luck in Hollywood:

> I was still connected with WLS. I was trying to get out of there; I was waiting until my contract ended. I wanted to go to Hollywood as soon as it did. . . . I left the Ramblers in 1940, and Patsy left about the same time too. I didn't want to die there. Everybody who'd gone out to Hollywood had made good: Gene, Smiley, Max Terhune, and all of 'em. And I was younger than the Prairie Ramblers, the others. You see, Jack and Chick were about ten years older than me, and Salty was about three years older than me. Patsy was just about my age.[20]

Though the Prairie Ramblers would record sporadically together through 1949, Patsy Montana became a solo act in 1940, while Atchison headed west, and Salty Holmes went solo in 1942, replaced by Rusty Gill (born Ralph Gill in St. Louis, Missouri, in 1919). The Ramblers remained together, with Alan Crockett (who died by suicide in 1947) and later Wade Ray (born in Griffin, Indiana, on April 6, 1906, and died on November 18, 1998) taking over fiddling chores. But the heyday of the Prairie Ramblers was over, and they turned increasingly to the novelty songs that went over so well in Chicago (a tack that also proved successful for the Hoosier Hot Shots, Homer & Jethro, and Captain Stubby & His Buccaneers). In 1954 Gill and his wife, Carolyn DeZurik (formerly of the DeZurik Sisters), Chick Hurt, and Jack Taylor brought in Stan Wolowic on accordion, and this outfit evolved into Stan Wolowic & His Polka Chips, who had the first network polka show, *It's Polka Time,* on ABC, from 1956 to 1957. Wolowic had tax troubles, and Hurt and Taylor—the last original members of the Prairie Ramblers—left the Polka Chips in 1960. With their departure, the last threads of the honored band unraveled. Lou Prohut took over the polka band, Rusty joined Captain Stubby & His Buccaneers for a few years, and Carolyn ("the Little Swiss Miss") became the Busch Bavarian beer girl from 1956 to 1963. Only Rusty and Carolyn Gill remain, in happy retirement.

For his part, Tex Atchison was relatively successful in his pursuit of the Hollywood dream. He appeared with Jimmy Wakely in films, recordings, and on radio, and when Wakely left the *Hollywood Barn Dance* radio show, Tex helped form an incarnation of the Riders of the Purple Sage with Foy Willing, Al Sloey, Art Wentzel, and Jimmy Dean. In the following years he recorded with Autry, Wakely, Ritter, Merle Travis, Johnny Bond, and others. He continued to lead western-swing bands, the Santa Fe Boys & the All Stars after the war, but he eventually drifted out of music and into horse training and died August 4, 1982.

As for the continuing career trajectory of Patsy Montana, she switched labels to Decca in 1941 and recorded first with the Light Crust Doughboys as Patsy Montana & Her Pardners, and with the Sons of the Pioneers, billed again as Her Pardners, in 1942, before returning to RCA in the late 1940s. But the earlier magic was gone, and though she worked steadily she had no more hit records; after a stint singing with Cowboy Slim Rinehart on border radio, she was in semi-retirement by the early 1950s. She became a fixture of folk festivals at home and overseas beginning in the 1960s, and she lived to see her "Cowboy's Sweetheart" become popular in recordings by Rosalie Allen, Patti Page, Dale Evans, Suzy Bogguss, and many others. She died May 3, 1996.

The other truly major cowboy singer to make his recording debut in 1932 was Woodward Maurice "Tex" Ritter, whose long career will be covered in chapter 7.

The year 1933 saw the first flowering of several other careers of note, and at least one interesting side excursion: Little Georgie Gobel (May 20, 1919–February 24, 1991), child star on WLS in Chicago, recorded "A Cowboy's Best Friend Is His Horse" and "Night Herding Song" on April 12. The label noted he was accompanied by Gene Autry on guitar. A child star on the *National Barn Dance* billed as "the Little Cowboy," Gobel became a nationally famous comedian and television star of the 1950s; however, this

Tex Ritter and his horse, White Flash, in their prime, the 1940s. (Author's collection)

childhood record and *National Barn Dance* appearances seem to have been his only forays into western music. In addition, Tex Hardin recorded "The Old Chisholm Trail" and "The Trail to California" in Richmond, Indiana, on January 16; the two sides were released on the Challenge label.

Frank Luther had a career that roughly paralleled that of his sometime partner Carson Robison; like Robison he wrote prolifically, recorded prolifically, and was a pivotal figure on the New York western scene. Born Francis Luther Crow on a ranch near Lakin, Kansas, on August 4, 1899, he began studying piano at the age of five and voice at fifteen. A tour as a tenor in a gospel quartet in 1917 whetted his interest in music as a career, and he dropped out of the University of Kansas to go on the road with another gospel quartet. He was ordained as a minister along the way and led a congregation in Bakersfield, California, before returning to Kansas to pursue a career in music and to marry Zora Layman, who was born in Hutchinson, Kansas, on March 12, 1900.

Layman went on to achieve her own distinction in the music field. Although Patsy Montana has long been credited as the first woman to have a major hit western record, Zora Layman's "Seven Years with the Wrong Man" (an answer to Bob Miller's popular "Seven Years with the Wrong Woman") was actually the first major hit, though not a million-seller, by a woman in what was then called the hillbilly field.

Under the name Frank Crow, Luther toured England with a pop quartet called the Revelers. Upon his return, he and Zora settled in New York, where he became a fixture in the New York country music scene of the late 1920s. As early as 1928 he was recording with Robison, the two appearing under numerous pseudonyms, most notably Bud & Joe Billings. Early in his solo recording career, which began in 1932, Luther cut a good bit of western material, but the bulk of his repertoire by far was hillbilly, country, event songs, novelty songs, and the like. As prolific in the studio as were Robison and Dalhart, he estimated he cut more than three thousand sides in his career. A good many of them during 1934 and 1935 were duets with Ray Whitley, whose star was then very much on the rise.

At the same time, Luther frequently recorded with his wife, and in addition he and a merry band of Manhattan cowboys filmed three musical shorts in 1934 and 1935 on Long Island. Though the music was of the sentimental or hillbilly variety and the skits hopelessly corny, there were appearances by some of the New York cowboy elite of the day, among them Ray Whitley (dressed in stereotypical Ozark hillbilly garb, complete with fake beard), an incredibly young-looking Elton Britt, and Zeke Manners. Luther looked and sounded splendid but a little too trained to be mistaken for a real range rider. The well-built Luther was decades ahead of his time as a physical fitness enthusiast; he ran and worked out at the gym, feeling that it gave him the stamina and endurance to handle his demanding recording and broadcasting career. In addition, Luther, Zora, Carson Robison, and others began

Country singer Red Foley with the yodeling Girls of the Golden West. They performed on radio as a trio sponsored by Pinex Cough Syrup from 1936 to 1938 but unfortunately never recorded. (Country Music Hall of Fame collections)

playing traditional and original mountain music on folklorist Ethel Park Richardson's popular NBC radio series *Hillbilly Heart Throbs.*

Beginning in 1934, Luther recorded a set of Mother Goose nursery rhymes for children for Decca Records, and its overwhelming success changed his career: He became a prolific interpreter of children's material. A good bit of it was western and proved to be enormously influential in introducing a generation of urban kids to the music of the West. He eventually began producing children's records for Decca and in time became Decca's head of children's, educational, sacred, and talking-book recordings. He wrote a book, *Americans and Their Songs,* in 1942. Though he lectured and gave the occasional children's concert, Luther gradually moved out of the performing limelight, and he ended his career as a Decca Records executive. He died November 16, 1980. Zora and Luther, who had made so many excellent records together, had divorced amicably by 1940; she remarried, becoming Zora Deramirez, and retired to upstate New York, where she died in November 1981.

Mildred Fern Goad was born April 11, 1913, in rural southern Illinois; her sister Dorothy Laverne was born December 11, 1915. They turned professional in their teens and came to the *National Barn Dance* in 1933 as Millie & Dolly Good, the Girls of the Golden West, cleverly taking the name of the familiar operetta for their stage name. Their western dress—fringed culottes, vests, scarves, and big hats—served as a visual complement to their heavily western repertoire and sweet, gentle, old-fashioned vocals, which were accented with gentle harmony yodeling. Young, pretty, and with a plaintive, sincere singing style, they quickly became *National Barn Dance* favorites and began a recording career on July 28, 1933, with "Colorado Blues" and "Started Out from Texas." They eventually recorded sixty-four sides, about two-thirds of which were western, for Victor's Bluebird label, a low-budget line that had been created to keep record sales from stopping altogether as the Depression squeezed tighter and tighter. Of those songs, many were traditional, but their simple, winning style made even modern western songs sound like hoary survivors of the last century.

In retrospect it is an appealing, winsome sound, but at the time their records were not big sellers; perhaps in the wide-open post-Prohibition 1930s their sound seemed just a little too quaint. They left the *National Barn Dance* in 1937, when John Lair opened the *Renfro Valley Barn Dance,* and they later were featured on the *Boone County Jamboree* and the *Midwestern Hayride* over WLW in Cincinnati. The Girls of the Golden West last recorded in 1938—about half the tunes were western—but their stage career lasted until 1949, when the public was wearying of singing cowboys and harder-edged honky-tonk was becoming the vogue in country music. Dolly died on November 12, 1967, and Millie passed away on May 2, 1993.

Elton Britt, he of the sky-high yodels, is another frequently recurring figure in the singing-cowboy story. Although he had success in popular and country music through the years, he was profoundly influential as a cowboy singer, especially in the range and fluid technical dexterity of his yodeling. Born to James M. and Martella Baker (who was forty-five at the time) in Zack, Arkansas, on June 27, 1913, James Elton Baker was the last of six children in a musical family. His dad played the fiddle (he once won the Oklahoma state championship), and his mom was a renowned ballad singer; two siblings, Arl and Vern, were accomplished musicians and singers who eventually recorded with their younger brother. Sickly for the first year of his life, the baby was not named until it seemed certain he'd survive, when he was given the name James Elton in honor of his father and of the physician, Elton Wilson, who nursed him to health. Young James Baker picked up the guitar at the age of ten and, enthralled by the recordings of Jimmie Rodgers as a teenager, first mimicked, then far surpassed, the yodeling of the Singing Brakeman.

Somehow Baker's reputation got to MacMillan and Rice, who had created and developed the Beverly Hillbillies at KMPC in Los Angeles, and they flew out to audition the high school student in the summer of 1930. Seventeen-year-old James Baker floored them with his pure, piercing version of "A Drunkard's Child." After negotiating with the family, they put

The Girls of the Golden West during their years with WLS Chicago, circa 1935. (Country Music Hall of Fame collections)

him on an airplane—his first such ride—for Hollywood, where MacMillan's publicity machine had stirred up so much interest over the radio that Baker was met at the airport by a crowd estimated at ten thousand. Like the rest of the Beverly Hillbillies, he was given a stage name, Elton Britt, and it stayed with him the rest of his career. He see-sawed back and forth between Arkansas and Hollywood for the next three years before landing in New York, where he began recording a number of sides for Conqueror with his brothers Vern and Arl, as the Wenatchee Mountaineers and also as the Britt Brothers, beginning August 8, 1933.

His first solo billing came with his first recording of the song with which he has been most firmly associated, "Chime Bells," on June 20, 1934, accompanied by the song's composer, Bob Miller, on piano. The song, about mountain lakes and the ringing of bells, was certainly not cowboy, nor was it really country or folk; rather, it reflected a peculiar European feel in its snappy 6/8 tempo. It was a showpiece for some of the most astonishing yodeling ever heard.

Britt recorded frequently with the Rustic Rhythm Trio (Vaughn and Roy Horton, with Paul Robinson on harmonica), and when he moved to RCA the Hortons went with him, billing themselves as the Skytoppers. Roy (born in 1914) became a well-respected executive with the music-publishing firm Peer International, while Vaughn (1911–1988) was the composer of dozens of successful songs, most notably "Mockingbird Hill."

The 1940s were heady years in Britt's career, with tours, hit records, and even a part in a Charles Starrett western at Columbia called *Laramie* (1949). Despite his success, he began a series of retirements in the early 1950s. By all accounts he preferred fishing to performing, and in 1952 he retired to his Maryland farm to devote himself to just that. It was, however, more a hiatus than a retirement. From 1953 to 1955 he hosted the *Hayloft Jamboree* over WCOP in Boston, and he had his own television show there as well. He once again chucked it all in 1955 to prospect and develop uranium mines in the Utah desert, and indeed he filed numerous claims.

Although Elton Britt's image and a few of his songs remained thoroughly western after he moved to RCA Victor in 1937, his style evolved into the smooth country-pop sound typical of Gene Autry and others of the era: violins and guitars and muted trumpet. These songs featured his liquid tenor and occasionally his phenomenal yodeling. He had a number of successful records in that style, including "I'm a Convict with Old Glory in My Heart" (1944), a fine Tin Pan Alley cowboy song called "Gotta Get Together with My Gal" (1946), "Detour" (1946), "Someday (You'll Want Me to Want You)" (1944), "Born to Lose" (1947), a rerecording of "Chime Bells" (1948), "Candy Kisses" (1949), and the delicious duet with fellow yodeler Rosalie Allen, "Quicksilver" (1949). But the song that put him on the national map was the ultrapatriotic "There's a Star Spangled Banner Waving Somewhere" in 1942. This sentimental song was published and co-written by Bob Miller, who continued to play a large part in Britt's career.

Britt returned to the stage in 1958 (he was only forty-five years old at this time) as a member of the *WWVA Jamboree,* but despite an active touring and recording schedule his career stalled, revived only briefly in 1968 by the surprising six-minute hit record "The Jimmie Rodgers Blues," which strung together Rodgers's song titles, punctuated by blue yodels. It was Britt's first chart record in eighteen years. He died of a heart attack while on tour on June 23, 1972, four days away from his fifty-ninth birthday.

Just days after joining the *National Barn Dance,* a New Mexico troupe called Louise Massey & the Westerners stepped before the Columbia mi-

Louise Massey & the Westerners, 1930s. *From left:* Allen Massey, Milt Mabie, Louise Massey, Larry Wellington, and Curt Massey. (Country Music Hall of Fame collections)

crophones on October 13, 1933. The session yielded three western songs ("The Cowboy's Dream," "Trail to Mexico" and "The Big Corral") and a rollicking hillbilly number, "New River Train." The Massey saga had begun in Texas, where fiddler Henry "Dad" Massey fathered three musical children: Victoria Louise, born in Hunt County on August 2, 1902; Allen, born in Midland on December 12, 1907; and Curt, also born in Midland, on May 3, 1910. The family moved to the Hondo Valley of New Mexico (just west of Roswell) in 1914, and within a few years Dad had a fine family act. He

An early Wilf
Carter song folio.
(Country Music Hall of
Fame collections)

fiddled, Louise sang and played the piano, Allen played the guitar, and
Curt played fiddle and trumpet. They were joined by teenage bride Louise's
husband, Milt Mabie (1900–1973); though he was a multi-instrumentalist,
Milt was enlisted to play bass. They were seasoned veterans of local performances before they turned professional around 1928, and they had toured
the country as part of a Chautauqua series before settling down on radio,
first at WIBW in Topeka, then at KMBC in Kansas City, where they added
Larry Wellington (1903–1973) on accordion.

It was this band (minus Dad, who had retired) that began recording and
appearing on radio over WLS in Chicago, where they became one of the
station's most popular acts. They broke away from time to time to appear
on programs—*Show Boat* over NBC in New York, and *Plantation Party* over
NBC from Chicago. In addition, they got their own show on NBC, *Log
Cabin Dude Ranch*, which cast Louise as the proprietress of a dude ranch,
with many musical interludes. Their sound was smooth and agreeable to
sophisticated as well as to rural ears; they were as slick as a pop band but
had that unmistakable ring of authenticity. They continued to record, with a
good bit of their repertoire western, producing more than 150 sides through
the years, and they appeared in at least one film, Tex Ritter's *Where the
Buffalo Roam* (Monogram, 1938). They had a national hit with "The Honey
Song" and with their signature song, "My Adobe Hacienda," which Louise

had begun writing as early as 1936. Their success allowed Milt and Louise to buy their dream house, their adobe hacienda, and while their career was still going strong they retired to it. "It was time for us to enjoy our own life," said Louise.[21] They lived there in happy retirement until Milt's failing health brought them to Roswell, where he died September 29, 1973. Louise Massey Mabie died there June 20, 1983.

As for the rest of the band, Wellington remained in Chicago, active in music, until his death in 1973. Allen Massey went west, worked on radio and with the Hoosier Hot Shots, and died March 3, 1983. Curt continued a long career as a musician, bandleader, singer, radio and television actor and host, and songwriter. Among his credits was the theme to the television series *Petticoat Junction,* which he also performed. Curt Massey died October 20, 1991.

The final days of 1933 brought a tall, strong-featured yodeler named Wilf Carter to the Victor studios in far off Montreal, Quebec. Born December 18, 1904, in Guysboro, Nova Scotia, Carter was profoundly affected by the yodeling of a now forgotten performer who was an "added attraction" at a stage performance of *Uncle Tom's Cabin.* Carter wound up in the cowboy town of Calgary—though his radio debut was on a U.S. station, KGY in Portland, in 1929—where he appeared on radio before auditioning for Vic-

A 1940 Victor advertisement featuring Wilf Carter, a.k.a. Montana Slim. (Author's collection)

tor with "My Swiss Moonlight Lullaby" and "The Capture of Albert Johnson" on December 30, 1933.

Carter continued to mix hobo, rounder, current-event, and hillbilly songs with his cowboy material—much of it original—and often featured his striking yodeling. He obtained a fifteen-minute program on CBS in New York, where he became known to American audiences as Montana Slim. Wilf Carter recorded quite prolifically for the next few years for Victor, in New York and Montreal, with cowboy songs predominant, and he continued his successful radio career until 1940, when on a leave of absence from CBS he was badly injured in a car accident in Montana, on his way to his recently purchased ranch near Calgary. This led to a nine-year recuperation and retirement from performing, during which he raised cattle and brought up two daughters.

Montana Slim returned to recording in 1947 and to touring and broadcasting in 1949. Although he had an extremely active career for a number of years, he never regained the prominence he'd reached in the 1930s. Except for brief stints with Decca and Starday, he was with RCA Victor for more than forty years, and he became a fixture of Canadian radio and television, only occasionally touring south of the border. His later years were spent in the less bone-chilling climes of Florida and Arizona. Like many singing cowboys, Wilf Carter was blessed with an iron constitution and lived a very long and full life, passing away on December 5, 1996.

Wilf Carter's story draws to a close the long list of singing cowboys who came to prominence (or at least earned some small attention) before 1934. Until this time the overwhelming portion of what we might call western songs focused lyrically on the life of the cowboy, upon events or outstanding characters or outlaws, and more rarely on love won or lost. Musically, the songs could be haunting or catchy, but they were seldom musically advanced. As late as 1934, cowboy music, for all its growing national popularity, was perceived and performed as folk music—music of and about the cowboy, the plainsman, the westerner. Only a few songs, like "Home on the Range," celebrated the West itself, but that was soon to change. There was, of course, no single person or group that caused the sudden and dramatic shift in what might be called western music. Several people combined at the right time, with the necessary ingredients of talent and timing, and discovered a huge national desire for this new sensibility that spoke not to the cowboy's actual life but to his romantic image: feckless and fancy-free, independent and proud, closer to nature than to civilization. Much of this was epitomized in, and celebrated by, the music of songwriter Billy Hill, and the act that came to embody the music, the Sons of the Pioneers.

# The Sons of the Pioneers and Billy Hill

## Painting the West in Song

Folksong scholar Alan Lomax once remarked, "I think the Sons of the Pioneers are the worst thing that ever happened to cowboy music." The remark was intended to get a rise, but Lomax may well have meant it. With the notable exception of "Home on the Range" and the songs of pop songwriter Billy Hill, western music before the Sons of the Pioneers was primarily concerned with the life of the cowboy on the range and trail. Again and again the focus of the folk poetry that became cowboy music, and of the music of the early cowboy recording artists, was the cowboy himself. He was often cast as a tragic hero, as in "The Cowboy's Lament," "Utah Carroll," "When the Work's All Done This Fall," or "Little Joe, the Wrangler," but he could also have a comic aspect, as in "High Chin Bob," "The Strawberry Roan," "The Zebra Dun," or "Tying Knots in the Devil's Tail." He could also be a feared outlaw, as he is in "Sam Bass," "Jesse James," or "Sam Hall." Love songs were less common, though "Red River Valley" endures. Songs written about the West for dance halls and minstrel shows, like "Dreary Black Hills," "Clementine," or "Betsy from Pike," reflected the western experience with tongue placed lightly in cheek, but the focus was on the westerner and his or her actions, the songs memorable for their jingling, dryly humorous lyrics and insistent melodies.

And Tin Pan Alley had come up with a number of fairly forgettable cowboy songs in the dawning years of the twentieth century, primarily popular love songs in a western setting, although clever, semi-mocking songs like "Ragtime Cowboy Joe" paved the way for a whole subtradition of western songs gently debunking the cowboy myth, such as "I'm an Old Cowhand" and "Wah-Hoo."

Recordings of these songs—the older quasi-folk tunes and the sassy, breezy Tin Pan Alley songs—remained a staple of recorded western music

The Pioneer Trio. *From left:* Tim Spencer, Len Slye (Roy Rogers), and Bob Nolan. (Courtesy of Lida Rose Maze.)

in the 1920s. Much of the recording was done with the emphasis on earthiness and authenticity, real or imagined. In the public mind the cowboy was a rough-hewn adventurer who lived in a country where cattle drives and Indian uprisings unfolded in a raw and untamed land, and who spoke an unusual and descriptive language all his own. Before the coming of the Pioneers, the public's expectation of the cowboy's music reflected that popular image.

The rise of Billy Hill (and, to be fair, Carson Robison) in the East and the Sons of the Pioneers in the West changed all that. They gave us a romantic, visionary West that turned the way the public thought of cowboy music upside down; at last the haunting beauty of the music matched the haunting beauty of the West.

Billy Hill's connection to the West began early. His father, George, was part Blackfoot Indian, a rambler and a rover who spent time cowboying in the West, sailing the seven seas, and sojourning in Alaska. He met a Latvian immigrant while in the port of Boston, and in the suburb of Jamaica Plain their son, William Joseph Hill, was born July 14, 1899. Though Billy studied violin at the New England Conservatory, he apparently had inherited his father's wanderlust, and he roamed all over the West as a laborer, cowboy, and musician before heading for Hollywood in the 1920s. On his way to New York in 1930, he wrote one of his classic tunes, "The West, a Nest, and You," for his new bride.

Whatever his hopes, he did not fare well in New York; he worked as a doorman while he struggled for a foothold in Tin Pan Alley. Recalling the death of a cowboy he'd seen in Texas some years before, he wrote "The Last Round-up" in 1931, but he was in such desperate straits that by the time his daughter was born he nearly sold the song for $25. He hung on to it, fortunately, and by the end of that year the song was introduced by Joe Morrison at the Paramount Theater. It was immediately recorded by a number of blossoming western artists, including Gene Autry, who had a substantial hit with it, as well as by Bing Crosby and other popular artists, and the song established Hill on Broadway—where "The Last Round-up" was featured in the *Ziegfeld Follies of 1934*, along with "Wagon Wheels"—on records, and in films. Billy Hill wrote or co-wrote a number of songs during these years, including "Prairie Lullaby" for Jimmie Rodgers, "The Old Spinning Wheel," "Wagon Wheels" (not really a western song but widely accepted in the western repertoire), "Rain," and "Empty Saddles" (first popularized by Bing Crosby in *Rhythm on the Range* [Paramount, 1936]). His final masterpiece was "Call of the Canyon," which Gene Autry first sang in *Melody Ranch* (Republic, 1940) and sang again as the title song of a 1942 Republic feature. It was also recorded by big bands and spent time on *Your Hit Parade* in 1940. His daughter claims that he was proud of his success in the western field and strove to separate it and his work from country music: "[He] just didn't want

The Gold Star Rangers—*from left,* Tim Spencer, Bob Nolan, Hugh Farr, and Len Slye—gather around their announcer at KFWB-Hollywood. (Author's collection)

to be connected with hillbilly music. He wrote genuine western and the comparison rankled him."[1]

Hill's sudden and overwhelming success with cowboy and rural, folklike material earned him the title the "Modern Stephen Foster." (This must have been an easy metaphor for journalists and publicists, for Bob Nolan was also billed by his publisher as the "Stephen Collins Foster of the Twentieth Century.") Regardless, Hill's stay at the top after his years of struggle was a relatively short seven years; he died in a Boston hotel room December 24, 1940.

As for the Sons of the Pioneers, surely no other group of performers had as profound an effect on the history of western music. A diverse collection of talents and personalities who coalesced in the early 1930s, the Pioneers raised the bar in terms of musicianship, harmony singing, and especially songwriting, where their lyrical musical portraits virtually define the romanticized West—a fierce and lonely place full of tumbling tumbleweeds, timber trails, waterfalls, everlasting hills, open ranges, rippling rills, and cataract spills—painting its colors as no one had done before or has done since.

Bob Nolan and Vern Spencer had met as early as 1932, when the indi-

Bob Nolan, looking like a leading man, in the 1940s. (Author's collection)

viduals—eventually brought together by another youngster named Len Slye, who later found fame as Roy Rogers—were attempting to find their place in the thriving cowboy and country music scene. It was a fertile era: semi-cowboy string bands like the Rocky Mountaineers, Jimmy LeFevre & His Saddle Pals, Jack LeFevre & His Texas Outlaws, Sheriff Loyal Underwood & His Arizona Wranglers, the Sierra Mountaineers, the Texas Ramblers, and—by far the most popular of them all—the Beverly Hillbillies crowded the airwaves and performance venues with string music, square dances, and cowboy and hillbilly songs. Bob Nolan, Vern Spencer, and Slye were trans-plants to the area; all had been drawn by the lure of plentiful work, sun-shine, and fitful hopes of careers in music and film.

Bob Nolan was the oldest, born Clarence Robert Nobles on April 13, 1908, in Winnipeg, Manitoba. He moved with his mother and brother Earl to British Columbia, then to New Brunswick, when his father, Harry Nobles, served in World War I. His mother abandoned the two boys and disap-peared; upon Harry's return his sons were sent to live with an aunt in Bos-ton for schooling, though Clarence was put on a train for Tucson almost immediately, where he joined his father in about 1922. Earl followed within the year. It was in Tucson that Harry Nobles changed the family name to Nolan. Earl became a football star at Arizona, but Clarence, though powerfully built and athletic as well, was artistic by nature. Inspired by the poetry of Keats, Shelley, and Byron, young Clarence Nolan applied their lofty tone, language, and rhythms to the astonishing beauty of the desert: "I was brought up in the back woods of Canada [and came] right from the tall timber, out to the desert. It was awe-inspiring, to say the least, to wake up in the morning to see the desert beauty with the sun shining through millions of drops of dew."[2]

Nolan's unstable early life delayed his schooling, and he did not graduate from high school until the age of twenty, in 1928—he preferred to be called Bob by this time. He married and moved to Santa Monica in 1929, rejoined his father, and began writing songs based on his earlier poetry. In October 1931, while working as a lifeguard, he answered a tiny ad tucked away in the "Wanted: Theatricals" section of the September 30 classifieds of the *Los Angeles Herald:* "YODELER, for old-time act. to travel. Tenor preferred. 1727 E. 65 st." He showed up barefoot, having blistered his feet in uncomfortable new shoes on the long walk to Sixty-fifth Street, to meet an astonished Len Slye.

Three years younger than Nolan, Leonard Frank Slye was an immigrant from Ohio who had traveled two thousand dusty miles the previous year with his whole family in a beat-up old truck reminiscent of scenes from John Steinbeck's *Grapes of Wrath.* The Slys (Len added an *e* to the family name when he began performing) had not found the land of plenty they had envisioned, and young Leonard found work as a truck driver and fruit picker. Music was very much on his mind, however, and he appeared with his cousin Stanley as a banjo-mandolin duet, finally joining a professional group, the Rocky Mountaineers, in mid-1931. Uncomfortable singing solo, he wanted to hire another singer for the act and placed the ad that brought Bob Nolan into his life.

Vern Spencer (who would later go by Tim) was three and a half months Nolan's junior, born July 13, 1908, in Webb City, Missouri. When he was five, his father moved the family to New Mexico, then moved the younger children—including Vern—to Oklahoma. Vern turned to mining after graduation, but an auto accident made heavy work impossible for a time, and he discovered he could eke out a small living as an entertainer, playing his banjo and singing at a night spot called the Bucket of Blood. Fired with ambition, he took a train to Los Angeles in 1931, where he stayed with an older brother, Glenn, who would later write or co-write, with Tim, several superb western songs in the Sons of the Pioneers' repertoire.

Slye and Nolan—and a third singer named Bill "Slumber" Nichols, whom Nolan had recruited to create a proto-Pioneer harmonizing and yodeling trio—had met with limited success in their efforts with the Rocky Mountaineers, but the mercurial Nolan left the group in the summer of 1932. Slye resorted again to advertising in the newspaper classifieds for a replacement, specifying a baritone who could yodel. "I wasn't a baritone, and I had never

The Sons of the Pioneers in *The Big Show* (1936). *From left:* Karl Farr, Bob Nolan, Tim Spencer, Hugh Farr, and Len Slye. (Author's collection)

yodeled, but I found out that I could," recalled Tim Spencer, "so I applied and was hired as a replacement for Bob Nolan" in August 1932.

The trio of Spencer, Slye, and Nichols left the Rocky Mountaineers to join Benny Nawahi & His International Cowboys, then left on a disastrous personal appearance tour of the Southwest as the O-Bar-O Cowboys. They scrimped along from date to date and barnstormed at radio stations, where they dropped strong hints about the kind of foods they liked; when the hints fell flat, they went hunting. The tour petered out in Texas, and the broke and dispirited cowboy trio limped back to Los Angeles. It was a momentous tour nonetheless: both Vern and Len met their future wives on this tour, Spencer in Lubbock, Texas, and Slye in Roswell, New Mexico. But for the moment, romance took a back seat to earning a living: Nichols got a job fiddling in Fort Worth, Spencer went back to a job at the Safeway store, and the future Roy Rogers got a solo singing job with Jack & His Texas Outlaws.

But Len Slye was not to be denied. Though shy about performing, and always a little uncomfortable about appearing in public, he was nonetheless ambitious and self-confident about his talent, particularly his yodeling. "From the beginning I could do a variety of yodeling, both fast and slow. . . . Jimmie Rodgers had some impact on my decision to make yodeling a strong part of my singing. By taking these yodels, changing the rhythm and breaks, I created a style all my own. I think we [the Pioneers] may have been the first to do trio yodeling; at least I had never heard any before."[3] He felt the O-Bar-O Cowboys had something unique, and though he had rejoined Jack & His Texas Outlaws, it was not long before he contacted Spencer about again forming a trio of their own. Len recalled the powerful voice and the vivid songs of the young lifeguard, Bob Nolan, he'd worked with the year before, and he and Spencer drove down to the Bel Air Country Club, where Nolan was working as a caddy, and persuaded him to join their newly minted Pioneer Trio. The three began intense daylong rehearsals, and according to Nolan they bought their way into an audition at KFWB. No one had heard western music anything quite like this: it was no loose and loopy string band in chaps, but a well-rehearsed trio with a precise blend, outstanding trio and solo yodeling, and stunning original songs. Their audition was successful, and before long they were appearing in the morning as the Pioneer Trio, in the afternoon as the Gold Star Rangers (after their sponsor, the Farley Clothing Company), and in the evening on a show called *Painting the West in Song* with the Jack Joy Orchestra. During one of these broadcasts their announcer, Harry Hall, unexpectedly introduced them as the Sons of the Pioneers, thinking they were far too youthful to be pioneers themselves. The name stuck.

All three men were adequate rhythm guitarists, but they soon felt the need of a soloist, and late in 1933 or early 1934 they added Texas fiddler Hugh Farr (1903–1980), formerly of Jack LeFevre's Texas Outlaws. These four made up the group of Pioneers that first recorded for Decca on August 8, 1934, cutting three songs that would shortly be used in movies, two of them as titles ("Tumbling Tumbleweeds" and "Moonlight on the Prairie"), as well as their triple-yodel train song "Way Out There," and the haunting "Riding Home." All were Bob Nolan compositions, though "Moonlight" was written with Spencer, and all portrayed not a picaresque westerner, but the West itself as a place of ethereal beauty and boundless freedom.

This represented a radical shift in the way the West was presented in song, and though their first recordings were somewhat rougher than the immaculate harmonizing that the vocal trio later mastered, they display technical brilliance far in advance of their time, and a vibrant sense of energy that differed from the drawling recitals of ranch life, horses, stampedes, and accidents that were the stock in trade of most previous western music. This was music of passion and excitement, music that took adventurous chances with harmony and structure, music of brilliantly lyrical flights that captured the vast majesty of the West. It was remarkably fresh, exciting, even breathtaking.

Their second session came March 7, 1935, when they recorded four more Nolan compositions that are similarly remembered for their vitality and poetry: "I Follow the Stream," "There's a Round-Up in the Sky," "I Still Do," and "The Roving Cowboy." Sessions later that month were of a sentimental and religious nature, but when the group returned to the studios in October it was Tim Spencer's turn to shine as composer, as they recorded his remarkable early efforts "The New Frontier," "Over the Santa Fe Trail," and "Song of the Pioneers" (co-written with his brother Glenn), as well as yet another Nolan tune, "Echoes from the Hills." The October sessions had something extra: Hugh's younger brother, the Django Reinhardt–influenced guitarist Karl Farr (1909–1961), who added a distinctive, red-hot jazzy sound to the group's vivid lyrics, sweeping melodies, and adventurous chord changes.

Their songs and their singing caused a sensation in Hollywood's western music community, and by the following year they had appeared in a musical short, *Way Up Thar* (Educational, 1935), in their first big-studio short film (MGM's *Slightly Static,* 1935), and in their first feature (Liberty's *The Old Homestead,* 1935), performing several other Bob Nolan songs. In short, their star was very much on the rise.

This quintet recorded for Decca through 1937, cutting many more of the classics of the genre, including their own compositions, among them, "Blue Prairie" and "One More Ride," as well as the works of other western composers, like "Hills of Old Wyomin'," "I'm an Old Cowhand (from the Rio Grande)," "A Melody from the Sky," and a couple of breakneck cowboy jazz instrumentals, "Cajon *[sic]* Stomp" and—presumably a tribute to the radio waves that were making them famous—"Kilocycle Stomp." The Farr brothers, in fact, recorded several sides on their own during this same period. The Sons of the Pioneers moved to the American Record Corporation (ARC), which became Columbia Records after September 1939, and recorded an interesting mix of original western and nonwestern material (love songs and religious music) beginning in October 1937.

Film work picked up as well, and over the course of the next couple of years the Sons of the Pioneers sang in westerns with Gene Autry, Dick Foran, and even Bing Crosby (*Rhythm on the Range,* Paramount, 1936). But their biggest move artistically—if not financially—was in signing on to add music to Charles Starrett's westerns at Columbia, beginning with *Gallant Defender,* released in November 1935.

Although Starrett had been a leading man in films since 1931, *Gallant Defender* was his first starring western. The tall, rangy, former Dartmouth football star would, in time, become the star of more B westerns than any other actor, 131, all for Columbia, 60 of them portraying a masked character called the Durango Kid, and he was ranked in the top ten most popular western actors in exhibitors' film polls every year but one from 1937 to 1952, with the single exception 1943. Born in Athol, Massachusetts, on March 28, 1904, Charles Starrett appeared on Broadway before breaking into films in 1930; when leading man Tim McCoy left Columbia, the studio took a chance on the young actor and made him a perennial western star.

Starrett did not sing, but he or Columbia or both believed in including music in his films, and singing sidekicks and trail hands, beginning with the Pioneers and eventually including a small galaxy of singers, appeared in many of those 131 films. Starrett certainly merits honorary inclusion among the singing cowboys, simply because so many of them appeared with him on screen. The heir to a manufacturing fortune, Starrett retired from films after the last Durango Kid release in 1952 and lived in extremely comfortable retirement in Southern California until his death on March 22, 1986.

The necessity of creating three to five songs each for eight Starrett pictures a year forced the Pioneers to write at a breakneck pace, and Nolan's output was astonishing. For awhile, he said, he tried to convert almost every phrase someone said to him into a song. Slye wrote a few very fine songs, but songwriting was not his forte, especially at that pace. Tim Spencer uncovered a genuine gift for songwriting—he had done none before the film work started—and he began turning out a large body of songs that are intriguing, poetic, and superbly crafted. The list of classic western songs created by Nolan and Spencer in these fevered few years runs into the dozens, forming the core repertoire of the entire western music oeuvre. In fact, to look at it backward, only a handful of the truly classic western songs ("Don't Fence Me In," "Riders in the Sky," "Back in the Saddle Again" and a few others) were *not* written by Nolan or Spencer. Though they continued to write many wonderful songs into the 1950s, the 1935–1941 period during the Charles Starrett westerns was by far their most prolific and productive.

These men were young, artistic, ambitious, and occasionally fractious; for all that was going well in their career, egos and personalities could collide, and in 1936 Tim Spencer quit the group for a while and moved to San Bernardino. To replace him as tenor (Slye was the middle voice, Nolan the distinctive baritone), the Pioneers recruited a brightly talented young nineteen year old who would remain the link in the ever shifting Pioneer lineup for the next forty-one years.

Born January 29, 1917, in Ruth, Arkansas, Lloyd Wilson Perryman headed west with his family in 1928, in search of a Promised Land. Even as a young man he had an exceptional voice, a beautiful tenor that had expression, power, and feeling; he had superb pitch and an exquisite ear for harmony, and he was a strong rhythm guitarist as well. It is little wonder he quickly found work in those early Southern California bands—the Sierra Mountaineers, Mack & His Texas Outlaws, Jimmy LeFevre & His Saddle Pals among them—before being brought into the Pioneer organization in 1936. This short-lived version of the trio made evocative music: Nolan's distinctive baritone stood out; the blend with Slye as melody singer and Perryman as tenor was sublime. More of Nolan's brilliant portraits of the West were recorded in their first ARC sessions: "Love Song of the Waterfall," "Song of the Bandit," and "Open Range Ahead."

Lloyd Perryman's exceptional talent quickly made him the obvious choice as vocal arranger of the Sons of the Pioneers; so great was his range,

The Sons of the Pioneers' association with Charles Starrett and Columbia Pictures led to the most productive period of their long career. In a typical film of this era (*Rio Grande*, 1938), the Pioneers—*from left,* Pat Brady, Bob Nolan, Karl Farr, Hugh Farr, and Lloyd Perryman —serenade Starrett, his costar Ann Doran, and assorted cast members. (Author's collection)

he could sing every harmony part (he even sang a solo bass part on "King of the River" in 1955), and he had an enormous repertoire of sentimental songs as well. Even after Nolan and Spencer both left the band in 1949, Perryman continued to lead the Pioneers, musically and spiritually, until his untimely death following heart surgery on May 31, 1977. He became known as "Mr. Pioneer" in his forty-one years as a member and leader of the Sons of the Pioneers.

Spencer returned to the Pioneers within a year, but the lineup was almost immediately juggled once again when Len Slye signed with Republic Studios and launched his solo career as Roy Rogers. He was replaced by comedian and bassist Pat Brady, and it was this six-man lineup—the trio of Nolan, Spencer, and Perryman, together with the Farr brothers and Brady— that made the majority of films, radio transcriptions, and recordings in this era. Singing cowboy Ray Whitley managed the group for a time and actually advised them to reject the Columbia contract, knowing their value was far greater than the penurious sum offered. The Pioneers, eager for film stardom, overrode his recommendation and started on one of the most musically fertile eras in their career.

By October 28, 1937, Len Slye was officially known as Roy Rogers, and a full session was cut as "Roy Rogers & the Sons of the Pioneers," which featured Roy's solo vocals and brilliant yodeling backed by his former band mates as instrumentalists. However, in December of that month they were back in the studio as a group, Roy Rogers leading the trio without extra credit or billing, recording a series of fourteen mostly religious songs on December 14 and 16, including some of Nolan's most moving compositions: "At the Rainbow's End," "The Touch of God's Hand," "Lord, You Made the Cowboy Happy," and the rollicking "What You Gonna Say to Peter?" There were religious standards, too ("Hear Dem Bells," "Leaning on the Everlasting Arms," and "Lead Me Gently Home, Father"), as well as up-tempo cowboy songs Nolan was writing for the movies ("The Devil's Great Grand Son" and "Hold That Critter Down").

During these Columbia years Bob Nolan began to have bigger and bigger parts in the Charles Starrett westerns. A handsome, strapping man with a unique voice, he seemed a natural for leading roles, an observation that has not escaped western film historians. "[In *Two Fisted Rangers*] Bob Nolan had a speaking role in tune with his abilities. (Nolan was a sure bet to star in his own series, but somebody missed the boat)."[4] "The most surprising aspect of the film *[The Durango Kid]*, in retrospect is, given Bob Nolan's physical resemblance to [dark haired, muscular cowboy star] George O'Brien, why no one ever attempted to capitalize on it and build him into a star in his own right, which had long been Nolan's ambition. Starrett, for his part, never begrudged Nolan the opportunity, itself rather an unusual posture among Western players."[5]

Whether starring parts had indeed been his ambition is a question still unanswered in the rare interviews conducted with the gracious but very private Nolan. Ray Whitley stated flatly that "Bob was always reluctant to take any kind of leading role. Aside from his humility, I think he had reservations about his ability to act."[6] And indeed he well might have, for despite his physique and dark good looks, he appeared stiff and ill at ease on camera, delivering his lines with an earnestness that came across as a great effort. Nolan himself has said that he was often uncomfortable onstage, and that this was one of the reasons he left the Pioneers in 1948. He truly had the soul of a poet, and he preferred writing songs and poems by the side of a rippling stream to the rigors and pressures of the stage, the microphone, and the sound stage.

Regarding Bob Nolan's desire for film stardom, one has the sense that even by 1940, when he was in his early thirties, his priorities were his songs, not a film career. He was doubtless as ambitious as the next young man, but he had been on enough movie sets to see enough gratuitous ego—the gracious Charles Starrett aside—to last a lifetime. He told a revealing story directly to this point: While walking from one part of the Columbia lot to another, he was spotted by studio head Harry Cohn, the Hollywood mogul who was trying to cast a much anticipated prizefighting movie. Taking in Nolan's broad-shouldered form, Cohn shouted, "I've found my 'Golden Boy'!" and excitedly approached him about testing for the role. Nolan wanted no part of it and recalled that he went out and got drunk for a week, basically shrugging off the opportunity as unappealing, even distasteful to him. William Holden got the part and launched his long career with *Golden Boy*. Nolan was a poet and songwriter first, a singer and recording artist second, and obviously he felt acting and moviemaking were just means to an end, a way to get paid to write songs.

After 1940 came a strange hiatus for the Sons of the Pioneers. Though they were active in films and on radio, they did not record again until March 1941, when they took a year off from Hollywood to appear on radio in Chicago. They returned to Decca Records, and their 1941–1942 sessions offered a mixture of country love songs ("I Knew It All the Time," "You Broke My Heart Little Darlin' "), western-pop music ("Lonely Rose of Mexico," a gorgeous rewriting of "South of the Border"), jazzy hoedown instrumentals ("Boggy Road to Texas," "Wagoner Hoedown"), standards ("There's a Long, Long Trail," "Cielito Lindo"), songs that reflected the upcoming war ("They Drew My Number," "Private Buckaroo"), and more brilliant western songs from the fertile minds of Tim Spencer ("He's Gone up the Trail"), Glenn Spencer ("So Long to the Red River Valley"), and Bob Nolan ("Tumbleweed Trail" and the all-time classic "Cool Water").

In 1940 their film contract with Columbia was up, and while the association with the popular Starrett had been an enjoyable one, the Sons of the Pioneers chafed under the low pay they were accorded. Their last Starrett film was *Outlaws of the Panhandle* (Columbia, 1941), and when they returned to Hollywood from Chicago, they joined Republic and Roy Rogers in *Red River Valley* (1941). There they continued to turn in distinguished performances and brilliant songs for a half dozen years. Again, Nolan was frequently given second-lead status, and often the group was billed as Bob Nolan & the Sons of the Pioneers. After their contract was up in 1948, they appeared in films only sporadically, most memorably as the regimental singers in *Rio Grande* (Republic, 1950).

World War II brought more changes to the Pioneers' lineup. Lloyd Perryman was called into service in the South Pacific, replaced by a new tenor, Ken Carson, formerly with the recently disbanded Ranch Boys. Pat Brady was soon drafted, replaced by bassist George "Shug" Fisher, although Brady made a final Decca session in December 1943 that featured Carson's floating tenor voice on several covers of popular cowboy/country hits of the day: Tex Ritter's "There's a New Moon over My Shoulder," Bob Wills's "Home in San Antone," and Gene Autry's "I Hang My Head and Cry."

The Pioneers had been recording for more than a decade before they hit their stride by signing with RCA Victor in 1945. The Nolan-Spencer-Carson trio, with the Farrs and Fisher, was backed by a small orchestra and recorded "Cool Water" and "The Timber Trail" on August 8. By the March 15, 1946, sessions both Lloyd Perryman and Pat Brady were out of uniform and back in boots and hats, and Ken Carson was kept on, making up a group with two outstanding tenors. One of them moved to counterpoint (Carson singing "water . . . water" on "Cool Water"), or Perryman dropped to melody (where his voice, by this time, was more comfortable), which moved Tim Spencer to background harmonist on ooohs and aaaahs. Tim's voice was sweet and pleasant, but never the powerful instrument possessed by the rest of the trio, and under the grueling traveling and recording schedule it was growing weaker. This lineup, again augmented with a small orchestra, recorded several more Nolan and Spencer classics in the spring and summer of 1946, many of which would form the nucleus of their influential 1952 *Cowboy Classics* album: "Tumbling Tumbleweeds," "The Everlasting Hills of Oklahoma," "Chant of the Wanderer," "Blue Prairie," "Trees," and "Cowboy Camp Meetin'."

This version of the Pioneers recorded for several years, although the small-orchestra experiment was not repeated. Instead, a steel guitar was often added, occasionally augmented by a small string section, in an attempt to achieve a kind of sophisticated country sound with a western feel, perhaps in emulation of the success then currently being enjoyed by Spade Cooley, with whom the Pioneers recorded in 1950, and with whom they later appeared in a film. They did a number of cobilled recordings with other RCA artists during this era, too. Some worked very well, for example, those with Perry Como, Spade Cooley, and of course Roy Rogers (including "Pecos Bill" and "Blue Shadows on the Trail"); others did not, like those with opera star Ezio Pinza and big-voiced bandleader Vaughn Monroe. Roughly half of the Pioneers' songs of those years were western; the other half were religious or country love songs, with the occasional burlesque thrown in—Tim Spencer's broadly farcical hillbilly song "Cigareetes, Whusky, and Wild (Wild) Women" became a surprise hit on juke boxes.

In 1948 Tim Spencer underwent a religious conversion. Exhausted from the road, weakened by heavy use of alcohol, and weary of voice, he quit the organization. He continued to act as manager for a number of years and built a very successful business as a music publisher, including the administration of the worldwide hit "How Great Thou Art." He suffered a stroke in 1970 and died April 26, 1974.

For Bob Nolan, the departure of Tim Spencer took the heart out of the group. "My God, once I lost Tim, for God's sake . . . I mean, he was the brains behind the whole thing, so I just lost interest. I just lost all heart in the whole thing when he left."[7] Within months Nolan too had left the group. He then became a semi-recluse, retreating for months on end to a small cabin at Big Bear Lake, a few hours east of Los Angeles. While his wife, Clara (known

A hearty welcome home for the Sons' returning servicemen Lloyd Perryman and Pat Brady. (Author's collection)

to all as P-Nuts), worked at a local cafe, Bob fished and wrote reams of songs and poetry, only a small portion of which has surfaced since. He recorded two sessions by himself at RCA's behest in 1952 and 1953 and continued to record with the Sons of the Pioneers on and off until 1957, at RCA's insistence. He was coaxed out of retirement by record producer Snuff Garrett and cut an intriguing, if overproduced, album for Elektra in 1979. Nolan died suddenly, while returning from a fishing trip, on June 16, 1980.

Spencer's place in the trio was taken by former Columbia Pictures singing cowboy and former Tommy Dorsey singer Ken Curtis, who was immediately featured on several Pioneer recordings, including "I Still Do" and "Room Full of Roses." Ken Carson left the organization, Lloyd Perryman returned to the tenor part, and Bob Nolan's place was taken by Lloyd "Spike" Doss (born in Weiser, Idaho, in 1920), who became known as Tommy to avoid the confusion of two Lloyds in the band. A western-swing singer briefly with Luke Wills's and Ole Rasmussen's bands, Doss's voice was strikingly similar to Nolan's, and the trademark Pioneer sound with the "bubbling baritone" continued without a hitch. Doss was a better singer technically than Nolan, and in some ways this trio of Perryman, Curtis, and Doss was the finest the Pioneers ever had, although many contend, with much justifi-

On *The Lucky U Ranch* radio set. *From left:* Sons of the Pioneers Karl Farr, Shug Fisher, Ken Curtis, Hugh Farr, Tommy Doss, and Lloyd Perryman. (Author's collection)

cation, that Curtis's eventual replacement, Dale Warren, elevated the trio to its smoothest ever.

Born in Rockford, Illinois, in 1925, Henry Dale Warren was a veteran of his father's old-time group, Uncle Henry's Kentucky Mountaineers, with whom he had sung since childhood; more recently he had sung with Foy Willing's Riders of the Purple Sage. In early 1953 he was brought in to replace Ken Curtis, who left the Pioneers to further his acting and producing career and went on to become Festus of TV's *Gunsmoke*. Through all the changes that have followed since Lloyd Perryman's death in 1977, it has been Dale Warren who has led the Pioneers; he has now been a member for nearly fifty years, and group leader for twenty-five.

Perryman headed the Pioneers during the difficult late 1950s, when cowboy singers and songs were passé. The cantankerous Hugh Farr left the group in 1958 and, as the oldest active member, tried to claim rights to the name. He lost, in a bitter court battle. His brother Karl chose to stay with the Pioneers, and the band was devastated when Karl suffered a heart attack and died on stage in Springfield, Massachusetts, in 1961. Although the heyday of the Sons of the Pioneers had come to a close, the group continued to make superbly sung albums for an audience of diehard fans throughout the 1960s, and it is a shame these have not enjoyed reissue, as have earlier Pioneers recordings. The Pioneers were finally dropped from RCA in 1969

In the late 1950s, the Sons of the Pioneers after Hugh Farr's departure. *From left:* George Bamby, Karl Farr, Dale Warren, Tommy Doss, and Lloyd Perryman. (Author's collection)

and did not record again until they made *Western Country* on Cliffie Stone's independent Granite label in 1976.

There have been numerous reissues on RCA, MCA (formerly Decca), and Columbia, and three massive boxed sets from Bear Family Records, but the Sons of the Pioneers (now Dale Warren, Luther Nallie, Sunny Spencer, Gary LeMaster, and Ken Lattimore) have not recorded, other than souvenir tapes and compact discs for on-site sale at shows, for a number of years. For all that, and despite Warren's advancing age and health problems, they are still going strong, one of the last vital direct links to the golden era of the singing cowboy and of western music.

A number of extremely talented and dedicated singers and musicians have appeared with the organization through the years (as well as frequent stand-ins or short-term members like Wesley Tuttle, Doye O'Dell, George Bamby, and Bob Minser), and the accompanying chart should help organize the tangled skein for those interested in a more detailed look at the group's long career.

## About the Time Line

I am deeply indebted to the Pioneers' longtime scholar and historian, Ken Griffis, for most of the information in the time line, and to Gary LeMaster and John Fullerton for additional generous help. The dates are somewhat approximate, since the various members' arrivals and departures did not occur in neat, year-end increments; all replacements came in midyear, and the frequent substitution of members for periods of days or weeks makes producing such a chart an inexact science at best. No disrespect is meant to the talented individuals whose stays were short. And the chart also cannot reflect that many of these singers—Perryman, Rogers, Nolan, Curtis, Warren, Doss, and Carson especially—were also superb soloists, and that in general each member of any of these trios frequently sang solos exceptionally well.

I have deliberately used the phrase "middle voice" rather than "lead" or "melody" because much of the smoothness of the Pioneers' harmony results from their conscious lack of a melody voice. Broadly speaking, each singer sang within a certain range, and if the melody was high the tenor took it, the other two harmonizing beneath that line; when the melody moved to a middle range, the harmony parts were one above and one below; and when the melody dipped low, the harmony would be two above. The harmony thus "shifted," sometimes many times within the course of a song, sometimes within the course of a line. A prime example of this shifting can be heard on the Pioneers' timeless 1946 recording of "Tumbling Tumbleweeds," where Carson sings the melody for the first two lines, with Perryman singing one below and Nolan two below; on the third line Carson jumps to tenor as the melody is taken over by Perryman in the middle, and Nolan sings what is traditionally called the baritone; the final line finds Nolan singing the melody deep in the baritone range, with Perryman singing tenor and Carson singing what some call a "high baritone," that is, the baritone "part" sung an octave above where it is normally found.

This intricate harmonizing is fundamental to appreciating the Pioneers' glorious blend and explains why I hesitate to call the middle voice a "lead" voice, because any voice, on any given line or even phrase within a line, could be said to be singing "lead" (melody) when singing western harmony, Pioneers style.

## Pioneers Time Line

| 1933 | Tenor Voice | Tim Spencer | Bass | Bob Nolan |
| | Middle Voice | Roy Rogers | | |
| | Baritone Voice | Bob Nolan | | |
| | | | | |
| 1934 | Tenor Voice | Tim Spencer | Fiddle | Hugh Farr |
| | Middle Voice | Roy Rogers | Bass | Bob Nolan |
| | Baritone Voice | Bob Nolan | | |
| | | | | |
| 1935 | Tenor Voice | Tim Spencer | Fiddle | Hugh Farr |
| | Middle Voice | Roy Rogers | Bass | Bob Nolan |
| | Baritone Voice | Bob Nolan | Guitar | Karl Farr |

| 1936 | *Tenor Voice* | Tim Spencer | *Fiddle* | Hugh Farr |
| | *Middle Voice* | Roy Rogers | *Bass* | Bob Nolan |
| | *Baritone Voice* | Bob Nolan | *Guitar* | Karl Farr |
| | | | | |
| 1937 | *Tenor Voice* | Lloyd Perryman | *Fiddle* | Hugh Farr |
| | *Middle Voice* | Roy Rogers | *Bass* | Bob Nolan |
| | *Baritone Voice* | Bob Nolan | *Guitar* | Karl Farr |
| | | | | |
| 1938 | *Tenor Voice* | Lloyd Perryman | *Fiddle* | Hugh Farr |
| | *Middle Voice* | Tim Spencer | *Bass* | Pat Brady |
| | *Baritone Voice* | Bob Nolan | *Guitar* | Karl Farr |
| | | | | |
| 1939 | *Tenor Voice* | Lloyd Perryman | *Fiddle* | Hugh Farr |
| | *Middle Voice* | Tim Spencer | *Bass* | Pat Brady |
| | *Baritone Voice* | Bob Nolan | *Guitar* | Karl Farr |
| | | | | |
| 1940 | *Tenor Voice* | Lloyd Perryman | *Fiddle* | Hugh Farr |
| | *Middle Voice* | Tim Spencer | *Bass* | Pat Brady |
| | *Baritone Voice* | Bob Nolan | *Guitar* | Karl Farr |
| | | | | |
| 1941 | *Tenor Voice* | Lloyd Perryman | *Fiddle* | Hugh Farr |
| | *Middle Voice* | Tim Spencer | *Bass* | Pat Brady |
| | *Baritone Voice* | Bob Nolan | *Guitar* | Karl Farr |
| | | | | |
| 1942 | *Tenor Voice* | Lloyd Perryman | *Fiddle* | Hugh Farr |
| | *Middle Voice* | Tim Spencer | *Bass* | Pat Brady |
| | *Baritone Voice* | Bob Nolan | *Guitar* | Karl Farr |
| | | | | |
| 1943 | *Tenor Voice* | Ken Carson | *Fiddle* | Hugh Farr |
| | *Middle Voice* | Tim Spencer | *Bass* | Pat Brady |
| | *Baritone Voice* | Bob Nolan | *Guitar* | Karl Farr |
| | | | | |
| 1944 | *Tenor Voice* | Ken Carson | *Fiddle* | Hugh Farr |
| | *Middle Voice* | Tim Spencer | *Bass* | Shug Fisher |
| | *Baritone Voice* | Bob Nolan | *Guitar* | Karl Farr |
| | | | | |
| 1945 | *Tenor Voice* | Ken Carson | *Fiddle* | Hugh Farr |
| | *Middle Voice* | Tim Spencer | *Bass* | Shug Fisher |
| | *Baritone Voice* | Bob Nolan | *Guitar* | Karl Farr |
| | | | | |
| 1946 | *Tenor Voice* | Ken Carson | *Fiddle* | Hugh Farr |
| | *Middle Voice* | Lloyd Perryman | *Bass* | Pat Brady |
| | *Baritone Voice* | Bob Nolan | *Guitar* | Karl Farr |
| | *Vocals* | Tim Spencer | | |

| 1947 | Tenor Voice | Ken Carson | Fiddle | Hugh Farr |
|------|-------------|-----------|--------|-----------|
| | Middle Voice | Lloyd Perryman | Bass | Pat Brady |
| | Baritone Voice | Bob Nolan | Guitar | Karl Farr |
| | Vocals | Tim Spencer | | |
| | | | | |
| 1948 | Tenor Voice | Ken Carson | Fiddle | Hugh Farr |
| | Middle Voice | Lloyd Perryman | Bass | Pat Brady |
| | Baritone Voice | Bob Nolan | Guitar | Karl Farr |
| | Vocals | Tim Spencer | | |
| | | | | |
| 1949 | Tenor Voice | Lloyd Perryman | Fiddle | Hugh Farr |
| | Middle Voice | Ken Curtis | Bass | Pat Brady |
| | Baritone Voice | Tommy Doss | Guitar | Karl Farr |
| | | | | |
| 1950 | Tenor Voice | Lloyd Perryman | Fiddle | Hugh Farr |
| | Middle Voice | Ken Curtis | Bass | Shug Fisher |
| | Baritone Voice | Tommy Doss | Guitar | Karl Farr |
| | | | | |
| 1951 | Tenor Voice | Lloyd Perryman | Fiddle | Hugh Farr |
| | Middle Voice | Ken Curtis | Bass | Shug Fisher |
| | Baritone Voice | Tommy Doss | Guitar | Karl Farr |
| | | | | |
| 1952 | Tenor Voice | Lloyd Perryman | Fiddle | Hugh Farr |
| | Middle Voice | Ken Curtis | Bass | Shug Fisher |
| | Baritone Voice | Tommy Doss | Guitar | Karl Farr |
| | | | | |
| 1953 | Tenor Voice | Lloyd Perryman | Fiddle | Hugh Farr |
| | Middle Voice | Dale Warren | Bass | Shug Fisher |
| | Baritone Voice | Tommy Doss | Guitar | Karl Farr |
| | | | | |
| 1954 | Tenor Voice | Lloyd Perryman | Fiddle | Hugh Farr |
| | Middle Voice | Dale Warren | Bass | Deuce Spriggins |
| | Baritone Voice | Tommy Doss | Guitar | Karl Farr |
| | | | | |
| 1955 | Tenor Voice | Lloyd Perryman | Fiddle | Hugh Farr |
| | Middle Voice | Dale Warren | Bass | Deuce Spriggins |
| | Baritone Voice | Tommy Doss | Guitar | Karl Farr |
| | | | | |
| 1956 | Tenor Voice | Lloyd Perryman | Fiddle | Hugh Farr |
| | Middle Voice | Dale Warren | Bass | Shug Fisher |
| | Baritone Voice | Tommy Doss | Guitar | Karl Farr |
| | | | | |
| 1957 | Tenor Voice | Lloyd Perryman | Fiddle | Hugh Farr |
| | Middle Voice | Dale Warren | Bass | Shug Fisher |
| | Baritone Voice | Tommy Doss | Guitar | Karl Farr |

| 1958 | Tenor Voice | Lloyd Perryman | Fiddle | Hugh Farr |
| | Middle Voice | Dale Warren | Bass | Shug Fisher |
| | Baritone Voice | Tommy Doss | Guitar | Karl Farr |
| | | | | |
| 1959 | Tenor Voice | Lloyd Perryman | Bass | Shug Fisher |
| | Middle Voice | Dale Warren | Guitar | Karl Farr |
| | Baritone Voice | Tommy Doss | | |
| | | | | |
| 1960 | Tenor Voice | Lloyd Perryman | Bass | Pat Brady |
| | Middle Voice | Dale Warren | Guitar | Karl Farr |
| | Baritone Voice | Tommy Doss | | |
| | | | | |
| 1961 | Tenor Voice | Lloyd Perryman | Bass | Pat Brady |
| | Middle Voice | Dale Warren | Guitar | Karl Farr |
| | Baritone Voice | Tommy Doss | | |
| | | | | |
| 1962 | Tenor Voice | Lloyd Perryman | Bass | Pat Brady |
| | Middle Voice | Dale Warren | Guitar | Roy Lanham |
| | Baritone Voice | Tommy Doss | | |
| | | | | |
| 1963 | Tenor Voice | Rusty Richards | Bass | Pat Brady |
| | Middle Voice | Lloyd Perryman | Guitar | Roy Lanham |
| | Baritone Voice | Dale Warren | | |
| | | | | |
| 1964 | Tenor Voice | Rusty Richards | Bass | Pat Brady |
| | Middle Voice | Lloyd Perryman | Guitar | Roy Lanham |
| | Baritone Voice | Dale Warren | | |
| | | | | |
| 1965 | Tenor Voice | Rusty Richards | Bass | Pat Brady |
| | Middle Voice | Lloyd Perryman | Guitar | Roy Lanham |
| | Baritone Voice | Dale Warren | | |
| | | | | |
| 1966 | Tenor Voice | Bob Minser | Fiddle | Billy Armstrong |
| | Middle Voice | Lloyd Perryman | Bass | Pat Brady |
| | Baritone Voice | Dale Warren | Guitar | Roy Lanham |
| | | | | |
| 1967 | Tenor Voice | Bob Minser | Fiddle | Billy Armstrong |
| | Middle Voice | Lloyd Perryman | Bass | Pat Brady |
| | Baritone Voice | Dale Warren | Guitar | Roy Lanham |
| | | | | |
| 1968 | Tenor Voice | Luther Nallie | Fiddle | Billy Armstrong |
| | Middle Voice | Lloyd Perryman | Bass | Luther Nallie |
| | Baritone Voice | Dale Warren | Guitar | Roy Lanham |
| | | | | |
| 1969 | Tenor Voice | Luther Nallie | Fiddle | Billy Armstrong |
| | Middle Voice | Lloyd Perryman | Bass | Luther Nallie |
| | Baritone Voice | Dale Warren | Guitar | Roy Lanham |

| 1970 | Tenor Voice | Luther Nallie | Fiddle | Billy Armstrong |
| | Middle Voice | Lloyd Perryman | Bass | Luther Nallie |
| | Baritone Voice | Dale Warren | Guitar | Roy Lanham |
| | | | | |
| 1971 | Tenor Voice | Luther Nallie | Fiddle | Billy Armstrong |
| | Middle Voice | Lloyd Perryman | Bass | Luther Nallie |
| | Baritone Voice | Dale Warren | Guitar | Roy Lanham |
| | | | | |
| 1972 | Tenor Voice | Luther Nallie | Fiddle | Billy Armstrong |
| | Middle Voice | Lloyd Perryman | Bass | Luther Nallie |
| | Baritone Voice | Dale Warren | Guitar | Roy Lanham |
| | | | | |
| 1973 | Tenor Voice | Luther Nallie | Bass | Luther Nallie |
| | Middle Voice | Lloyd Perryman | Guitar | Roy Lanham |
| | Baritone Voice | Dale Warren | | |
| | | | | |
| 1974 | Tenor Voice | Rusty Richards | Bass | Dale Warren |
| | Middle Voice | Lloyd Perryman | Guitar | Roy Lanham |
| | Baritone Voice | Dale Warren | Accordion | Billy Liebert |
| | | | | |
| 1975 | Tenor Voice | Rusty Richards | Bass | Dale Warren |
| | Middle Voice | Lloyd Perryman | Guitar | Roy Lanham |
| | Baritone Voice | Dale Warren | Accordion | Billy Liebert |
| | | | | |
| 1976 | Tenor Voice | Rusty Richards | Bass | Dale Warren |
| | Middle Voice | Lloyd Perryman | Guitar | Roy Lanham |
| | Baritone Voice | Dale Warren | Accordion | Billy Liebert |
| | | | | |
| 1977 | Tenor Voice | Rusty Richards | Bass | Dale Warren |
| | Middle Voice | Lloyd Perryman | Guitar | Roy Lanham |
| | Baritone Voice | Dale Warren | Accordion | Billy Liebert |
| | | | | |
| 1978 | Tenor Voice | Rusty Richards | Bass | Dale Warren |
| | Middle Voice | Rome Johnson | Guitar | Roy Lanham |
| | Baritone Voice | Dale Warren | Accordion | Billy Liebert |
| | | | | |
| 1979 | Tenor Voice | Rusty Richards | Bass | Dale Warren |
| | Middle Voice | Rome Johnson | Guitar | Roy Lanham |
| | Baritone Voice | Dale Warren | Accordion | Billy Liebert |
| | | | | |
| 1980 | Tenor Voice | Rusty Richards | Fiddle | Doc Denning |
| | Middle Voice | Luther Nallie | Bass | Dale Warren |
| | Baritone Voice | Dale Warren | Guitar | Roy Lanham |
| | Accordion | Billy Liebert | | |

| 1981 | Tenor Voice | Rusty Richards | Fiddle | Dale Morris |
| | Middle Voice | Luther Nallie | Bass | Dale Warren |
| | Baritone Voice | Dale Warren | Guitar | Roy Lanham |
| | Accordion | Billy Liebert | | |
| | | | | |
| 1982 | Tenor Voice | Rusty Richards | Fiddle | Dale Morris |
| | Middle Voice | Luther Nallie | Bass | Dale Warren |
| | Baritone Voice | Dale Warren | Guitar | Roy Lanham |
| | | | | |
| 1983 | Tenor Voice | Rusty Richards | Fiddle | Dale Morris |
| | Middle Voice | Luther Nallie | Bass | Dale Warren |
| | Baritone Voice | Dale Warren | Guitar | Roy Lanham |
| | Drums | Tommy Nallie | | |
| | | | | |
| 1984 | Tenor Voice | Sunny Spencer | Bass | Jack Nallie |
| | Middle Voice | Luther Nallie | Guitar | Roy Lanham |
| | Baritone Voice | Dale Warren | Accordion | Billy Liebert |
| | Drums | Tommy Nallie | | |
| | | | | |
| 1985 | Tenor Voice | Luther Nallie | Bass | Jack LaRoux |
| | Middle Voice | Sunny Spencer | | (Jack Nallie) |
| | Baritone Voice | Dale Warren | Guitar | Roy Lanham |
| | Multiple | Sunny Spencer | Drums | Tommy Nallie |
| | | | | |
| 1986 | Tenor Voice | Gary Foster | Bass | Gary Foster |
| | Middle Voice | Sunny Spencer | Guitar | Gary LeMaster |
| | Baritone Voice | Dale Warren | Drums | Tommy Nallie |
| | Multiple | Sunny Spencer | | |
| | | | | |
| 1987 | Tenor Voice | Gary LeMaster | Keyboards | Daryl Wainscott |
| | Middle Voice | Luther Nallie | & keyboard | |
| | Baritone Voice | Dale Warren | bass | |
| | Guitar | Gary LeMaster | Drums | Tommy Nallie |
| | Multiple | Sunny Spencer | | |
| | | | | |
| 1988 | Tenor Voice | Gary LeMaster | Keyboards | Daryl Wainscott |
| | Middle Voice | Luther Nallie | & keyboard | |
| | Baritone Voice | Dale Warren | bass | |
| | Guitar | Gary LeMaster | Drums | Tommy Nallie |
| | Multiple | Sunny Spencer | | |
| | | | | |
| 1989 | Tenor Voice | Gary LeMaster | Keyboards | Daryl Wainscott |
| | Middle Voice | Luther Nallie | & keyboard | |
| | Baritone Voice | Dale Warren | bass | |
| | Guitar | Gary LeMaster | Drums | Tommy Nallie |
| | Vocals | David Bradley | | |

| Year | Role | Performer | Instrument | Performer |
|------|------|-----------|------------|-----------|
| 1990 | *Tenor Voice* | Gary LeMaster | *Keyboards &* | Daryl Wainscott |
|      | *Middle Voice* | Luther Nallie | *keyboard* | |
|      | *Baritone Voice* | Dale Warren | *bass* | |
|      | *Guitar* | Gary LeMaster | | |
|      | *Vocals* | David Bradley | | |
| 1991 | *Tenor Voice* | Gary LeMaster | *Keyboards &* | Daryl Wainscott |
|      | *Middle Voice* | Luther Nallie | *keyboard* | |
|      | *Baritone Voice* | Dale Warren | *bass* | |
|      | *Guitar* | Gary LeMaster | | |
|      | *Vocals* | David Bradley | | |
|      | *Multiple* | Sunny Spencer | | |
| 1992 | *Tenor Voice* | Gary LeMaster | *Keyboards &* | Daryl Wainscott |
|      | *Middle Voice* | Luther Nallie | *keyboard* | |
|      | *Baritone Voice* | Dale Warren | *bass* | |
|      | *Guitar* | Gary LeMaster | | |
|      | *Vocals* | David Bradley | | |
|      | *Multiple* | Sunny Spencer | | |
| 1993 | *Tenor Voice* | Gary LeMaster | *Fiddle* | Roy Warhurst |
|      | *Middle Voice* | Luther Nallie, John Nallie | *Keyboards & keyboard* | John Nallie |
|      | *Baritone Voice* | Dale Warren | *bass* | |
|      | *Guitar* | Gary LeMaster | | |
|      | *Multiple* | Sunny Spencer | | |
| 1994 | *Tenor Voice* | Gary LeMaster | *Keyboards & keyboard* | John Nallie |
|      | *Middle Voice* | John Nallie | *bass* | |
|      | *Baritone Voice* | Dale Warren | | |
|      | *Guitar* | Gary LeMaster | *Fiddle* | Roy Warhurst |
|      | *Multiple* | Sunny Spencer | | |
| 1995 | *Tenor Voice* | Gary LeMaster | *Keyboards & keyboard* | John Nallie |
|      | *Middle Voice* | John Nallie | *bass* | |
|      | *Baritone Voice* | Dale Warren | | |
|      | *Guitar* | Gary LeMaster | *Fiddle* | Roy Warhurst |
|      | *Multiple* | Sunny Spencer, Luther Nallie | | |
| 1996 | *Tenor Voice* | Gary LeMaster | *Keyboards & keyboard* | John Nallie |
|      | *Middle Voice* | John Nallie | *bass* | |
|      | *Baritone Voice* | Dale Warren | | |
|      | *Guitar* | Gary LeMaster | *Fiddle* | Roy Warhurst |
|      | *Multiple* | Sunny Spencer, Luther Nallie | | |

| 1997 | Tenor Voice | Gary LeMaster | Keyboards | John Nallie |
|------|-------------|---------------|-----------|-------------|
|      | Middle Voice | John Nallie | & keyboard | |
|      | Baritone Voice | Dale Warren | bass | |
|      | Guitar | Gary LeMaster | | |
|      | Multiple | Sunny Spencer, | | |
|      |  | Luther Nallie | | |

| 1998 | Tenor Voice | Ken Lattimore | Bass | Dale Warren |
|------|-------------|---------------|------|-------------|
|      | Middle Voice | Rudy Rudd | Guitar | Gary LeMaster |
|      | Baritone Voice | Dale Warren | | |
|      | Multiple | Sunny Spencer, | | |
|      |  | Luther Nallie | | |

| 1999 | Tenor Voice | Ken Lattimore | Bass | Dale Warren |
|------|-------------|---------------|------|-------------|
|      | Middle Voice | Rudy Rudd | Guitar | Gary LeMaster |
|      | Baritone Voice | Dale Warren | | |
|      | Multiple | Sunny Spencer, | | |
|      |  | Luther Nallie | | |

| 2000 | Tenor Voice | Ken Lattimore | Bass | Dale Warren |
|------|-------------|---------------|------|-------------|
|      | Middle Voice | Rudy Rudd | Guitar | Gary LeMaster |
|      | Baritone Voice | Dale Warren | | |
|      | Multiple | Sunny Spencer, | | |
|      |  | Luther Nallie | | |

| 2001 | Tenor Voice | Ken Lattimore | Bass | Preston Eldridge |
|------|-------------|---------------|------|-------------|
|      | Middle Voice | Rudy Rudd | Guitar | Gary LeMaster |
|      | Baritone Voice | Dale Warren | | |
|      | Multiple | Sunny Spencer, | | |
|      |  | Luther Nallie | | |

| 2002 | Tenor Voice | Ken Lattimore | Bass | Preston Eldridge |
|------|-------------|---------------|------|-------------|
|      | Middle Voice | Rudy Rudd | Guitar | Gary LeMaster |
|      | Baritone Voice | Dale Warren | | |
|      | Multiple | Sunny Spencer, | | |
|      |  | Luther Nallie | | |

[N.B.: This time line is based on Ken Griffis's pioneering research and the recollections of several Pioneers and scholars. Given the nature of human memory, errors are possible. The author welcomes corrections.]

# Western Music Rides to the Big Screen

The coming of sound to motion pictures was big, big news in the late 1920s, although in some ways it is surprising that it didn't come sooner. Edison's kinetophone was designed with sound in mind as early as 1889, and various other schemes were tried out in the early years of film, including synchronized sound on discs. On Christmas Day, 1926, Warner Bros. presented an entire program of talking short subjects, and on October 6 of the following year Al Jolson's *Jazz Singer* became the first full-length feature sound film, and the first musical, presented in theaters. The public's reaction to sound was profound and intense, and there was enormous and immediate pressure for studios to create sound films and for theaters to install sound systems.

However, the technology for recording was in its infancy, and many felt that sound could not be used successfully in outdoor films due to aural static from wind and background noise, as well as the distraction of airplane, locomotive, and highway sounds. The earliest sound films were recorded on sound stages—many of them in New York—but by 1928 Fox had developed its Movietone sound-on-film system (at first used exclusively for newsreels) to such a point that the first sound western, the first outdoor musical, and in a loose sense the first singing-cowboy film, *In Old Arizona* (Fox), was released in January 1929. Raoul Walsh was set to star in and direct this lively tale of the Cisco Kid, a character created by O. Henry. However, Walsh lost an eye in a shooting accident while scouting locations for this film, and although he went on to a long career as a director, his acting days were over. Warner Baxter took over the role and earned an Academy Award for his efforts. Baxter was not the only one to sing ("My Tonia," which became a popular record for Vanderbilt-educated classical tenor James Melton as well)—so did his costar, Dorothy Burgess, as did the men who played the cavalry, who delivered a manly version of "A Bicycle Built for Two" early in

Dashing Warner Baxter serenades the lovely but treacherous Tonia (Dorothy Burgess) in Fox's *In Old Arizona* (1929), the first sound western and the first musical western. Baxter won an Oscar for his role as the Cisco Kid. (Author's collection)

the film. The story concerned the cavalry's attempt to settle Arizona, so many of the eastern soldiers sang hits or snatches of hits from the turn-of-the-century period, still well within memory of many of the film's first viewers.

This film was followed, in short order, by Tim McCoy's first sound effort. A ramrod-straight silent-film star, McCoy took a short break between his silent series for M-G-M and his first talking series for Columbia to film a one-reel musical short for Fox called *A Night on the Range,* in which he sang around the campfire with some other anonymous cowpokes and range riders. Film scholar Buck Rainey claims it was "made as a voice test for McCoy and received very limited distribution." Colonel McCoy was never known to sing at any other point in his long career in film or television, but clearly he, or the studio (Rainey again reports that "sources disagree as to releasing company and the film was not copyrighted"), or both, understood the power or at least the novelty of cowboy music on-screen.[1] An obscure one-reeler called *Cow Camp Ballads* (Robert C. Bruce Outdoor Talking Pictures/Paramount, 1929) starred veteran cowboy, rodeo contestant, and dude wrangler Everett Cheetham. It is presumed but not known for a fact that *Oklahoma Bob Albright and His Rodeo Do Flappers* (Vitaphone/Warner Bros., 1929), released in June, contained music. And *Otto Gray and His Oklahoma Cowboys* was released that year as well by Veribest of New York. Thus the musical western came to the screen; westerns were a proven moneymaking genre, and cowboys were associated with singing. While for years directors, actors, and technicians had been able to tell a good story with a little printed dialogue on-screen, the one thing they could not deliver in subtitles was a song. The novelty of talking pictures was not wholly in the dialogue, or even in the music, for pianists or orchestras had provided music for silents for years. The real novelty was in the singing, and it is little surprise that much of the success of *The Jazz Singer* and *In Old Arizona* was based on their songs. For the public to hear their favorite actors talk was revelatory; to watch and hear their favorite radio and record stars sing was a greater novelty by far.

The effect on the film industry was profound: Attendance at movie houses nearly doubled between 1927 and 1930, a boom brought to a shuddering halt by the stock market crash of late 1929 and the coming of the Great Depression. Yet even this catastrophe opened the door for the singing cowboy, for in a desperate attempt to lure customers back into theaters many theater owners slashed prices and came up with the double feature—two films for one low price. A longer and more expensive A picture was coupled with a shorter, cheaper, more formulaic feature that came to be known as the B picture. The A pictures normally were exhibited on a percentage basis, while the theater owners typically paid a small flat rate for the Bs, which were ground out cheaply and efficiently to feed the growing demand. Crime films, light comedies, horror films, adventure films (which featured action figures such as pilots and explorers and race car drivers), and westerns be-

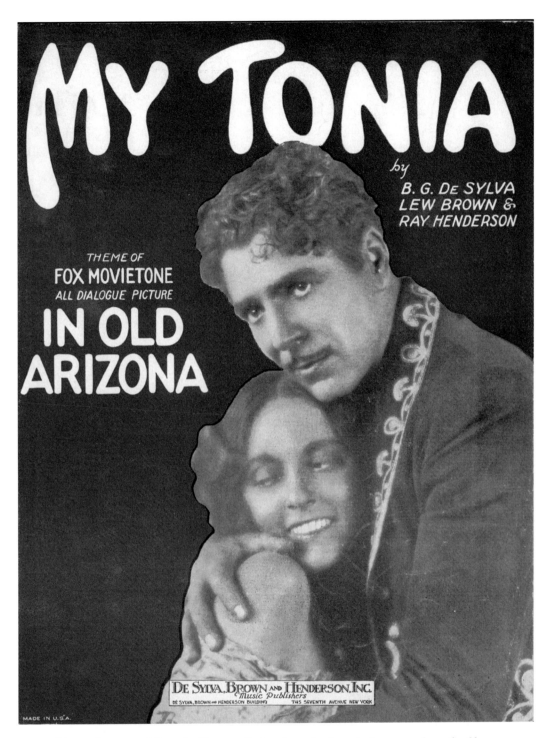

Warner Baxter and Dorothy Burgess, featured on sheet music for a song from the film *In Old Arizona*. (Author's collection)

came the staples of the B studios, and many of the studios that produced them the most efficiently—primarily Republic and Monogram—came up with their own series of singing-cowboy films in the following years. These "Gower Gulch" studios (nicknamed for the many offices and studios located on Gower Avenue in Hollywood) included Monogram, Grand National, Tiffany, Producers Releasing Corporation (PRC), and Mascot. Indeed, virtually every studio, major or minor, had a singing cowboy in the B-film entries at one time or another, including Warner Bros. and Twentieth Century-Fox. The one exception was M-G-M; the closest that studio came was Nelson Eddy–Jeanette MacDonald operettas, which shared with the singing-cowboy films the dreamy unreality of the musical but were definitely A features.

The B picture was a nationwide standard by 1935, just as the singing-cowboy genre was taking off. Although a very few singing-cowboy films could be classified as A pictures due to length and production values—most notably the Roy Rogers and Monte Hale Republic films of the mid-1940s, shot in Trucolor, and a couple of the later Gene Autry Columbia movies shot in glorious Cinecolor—the singing cowboy was almost universally a B-picture phenomenon.

Another event that opened the door for the introduction of the singing cowboy was the industrywide imposition of the controversial Production Code, a rigid code of ethics for filmmakers that went into strict effect on July 1, 1934. The Production Code was instituted in reaction to the increasingly salacious content of films as the Depression deepened, Mae West's in particular. The office of Will H. Hays (1879–1954), president of the Motion Picture Producers and Directors Association of America, had censored and imposed morality on films since 1922, but the profound power of what came to be called the Hays Office and the new, much stricter standards insisted upon sent Hollywood scrambling for films that exemplified wholesomeness. The timing was perfect for the introduction of the epitome of wholesomeness: sunny, smiling Gene Autry, a cowboy with the ability to restore law and order with a song, a smile, and a good heart.

The grip of the Production Code was not broken until after World War II, when noir films such as *The Postman Always Rings Twice* and *Double Indemnity* exposed the darker side of our psyche. There were, to be sure, adult westerns in the 1930s, most notably John Ford's *Stagecoach* (United Artists, 1939), which not only heralded the birth of a darker, more complex adult western, but also launched John Wayne on the path that would make him the most iconic cowboy figure in American culture. Once the shackles of the Production Code were thrown off, Ford could explore these darker themes with more overt violence and sexuality, which led to much of the rest of his stunning oeuvre, including *The Searchers* (Warner Bros., 1956) and *The Man Who Shot Liberty Valance* (Paramount, 1962). Similarly dark in tone and theme were the influential westerns of his peer Howard Hawks, including *Red River* (United Artists, 1948) and *Rio Bravo* (Warner Bros., 1959). Also influential in the coming years were such mature, artful interpretations as George Stevens's *Shane* (Paramount, 1953) and *The Magnificent Seven* (United Artists, 1960), a western adaptation of Akira Kurosawa's *The Seven Samurai*. In particular, *The Magnificent Seven*'s rousing score by Elmer Bernstein embodied a bracing, orchestral vision of the West. These films were followed by such graphic, latter-day revisionist westerns as Sergio Leone's mid-1960s *Fistful* series (released in the United States by United Artists), Sam Peckinpah's *The Wild Bunch* (Warner Bros., 1969), *The Long Riders* (United Artists, 1980), and Clint Eastwood's *Unforgiven* (Malpaso Productions/Warner Brothers, 1992). Ultimately, the rise of the adult western in the post–World War II era symbolized the shift in public sentiment to more morally ambivalent, graphic, and violent films, a trend that would ultimately relegate the infectious optimism of the singing cowboy to the antiquated halls of history.

But to return to 1930, although the term A or B picture was not in use yet, there were expensive big-studio productions and small, cheap, independent films, many of them westerns. A curious footnote in the history of the singing cowboy is one of these cheap independents, *Oklahoma Cyclone,* released by Tiffany in 1930. Its star was a wiry young up-and-comer known for screen purposes as Bob Steele. Bob and his twin brother, Bill (born Robert Adrian Bradbury and William Curtis Bradbury in Portland, Oregon, January 23, 1907), were the sons of prolific silent action director and screenwriter Robert North Bradbury, who had been born Ronald E. Bradbury, March 23, 1886, and who himself had aspired to a career in opera. As early as 1920 the senior Bradbury had cast his teenage sons in *The Adventures of Bob and Bill,* a series of semi-documentary nature shorts. Although Bob was small in stature, he had a tough, athletic look about him, and he naturally moved into westerns. He and his brother both sang, and, although young Bob did not have a particularly melodious voice, Bill did, and dubbed the singing for John Wayne in his Singin' Sandy film, *Riders of Destiny* (Monogram, 1933). When Bob Steele landed a contract with little Tiffany in 1930, his first sound films contained music. Bob and Perry Murdock portrayed (in disguise) a dudelike song-and-dance team in *Headin' North* (Tiffany, November 1, 1930), and Bob sang five western-oriented songs in *Oklahoma Cyclone* (Tiffany, August 8, 1930). The songs themselves were not great successes; according to one film historian, Steele "was an even worse singer than [Ken] Maynard was."[2] Steele went on to star and costar in dozens of B westerns and even took a turn in big films from time to time, playing Curly in *Of Mice and Men* in 1940, and Canino in *The Big Sleep* in 1946. He turned to character roles in the late 1940s and appears in uncounted westerns of the 1950s and 1960s, and on television, as well, where in addition to his character roles he became a regular on *F Troop*. Steele died December 21, 1988, in Buena Park, California. One of the most charismatic and exciting of the B-movie heroes, and later a highly respected character actor, he was never known to sing again on film after *Oklahoma Cyclone.* His twin brother, Bill, did no professional singing after providing the voice of Singin' Sandy; he went on to college, became a doctor, and enjoyed a long and successful medical practice in Southern California before his death in 1971. The twins' visionary father died November 24, 1949.

Steele was not the only musical cowboy to ride onto the screen in 1930, or even the first. Tiffany also featured a western duet in *Border Romance* (1930), while a Jack Perrin film, *Phantom of the Desert* (Syndicate, 1930), had an extended campfire scene featuring cowhands singing "The Great Roundup." That same year a Ken Maynard western, *The Fighting Legion* (Universal, released April 6), featured a trio billed as the Hook Brothers—actors Les Bates, Bill Nestell, and Slim Whittaker—singing in a saloon. Music and singing cowboys appeared in other films of the same era: Hoot Gibson and some cowhands make some raucous campfire music in *The Mounted Stranger* (Universal, 1930), and a villain sang in Buck Jones's *Men without Law* (Columbia, 1930), in which a Mexican love song was sung as well. Interestingly, Jones would later become outspoken in his dislike of the musical western: "They use songs to save money on horses, riders, and ammunition. Why, you take Gene Autry and lean him up against a tree with his guitar and let him sing three songs and you can fill up a whole reel without spending any money. That's why they've overdone the singing."[3] There was a touch of irony in Jones's prickly stance—he was not above putting out a songbook of familiar cowboy tunes in 1940. His reaction is understandable, however, given that a number of western purists regarded hard riding and hard fighting as the hallmarks of the screen western and had little sympathy and understanding for the new order.

Among the earliest and most interesting of these early singing-cowboy films is *Riders of Destiny,* the Singin' Sandy film John Wayne made in 1933. Wayne's first big starring picture, *The Big Trail* (Fox, 1930), had not been a success, and Wayne spent the rest of the decade working his way back in B westerns before launching his second A-film career with *Stagecoach* (United Artists, 1939). Singin' Sandy Sanders was a role created for Wayne by Robert N. Bradbury, who clearly foresaw a market niche for a singing cowboy, although he did not pursue it with particular vigor beyond directing a great many such westerns in a long career.

John Wayne's Singin' Sandy film was a pleasant effort, though it was obvious that his singing voice did not match his spoken voice. It was planned as the first of a singing-western series, but Sandy sang in only the first of these productions, and the character of Sandy Sanders was not used again. When Monogram was absorbed by the newly formed Republic in 1935, Wayne did his last lip-synching, in *Westward Ho!* (Republic, 1935), where it is thought that veteran character actor Jack Kirk provided Wayne's singing voice.

The dominant figure of this early period was, however, Ken Maynard.

His rags-to-riches and back-to-rags saga began on July 21, 1895, when he was born the first of five children to William H. and Emma May Maynard in Vevay, Indiana. A second son, Kermit, was born in 1897, and while he was not musical, he was also to appear in hundreds of B westerns in roles from extra to bad guy to sheriff to Mountie to stuntman to star. Although singing was never Kermit Maynard's forte, he strummed a tenor guitar in *Roaring Six Guns* (Ambassador, 1937).

Both Maynard boys were athletic and restless, and at the age of twelve Ken ran away from home to join a third-rate Wild West show. His father, a building contractor, went after the show and dragged his wandering boy home, but it remained Ken's dream to travel and star in a touring Wild West show or circus, and at the age of sixteen he got his father's permission to do so. By 1914 Maynard, an outstanding athlete, was a star of the Kit Carson Show, and he developed into a superb horseman. In addition, he worked hard at learning showy rope tricks from the famous Mexican rope artist Oro Peso. Somewhere along the way he developed rudimentary skills on the guitar, fiddle, and harmonica as well. He joined the Hagenbeck-Wallace Circus in 1915, left it to serve in the army during World War I, then rejoined the circus at war's end. He hooked up with Pawnee Bill's Wild West Show,

Young Bob Steele on-screen with a willing señorita, circa 1930. (Author's collection)

Ken Maynard in a scene from one of his many films. (Author's collection)

which was still touring in 1920, won World's Champion Trick Rider honors that year, and as a result was signed by Ringling Brothers as a star attraction in 1921, earning an astonishing $40,000 per year.

The next stop was Hollywood, where his spectacular riding ability won him the role of Paul Revere in *Janice Meredith* (Cosmopolitan, 1925). He was quickly signed by Fox, where it is thought he was brought in to put pressure on reigning stars Tom Mix and Buck Jones. When Mix and Jones relented to studio pressure and signed again, without raises, Maynard became expendable and was dropped. He then began making his own series of westerns for the small Davis Distribution Division Company in 1924, which established him as an up-and-coming cowboy star. Ken Maynard's success continued to grow throughout the 1920s, and he moved up to bigger studios and bigger budgets, particularly with Universal. Most of the films concentrated on his spectacular horsemanship, but they had their share of shooting, fisticuffs, romance, and humor, as well. Maynard was a capable actor, but he was most at home in the saddle, and vivid and sometimes astonishing riding scenes would remain a hallmark of his pictures.

During his first (1929–1930) stint with Universal, Maynard and studio head Carl Laemmle (1867–1939) saw the premier screening of *In Old Ari-*

Ken Maynard and his horse, Tarzan. A former featured circus act, Maynard was by far the best horseman among the singing cowboys. (Country Music Hall of Fame collections)

*zona* in 1929, and both became convinced that sound westerns, including music, were a possibility worth exploring. After a couple of films with partial sound, Ken's first all-sound feature was *Mountain Justice,* sometimes titled *Kettle Creek* (Universal, 1930). Set in Kentucky, it featured not only several songs but also some of the most harrowing stunts Maynard ever performed on film. In addition, *The Fighting Legion* (April 6, 1930), *Song of the Caballero* (June 29), and *Sons of the Saddle* (August 3) featured music as well. In the last, Maynard sang "Trail Herd Song" and "Down the Home Trail with You," and he and his studio probably hoped the roughness of his performances could be chalked up to authenticity.

Maynard was hotheaded and consistently over budget, however, and Universal dropped him. The little Tiffany Studios pulled off a coup by signing him; the small studio introduced him in one of their *Voice of Hollywood* filler shorts, in which Maynard leads his horse Tarzan to the stage, then takes up a fiddle and sings "The Drunken Hiccoughs."

Maynard's fascination with western music led to a recording contract, as well. He recorded eight sides for the soon to be bankrupt Columbia Graphophone Corporation in Hollywood on April 14, 1930. Only two sides, "Cowboy's Lament" and "Lone Star Trail" (which featured a lonesome "whee, whee, whee" sort of proto-yodel), were released at the time. Although Maynard was a capable guitarist and sang in a rather stiff authentic-sounding tenor, the unrelieved nasality of his vocal timbre quickly became monotonous and was a poor fit for his masculine, robust screen image. Though this was to be his only recording session, Ken Maynard put out a fine songbook in 1935 consisting of two of his own compositions ("The Trail Herd" and "Wheels of Destiny") and several western classics. He clearly felt he had something to offer as a musician and singer as well as an actor and movie star.

Yet, despite his apparent desire to include music in his films, none of his eleven Tiffany westerns (1929–1932) had music in them. Maynard then moved to another small studio, World Wide, for seven films, while Universal realized to their dismay that Maynard's popularity had only increased since they had dropped him. Carl Laemmle re-signed him in 1933 for $10,000 a week for each week of shooting, his own production unit, and a percentage of the profits. Although the emphasis was on action, as always, music became prevalent in these films. In *Fiddlin' Buckaroo* (Universal, 1933), for example, Maynard fiddled while the townspeople danced in the opening sequence, during which the bank is being robbed. In *The Trail Drive* (Universal, 1933), he wrote and performed the theme song, "The Trail Herd," and played the banjo by the campfire. Maynard bought the film rights to Curly Fletcher's cowboy ballad "The Strawberry Roan" and sang that clever tale of an unridable horse in his 1933 film of the same name. Not only did the film help make the song a western classic, but also it featured a trio with Maynard, Frank Yaconelli, and Charlie King, who is best remembered for

Ken Maynard saws his fiddle in a scene from *The Strawberry Roan* (1933), accompanied by Frank Yaconelli, *left,* and Charles King. (Country Music Hall of Fame collections)

his classic role of henchman in hundreds of westerns. Whatever the merits of Maynard's music, *The Strawberry Roan* is often cited as "the first full-fledged realization" of the musical western.[4]

A young producer and film company executive named Nat Levine had seen *The Strawberry Roan* and was apparently as excited as Maynard was about a series of musical westerns. He contacted Maynard about coming over to Mascot to do musical films, and Maynard kept the offer at the back of his mind. When his consistently over-budget films and his famous surliness when abusing alcohol caused another rift at Universal, Maynard stormed out of a meeting with Carl Laemmle, walked out on his contract, and contacted Levine. Levine agreed to match the whopping $10,000 per week salary and later reflected, "When I signed Ken Maynard for a serial at forty thousand dollars, his name value justified the investment."[5] He was the highest-paid western actor in Hollywood.

Although serials were Mascot's domain, Maynard's first film for the studio was a feature, *In Old Santa Fe,* released November 15, 1934. It was a landmark film in several ways. First, longtime character actor George Hayes developed a new, textured character as a cranky but lovable sidekick to Maynard, and he catapulted this character into an extremely popular side-

*In Old Santa Fe* (1934) was Ken Maynard's first film for Mascot Pictures. Unfortunately for him, it was also Gene Autry's first film for the studio. Autry soon became the leading singing cowboy at the studio and in America. (Country Music Hall of Fame collections)

kick role in Hopalong Cassidy westerns, then into singing-cowboy immortality as Gabby Hayes in the Roy Rogers films.

A second landmark was the modern West setting of *In Old Santa Fe:* a dude ranch that blended horses and six-guns with roaring roadsters and gaudy contemporary western fashions. Apparently this was Levine's creation, and it would be a hallmark of many of the Gene Autry and Roy Rogers films made at Republic in the following decade. Western purists often vilified the approach as ludicrous, but it proved popular with the public, who apparently enjoyed watching their heroes portraying radio stars or touring entertainers who happened to foil evildoers in their spare time, rode powerful, intelligent horses, and formed posses composed of guitarists, fiddlers, and harmony singers. Several of the more traditional western artists used this anachronistic plot device as well: Buck Jones in *The Thrill Hunter* (Columbia, 1933) and Tim McCoy in *Speed Wings* (Columbia, 1934) piloted automobiles and airplanes in the modern West. "Perhaps some of the producers are suffering from over-productions of Westerns," said Mascot production manager J. L. Wickland at the time, adding dryly, "We are modernizing them."[6] The third influential aspect of *In Old Santa Fe* was the singing-film debut of a young radio singer named Gene Autry.

The serial Levine had promised Maynard came next. Entitled *Mystery Mountain* (released on December 1, 1934, just two and a half weeks after *In Old Santa Fe*), it was devoid of music, and in fact Gene Autry—now under contract to Levine, and taking riding lessons from stuntman, actor, and director Yakima Canutt—and Smiley Burnette played small nonsinging roles as wagon drivers. Although Maynard negotiated control of the picture, he was personally spinning out of control. Not only did he go well over budget, which aggravated the cost-obsessed Levine, but worse yet his alcohol abuse and volatile behavior alienated cast, crew, and staff. Several of the horses who played Maynard's Tarzan on-screen bore the brunt of Maynard's violent outbursts, and one such episode was recorded by a sound man and played for a horrified Levine. Maynard reached a nadir when he pulled his six-guns on director Joe Kane over a perceived insult, and it was young Gene Autry, who idolized Maynard, who pulled the choleric and potentially dangerous star aside and calmed him down.

For Levine, at this point, Maynard's liabilities outweighed his considerable assets, and Mascot cut him loose. Ironically, *Mystery Mountain* became the second-largest-grossing serial in Mascot's history. With Maynard now dropped from Mascot, the studio assigned his next serial, *Phantom Empire,* to the unproven radio star Gene Autry. Though Maynard's reputation was getting tarnished within the industry, he was still very popular with the public, and he had a long career in films, making the rounds of most of the major and minor studios. He quickly signed with Columbia in 1935, then Grand National in 1937, Colony in 1939, Monogram in 1943, and Astor in 1944, but music played little if any part in these westerns. Maynard made some highly profitable circus tours between film contracts until bowing out of the B western in 1945. The success of Gene Autry and the singing cowboys who followed rendered Maynard's more crude musicmaking obsolete, a little too authentic for the fantasy singing westerns, and singing was never a factor in his films again. Maynard worked again in circuses after his film days, but age and alcohol abuse eventually destroyed his legendary riding ability, and his finances dried up as well—for all the money he made as a star, he spent the remainder of his years in a small trailer, living on social security and a monthly stipend regularly sent by an anonymous admirer, long presumed to be Gene Autry, who loved his flawed idol. He was finally moved to the Motion Picture Country House and Lodge in Woodland Hills in 1973, where he died within weeks.

Ken Maynard, Carl Laemmle, and Robert N. Bradbury clearly had a vision that musical western pictures could work, and they all had groped toward a formula that would click. But the man with the passion for the form, who shaped and developed it in its infancy, and who had the clout to put it on the silver screen, was the young Mascot executive, Nat Levine, a gambler in every sense. There is no evidence he cared particularly for cowboy, folk, or country music; what he did care for was black ink on the bottom line, and he correctly judged that the public would pay to see attractive young radio stars sing in films that traditionally had featured action, scenery, and more action.

Nathaniel Levine was born in New York City on July 26, 1900. Enthralled by a summer job with Marcus Loew in 1913, he gave up the idea of going to high school and worked with Loew's theater chain for six years, rising to the position of Loew's personal secretary. He left Loew in 1919 and ended up in Kansas City as a sales manager for the Margaret Winkler organization, which distributed a number of cartoons, including *Felix the Cat* and some by the young Walt Disney. Passionate about the film industry, Levine learned fast and wound up in Hollywood in 1921, eager to test the skills in independent marketing he'd learned in Kansas City, and the savvy he'd learned with Loew. He spent the next few years buying up pictures that had been made but were entangled with liens or other financial troubles, and distributing them himself. He began producing on a shoestring in the mid-1920s and became adept at creating cheaply produced action-packed serials that were enormously profitable. To that end he formed his own studio, Mascot Pictures, devoted to the art of the serial, which released its first effort, *The Golden Stallion,* in 1927. Mascot quickly became known for serials light on logic and heavy on breakneck action. Levine moved easily (and early) into the sound era with *The King of the Kongo,* the first sound serial, in 1929, and became extremely successful with a series of Rin-Tin-Tin serials, which helped little Mascot Pictures weather the Depression in fine style. John Wayne, Ken Maynard, Tom Mix, Harry Carey, and Gene Autry all worked for a time under the Mascot banner.

Levine was flying high in the early 1930s. Still in his early thirties, he was a millionaire on paper, was a highly regarded independent producer, and was able to make a single product—the serial—cheaply and well. It was not art, but vivid, fast-paced entertainment that filled a niche. Upping the stakes, he obtained the Mack Sennett studios in North Hollywood/Studio City in 1933, but because his money was so tied up with production he chose to lease with an option to buy, then never exercised the option. This proved to be an extremely unfortunate decision. Overextended yet eager to expand, he pondered two career choices in 1935. The first offer was from Louis B. Mayer to join M-G-M as an associate producer at $3,500 a week. The second was from Herbert J. Yates, a film-processing laboratory owner, to merge Mascot, Monogram Pictures, and Consolidated Film Industries to form Republic Pictures, an entity that would then buy out Liberty Pictures, Majestic Pictures, and Chesterfield Pictures, all of which owed staggering sums to Yates for film processing.

Levine, along with Monogram heads W. Ray Johnston and Trem Carr, opted to join Yates in his grand plan. None of them realized that Yates's hidden agenda was first to merge, then to buy out and discard his erstwhile partners when he was financially able. Levine admitted the grand sweep of

Nat Levine, the visionary who brought Gene Autry, and the singing-cowboy genre, to the screen. (Author's collection)

his mistake to film historian Jon Tuska much later, admitting that the merger with Herbert Yates

> was taking me from an operation that I owned with complete control to an operation of being subject to partners and ones who knew very little about production. When I joined Republic, my serials were the most successful on the market, Autry and the musical Westerns were completely my own venture, and the studio in North Hollywood was mine . . . my thoughts were to remain with Republic for five years and establish it as an important entity, then to sell out and become an independent producer. . . . Prior to becoming Herb Yates' partner, I was considered the leading independent producer and my ambitions were to become the leading *major* producer, divorcing myself from distribution.[7]

Yates showed his colors quickly, buying out Trem Carr's shares for $1 million but holding on to the distribution system Monogram had brought to the table, as well as Monogram's major star, John Wayne. In true corporate raider fashion, Yates then turned on Levine and bought him out for $2 million, to remain sole head of Republic Studios until he retired in 1959. In 1937 Levine left Republic and was replaced by Moe Siegel, whose brother Sol Siegel was brought in to the studio to oversee serials and the Autry westerns.

Nat Levine, just thirty-seven years old, was at a loss. He did not care to start over, for Republic and the quickly re-formed Monogram now dominated the field of B action pictures he knew how to make, and the public's infatuation with the serial was on the wane. He eventually accepted the M-G-M offer, but his association lasted less than a year; then, after a few months of drifting he returned to M-G-M as an independent producer, but this too lasted only a couple of years. A passion for gambling kept him at the Santa Anita race track when he might have been wheeling and dealing, and by the mid-1940s, in desperation, he sold all the Mascot negatives he still owned to Irvin Shapiro, who would later make a fortune renting them to television. Levine's wife and business partner, disgusted with his compulsive gambling, divorced him, and he drifted downward in the industry. He worked for a time as a TV studio manager, then managed theaters for California Sterling Theaters and ended his working days in the 1970s managing a nondescript movie theater in Torrance, California. "When I gambled making movies, I made money. When I began playing the horses, I lost . . . I lost everything."[8] He died, on Social Security and in a nursing home, August 6, 1989.

As for Herbert J. Yates, the ferocious corporate raider, this ruthless businessman was later described by Roy Rogers as so tight "he wouldn't pay a nickel to see an ant eat a bale of hay."[9] He is a recurring figure in the singing-cowboy saga, for in running Republic Pictures for two decades he set the standard for singing-cowboy films in production and in presentation. In doing so, he set the tone for all B-picture studios; with few exceptions, Republic's output was superior in photography, pacing, special effects, and excitement. As Republic touted in a 1938 *Hollywood Daily Reporter* special: "There is little about Republic Pictures that is not built upon a cold 'business' basis. The barometer of its bank balance is truly the box office." Yet the studio was famously insistent on quality within that small budget, and Republic made fast, exciting westerns far more quickly and efficiently than larger studios made the A westerns. As character actor I. Stanford Jolley commented: "The high professionalism and teamwork at a small studio like Republic, with limited finances, could result in up to 100 scenes a day. While over at, say, M-G-M, if they got ten scenes a day it was a small miracle!"[10] Composer Stanley Wilson, who started his career at Republic, concurred: "We were a very good highly overworked underpaid group of dedicated people. . . . It was the best training anyone ever had."[11] Director Spencer Gordon Bennet echoed the feeling that was, one must assume, typical of all those who worked at Republic: "All personnel, all the equipment were geared to that fast pace production style. Everyone whom Republic placed in the serial productions, for instance—assistant directors, cameramen, sound engineers and others—were capable of doing the work under pressure, doing maybe forty or more 'setups' per working day."[12]

Herbert J. Yates, the heart and soul of Republic, was born in Brooklyn on August 24, 1880, and educated at Columbia. By the turn of the century he was a sales executive at the American Tobacco Company, and later at Liggett and Myers. Cannily sensing a future in the film industry, he invested in a processing outfit called Hedwig Laboratories in 1915, and then Republic Laboratories in 1918. By 1924 he had combined his holdings and assembled a complete film laboratory service he called Consolidated Film Laboratories, which became a major client of many of the smaller and independent film studios. In time many of these independents, struggling through the Depression, came to owe Yates and Consolidated considerable sums of money. Seizing the opportunity to become a studio head himself, Yates called in those debts by absorbing these small studios into the entity he, Levine, Johnston, and Carr had formed, an entity that would quickly spit out Johnston and Carr, and then Levine, leaving Yates as president and chairman of the board, a minimogul running the top small studio in Hollywood.

Of the many associated businesses that Yates came to acquire under the umbrella of Consolidated Film Industries, one of the most fortuitous was Plaza Music, which became the American Record Corporation, a major record label that made Conqueror records for sale at Sears, Roebuck, and released the same masters for other mass marketers under the Perfect, Banner, Melotone, and Oriole labels. Many of the early cowboy singers, including Gene Autry, recorded for ARC. With either phenomenal foresight or phenomenal luck, Yates had poised himself to create a singing cowboy with a dual career on record and film. With the producer Art Satherley at the helm of his recording operation, Yates developed a profitable recording business in the heart of the Depression, selling western, hillbilly, folk, and blues records. At the same time, he gained full control of Republic Pictures and turned it into a minimajor by a similar approach, that is, by developing

Herbert J. Yates, longtime head of Republic Pictures. (Author's collection)

stars and themes that appealed to a huge rural audience ignored or even scorned by the major studios.

Yates ran Republic with an iron hand and an exceedingly tight budget, something that would cost him dearly in personal relations and legal actions with his major stars, Gene Autry and Roy Rogers. In his defense, Republic unquestionably made the finest, most consistent B pictures. Republic's occasional forays into longer, more expensive A pictures were usually not terribly successful, although some were well received, including *Dark Command* (1940), which featured Roy Rogers in a strong supporting, nonsinging role, and at least three John Wayne films—*Wake of the Red Witch* (1948), *Sands of Iwo Jima* (1949), and *The Quiet Man* (1952). But the B movie was Republic's strength and its bread and butter. As veteran Republic writer Sloan Nibley said: "What Republic did better than anyone else was good, fast action shows for a price."[13]

If the hard-as-nails Yates had a weak spot, it was for the Czech ice-skating star Vera Hruba Ralston, whom he discovered in 1940, married in 1952, and developed into Republic's top star during the 1950s. After the departure of Wayne, Autry, and Rogers, she headlined the studio's biggest-budget releases. The lovely, athletic Ralston (considerably taller than the 5' 4" Yates, and forty years his junior) had taken the silver medal in the 1936 Olympics, bested only by Norway's Sonja Henie, and she was destined to remain in Henie's shadow as both women entered pictures. Despite Yates's energetic backing, most of Ralston's films were not financial successes, unable to recoup their big budgets. The studio began to flounder in the 1950s as events conspired against Republic, among them the financial failure of Ralston's movies; the evaporation of the B-picture market; the defection of Yates's moneymaking singing cowboys and the decline of public interest in singing-cowboy pictures in general, along with a seemingly endless string of legal battles with stars, writers, and craft unions; and the rise of television. In addition Yates was growing old and was not in the best of health. A few years after a protracted lawsuit with Roy Rogers, he was sued by his stockholders, who came together, as the *New York Times* headlined its October 30, 1956, article, to "Charge He Used Film Company Funds for Wife's Career." As John Wayne said about the situation, "Yates was one of the smartest businessmen I ever met . . . but when it came to the woman he loved, his business brains just went flyin' out the window."[14]

It is unfair to blame Ralston's films for Republic's demise, as some film historians have insinuated. Yates's and Republic's problems were many, and they worsened when he faced an unpleasant strike in 1958 by the Screen Actors Guild and the Writers Guild of America over the issue of residual payments, payments Yates was loathe to make. With the exception of 1948, Republic had turned tidy though unspectacular profits every year from 1940 to 1956, but much of the 1950s profit was not from current films, but from the sale of Yates's older catalogue to television. This action infuriated Rogers and Autry, who brought lawsuits against Republic. Small-theater owners, long the bread and butter of Republic, were infuriated as well. They felt Yates was selling out to the enemy: Why would youngsters pay to see a reissued Roy Rogers film when they could see the same thing at home for free? Would they come to see the new Rex Allen movie if Roy, Gene, and Hopalong could be had without leaving the living room?

By the mid-1950s what profit Republic generated was not from its current film releases but from those sales of old films to television, from renting out the studio's well-equipped lot, and from the film-processing arm of the business. Having given up on the kinds of films that had built the studio—serials, B westerns, and singing cowboys—Republic concentrated solely on A features after about 1955 and more than once considered suspending film operations altogether. After losing $1.36 million in 1957 and $1.48 million in 1958, the flow of red ink was too much for the ailing Yates, who sold the firm on July 1, 1959. Ownership of the studio has passed through various hands, and while Republic still exists on paper to this day, it no longer produces feature films. Yates, whose defiant and independent spirit guided and defined Republic, only briefly enjoyed his retirement, due to failing health, and he died in 1966 in Sherman Oaks, California.

The story of Herbert J. Yates and Nat Levine—and the absorption of the Mascot film company into what would become Republic Pictures—sets the stage for a closer look at the emergence of Gene Autry. Although in time Autry would become Republic's biggest moneymaker and the top singing cowboy in history, he was still just a radio star on WLS with no screen experience when he made his debut in *In Old Santa Fe*. Although he had a small role, Autry's appearance heralded the arrival of a new force, a singing cowboy on film who would eventually take the country by storm.

Why Gene Autry, of all the vocalists on both coasts, of all the radio stars across the country, of all the recording artists, of all the competent singing actors in Hollywood? It is a fascinating story clouded by failing memory and conflicting recollections. Autry had one version; Nat Levine had another; Herbert Yates left no recollections (although Autry had been discovered before Yates absorbed Mascot, Yates quickly became intimately involved in Autry's career); and Arthur Satherley also claimed to have had a role.

In his 1978 autobiography, *Back in the Saddle Again*, Autry addressed this crucial juncture in his career. He recalled that in 1934 he was not particularly interested in getting into films—he knew nothing of screen acting and was in the midst of a surging recording, broadcasting, and touring career. However, Autry recalled that Herbert Yates himself felt the straight-action western "was a thing of the past," and that when young Nat Levine—then running his scrappy and thriving Mascot operation—approached Yates for financing, Yates told Levine: "Look, I think that the straight western picture, the shoot-'em-up western with chases and fights and that kind of stuff has kind of had its run. Why don't you think of putting some music and songs in the picture?"[15] Yates—who at that time controlled Autry's label, ARC—was likely aware of Autry's emerging success and, according to Autry's version, concocted the notion of bringing that firm's top record-seller to Hollywood with ARC president Moe Siegel, with assistance from ARC vice-president and Autry's record producer, Arthur Satherley. This version seems to contain a small chronological discrepancy, for Autry had been working with Levine many months before Yates formed Republic Pictures in 1935. However, as an inveterate string puller at Consolidated, Yates would likely have been doing business with Levine for some time, and he may indeed have been advancing him production money as well.

Although Autry was not present for these discussions, he related several secondhand stories through the years. According to Autry, Yates instructed Levine to consider the young singer for film roles. Autry quotes Yates as approaching Levine with " 'Nat, I'll give you the money, but on one condition. We have a fellow who sells a helluva lot of records for us. He's on radio in Chicago, on a national hookup, does the Barn Dance. Nat, it would be worth your while to take a look at Gene Autry.' " To get the financing for his pictures, Autry continues, "Nat Levine would have looked at a singing kangaroo. A day later I received a call from Yates and [ARC president Moe] Siegel, telling me Levine was on his way to Chicago and wanted to meet with me. I had finished my show at WLS when he arrived . . . *blew in* is the phrase I meant to use." When Levine met the shy young singer, he explained his plan to Autry: "I'm going to make this picture with Ken Maynard. Cowboy picture. Low budget. Usually, we try out a new actor, we give you a screen test, read lines, things like that. No need to bother. If you'd like to come out and appear in it, we've written in a Barn Dance scene. You can call the square dance, do a few songs. That can be your screen test. We'll see what kind of reaction we get when the movie plays." Autry replied, "Sounds okay to me," and Levine blew out as fast as he'd blown in, pausing briefly to say "Good. Call me before you come. . . . You're a nice boy. You may call me collect."[16] It is interesting in this last regard that—although Autry remembers Nat Levine as a bluff, no-nonsense tycoon who called him a "nice boy"—Levine was only seven years Autry's senior.

Autry told a similar, but significantly different, story to biographer David Rothel, using many of the same quotations ("We have a young man . . . who is selling a hell of a lot of records"), but he puts them in the mouth of Moe Siegel, who in this version was "sitting in [at this historic meeting] with Levine and Yates." According to this version it was Siegel who created the concept: " 'Everybody is making movies of regular program Westerns—Hoot Gibson, Buck Jones, Ken Maynard. Why don't you try something musical? We have a young man out of Chicago,' " and so on.[17] In many ways it really makes more sense for such a suggestion to come from a record executive than from a film executive, so this could well have been the case.

Because Autry was not present for these discussions, it is little wonder that, recounting the events many years later, he contradicted himself on who said what. Art Satherley's version has harmonies and dissonances with Autry's, and he recalled these events when he was well into his eighties:

> Herbert Yates said to me one day, "Who is this cowboy guy that you've got selling records?" I said, "Gene Autry." He said . . . , "Let me hear this fellow's records." So I took them upstairs to his fabulous office, he played them, and . . . said, "Is *that* what you're talking about?" I said, "Yeah. Don't you like it?" He said, "What is it?" I said, "That's America! Country America! That's what we're selling, and this man is a star!" . . . "Well, I can't use the stuff!" [However,] about two days later he called me back and said . . . "The guy's fabulous. I don't know what the hell he's singing about, but there it is. Where is he?" I said, "He's in Chicago. He's on the air every day, and he's getting fantastic publicity! Money can't *buy* the publicity that Sears, Roebuck has given to us! For the thirty bucks a week we're paying him!"
>
> "Well," he said, "I've got a fellow at the Blackstone Hotel's just come in from Hollywood. His name is Nat Levine. Could you have Gene clean himself up a little bit and go and see him and sing a little bit of 'That Silver Haired Daddy?' And, of course, I said sure. I got on to the phone to Gene and I said . . . "Get yourself ready, get your hair done nicely, get your pants pressed, go in there as a spic-and-span cowboy from the West." So he did. So Nat Levine signed him for the usual contract—think it was a $175 a week, which was the average in those days—and Gene signed. So that was the beginning of Gene going to the West.[18]

In this version, Satherley has put himself in the position Siegel occupied in one of Autry's versions, and a later conflicting account by Autry puts Satherley back in the picture: "I think Art Satherley called me and said that Nat Levine would be in Chicago on a certain day and . . . we arranged a meeting and I sat down and talked with Levine."[19]

For his part, an elderly Nat Levine, interviewed at length by film historian Jon Tuska, had a far different, and equally self-serving, remembrance of events:

> I received a half dozen letters from Autry during 1933 asking for an opportunity to work for me in anything I would suggest in pictures. Autry's name value at the time was limited to an independent radio station in Chicago, practically an unknown with questionable ability. On one of my trips east I stopped off in Chicago, not to meet Autry but for business I had with my distributor. But I did get to meet Autry and he virtually begged me for an opportunity to come to Hollywood and work in pictures. While he was nice looking, it seemed to me he lacked the commodity necessary to become a Western star: virility! I was not impressed and tried to give him a nice brush-off, telling him I would think about it. For a period of six months he wrote to me continually, conveying that he would do anything for the opportunity.[20]

According to Tuska, Autry importuned Yates to intercede in his behalf, and although Levine himself never explained why he chose to eventually sign the young singer, sign him he did, along with Smiley Burnette and Frank Marvin.

> "Gene was completely raw material," Levine continued, "knew nothing about acting, lacked poise, and was awkward. . . . All my staff questioned my judgment in putting him under contract. They thought I was slipping. But I persisted, and for the first four months he went through a learning period. We had at that time, in our employ, a professional dramatic and voice teacher, and Autry became one of her pupils. He wasn't much of a horseman either, so I had Tracy Lane and Yakima Canutt teach him how to ride. . . . I don't believe he ever acknowledged my contribution to his career, nor did I ever receive thanks."[21]

Tuska goes on to say that Levine's version is confirmed by many who were there, including Yakima Canutt, director Joe Kane, screenwriter Maurice Geraghty, Smiley Burnette, and Ken Maynard, but Levine still does not explain what changed his mind, or why he took a chance on the young man he politely brushed off and thought lacking in virility. When asked directly to clear up the matter of credit, Gene Autry said flatly that he'd always given Levine the credit, stating that of the two of them, Levine and Satherley, "I think that Art Satherley recommended me. Naturally. But the man that actually took the big chance and put up all the money was Nat Levine."[22] Here Yates is not mentioned at all.

And this last may be closest to the truth. Despite Levine's claims of a half dozen letters (none of which have come to light), it seems odd that young Autry would importune relatively lowly Nat Levine, of all the studio heads in Hollywood. Mascot was still a fairly obscure studio in 1933 specializing in serials and had never made a musical Western. If Autry was writing anyone out of the blue, would it not logically have been Robert N. Bradbury at Tiffany or Carl Laemmle at Universal, where his idol Ken Maynard was singing on-screen, or Monogram, where John Wayne was singing? Autry claimed he wrote Levine a letter explaining that he'd just had an offer from Monogram and asking Levine "if he'd given up on his idea. Because if he had, I was going to talk with these other people."[23] According to this version, Levine wrote him back immediately and offered him a part in *In Old Santa Fe*. Perhaps some day a letter or two will surface, though none now exist, according to Autry's office, and Gene Autry was famous for never throwing anything away.

Regardless, the young radio star was thrust into films, though he was in fact unprepared for this transition. Although he had grown up around horses, he was not an accomplished rider in the vigorous, aggressive, western-movie style. He had no training as an actor. It was not to his advantage, on-screen, that he was only in his midtwenties; his appeal was that of the shy boy next door, not the rugged, dashing action hero. He was awkward on-screen, and he himself strongly disliked what he saw: "I was ready to call it quits. I moved like my parts needed oiling, and I didn't like the way I looked or sounded."[24] "After I saw the picture, why, I remember telling Ina, I said, 'Look, let's go back to Chicago. Far as I'm concerned, I don't think that I'm cut out for the movies, and I can do all right on radio and with my records. And I think I'll let somebody else do the pictures."[25] As he often said of his first performances in later years: "I had to get better. I couldn't get any worse."

When it came to his career, however, Gene Autry was never afraid of hard work, and he strove mightily to improve his presence on-screen. In his middle and later career he eventually became a quite competent cowboy hero, with the proper amount of authority and presence, but in his early

Gene Autry on the Republic lot with his mentor and record producer Arthur "Uncle Art" Satherley in the mid-1940s. (Country Music Hall of Fame collections)

Sally Payne does a turn in *The Big Show* (1936) as many of the western notables of the era look on. *From left:* Smiley Burnette, the Sons of the Pioneers (Bob Nolan, Karl Farr, Tim Spencer, Hugh Farr, Len Slye), Kay Hughes, Gene Autry, Little Elmer, Max Terhune, and Frank Marvin. Slye, as Roy Rogers, would within a few years challenge Autry for the title of most popular singing cowboy. (Author's collection)

films he appeared often to be uncomfortable and out of his element. This is no doubt why he was so often dismissed by the industry in which he worked in the early years (and by action-western critics ever since), but in other ways his shy, unassuming demeanor worked greatly to his advantage, for the boy next door could easily be seen as a buddy, a favorite uncle or big brother for the kids, a sweet young man for the ladies. And then of course there was his singing—his gentle, relaxed, earnest vocals seemed genuine and heartfelt and conveyed the spirit of the West without being corny on the one hand, or pretentious on the other. In other words, he seemed very much like the real thing, his accent and attitude just right, and if he looked a little out of his league in fistfights, he was quickly and easily forgiven when he sang. That this could be has astounded and frustrated action-western fans and critics ever since, but the public loved the novelty of a singing cowboy, and they loved Gene Autry as that singing cowboy.

And, as is so often the case, being first meant a great deal. As he himself said, "I never claimed and never thought that I was the greatest actor in the world. I knew that. I was strictly a personality. But being the first of the singing cowboys, well, who ever followed had to be probably ten times better than I was, or they would always be a copy. Now that's a hard thing to say. . . . That was like Sonja Henie coming along and was the first ice-skating star. There was others that tried to follow her, I could name you half a dozen of them that tried to follow her, and some of them was probably better than she was, but they wasn't Henie."[26]

Despite Autry's own deep reservations about his movie debut, reports from film exhibitors to the *Motion Picture Herald* were glowing: "Good story, plenty of thrills, and some good music and singing by Gene Autry and his band. This is the kind of Western that pleases my patrons"; "Why, oh, why doesn't some company produce more westerns like this one and give us small-town exhibitors something to make money on"; "A good western with music and fun . . . give us more of this type"; "some really delightful Gene Autry music to lift it out of the rut of the common-place shooting and fighting. . . . [With] a little music and cowboy singing, Westerns go over well weekly in my town."[27]

Although *In Old Santa Fe* featured a Ken Maynard song at the beginning (which was dubbed, after Levine ruled Maynard's voice inadequate), it was the songs by the young dude-ranch performer played by Autry (backed by Smiley Burnette and Frank Marvin) that provided the pivotal moment in the history of the singing cowboy. This was the transition between cowboys who sang (such as Steele, Wayne, and Maynard) and singing cowboys. The Gene Autry phenomenon, and with it the singing-cowboy phenomenon, truly began with this movie. The die had been cast. Gene Autry was now in the movies, and the era of the singing cowboy had begun.

# Gene Autry

## Public Cowboy #1

Gene Autry's rags-to-riches saga begins in the quiet crossroads of Tioga, Texas, about two-thirds of the way between Dallas–Fort Worth and the Oklahoma border. The first of four children, Orvon Grover Autry was born to Delbert and Elnora Ozment Autry on September 29, 1907.[1] He was exposed to the life of the cowboy and the traditions of the West by his father, a livestock dealer and horse trader, and to music by his mother, who taught him to play the guitar, and then by his grandfather, William Autry, a Baptist minister who enlisted five-year-old Gene in the church choir. In addition he absorbed the music he heard on record and on trips to Fort Worth and Kansas City with his father.

Growing up in the West shaped Gene Autry's life, as did his mother's frail health (she died in 1930 at the age of forty-five) and his father's boom-or-bust occupation, which left the family alternately flush or broke and often on the move. The horse trader and his family moved to Achille, Oklahoma, then back to Tioga; they lived high, wide, and handsome, then went back to scraping and scratching. It was a feast-or-famine lifestyle, one that made young Gene both fiercely independent and eager to establish security and consistency in his own life.

Although he had talent as a musician and as a baseball player, he considered any given career not as a passion but as a means to escaping this cycle of instability. Not that Gene Autry's life was one of desperate hardship, but from an early age he developed a determination to create order from this chaos, to achieve stability and stature and financial security. He said in his autobiography: "It always surprises me when people seem surprised by my success in business. Actually working with numbers was what I did best. What I did less well was sing, act, and play the guitar."[2] Even as a young man he was driven to succeed, and by his midteens he reportedly toured as a singer with the Fields Brothers Marvelous Medicine Show. Around the same time he took correspondence courses in accounting and taught himself Morse code to better his chances of getting a job with the railroad. After leaving high school in 1925, he took a series of positions with the St. Louis & Frisco Railroad in Oklahoma, eventually rising to the post of relief telegrapher.

In an oft-told Autry story that may be apocryphal, fate intervened in the summer of 1927. During a visit to his sister, humorist Will Rogers stopped by a small railway station in Chelsea, Oklahoma, to telegraph his newspaper column (the town varies in different retellings of the story, but Chelsea makes the most geographical sense as it is nearest to Rogers's sister's ranch). The relief telegrapher that night was young Gene Autry, who whiled away the empty hours singing and playing his guitar. Gene later recalled Rogers's words to him: "You know, with some hard work, young man, you might have something. You ought to think about going to New York and get yourself a job on radio." Rogers's compliments stoked a fire burning deep within the young man. Radio had swept the nation, and Autry knew that there was a wide world out there to be conquered. After nearly a year of thinking it over, practicing, and dreaming, Autry used his small savings, a free round-trip railroad pass, and some vacation time to take his guitar and dreams to New York. Whether it happened quite this way is unclear—Autry only began telling this story after Rogers's untimely death in a 1935 airplane crash, as a tribute to the influence of the beloved humorist. It is not mentioned in his 1934 song folios, where Autry credits Jimmy Long with mentorship and inspiration. What is certain is that Autry's music turned from hobby to passion, and he saw it as a way out of the dusty Oklahoma prairies and into the glittering good life the Jazz Age promised.

Gene Autry had been to cities before, visiting the stockyards and hotels of Kansas City and Fort Worth with his father, but these were a far cry from New York, one of the most sophisticated cities on earth, at the very height of the Roaring Twenties. Surely he was daunted, at least at moments, but unshakable optimism and burning ambition—so much a part of Autry's character—sometimes allow the young to do the impossible simply because they haven't learned yet that it can't be done.

Gene knew no one in New York; his only lead was from a woman he'd met in a cafe in Butler, Oklahoma, who had recommended that Gene look up her sons, Frankie and Johnny Marvin, when he got to the city. Acting on her tip, Gene knocked on their door and introduced himself, beginning a lifelong relationship with both men. Frank Marvin, Gene's contemporary, was trying to break into the business and had started a small career as a musician, singer, and comedian. Thirty-year-old Johnny was already successful in New York as a singer and songwriter and had made a name for himself on radio as "the Lonesome Cowboy of the Air." After his star faded on Broadway, and Gene's rose in Hollywood, Johnny came to work for the

Autry organization and remained as musical director until his death from a disease contracted on a wartime USO tour of the South Pacific. Frank went on to provide the haunting and instantly recognizable steel-guitar fills in dozens of Autry movies, hundreds of records, and uncountable radio shows and live appearances. Frank was born January 27, 1904 in Butler, Oklahoma, and died in Frazier Park, California, in January 1985.

In the late summer and fall of 1928, Gene and Frank became immediate buddies, shared a small apartment, and even, according to Gene, shared one overcoat between them as the weather grew cold. Frank had a recording contract and a career, and using his and his brother's contacts, he and Gene made the rounds of every record company they could think of: "The days turned into weeks as I lugged my guitar up and down Broadway," Autry recalled, "to the rhythm of the record companies doors slamming in my face. At the time there were only a handful of companies—Victor, Columbia, Brunswick, Edison—and I tried them all, day after day, trying for an audition. My first problem was to get past the reception desk."[3]

Autry's persistence finally paid off. Although Frank Marvin recalled the big break happening at Edison, and Autry clearly recalls it happening at Victor, the scenario and the result were the same. According to Marvin: "I took him down to the old Edison Company and one of the sound men there played the piano, and he tried to make a test record of [Al Jolson's recent hit] 'Sonny Boy.' He couldn't sing 'Sonny Boy' yet! I told him, when we got back to the hotel, that if I was him I'd try to do some of those western-type songs. . . . I told him, 'Go back home and practice your singing and yodeling and come back here and I'll get you another test record.'"[4] Autry recalled his break coming at Victor, where executive Nat Shilkret heard him auditioning, in youthful desperation, for a secretary. According to Autry, the song, "Jeanine, I Dream of Lilac Time," caught Shilkret's ear because it was one of Shilkret's own compositions. Bringing Victor's vice-president, Leonard Joy, into the small reception room, they auditioned Autry and invited him to make a test recording the following morning. The divergent versions agree on the test song, "Sonny Boy" ("probably not the smartest choice on my part," reflected Gene), and Autry also recalled recording "The Prisoner's Song."

According to Autry, Shilkret urged him to get experience and choose material more wisely: " 'You got a nice voice for records,' he said, 'but you need experience. My advice is go home. Take six months, a year. Get a job on a radio station. Learn to work in front of a microphone.' "[5] Marvin told him flatly, "Forget that Jolson stuff. Learn to sing some yodel songs. That's more to your style."[6]

Autry swallowed his pride, took the advice, and went back to Oklahoma with a kind letter of recommendation from Shilkret, which he parlayed into a job on KVOO radio in Tulsa. There he was billed as "Oklahoma's Yodelin' Cowboy," appearing as a solo artist and with Jimmy Wilson's Cat-

Brothers Frank and Johnny
Marvin onstage in the
late 1920s around the time
they met Gene Autry.
(Author's collection)

fish String Band. Yet he was both wise and cautious in keeping his position as relief telegrapher with the Frisco railway. He wasn't ready yet to give up his day job.

In the months that followed Autry recalled that he "traveled more back roads than a bootlegger, singing at Kiwanis clubs and high schools and private parties all over the state."[7] He also began to perform and write songs with a night dispatcher on the railroad, a man named Jimmy Long. Eighteen years his senior, Long was in similar thrall to the music of Jimmie Rodgers, and the two hit it off well, practicing, performing, and writing together. Long eventually recorded and appeared with his young friend on the *National Barn Dance,* and in 1932 he introduced Autry to his niece (and Gene's future bride), Ina Mae Spivey. Long was co-billed on many early Autry records, including the million-selling "That Silver Haired Daddy of Mine" (which he had written), and he toured with Autry a bit during Depression-era layoffs. But Long was older and settled, and apparently did not care for the vagabond life of the touring performer. Though a million-selling songwriter and recording artist, he returned to his job with the railroad in Springfield, Missouri, where he retired in 1950 and died in 1953.

Autry had made great strides as a performer, singer, guitarist, and yodeler in the eleven months since he'd returned from New York, and in the fall of 1929 he once again took some vacation time and headed back in search of a record contract. Frank Marvin recalled: "So next time he came back . . . I was going over to the old Gennett Company in Flushing, Long Island, and he made a test record and they liked him. Then we went to Victor, and Johnny and I played guitars for him. He couldn't yodel yet, but I did some yodels for him. So we kind of helped, and Johnny even brought him out on stage at the Palace, and they liked old Gene there, by golly!"[8] Autry's autobiography makes no mention of the trip to Gennett but does report that "backed up by the guitars of Frankie and Johnny Marvin, I cut my first record for Victor. Johnny had written one of the sides, 'My Dreaming of You.' Jimmy Long composed the other, 'My Alabama Home.' "[9] The date of those Victor sessions was October 9, 1929, just fifteen days before the wildly careening Jazz Age would collide head on with the Depression. Autry made several other recordings before the new year, a telling mix of the music influencing him, with Jimmie Rodgers songs predominant ("Blue Yodel #5," "Waiting for a Train," "California Blues," and "Daddy and Home"), as well as Carson Robison's hillbilly hit "Left My Gal in the Mountains." Then he headed back once more to Oklahoma.

The Depression cut quickly and deeply into the booming recording business, but undaunted by the growing despair around him, Autry took advantage of another free pass and took a sixty-day leave of absence from the St. Louis & Frisco Railroad—to which he never returned—and ventured once again to New York. He was soon recording for a host of labels, including Victor, Columbia, Grey Gull, Cova, OKeh, and Gennett.

By the later sessions his shaky guitar playing had improved noticeably, and his voice, particularly his yodeling, had more authority. Despite his billing on KVOO, he was still no singing cowboy. His eclectic musical tastes ran the gamut on these early sessions: one or two cowboy songs, to be sure ("Cowboy Yodel"), but also sentimental songs ("The Tie That Binds"), minstrel songs ("Methodist Pie"), topical songs ("A Gangster's Warning"), a labor ballad ("The Death of Mother Jones"), and a heavy dose of blue yodels in the style of Jimmie Rodgers, who was at the peak of his career. Autry also began to develop his talents as a songwriter, although these early efforts were basically Rodgers-style blue yodels that would have fit unobtrusively into the repertoire of the Singing Brakeman. Autry even recorded two of Rodgers's most intensely personal songs, "Jimmie the Kid" and "T. B. Blues," on Victor's budget label Timely Tunes in the spring of 1931. Despite his intense early emulation of the Singing Brakeman, Autry recalled little of Jimmie Rodgers in his later years and did not mention him at all in his 1977 autobiography, *Back in the Saddle Again.*

This omission points out a consistent problem in studying the Autry phenomenon: Throughout his long life, Autry remained indifferent about discussing his music and the passion that drove him as a youth. His autobiography hardly touched on his musical origins. He corroborated some of the familiar stories and dispelled others as fiction, but in the end we are left

A debonair Gene
Autry at the dawn of
his career. (Country
Music Hall of
Fame collections)

with precious little more knowledge of the music that inspired him, and the music he created, than we began with. Autry appeared to be a little starstruck himself—in his book he fondly recalled his meetings and interactions with such luminaries as Kate Smith and Will Rogers—but he never referred to the music and musicians who touched his soul. Many musical figures of paramount importance in his career were scarcely covered: Johnny Marvin was mentioned just a handful of times, as were Fred Rose and Johnny Bond; Art Satherley only three times (his name misspelled with rigid consistency, as was Autry's "good friend" Carson Robison's); Ray Whitley just once; and Jimmie Rodgers not at all.

The main creator of this vague, enigmatic Gene Autry was Autry himself. In his later years he became protective of his image and was notoriously leery of interviews, best demonstrated in James Horowitz's amusing account in *Rolling Stone* (October 25, 1973) entitled "In Search of the Original Singing Cowboy," an article that chronicled Horowitz's endless and ultimately unsuccessful attempts to obtain an in-depth interview with the star. Journalists who were able to break into the cocoon created by Autry's family and staff came away with the familiar stories, such as the Will Rogers meeting, and minor reminiscences about Autry's films and records. They heard about his deft combination of luck and skill in business (calculated,

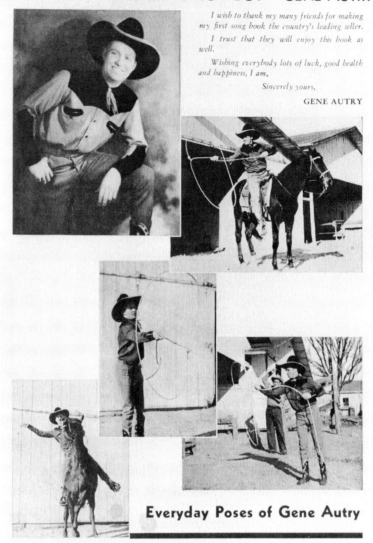

OKLAHOMA'S YODELING COWBOY—GENE AUTRY

*I wish to thank my many friends for making my first song book the country's leading seller.*

*I trust that they will enjoy this book as well.*

*Wishing everybody lots of luck, good health and happiness, I am,*

*Sincerely yours,*

**GENE AUTRY**

**Everyday Poses of Gene Autry**

A page from a Gene Autry songbook, 1930s. (Author's collection)

after three-quarters of a century in public life, to prove both his humility and his business acumen); how his wife, Ina, insisted he record "Rudolph the Red-Nosed Reindeer," a song he personally disliked; and how the California (now Anaheim) Angels would fare in the upcoming year's pennant race.

Gene Autry remained singularly unreflective concerning both the origins of his inspiration and the effects of his music and film careers. Late in his life, when broadcaster Mike Oatman asked directly about the influence of Jimmie Rodgers, Autry replied: "I've had a lot of people to say that I did

An early WLS publicity shot of Gene Autry. (Country Music Hall of Fame collections)

sound like Jimmie Rodgers, and not intentionally I didn't. But I can see now where it would be very easy to fall into a pattern such as Jimmie Rodgers or even probably Vernon Dalhart when you would sing some of those songs. I think why especially when you would learn them off a record, why it would be very, very easy to fall into a pattern. I can see that."[10]

It is clear, however, that Autry's sound and repertoire owed far more to Rodgers than to Dalhart: Autry recorded such Rodgers numbers as "My Rough and Rowdy Ways," "Hobo Bill's Last Ride," "My Carolina Sunshine Girl," "Anniversary Blue Yodel," "Any Old Time," and "In the Jail House Now," as well as such Rodgers sound-alike cuts as "High Steppin' Mama Blues," "Dallas County Jail Blues," "Bear Cat Papa Blues," and "She's a Low Down Mama."

By the end of 1931, however, Autry had clearly become aware that he must forge his own identity if a long-lasting career in entertainment was to be had. His voice began to become recognizable as a young version of that friendly, sun-warmed voice that would fill theaters and sell millions of records later in the decade. Sentimental songs of the southern highlands began to show up in his recorded repertoire, such as "There's a Good Gal in the Mountains" and "Missouri Is Calling," and it was at this time that Autry and Long recorded their composition "That Silver Haired Daddy of Mine," which became the runaway national hit Autry had worked so hard for.

By this time he had become a member of the *WLS Barn Dance* in Chicago, then the hottest rural-oriented radio program in America, and he had also obtained a radio show of his own, *Conqueror Record Time.* He now signed exclusively with Arthur Satherley of the American Record Corporation, the renowned producer of many of the most influential folk, country, cowboy, and blues artists of the 1930s and 1940s, including Bessie Smith, Roy Acuff, Big Bill Broonzy, Bob Wills & His Texas Playboys, Blind Lemon Jefferson, Al Dexter, Ma Rainey, Carl Smith, Little Jimmy Dickens, Roy Rogers, Bill Monroe, Bob Atcher, and the Sons of the Pioneers.

Satherley apparently first signed Autry as the American Record Corporation's answer to Victor's Jimmie Rodgers, but he came to realize that Autry's potential lay with the songs of the prairies and rangelands. Although there were plenty of cowboy records on the market, most of them presented the song itself as the appeal. Satherley seemed to realize there was or would be a market for a singer with personality, a likable voice as opposed to Vernon Dalhart's stentorian approach, or Carl T. Sprague's reedy tenor, or the folksy geezer charm of Haywire Mac. The successful country recording artist of the day was Jimmie Rodgers, whose voice was untrained but intimate. Beyond the striking yodels there was a warmth and humanity to Rodgers's voice; listening to Jimmie Rodgers was like sitting on the front porch with an old friend.

The introduction of electrical recording in 1925 in some ways made popular singing possible, for it meant that singers no longer needed enormous force and volume to be heard. The era of the belter was out, and the era of the soft, Bing Crosby style was here to stay. This palpable intimacy was what was driving the Rodgers phenomenon, and something in Autry's gentle, unthreatening voice suggested to Satherley that, with guidance, a similar ability to sell records could be developed in the kid from Oklahoma.

Satherley got Autry the exclusive record contract and sponsored *Conqueror Record Time,* but he attached exacting terms: Autry was to be a cowboy singer, presented as fresh from the Oklahoma plains, ready to sing cowboy songs in a shy, aw-shucks manner. It was not an approach with which Autry was at first comfortable: "That sort of stuff didn't sound very glamorous to me, as my recollections of ranch life included aching muscles and endless days in the sun and dust. I wanted to be a dreamy eyed singer of love songs like Rudy Vallee."[11]

Ann Williams, the announcer on *Conqueror Record Time,* made much of the romantic cowboy image, building the cowboy up as "bringing the West back East with bright talk of the wind-swept plains, of coyote howls in the moonlight, and cowboys on galloping horses." Autry recalled that he began to leave behind the mountain ballads and blue yodels and "sang cowboy songs, not because I felt the listeners liked 'em better, but because Arthur insisted upon it. Ann began to build-up my Oklahoma-Texas background and sprinkled the program with talk of sagebrush and tumbleweed. So between the three of them, Marvin, Satherley, and Ann Williams, they finally got it through my ornery skull that instead of doing poor imitations of all the

Gene Autry at the peak of his film and radio career, circa 1940. (Country Music Hall of Fame collections)

popular singers of the day, I should stay in my own backyard and sing the songs I knew best."[12]

Although there is no indication that Autry grew up immersed in cowboy songs, his gentle, soothing voice was well suited to painting musical pictures of the Western landscape. It was a modern voice, intimate and friendly, compatible with the demands of radio and record. Smooth and warm enough to appeal to those used to popular music, it yet retained the accent of the West and the unstudied sincerity that rural audiences demanded.

Gene Autry and Champion. (Author's collection)

He had developed an unbeatable combination. While Autry could be force-ful and even demanding in person, his voice on records and radio conveyed bashfulness and sincerity. This vulnerable quality had great appeal to fe-males, who historically make up a majority of the record-buying audience, and his songs of outdoor life and wide-open spaces in the heart of the De-pression appealed to all sexes and all ages.

Autry's three years on WLS and the network *National Barn Dance* (1931–1934) redirected his career in several other ways. He got a boost when Sears, Roebuck—the Chicago-based retail giant that owned WLS from 1924 to

October 1928—began carrying a Gene Autry Roundup Guitar for $9.95. Sears also teamed Autry with the M. M. Cole music-publishing company for two songbooks, the first called *Mountain Ballads and Cowboy Songs.* The second, significantly, reversed the wording in the title: *Cowboy Songs and Mountain Ballads.*

These WLS years were heady ones for the young Gene Autry, still only in his midtwenties. He was a regional star on radio with a national hit record, was on the most prestigious barn dance program in the nation, had his own extremely popular radio show on one of the country's biggest stations, and commanded good money on tour in those desperate Depression times. Then Hollywood came calling. By 1934 Ken Maynard, Bob Steele, and even John Wayne had done some singing on film; some of Maynard's films came perilously close to becoming singing-cowboy pictures. But in no sense were they a series: Maynard simply featured music as incidental to the action in several of his standard western films. Fortunately for Gene Autry, Ken Maynard was not a gifted singer. His rough-hewn voice may have projected authenticity, but it was not particularly pleasing. Though Maynard was a harbinger of things to come, it was up to Gene Autry to personify the personality and warm appeal that made the singing-cowboy genre possible.

Although Autry strongly disliked himself on-screen in *In Old Santa Fe,* the public and the studio executives approved of what they saw, and he and Burnette were signed to star in a bizarre twelve-part western-cum-science-fiction cliffhanger serial called *Phantom Empire* (1935), wherein a radio star named Gene Autry discovers the scientifically advanced empire of Murania hidden 25,000 feet beneath the earth, a plot used previously by the likes of Jules Verne and Edgar Rice Burroughs. (Here was another film innovation: Gene Autry, with a couple of minor exceptions, always played himself on screen.) The Muranians have robots, television, and other scientific marvels, such as the death ray that eventually destroys their empire. Much of the time the tension in this series of cliffhangers arises because of a deadline never before used in movie serials: Gene has to get back to the surface to do his scheduled radio broadcast. Whether it was this peculiar mix of film genres or Autry's appealing singing, this serial was popular as well, and his film career was on its way.

In 1935 Gene, Ina, and Smiley Burnette returned to Hollywood to stay. Autry was quickly thrust into a series of westerns for the newly formed Republic Pictures Corporation, into which Mascot was being folded. His first full-length feature, *Tumbling Tumbleweeds,* began, in fact, as a Mascot production and was named, as were many of his films, for his currently popular record. The song, written by Bob Nolan, became Autry's second million-seller, and his string of hit records continued unabated while his film career bloomed. The public couldn't get enough of Gene Autry's films, and Republic Pictures ground them out at a hectic pace. Just three weeks after the September 5 release of *Tumbling Tumbleweeds* came *Melody Trail,* which was followed by *Sagebrush Troubadour* on November 19, and *Singing Vagabond* on December 11. The titles of these films served notice that here were westerns with a big difference. While there was action, comedy, and wide-open spaces aplenty, the focus was on the music and on the hot young music maker. The following year was nearly as hectic for Autry, and in 1936 his tenth film finally named the phenomenon that was becoming a film genre of its own: *The Singing Cowboy.*

All these movies were produced by Nat Levine, costarred Smiley Burnette, were directed by Joseph Kane, prominently featured Autry's horse, Champion, and each was loaded with five to eight songs. These pioneering films gradually developed a format and a feel of their own, and their success virtually built Republic. In the words of Nat Levine, *Tumbling Tumbleweeds* "cost only $15,000 and brought in $500,000. That was in the middle of the Depression and consisted mainly of fifteen-dollar flat rentals per engagement."[13] Another source quoted the cost as $18,000, the eventual gross "nearly $1 million."[14]

Autry's real film career was in full swing, and he embodied a charming Depression fantasy—troubles and problems could be dispelled with songs, good cheer, and innocent honesty. From this point on, musical westerns made up a high percentage (though not a majority) of B-western releases, and even many action stars like Charles Starrett, Johnny Mack Brown, Hopalong Cassidy, George O'Brien, and Tim Holt stepped aside during their films while the Sons of the Pioneers, Jimmy Wakely, Eddie Dean, or

Lovable, bumbling, and musically gifted Smiley Burnette astride Ring Eye Nellie. (Author's collection)

Gene Autry toward the end of his film career. As the singing-cowboy films vainly tried to compete with the hard-edged "new westerns," cowboys' once gaudy outfits got toned down. (Author's collection)

Ray Whitley added musical texture for a few moments before the head-liners returned to action. After Gene Autry, the musical western film would never be the same.

Autry's early films broke ground in a number of other ways. Comedy (usually in the person of Smiley "Frog Millhouse" Burnette) was featured to a degree rarely if ever seen before in westerns; women were usually not portrayed as helpless prairie flowers in need of a good rescuing, but instead as independent, sassy, and intelligent; and, with a few exceptions, the time period was the present. Once the viewer could accept a West where six-guns and saddles coincided with radios, telephones, and Lincoln convertibles, scripts could touch on a number of contemporary social issues, such as the Dust Bowl and the treatment of Native Americans. The films often reflected the populist sentiment of the day: Gene Autry portrayed an Everyman, championing the rights of the small ranchers, farmers, or towns-people against heartless business conglomerates, corrupt politicians, or the injustices of "the system."

By 1937 Autry's relationship with Republic was coming unglued over money. He had been hired by Nat Levine for $75 a week in 1934—good money in those Depression years, but not nearly what he could be making on tour in the Midwest—and had risen to $100 a week when Mascot merged into Republic. His contract called for raises of $50 a week every six months that he remained with Republic, which brought him up to a couple of hundred dollars a week by mid-1936, but his films were grossing hundreds of thousands. In addition, he was forced by contract to split personal-appearance fees with Republic.

Working under Herbert Yates surely provided a virtual M.B.A. in tightfisted business practices, and Autry learned a great deal in his several long and bitter contract disputes with Yates. He re-signed with Republic in July 1936 and negotiated to receive $2,000 per picture and all income from his personal appearances. When 1937 came along, his salary doubled to $4,000 per film, but he was well aware that his worth to the studio was far greater than that. At this point he was making some of the most popular films in the country, raking in money on personal appearances, and selling thousands of records, yet he was seething over his dealings with Yates, which would have profound consequences later in the year.

This suppressed resentment came to a head in the fall, when Autry walked out on Republic, still not satisfied with a contract he found too confining. Though young, he was already a canny businessman and was well aware of his worth to Republic, and he felt a hefty raise was due. He also heartily disliked Republic's practice of block booking, which forced theater owners to sign up for Republic's entire set of releases rather than allowing them to pick and choose. Many of these owners wanted only the Autry pictures, which filled their theaters, and were not always thrilled about taking on the rest of the studio's offerings, which may not have appealed to their audiences. "Many of them had gone along with the block buying," recalled Autry, "to the extent that they would buy a package of twenty, my eight plus twelve others, and ship back the ones they didn't want without using them."[15]

In later years the Autry spin machine emphasized that Autry's walkout was due to Gene's unwillingness to allow Republic to continue the block-buying practice with exhibitors. But everyone knew then, and they know now, that it was about money. As Autry later put it, "I wanted that practice stopped, and, while I was about it, a fairer share of the profits my pictures were producing." Autry "hurried back to Hollywood and confronted Herb Yates. . . . That was the wrong approach to take with Yates. But if there was a better one I didn't know it then, and I don't now" (p. 60).

After an angry meeting with Yates, Autry gathered his band and went on a lengthy personal appearance tour of the Southwest, failing to return to the set for scheduled shooting:

> When I walked out of his office, we both knew I wouldn't be there when the cameras rolled. . . . Of course, when I failed to show up for the first day's

All smiles for the camera, Republic's three biggest stars were frequent adversaries in and out of court with their irascible boss, Herbert Yates. *From left:* Gene Autry, Yates, Roy Rogers, and Bill Elliott. (Photo courtesy of Gene Autry's office)

> shooting on *Washington Cowboy,* the studio suspended me. Yates said he would make the film without me and create a new cowboy star. . . . Yates had threatened to break me—"if you won't work here you won't work anywhere." The studio took out an injunction to prevent me from appearing on stage until my contract had been fulfilled. We hit the road . . . always one step ahead of the process server. (p. 61)

Angered by Autry's walkout, Yates set out to find another singing-cowboy star, hoping both to pressure Autry back to work and to replace him if need be. While Yates's search brought young Roy Rogers to the screen, Rogers was not big enough yet to fill the vacuum left by Autry's defection from Republic.

As Roy's star ascended in films, Autry actively toured, and he recorded three of the biggest pure-western records of his career in 1938: "Gold Mine in the Sky," "Take Me Back to My Boots and Saddle," and "When It's Springtime in the Rockies." All of this dramatically upped his worth to Republic—much to Yates's chagrin—and Autry received an unexpected boost from Republic's film distributors. At their annual convention they "climbed all over Herb Yates" because they had gone six months without an Autry release (p. 63). For many small theaters, the Autry movies were their only proven moneymakers. Autry later recalled:

> At that point Yates called. While our attorneys got together and worked out a compromise, we went off to play golf. In a curious way, there were no hard feelings. All he had done was call me disloyal and threaten to ruin me. In return I had called him a cheapskate and a tyrant. In those years, in Hollywood, no one took anyone else seriously. So we played golf. My salary was raised to ten thousand dollars a film (escalating to fifteen and twenty over the next seven years), and the clauses I found objectionable were removed. The package deals continued; they were by then too entrenched to undo. (pp. 62–63)

So Gene went back to work at Republic, and by fall he was back in theaters with *Gold Mine in the Sky,* supported by Pee Wee King & His Golden West Cowboys. Although the block-booking practice was not rescinded, Autry's point was well taken, as it eventually turned out. By 1940 the Department of Justice, having investigated the practice after restraint-of-trade allegations, reduced the number of films that could be block booked to a series of five. In 1946 a federal consent decree outlawed the practice altogether.

The string of Autry films continued, usually eight a year. Between films there were tours and appearances at rodeos in which the canny Autry owned stock. And Autry's prewar years had also yielded an astonishing number of hit records, including "The Yellow Rose of Texas" (1933), "The Last Roundup" (1934), "Ridin' down the Canyon" (1935), "Nobody's Darling But Mine" (1935), "You're the Only Star (in My Blue Heaven)" (1935), "Mexicali Rose" (1935), "Take Me Back to My Boots and Saddle" (1937), "There's a Gold Mine in the Sky" (1937), "Back in the Saddle Again" (1939), "South of the Border" (1939), "Tears on My Pillow" (1940), "You Are My Sunshine" (1941), "I Hang My Head and Cry" (1941), "It Makes No Difference Now" (1941), and "Tweedle-O-Twill" (1942). The extent of Autry's popularity becomes apparent in this list of hits, many of which remain standards. Excluding Bing Crosby's output, it is a list unequaled by any other recording artist of the period.

One of the most fascinating aspects of 1940 was the reemergence of Gene Autry on record. He was still king of the hill on-screen and was a major ticket seller in personal appearances across the country, and his records were still popular. But his sound had become somewhat dated, reedy, and creaky. Jimmy Long's old-fashioned tenor (and Smiley Burnette's similar style) often rose above the melody, and Burnette's chugging accordion accompaniment was herky-jerky.

It was time for a musical makeover, and Gene Autry, ever ready to reinvent himself, undertook one, beginning with his March 12, 1940, session. Carl Cotner and Spade Cooley played ultrasmooth twin fiddles, the fluid Paul Sells replaced the huffing and chuffing of Burnette on accordian, and Frank Marvin, outfitted with a buttery-sounding electric steel guitar to replace the harsher metallic tones of his acoustic resonator guitar, began to supply the haunting pads and fills that supply so much of the trademark Autry sound. The only two things missing from the swinging small-band sound associated with Autry at his peak were the acoustic guitar runs of Johnny Bond, which became a fixture of the Autry sound beginning with his June 18, 1941, session (which included the classic recordings of "It Makes No Difference Now" and "You Are My Sunshine"), and the plaintive, muted trumpet of Don Linder, who began recording with Autry the following month.

This hot little orchestra (often augmented with the clarinet of studio musicians Thomas Retraff, Jack Mayhew, or Joe Krechter) combined a tangy western flavor with the breezy feel of a solid jazz combo. It suited Autry's maturing vocals perfectly, and many of his finest records date from 1940 to his final prewar session in June 1942. They included "Amapola (Pretty Little Poppy)," "Lonely River," "Sweethearts or Strangers," "I Hang My Head and Cry," "Rainbow on the Rio Colorado," "Call of the Canyon," and "Be Honest with Me." Autry had caught up with the times, and this lovely sound would soon be emulated by many of the popular western record sellers of the period.

Autry took on another chore in 1940: *Melody Ranch,* a radio show sponsored by Wrigley's chewing gum, which aired through 1956. It began as a fifteen-minute show on CBS; the initial show had just enough time for a song, a retelling of the apocryphal meeting with Will Rogers, and a version of "Back in the Saddle Again," then his current hit. In short order it became the theme song for the program.

*Melody Ranch* existed in fifteen-, thirty-, and forty-five-minute formats in these early years, always on Sunday evening, and the format settled on music, comedy, and a necessarily brief dramatic adventure in which Gene saved the day.

A highlight of the early broadcasts was the inclusion of the Rough Riders (Jimmy Wakely, Johnny Bond, and Dick Reinhart) as the featured trio. Mary Lee, the juvenile who appeared in several Autry films of the era, was featured on the show, as was Horace Murphy as sidekick. The orchestra was led by Lou Bring, assisted by Autry's old mentor Johnny Marvin. Female singers came and went, and eventually Jimmy Wakely left to pursue a solo career, so the trio became Johnny Bond with brothers Eddie and Jimmy Dean. When Eddie left after some months to take a costarring role in radio, an interesting short-term trio consisted of Jimmy Dean, Wesley Tuttle, and Merle Travis. This fluid situation settled down with the coming of the Cass County Boys after World War II.

World War II changed the country forever, and no one's career was affected more than Gene Autry's. In a surprising move, Autry marched into Herbert Yates's office and announced that he planned to enlist. Yates tried to mollify his biggest cowboy star; he had ways, he claimed with justification, of delaying or deferring or exempting Autry from service, but Autry would have none of it. As he later recalled:

> Yates thought he would be doing us both a favor. But I didn't see it quite that way. My mind was made up. . . . He thought I was being a fool or, worse, that I was grandstanding. "If you do this to us," he said, "you know what will happen. By the time you get back, you'll be forgotten. You could be throwing away your whole career. And it won't hurt us. No sir. If we have to we'll spend a million dollars to promote Rogers. A million. And we'll make him bigger than you ever were." He was trying to get under my skin. There may have been some truth in what he was saying, but I wasn't going to lose my temper. "Herb," I said, "do what you have to do. But I'm telling you, I can't stay out. It would make me look bad and the movie business look bad. . . ." After that we did four movies in six months. . . . I played my last date in Chicago's Soldier Field on the Fourth of July, 1942, and . . . by the end of the year I was living it up on a tech sergeant's pay of $135 a month. (pp. 81–83)

Yates reportedly was apoplectic over Autry's decision to enlist. Autry was just as firm in his patriotic conviction, and he was officially inducted into the Army Air Corps during a *Melody Ranch* radio broadcast on July 26, 1942. His last prewar film, *Bells of Capistrano,* was released in September 1942. While he did some of the obligatory fund-raising and high-profile celebrity touring while in the service, he also did not get a cushy officer's commission. Autry was a tech sergeant, and he paid for his own flying lessons, on his own time, to improve his ratings as a pilot in order to qualify to fly twin-engine planes. He subsequently spent a good amount of time flying C-109 transport supply planes in the Far East and in North Africa and ended up flying supplies in DC-3s in Burma, a dangerous and tricky assignment that used his pilot's skills effectively.

Autry was a changed man upon his return. The country had changed as well. Both the man and the American people were more serious, touched by the horrors of war, and less interested in the escapist fantasies that had so charmed prewar audiences. Though it took a number of years to play out, the singing-cowboy genre had peaked and was never the same after the war. While kids still flocked to westerns and adults still bought Autry's records, the singing-cowboy heyday was over.

His stint in the military gave Autry cause and time to reflect on his future. He often maintained that his awakening to the world of business came when he entered the Army Air Force, when his salary dropped from $600,000 a year to $135 a month. While still in the service he began to take steps to ensure a comfortable retirement once his voice gave out or the public tired of him. He surely knew that audiences would not be the same upon his return—there was always some new star or sound to captivate the public's attention—and he had for years planned for the inevitable day when his celebrity would "cool off." He could have envisioned a future much like that of many entertainers of the time: an endless trail of stage shows, recordings, and nights on the road. A darker picture in that crystal ball would have shown his old idol Ken Maynard, who had earned $10,000 a week in 1934 but was washed up and out of films by 1946.

None of these possibilities appealed to Autry, and he began in his methodical and hardworking way to prepare for a career in business. He began by buying a radio station in Phoenix while he was still in the Army Air Corps, then another in Tucson. When it became obvious that television was going to be a major force in the entertainment business, he applied for and received a TV license for his Phoenix radio station. He hired a trusted and efficient staff and made sure all aspects of his career were tightly handled. As he continued to obtain rights or partial rights to songs, he built a profitable song-publishing business. Although Republic suggested he step into noncowboy roles, he refused to. Autry knew his audience and stayed with the westerns that had made him a star.

And of course there were the records. Autry returned to the recording studio with a vengeance, cutting dozens of sides, including originals, covers of popular tunes, and rerecordings of his 1930s classics. His singing had matured, and thanks to arrangements by Carl Cotner, both the new songs he recorded in the postwar years and the rerecordings of his earlier hits showcased Autry at his best. He had several postwar hits ("At Mail Call Today," "Have I Told You Lately That I Love You?," "Sioux City Sue," and "Mule Train" among them), but he didn't strike gold again until 1949, when "Rudolph the Red-Nosed Reindeer" went on to sell more than eight million copies. Though Autry had continued to record country, cowboy, and pop tunes all along, he now found a whole new avenue to explore in children's seasonal songs. He hit again in 1950 with "Peter Cottontail" and had contributed to this genre by co-writing and recording "Here Comes Santa Claus" in 1947.

Autry's radio program *Melody Ranch* picked up right after the war, popular as ever. The show had become *Sgt. Gene Autry* for a while, broadcast remote from various military installations, with a strong accent on patriotic songs and themes. Eventually it left the air for a time, when Autry went overseas to fly transport aircraft, only to return bigger and better (again as *Melody Ranch*) on September 23, 1945.

The cast and orchestra on *Melody Ranch* were bigger in those heady postwar years. Johnny Bond became the laconic sidekick, dry of wit and delivery, and Carl Cotner led the orchestra, delivering over the air waves the same sound found on Autry's records: muted trumpet, small string section, clarinet, Johnny Bond's acoustic guitar, and Frank Marvin's steel guitar. A female trio called the Pinafores was featured, consisting of the three Kettle sisters, Eunice, Beulah, and Ione, and the obligatory bunkhouse trio was the Cass County Boys. Lou Crosby joined as announcer, providing his famous introduction that opened: "Out where the pavement ends and the West

## Gene Autry on the Road

When most of the singing cowboys hit the road for personal appearances, the shows were similar: a few songs, a few tricks with the horse, a bit of patter, some gun or whip and rope tricks. Performed at a theater between showings of the latest movie, the live twenty-minute shows occurred about four times a day. As always, Gene Autry's show was the biggest and grandest, and thanks to the detailed memories of Johnny Bond, we have a glimpse of a typical postwar Autry road show.

It invariably began with Autry himself coming out on-stage, welcoming the crowd, and singing a few signature bars of "Back in the Saddle Again." Trick roper Barbara Bardo (married to Autry's brother Dudley [1920–1962]) then did a short routine, followed by a few jokes from Autry. He then introduced the female trio the Pinafores, backed by the Cass County Boys, who harmonized on a hit or two of the day. (Later, the Candy Mountain Girls, then the King Sisters with Norma Zimmer, would perform the same function in the show.) Chief White Cloud followed with a short demonstration of Indian dances. Then Johnny Bond himself came out, did a few jokes, and sang a country hit of the day; some of those he recalled were "Don't Let the Stars Get in Your Eyes," "If You've Got the Money (I've Got the Time)," "Alabama Jubilee," and "Oklahoma Hills." Next came, in Bond's words, an "outside musical attraction" such as the Hoosier Hot Shots or banjoist Eddie Peabody, and then came a song or two by a female soloist, usually Ginny Jackson, Judy Clark, Gloria Grey, or Gail Davis, a limited singer but Autry's frequent film costar and television's Annie Oakley.

A series of tricks with Champion came next, followed by Jack Knapp, a rope trick specialist, who was joined after a few moments by his wife, Bobbie, for a series of rope and whip tricks, as well as acrobatics.

Then at last Gene himself sang, backed by Bond, Carl Cotner, and the Cass County Boys, beginning with "Back in the Saddle Again," followed by a few popular tunes such as "Don't Fence Me In," "Have I Told You Lately That I Love You?," "Return to Me," and "Be Honest with Me." Autry invariably closed with a western classic, which might have been any of a dozen of the most familiar examples of the genre. Some had been Autry hits, such as "Tumbling Tumbleweeds," "South of the Border," "The Last Roundup," or "You Are My Sunshine," while others were associated with other performers, such as "Riders in the Sky," "Jingle Jangle Jingle," or "Deep in the Heart of Texas." And all of this came in only the first half.

Merchandise was offered at intermission, including songbooks, souvenir books, and photos of the star; 78 rpm records were not sold, for they were far too fragile and susceptible to heat to transport across the country on tour. The Cass County Boys opened the second half of the show, singing such songs as "See That You're Born in Texas," "Room Full of Roses," or "El Rancho Grande." Carl Cotner then stepped forward and played "Listen to the Mockingbird" and "The Hot Canary" on his violin, and then Rufe Davis presented a few minutes of comedy and music. Pat Buttram followed with more of the same, offering a homey solo monologue in his cracking voice before being joined by Frankie Marvin for some banter. Frank then sat down at his steel guitar to play "Steel Guitar Rag," and if Smiley Burnette was on the show he then came out to do a little comedy and sing one of his original classics, "Hominy Grits" or "It's My Lazy Day." Champion (or one of several Champion doubles) did some more equine tricks, then Gene returned to say farewell and sing a final version of "Back in the Saddle Again."

The cast was a little fluid over time (Merle Travis came and went, Ray Whitley occasionally appeared, the Riders of the Purple Sage did one tour in place of the Cass County Boys, Johnny Western replaced Johnny Bond in the late 1950s, and there were many "girl singers" and comedians who were part of the show), but the structure was the same. Bond reported, with evident regret, that the show too began to suffer in the late 1950s, when the films were no longer being made and rock & roll dominated the airwaves:

"We didn't have the full crew that we'd had before: here it was just Autry, myself, Merle Travis, Carl Cotner leading a local band, plus a few circus type acts brought in from other sources. It was mostly an outdoor affair giving us all the feeling that we were now in Carnival, sometimes considered by some to be a second rate class of the show business. The smaller shows coupled with the smaller crowds made it obvious to all of us that the end of the line was well within sight." *

Autry's interest at that time was devoted to his business. Bond, with typical irony, remarks that after yet another disappointing show in those waning years, he caught Autry reading a copy of *Variety* on the airplane with the headline "Autry Sells TV Re-Releases for 5 Million." **

Many of the movie cowboys continued to tour after the glory days, but they too scaled back. Their horses were no longer part of the tours, the supporting acts and comedians grew fewer or nonexistent, and the shows increasingly became musical performances much like the country acts of the era.

The big-scale shows were considered passé in this era when raw and primitive rock & roll was in its infancy. Huge concerts of a different type emerged as rock grew through the years, with light shows, flash pots, and smoke and mirrors a part of the multisensory experience, a far cry from the homey variety shows the singing cowboys provided in their touring heyday. We can be grateful to Johnny Bond for preserving a look at what the biggest show of its time looked like.

*   Bond, *Champion,* p. 388.
**   Ibid., p. 391.

begins." When the show went back to half an hour in 1946, the western dramas were reintroduced, and this successful format was part of the fabric of American life for the next decade.

The addition of Pat Buttram as comedian and sidekick in 1948 (Johnny Bond took a lesser role as backup musician, occasional singer, and folksy humorist) was the final link in the stabilization of the cast. The only major change in the following years was the replacement of the original Pinafores when Eunice Kettle left the group to marry and the sister act disbanded. Gloria Wood, Sue Allen, and Dorothy McCarty then became the Pinafores, seamlessly continuing the Kettle sisters' sound and style. Johnny Bond left for more than a year but returned, and guitar legend Merle Travis became part of the cast on later shows, evidently attempting to update Autry's musical sound.

Gene Autry also came back from the war ready to do battle once again with Herbert Yates at Republic. By 1947, Autry felt, in Jon Tuska's words, that "as a western property he was worth more than any player on the screen. He refused to put up with Yates's attempts to humble him and negotiated himself an excellent package with Columbia."[16] Yates, it seems, knew the moment might come when Autry would permanently jump ship, but he felt prepared: He had leading western stars John Wayne and Bill Elliott and felt he could challenge the majors, and to keep Gene firmly in his place he had established Roy Rogers as the King of the Cowboys. Yates, always adversarial, apparently did not realize the value of Gene Autry and thought him replaceable. In the long run he was right, of course, but in the short run the loss of Autry cost Yates dearly both in financial terms and in goodwill. Autry sued for release from his contract, contending that his seven-year contract had run out while he was in the service. Republic felt the contract was suspended while Autry served, and claimed Autry owed them twenty-one more films. Republic lost the suit, and with it, the goose that had laid all those golden eggs.

Evidently Yates did not learn much from his errors in judgment. An argument with John Wayne in 1952 ended their twenty-year relationship in bitterness and anger, this on the heels of the great critical and commercial success of *The Quiet Man*, which was Wayne's last film for Republic. Roy Rogers had a litigious relationship with Yates as well, and thus Herbert Yates ended up thoroughly alienating the three biggest stars Republic ever had—Wayne, Rogers, and Gene Autry—who went on quickly to bigger and better deals. Autry recalled his final break with Republic:

> By the time *Robin Hood of Texas* had reached the movie houses, I had parted ways with Republic. The courts had upheld my suit and I was now free to make my own deals and pick my own friends. We had offers from several studios. But I wanted to form my own company, frankly, because of the tax angles. If you earned over $100,000 in those days, 85 per cent of it was

Gene Autry, for years one of Columbia's top record-sellers, in a November 1947 ad in *Life* magazine featuring the company's foremost popular artists. (Author's collection)

taxable. The only way to hang on to your money was to form a corporation. So I became the president and executive producer of Gene Autry Productions, and we signed a contract with Columbia to release our pictures. It was as good a deal as anyone in Hollywood had at that time. I had complete say over my films and I could take home half the profits.[17]

It was quite a deal, though people warned Autry that Columbia Studio boss Harry Cohn might be every bit as hard to deal with as Herbert Yates. "When I first went to Columbia Pictures, why a lot of people said 'you think you've had trouble with Herb Yates over at Republic? Just wait 'til you get to Columbia and some of the trouble you'll have over there!' Well all the time I was with Columbia I had no problems with anyone. . . . It was just that I thought when I went to Columbia that they would probably spend more money on the pictures and maybe make bigger pictures than I had made at Republic."[18]

After some legal wrangling, Autry agreed to five more films for Republic before the November 1947 release of *The Last Roundup,* the first Gene Autry Production for Columbia. Although it was not in color, the film's production values were high, the songs were many, and forty-year-old Autry showed great growth as an actor. The story line dealt with water rights and the mistreatment of Indians in the modern West. It was typical of the several Columbia films to follow, although, to Autry's disappointment, only two were filmed in color: *The Strawberry Roan* and *The Big Sombrero* (which even included an animated sequence). Even though Autry was producing his own films, the color process was too expensive, and the wait for color processing too long, to make economic sense.

Even as his long-range thoughts turned to other horizons, Autry was at his artistic peak during those postwar years. His films show a maturity of presence, a far cry from the self-conscious kid who had made his first films a decade before. While the charm was still there, his screen image was no longer boyish. Although he had gained weight in the Army Air Corps and had a fondness for scotch that kept him from looking like a stereotypical action hero, he still had that Autry magic, the warm smile, and the sunny voice, with the gravity and authority that only experience and age can bring. The final Republic films and the subsequent Columbia releases revealed a man at the height of his powers: confident, assured, likable, and far more credible as a western hero. Although he still played Gene Autry, he played Gene Autry to perfection.

But film stardom had lost its appeal for him. It had become a means to an end, and that end was the building of a financial empire. He clearly saw Gene Autry as a product to be merchandised, and he continued to merchandise his image while he invested in businesses both inside and outside show business, including radio and television studios, television production, oil wells, ranches, and hotels.

He elaborated on this process with a folksy homily:

I was reminded once by Johnny Bond . . . of a tradition of the Old West. Whenever a lone cowboy or Indian needed to take a long journey by horseback, it was customary for him to ride one saddled horse while leading another bareback. When his mount began to tire, instead of stopping for a rest, he merely slipped the saddle onto the spare horse and rode on. In just about that way I eased out of my life as a performer and began to devote my full energy to business. I just changed horses. I had discovered during the war how quickly your security can be threatened by conditions beyond your control. It was a jolt to the nervous system to find myself starting at an Air Force salary of less than two thousand dollars a year, after earning up to ten thousand dollars a week. I thought to myself, well, as long as I can work I know I can make money. But what if something happened to my health? Or my voice went haywire? Times change, too. If you don't part your hair right, they, the public, will find someone who does. I knew the time had come to start looking for an interest that did not depend on my being able to perform.[19]

While Autry may mentally have switched to that second horse during the war, he was no financial naif when he entered the service. He simply began to spend more and more time on business activities. It served him well—through the years his personal fortune grew from hundreds of thousands of dollars to millions to hundreds of millions. Yet regardless of his intense devotion to business, his love of performing never left him. Those who worked with Autry even at the very end of his performing career—Johnny Bond and Johnny Western in particular—remarked that Autry was always eager, even impatient, to hit the stage. Despite the increasing difficulty of running a business empire from the road in those days before cellular telephones, facsimile machines, and the Internet, he loved and looked forward to live performances to the last.

It is ironic and more than a little prophetic that Gene Autry's first starring serial, *Phantom Empire* (1935), and one of his first starring films, *The Singing Cowboy* (1936), both prominently featured television. It was an idea whose time had been coming, and those with foresight saw it bearing down like an onrushing express train. There had been cowboy singing televised as early as 1932, when experimental station W9XAL, in cooperation with radio station KMBC, broadcast a reading of the news by Kansas City radio reporter John Cameron Swayze (later to become a leading network news anchor) and an appearance by Tex Owens doing his famous "Cattle Call." Red River Dave's cowboy songs had been broadcast from the New York World's Fair in 1939, but these were just experiments, demonstrations, test runs; indeed there were only four hundred television sets in all of the United States at that time. Early in the game Gene Autry, ever the astute businessman, saw that there was a future in television, and he wanted his organization to be part of it.

Autry formed Flying A Productions to produce a series of television shows in 1949 and 1950, and ultimately it produced four in the heyday of early television, including *Annie Oakley,* which starred his former movie costar Gail Davis, and *The Range Rider* starring Jock Mahoney and Dick Jones. Autry even produced a short-lived series starring his horse, *Champion.* In the next few years Autry bought property (most notably Melody Ranch, where his television series were filmed, and which is used to this day as a western location for such TV productions as *Dr. Quinn, Medicine Woman*). He also acquired hotels, cattle ranches, real estate, oil wells, the rodeo stock, and more radio and television stations: KMPC in Los Angeles (the flagship station for Golden West Broadcasting), and later KTLA television. He formed his own record label, ironically called Republic, and although he did not record for it himself, the independent label had numerous hits during its heyday, among them Johnny Bond's 1960 foray into rock & roll, "Hot Rod Lincoln."

Autry's move into television was not a popular one in the film industry. If movie studios were uneasy about the effects television would have on their industry, theater owners were anxiety ridden. Autry recalled telling a convention of theater owners to accept the change, that television would build and develop film stars as radio had with himself, Bing Crosby, and others, and despite resistance within his industry, Autry went ahead with his plans. By 1950 Autry surely saw television as yet another opportunity to squeeze the remaining juice from the Gene Autry juggernaut of the past, and to develop a whole new arm of his rapidly growing business empire.

*The Gene Autry Show* premiered as a TV series at 7 P.M. on July 23, 1950, on the CBS Television Network. A crack team was in place: longtime film producer Armand Schaefer was at the helm, Carl Cotner provided the music, and Pat Buttram played the sidekick. The shows, numbering ninety-one in all, were beautifully filmed, many of the later ones in color. Frank Marvin and the Cass County Boys could often be seen in the small casts, along with a variety of stock Hollywood villains (Harry Lauter seemed to be in every other show), as well as such former leading men as Robert Livingston and Kermit Maynard in character parts.

Unlike the Roy Rogers series that followed, the Autry shows prominently featured music—usually one, sometimes two, songs per half-hour segment—although a few had no music at all. And unlike Rogers's show, which had a single locale from week to week, Autry's show featured him in a wide variety of places and jobs. One week he could be a border ranger, the next a ranch foreman, the next a ranch owner, the next a stage line superintendent, the next a former Texas Ranger, the next an undercover investigator for a government agency. Regardless of his job of the week, there was always a problem to be solved with a smile, some common sense, and a song, and grizzled Pat Buttram was always there to provide laughs in his cracked voice.

Although he embraced the future of television, Autry recalled he "caught all kinds of hell from theater owners, exhibitors, and even from Columbia Pictures! They were all over me for making this first series."[20] The film studios saw series television shows as competition to their own movie series, and they were right. Within a few years the B movie was dead, for television was able to provide the action-filled, unpretentious formula stories about detectives, spacemen, and cowboys that had formerly drawn the same audience into theaters.

Gene sang "Sing Me a Song of the Saddle" in the opening show—although "Back in the Saddle Again" was of course the show's theme song—and "Sierra Nevada" in the final color episode, "Dynamite," broadcast December 24, 1955. It was a good run; the shows were efficiently produced miniatures. Autry himself had developed into a confident and capable actor and had matured as a singer, and after twenty-five years of singing cowboy songs he was comfortable and relaxed with his material. The whole series had a warm, pleasant feel that was an extension of the Gene Autry personality the public had loved for all those years.

The cultural changes wrought by television and rock & roll in the 1950s affected Autry's radio show, *Melody Ranch,* as well. In 1953 the show had been overhauled. The cast and band became much smaller, and more pop songs were featured. Although it was still popular, the show was fading when the final installment was broadcast on May 13, 1956. *Melody Ranch* was the epitome of the cowboy radio show of its era, the template upon which others were designed. It was by far the most successful, and the best remembered.

At this point in his career, for all his love of the stage, Autry's main focus was now on his growing business empire. The mythic image of Gene Autry, the common man on the blazing stallion, had run its course, and Gene Autry the businessman was wise enough to realize it. He had never wanted to end up just another old performer reliving his past in smaller and smaller venues. By the end of the series he was almost fifty and out of shape, with plenty of other fish to fry. He had television shows to produce, hotels to run, oil and cattle investments to oversee, a set of radio and television stations to manage, and in just a few years, a baseball team to buy. Although he continued limited touring—a proven moneymaker—for a few more years, with the end of *The Gene Autry Show* series and the closing down of *Melody Ranch* on radio the following year, Autry pretty well took off his spurs and put on his corporate cowboy suit.

With a growing empire to manage, it was easy enough for Autry to gradually slip out of the limelight and concentrate on his business endeavors. "I knew," he wrote in his autobiography, "I would never grow old on a sound stage."[21] His performing career had been long and studded with highlights: he is the only performer represented by five stars on Hollywood's famous Walk of Fame, one each for records, radio, films, stage appearances, and television. But times were changing, and so were the public's tastes, and Gene Autry, a class act, bowed out gracefully.

The handwriting was on the wall for the singing-cowboy western anyway, and indeed for the B western in general. Most of the great singing cowboys and all of the lesser ones had finished making singing-cowboy movies by the time *Last of the Pony Riders*—Gene's final of ninety-one starring roles—was released in November 1953.

Even Autry's recordings, the staple of his career, slowed down markedly after 1954, with just a handful of releases in 1955 and 1956, a couple of singles and a Christmas album in 1957, and nothing at all in 1958. A 1962 greatest-hits album on RCA essentially closed out one of the most remarkable recording careers of all time. The remainder of Autry's output included a solitary 1964 single, a number of reissues (mainly on Columbia) in later years, and an ambitious multi-album set of cuts of *Melody Ranch* material (with unfortunate overdubbing) on Autry's own Republic label in the 1970s. Very recently his office has been releasing a fine series of remastered cuts from his films and television shows.

Autry appeared on his last bona fide tour in 1961, along with Foy Willing & the Riders of the Purple Sage. Except for a couple of television appearances in subsequent years, he was mainly known through occasional television reruns of his old films. During 1987 and 1988 he cohosted, with Pat Buttram, The Nashville Network series *Melody Ranch Theater,* in which he introduced his old films.

Although his financial dealings generally were low profile, he became a major public figure in the business world when he brought the Angels baseball franchise to Southern California in 1960. In his final years Autry largely divested himself of his business empire, focusing the bulk of his enthusiasm on the California Angels baseball club in their yearly chase for the pennant and on an entirely new endeavor. Driven by his lifelong passion for the American West, and having amassed a valuable collection of western artifacts, he built the Autry Museum of Western Heritage in Los Angeles's Griffith Park.

Late into the 1990s Gene Autry enjoyed his retirement, his museum, his wife, Jackie (Autry's first wife, Ina Mae, died in 1981), and his remaining friends. With his iron constitution he had outlived most of his peers, and he frequently joked that "if I'd known I was going to live this long I would have taken better care of myself." The Singing Cowboy finally passed away, from the complex ailments of great old age, on October 3, 1998, a week after his ninety-first birthday.

# 7

# The Next Generation

## Tex Ritter, Roy Rogers, Dick Foran, Ray Whitley, and the Rest of the Posse

The impact and influence of Gene Autry's films on other cowboy singers and other film studios can hardly be overestimated. As the year 1936 dawned, Autry was well on the way to becoming a national sensation, and his rising stature made the infant Republic Pictures a genuine player, if not a major one. His stardom solidified the phenomenon that was coming to be called—like the title of one of those 1936 entries—the singing cowboy. Autry's surprising and immediate success in movies opened a floodgate, and dozens of cowboy hopefuls followed, including two future singing-cowboy titans, Tex Ritter and Roy Rogers.

Autry's films featured a number of interesting flourishes and innovations, among them the casting of regionally popular bands to provide musical backup, in order to help boost the films in areas where the bands were popular. Autry did this again and again in his films, and in 1936 filmgoers saw the Light Crust Doughboys (twice), the Sons of the Pioneers (twice), the Tennessee Ramblers, and the Beverly Hillbillies provide music in addition to the songs featured by Autry and Smiley Burnette.

Nothing breeds competition like success, especially in Hollywood, and given Autry's sudden success it should come as no surprise that a host of cowboy films came out in a rush to fill a perceived void for musical westerns. Most were imitators—of the nascent genre, not of Autry himself—but the very first came just two months after Autry's first picture, so soon that it is impossible to imagine that a decision could have been made, a star selected, a film script written, a cast and crew scheduled, and a marketing plan put in place in so short a time. More likely, Warner Bros. came up with virtually the same idea as the team that had launched Autry and was just a hair slower, in its big-studio way, to exploit it than was the scrappy and efficiency-oriented Mascot.

In fact, Warner Bros. was not shy about claiming the singing cowboy as its invention. Aimed at theater owners, the studio's bombastic advertisement on page 2 of the November 9, 1935, issue of *Motion Picture Herald* declared: " 'Our hat's in the ring with Westerns that sing': Dick Foran, 'The Singing Cowboy.' Yessir, men, we've got the first new idea in Westerns since Broncho Billy Anderson learned to ride! All the rarin,' tearin,' ridin' and shootin' of the best of the old-time series—plus those Cowboy Songs the country's crazy over, featured in every release! That's why you'll have the edge on the other fellow if you'll grab Warner Bros. six Westerns presenting the screen's New-West star Dick Foran."

Perhaps Warner Bros. executives had been as impressed by *In Old Arizona* as Ken Maynard and Carl Laemmle had been; perhaps they had seen possibilities in Maynard's singing in his Universal films; perhaps the buzz from exhibitors in *Motion Picture Herald* about *In Old Santa Fe* was so great they put their big machine in gear and got a series up and running in a hurry. Perhaps it dawned on them that with hit songs like "The Last Roundup" coming out of New York, there was a market for western musicals. Regardless, their singing-cowboy B westerns (the only ones Warner Bros. ever made) were far from carbon copies of the Autry films. Their star, Dick Foran, was a different screen presence than Autry, played a different character, and was a different kind of singer; the music was more sophisticated and production values far higher. These movies were clearly another studio's idea of what a singing-cowboy film should be, and they enjoyed fairly successful runs. The first three of the series made an average profit of almost $49,000 on films with average budgets a hair over $80,000. On the other hand, while this was a good profit, it "pales in comparison to the hundreds of thousand of dollars brought in by Autry's *Tumbling Tumbleweeds*." [1]

Dick Foran appeared in these singing-cowboy adventures very early in a long and respected career in films. Born in Flemington, New Jersey, on June 18, 1910, John Nicholas Foran was an eastern blue blood, the son of future New Jersey state senator Arthur F. Foran, and was educated at Princeton, where he excelled in athletics and theatricals. His early goal was to become a geologist, but his beautiful singing voice brought him into the realm of amateur musicals, and he was soon bitten by the show business bug. Foran found quick success upon moving to Hollywood and starred in several B pictures for Fox, though they were not westerns, including the Shirley Temple musical *Stand Up and Cheer* (1934). He left Fox to go over to Warner Bros. to star in this singing-cowboy series and changed his billing from Nick Foran to Dick Foran.

Dick Foran was extremely athletic and handled himself well in the physical scenes as well as the vocal. In addition, he was a good horseman. Even younger than Autry, he nevertheless projected a greater maturity and confidence on-screen, though it could shade into a kind of smugness at times. Yet like Autry, Foran seemed more like an older brother than a rugged cowboy

Dick Foran was Gene Autry's first rival and almost beat him to the punch, as his first singing-cowboy film was released just weeks after Autry's first. (Author's collection)

hero in the flinty William S. Hart or flashy Tom Mix mold. The budgets, huge for B pictures, showed in the smooth and classy production values, and in the orchestral music in the background—unlike those of most cheaper westerns, the scores were not drawn from the stock arrangements in the studio library but frequently were symphonic arrangements of the songs used in the film, most written by studio songwriters M. K. Jerome and Jack Scholl. One of their songs, "My Little Buckaroo," became a standard; it was introduced in Foran's *Cherokee Strip* in 1937.

Foran's first feature was *Moonlight on the Prairie,* in which, interestingly, he is cast not as a lonely cowpoke but, like Gene Autry in *In Old Santa Fe,* as a medicine show singer, which would certainly indicate that Warner Bros. understood something of Autry's formula. Unlike Autry, however, Foran did not play guitar (though he occasionally posed with one); accompanist chores went to George E. Stone. *Moonlight on the Prairie* was followed by *Treachery Rides the Range* and *Trailin' West,* both released in 1935 as well. Like many B titles, they tended to be interchangeable. A kid sidekick—usually Dickie Jones—was a unique feature of the Foran films, which some critics thought clever and endearing, and others found condescending or even nauseating. Most felt that kids in the audience would rather look up to a hero, imagining themselves in his place, than look with envy upon someone their own age enjoying the excitement.

Historian and critic Peter Stanfield succinctly caught the essence of the Foran western in comparison to the Autry version:

> His films . . . had good production values and the narratives followed the predictable formula of rescuing a distressed maiden, but they are in the historical West, not the contemporary West that Autry inhabits. His songs are also rather overblown compared with Autry's, lacking the intimacy, if not the bonhomie. There is also too great an emphasis on him as the star; in Autry's films a great deal of screen time is given over to the comic antics of Smiley Burnette, and there was always a featured performance by a musical guest star or stars who have made a name for themselves on radio.[2]

The Foran features remained consistently though unspectacularly profitable, but they caused no wave of excitement as Autry's series had, and after a dozen, Foran left the series to pursue a long career as a B star and an A-feature second leading man, sometimes singing and sometimes not, sometimes in westerns and sometimes not. He left Warner Bros. for Universal in 1938, where he appeared in every kind of feature—from comedy to horror to adventure to nonsinging westerns—but he still looked good in his cowboy clothes in Abbott and Costello's *Private Buckaroo* in 1942 and in their farce *Ride 'Em Cowboy* the same year, where he introduced the pop standard "I'll Remember April." He also starred and sang in the most expensive western serial of its time, Universal's self-proclaimed "million-dollar serial" *Riders of Death Valley* (1941), with Buck Jones and a host of other western notables. His real career highlight probably came with the light romantic comedy *Guest Wife* in 1945, with Don Ameche and Claudette Colbert, although he was justifiably proud of his singing role in John Ford's *Fort Apache* (RKO-Radio, 1948), with John Wayne and Henry Fonda. Foran stated, "I think *Fort Apache* was the best Western ever made."[3] He appeared on Broadway and was frequently seen in early television, and his film career straggled along in character roles well into the 1960s, ending with *Brighty of the Grand Canyon* in 1968. He recorded sporadically, very little of it in the Western style, although he did do a fine pop version of "Mexicali Rose" for Decca in the 1940s. Late in his life Dick Foran tended to casually dismiss his singing-cowboy years as a short and insignificant phase of his long career, and he declined repeated attempts to obtain interviews on that long-ago aspect of his professional life. He died August 10, 1979, in Panorama City, California.

If smoothly professional film making, an early start, a handsome and very talented star, and sweet popular music with a western flair made for hit singing-cowboy films, surely the Foran series would have been a whopping success, not the profitable but financially unspectacular films they were. The public just did not flock to theaters to see them in nearly the numbers they were flocking to Autry's cheaper, homier singing-cowboy films. Autry, a less talented singer and actor, nevertheless had a great deal more appeal. His boyish charm and winning smile, his authentic Texas/Oklahoma drawl, appealed far more to the ticket-buying public. Dick Foran felt more like a B version of Nelson Eddy. Gene Autry may not have been a trained singer or traditional action cowboy, but he projected a bashfulness, a sincerity, and an honesty that the public just loved.

Many other studios would miss this same point: singers like Gene Autry—and later Tex Ritter and Roy Rogers—felt like the real thing to moviegoers of all ages, while the singing cowboys some studios plucked from the legit stage, even in some cases from the operatic stage, seemed strangely out of synch, no matter how well they handled their horses, their guns, their fists, and their acting chores. They didn't come across as singing cowboys, but as professional singers dressed as cowboys, and while many had good careers in and out of westerns, none would come close to approaching the success of Autry, Ritter, or Rogers.

Many critics feel, with Bobby Copeland, that the reason was simple: "B Western films flourished in the rural South, where [Autry's] type of music had its stronghold. Ritter and [Bob] Baker's style fit the bill for this area, but Foran, Scott, Houston, Newill, Ballew, and Randall's operatic style brought howls of ridicule from the Southern youths who frequented the Saturday matinees."[4] The point is well taken, although it should be quickly pointed out that the films were extremely popular outside the South as well. Ultimately, pure tone, suave phrasing, and accurate pitch meant little to audiences—both youth and adult—who paid hard Depression money to see these films; they simply wanted to see cowboys who they felt sounded like cowboys.

Yet time and again the studios chose training and projection over simplicity and naturalness. In the context of the times, this missed point is understandable—after all, the public accepted, even expected, trained singers in costume dramas and musicals. If Nelson Eddy worked so well in A pictures, why not Dick Foran in B movies? B westerns, however, turned out to be a different world, and only Republic and Monogram seemed to have intuited this from the start.

Regardless, if a big outfit like Warner Bros. saw the possibilities of a singing-cowboy series so quickly, it is little wonder that the small independents would rush in to fill the screen with singing cowboys. Chronologically, the next series to reach the screen began with Spectrum's *Romance Rides the Range* (1936), starring Fred Scott. Spectrum was a tiny shoestring Gower Gulch outfit, and unfortunately for the likable Scott this series was probably doomed from the start by its poor production values. The outdoor scenes were good, but apparently second takes were considered an unnecessary expense, making for some amusing and cheesy moments.

Scott was a strapping, handsome fellow, had experience in films and on horseback, and was a magnificent singer. Although he looked the part of the cowboy hero, he did not sound a bit like one when he sang. His classical training was all too obvious, and wholly inappropriate to the pleasant, gentle cowboy songs in his films, many of them, including his theme song, "Riding down the Trail to Albuquerque," written by the husband-and-wife team of Don Swander and June Hershey, who would write the wartime hit "Deep in the Heart of Texas."

A native Californian, Fred Leedom Scott was born in Fresno on Valentine's Day, 1902, and learned to ride on ranches in the San Fernando Valley. Enthralled by the recordings of singers like Enrico Caruso and John McCormack, he taught himself to sing by vocalizing along with their records, and by the age of twelve he was onstage. As a teenager he acted and sang in local theatrical productions, and first went to Hollywood in the early 1920s to enter a fencing championship, in which he won a bronze medal. The team returned to Fresno, but Scott stayed, enrolled in acting school, and first appeared on-screen in *Bride of the Storm* in 1926 for Warner Bros.

He happened to be taking vocal coaching from the same teacher as

The cover of Fred Scott's 1939 song folio. (Country Music Hall of Fame collections)

popular silent star Bebe Daniels, and after hearing him sing, Daniels recommended him for a part in her first talking picture, a musical called *Rio Rita*. Scott made a few nonwestern films under contract to Pathe in 1930 and 1931, then gave his full attention to singing and joined the San Francisco Opera Company in 1932. He returned to films in 1936 in a small part as a singing cowboy in a Harry Carey–Hoot Gibson film called *The Last Outlaw* (RKO, 1936) and was quickly signed by producer Jed Buell of Spectrum for a western series.

Spectrum's approach to the singing cowboy was a bit different from Autry's or Foran's. Scott was in his early thirties, taller and more mature looking than his more boyish counterparts. The title of his first starring film, *Romance Rides the Range,* announced that the appeal of his westerns was to be at least partially to the ladies, not just to the kids. He did a capable job on screen, was a good actor and rider, handled the action scenes well, was an attractive male lead for his female costars, and from films number three through ten was blessed with one of the greatest movie sidekicks, the acrobatic geezer Al "Fuzzy" St. John. That he was to be a *singing* cowboy was clear, for music as well as romance was stressed, and several titles emphasized the point: *The Singing Buckaroo* and *Melody of the Plains* in 1937, *Songs and Bullets* in 1938, and *Two Gun Troubadour* in 1939.

However, his commanding operatic voice (he was billed as "the Silvery-Voiced Buckaroo") missed the point of what was making Autry's pictures so popular, and the threadbare look of the Spectrum product doomed the series. "It was never how good, but how quick. You did everything in one take because the schedule and budget allowed for no more. . . . [E]verything was done on the cheap and it often showed."[5] The seat-of-the-pants quality of these films haunted Scott in his later years, and he remarked on it often, citing instances such as the time "we packed up and went on location not too far from Los Angeles, and the cameraman had brought the camera but no film. Having to wait for him to go and get the film caused us to go over budget!"[6]

An interesting note was the behind-the-camera presence of comedian Stan Laurel, who, though busy making films of his own with Oliver Hardy, was stretching his talents by producing other films. Three of the Scott entries were officially Stan Laurel Productions, but despite the gifts of Laurel, Scott, and St. John, the budgets remained minuscule, and the series never really took off. After St. John left the series, the final four films did not have even the element of humor that made the earlier ones enjoyable, and Spectrum itself was a ramshackle, day-to-day operation that finally folded. The studio's final Scott western, *Ridin' the Trail,* was completed in 1939 but not released until 1940, when it was picked up by an independent distributor named Arthur Zeihm. Scott toured as a singing cowboy in these years, "play[ing] all the Western houses, singing a few songs, putting on a show before the movie started or at intermission."[7] He made one more western,

*Rodeo Rhythm,* for Producers Releasing Corporation, which released it in 1942, but it was even cheaper than the rest. With that film, his career on the screen, and his contribution to the singing cowboy, ended. He took off his huge Stetson to return to popular singing.

During the war Scott sang at the Florentine Gardens on Hollywood Boulevard and managed the club as well. He became a realtor after the war, about which he famously said: "I don't ride any more. I have a deal with the horses—I don't get on them and they don't sell any real estate!"[8] He did very well in his new career, retired in Palm Springs, California, and remained an extremely gracious gentleman until his death in 1991.

*Rhythm on the Range* (Paramount, 1936), starring Bing Crosby, star-crossed Frances Farmer, and the Sons of the Pioneers, is a film that deserves a closer look. Though born in the West, Harry Lillis Crosby (1904–1977) was anything but a cowboy. Yet he was one of the most influential performers in the style, for while earnest and sincere Gene Autry was appealing to middle and rural America, the ultrahot Crosby roped in the sophisticates with his frequent performances of western songs on film, on record, and especially on radio, where he was a national sensation. Though Crosby could deliver a western song with sincerity—he introduced "Empty Saddles" in *Rhythm on the Range* and had the true national hit recording of "Home on the Range"—he was at his best when mocking himself. Urbane and hip, he was no cowboy and he knew it, and when he poked fun at his image in a song like "I'm an Old Cowhand (from the Rio Grande)," he was at his most charming. Urbanites appreciated his cool irony and distancing, and yet while they smirked they could still enjoy the kitschy glamour of the West and the singing cowboy. Although Crosby attracted an audience entirely different from Autry's, both singers contributed enormously to the interest in cowboys, the West, and western music that permeated the country in the middle 1930s. Though the broad scope of Crosby's career extends far beyond western music, it is important to acknowledge his impact on the sudden and sustained interest in the singing cowboy during the formative years of the genre. *Rhythm on the Range* was a big-budget film and exemplified more than any other easily discerned landmark the embrace of the singing cowboy by Hollywood and by popular culture.

It was also in 1936 that the cohosts of the *WHN Barn Dance* in New York City headed west—independently of each other—to seek film success in Hollywood. The first was Ray Whitley, whose debut speaking role was in *Hopalong Cassidy Returns* (Paramount, 1936), and who had a number of small roles before landing a series of musical shorts for RKO in 1937. The advent of the double-feature A and B film sharply curtailed the use of short subjects, but they remained a factor at the classier film houses, and it was via this vehicle that RKO chose to enter the singing-cowboy sweepstakes. The stories were minimal, really just excuses for Whitley to sing, but they were well shot. Whitley had a very nice voice with a slight southern accent, and

Popular culture embraces the West: Bing Crosby and the Andrews Sisters in Wild West attire, as depicted on sheet music from 1945. (Country Music Hall of Fame collections)

he was in addition an accomplished yodeler. He also came from a folk, not an operatic, background, and his unpretentious vocals and enjoyable songs came off as the real thing.

Ray Whitley toured between films in these years, but more importantly he wrote songs, several with country-songwriting legend Fred Rose, who lived with the Whitleys for a time while trying to climb on the Hollywood songwriting merry-go-round. Whitley came up with a number of western classics with Rose ("Lonely River," "Ages and Ages Ago," "I Hang My Head and Cry"), and his solo effort, "Back in the Saddle Again," became Gene Autry's theme song on *Melody Ranch,* the title of an Autry movie, and a million-selling Autry record.

Backed by his Six Bar Cowboys (the Phelps brothers and Ken Card in the earlier films; later, off-screen, Lloyd Perryman and the Farr brothers from the Sons of the Pioneers), Whitley kept RKO's toe in the water of the singing-cowboy pool, but the studio never took the plunge. RKO developed no other singing cowboys and never allowed Whitley a full-fledged series of his own; instead the studio continued to cast him as a singing sidekick with action stars George O'Brien (six films) and Tim Holt (twelve films).

Ray Whitley and
Elvira Rios in *Cupid
Rides the Range* (1939).
(Author's collection)

Whitley later recalled this part of his career with a laugh: "I played . . . a
character called Smokey. He was kind of a dumb character that did things
unwittingly to throw the lead into an awkward spot, so he'd always have
some work to do to come out with shining armor. . . . I always managed to
sing . . . in each picture, and usually I would be the leader of the band in
some saloon. . . . Didn't show me off as too brilliant, but that was all right."[9]

All in all, Whitley made eighteen shorts for RKO between 1937 and
1942, and as one film historian discovered, these turned a tidy profit on the
studio's investment. Richard W. Bann reported that a typical example, *Cupid Rides the Range* (1939), was shot in two days for $13,583.50 and, after its
original issue and a reissue in 1946, grossed $58,410.35. It was reissued yet
another time in 1954.[10]

Why RKO failed to promote Whitley to a series of his own remains a
mystery. As one film historian succinctly put it: "The general consensus
among film historians is that Whitley had far more looks, talent, and charisma than many of the actors who were promoted by studios and starred in

Western epics, yet Whitley never made it above the co-starring rung on the Western success ladder."[11]

Whitley left RKO after 1942 to move over to Universal, perhaps hoping for a better break, but he was immediately cast into similar sidekick roles with up-and-coming Rod Cameron, and his last costarring film with Cameron was *Renegades of the Rio Grande* in 1945. By then, though a few new singing cowboys would be introduced to the screen, the novelty of the phenomenon had worn off, and Whitley, by then in his early forties, was not a new face. He turned to his active musical career and toured almost constantly for several years, often as musical support for Tim Holt. He later toured with Monte Hale as well, and with his wife, Kay, and their daughter Judy, with band backup from Herb Adams and Dick Morgan. Whitley continued to write songs and record, and fronted a large western-swing dance band for a while, at the same time that Bob Wills, Spade Cooley, and Ole Rasmussen were also experiencing a surge in popularity, during the war and immediate postwar period. He even managed his friend Jimmy Wakely for a short time, but eventually he settled down and opened a succession of businesses. He intermittently appeared onstage and on-screen, including a small role in Wakely's *Brand of Fear* (Monogram, 1949), and in character roles on Roy Rogers's television show. His final film appearance was in the role of Watts, James Dean's manager, in *Giant* (Warner Bros., 1956).

Unpretentious and genuine, Ray Whitley was rediscovered during the heyday of western film festivals in the 1970s, and he relished the renewed attention to his long career. He had battled diabetes since middle age and died of diabetic shock on February 21, 1979, while on a fishing trip to Mexico.

Tex Ritter, who would become one of the singing-cowboy titans, was a regional radio and recording star when he made his first film, *Song of the*

Ray Whitley and legendary songwriter Fred Rose. (Author's collection)

*Gringo,* for Grand National in 1936. As with Gene Autry, Ritter on-screen was instantly appealing to the public. Although he was not a genuine cowboy, he was a Texan with a great love and knowledge of cowboy song and lore, and his rough-hewn voice had an authority and authenticity unmatched among singing cowboys. Though not a great singer, he was an extraordinarily effective one, and this unique quality helped make him not only a film star, but also one of the country's most popular and most frequently recorded performers, particularly after he signed with Capitol in 1942. He was also the best brawler of the singing cowboys. Where Autry solved problems with sweet reason and a song, and Roy Rogers's athleticism occasionally made his fights look like Olympic gymnastics, Tex Ritter (and his frequent nemesis, the hulking Charles King) was convincing with his fists. With his lank hair dropping over his face as he stood over the pulverized remains of a film's villain, he was the very picture of the tough, two-fisted cowboy of the historical West that he played on film, in contrast to the dreamy, contemporary West that Autry, and later Roy Rogers, inhabited at Republic.

Woodward Maurice Ritter was born January 12, 1905, in the piney woods of East Texas near the tiny community of Murvaul in Panola County. A fourth-generation Texan, he was one of six children born to James Everett Ritter and Martha Elizabeth "Lizzie" Matthews Ritter. "My family sang a lot. My two older brothers were very good singers. There again it was mostly church music, but usually they wouldn't let me sing with them because I couldn't sing well enough. I remember once my mother said it would be nice if her boys would sing so we got up in front of the fireplace and sang about half a song and the others stopped and said 'Mama, would you make him sit down?'"[12]

His family moved south during his teen years, first to Carthage from 1917 to 1920, then to Nederland. There he attended South Park High School in nearby Beaumont, where he participated in athletics, debate, and theater and was the senior class president. After graduation in 1922 he attended the University of Texas in Austin, where he appeared in several theatrical productions and shocked his family and friends by leaving the UT law school just shy of his degree to go on the road, appearing in the chorus of a play called *Maryland, My Maryland* in 1928.

Ritter had been preparing for such an opportunity all through college, however, for he had been active in Glee Club and in theater and helped put himself through college doing a thirty-minute weekly show of cowboy songs on KPRC in Houston. In Austin, the academic tradition of folk song study meshed perfectly with his commercial ambitions: "I had benefit of association at the University with three men who encouraged me to sing and they helped direct my career. One was J. Frank Dobie, renowned authority on Southwestern folk lore; the second was John A. Lomax, well known collector of American folk ballads; and the third was Oscar J. Fox, composer of cowboy songs and director of the Glee Club, who also gave me lessons in

*Headin' for the Rio Grande* (1936), Tex Ritter's second Grand National release. (Author's collection)

voice." These respected scholars and researchers found in young Woodward Ritter a bright young man who eagerly absorbed all they had to teach. The mark they made on him was indelible. Of all the singing cowboys, Ritter was the most knowledgeable and passionate about cowboy folk songs and the roots of his own musical style. He learned vocal and guitar technique from Fox, discussed folklore with Lomax, and collected folk songs

## Tex Ritter on the Road

A song on a spinning plastic disc or a performance on flickering celluloid is a moment frozen in time, a bit of history preserved, unchanging and intact. These are the parts of a performer's career we remember, study, savor. But the bulk of an artist's career is made up of live performances, the string of endless one-nighters in towns small and large across the country and around the world.

The singing cowboys considered touring an indispensable part of their lives. They were musicians first, having come from a background in radio and record. Indeed, several nonsinging film cowboys found it lucrative as well. A few rope and horse tricks and some musical support by a cowboy singer provided a nice income and promotion for their films.

Ken Maynard toured with a full circus, and Gene Autry operated full rodeos, but the bread-and-butter work was the small-town theater stage, where a radio and recording star could present a stage show, or a film star could appear in between showings of his latest movie, sometimes doing as many as five or six appearances in a day. Outdoor parks such as Sunset Park in Pennsylvania, Frontier Ranch in Ohio, and Buck Lake Ranch in Indiana eventually became popular venues for western and country entertainers, and state (and later county) fairs also provided stages, often in conjunction with rodeos.

This was the time the cowboy singers took to the road, and judging by existing records they took to it with a vengeance. Gerald F. Vaughn has documented Ray Whitley's prodigious touring, sometimes in support of Tim Holt or Monte Hale, sometimes with a full band of his own; Whitley's abilities with a whip and his sense of humor added to his musical appeal. Gene Autry was a seasoned road warrior, consistently pulling the highest grosses of all of the cowboy singers. Bob Nolan long maintained that one of the primary reasons he left the Sons of the Pioneers in 1948 was that in the previous year the Pioneers had been on tour 350 days. But legend has it, and documents support it, that Tex Ritter was the champion, a tireless tourer throughout his career, first in support of his films, then in support of his recordings.

A sample itinerary that covered September 10–27, 1939, has Ritter doing fifteen shows in seventeen days, with the two days "off" being an unpaid appearance at a film distributors' convention in Memphis. The dates were in the Southeast, where attendance at musical westerns was always strong, and Tex & His Tornadoes appeared in five states during this rather typical run. Many appearances brought him a flat $100 or $150, but where he appeared on percentage (as Autry always did), the results were mixed. His highest take was at the Royal Theater in Chillicothe, Ohio, for $138.30; his least successful was at an unnamed theater in Monticello, Arkansas, where he raked in just $50.55. He averaged about $800 a week, out of which he paid commissions to his manager (Edward Finney) and agent (William Morris), as well as his band and travel expenses. It was hardly the path to riches, but it was a solid income in 1939.

Tex kept a log with brief comments on the shows, theaters, and managers, some of which are telling, some simply poignant.

Baldwin, Mississippi: "There were more people in the town than I have ever seen in my life in a small town. It is a terrific Saturday town and you really could not move on the streets."

Tex Ritter on the road in the 1940s. The trailer was presented to him by Monogram in 1938. (Author's collection)

Scottsboro, Alabama: "Manager expected to do a little more but thought the rain had hurt him."

Woodbury, Kentucky: "Town too small and in a poor section. Only two of my pictures had ever played here but the last one drew $80.00 and the average Western business is $55.00 or $60.00. The last Autry picture drew $100.00 for his Saturday record. Reason for this it was published that Autry sings 'It Makes No Difference Now' in the picture." (Ritter was continually frustrated that Republic allowed Autry to sing current hits in his movies, while Monogram relied on lesser-known, and consequently cheaper, song material.)

Livingston, Tennessee: "Played here too soon after my first appearance. . . . Since my personal appearance here my pictures have doubled in gross."

Carrollton, Kentucky: "Came a thunder storm in the morning, but had stopped raining by night. Autry, Ritter, Starret [sic], and Rogers are the four top drawing in the order named."

Frankfort, Kentucky: "Business was great here. Pictures go well."[*]

Speaking of Ritter, longtime local bandleader Joe Taylor described in his diary a memorable 1954 appearance at Buck Lake Ranch (he misnames Ritter's horse White Cloud—his name was White Flash):

Tex . . . got his horse on stage and sat astride, waiting in wings for introduction. (Stage was above dressing rooms, office and refreshment stand.) Nature called and White Cloud relieved himself! The body waste seeped down through cracks in stage's rough timber floor onto carmel [sic] corn machine below. Whew—what an odor! Brought screams from young girl manning stand. [Owner] Harry [Smythe] flew up stairway to stage in snit. Yelled at Tex for White Cloud's action. Tex replied telling Harry if White Cloud could talk and tell him of his need, he [Tex] certainly wouldn't be working parks like Buck Lake. Even still upset, Harry had to laugh.[**]

---

[*]   From material in the Edward Finney collection at the Autry Museum of Western Heritage in Los Angeles.

[**]  Taylor and Corbett, *50 Years Together,* p. 17.

like "Rye Whiskey" with Dobie, who "played a large part in making me what I am today."[13]

The effects of these three scholars were profound, but for all his passion and insight into cowboy folk songs, Woodward Ritter was also young, restless, and ambitious. When the cast of *Maryland, My Maryland* returned to New York, Ritter went with them, quickly landing a spot in the chorus of *The New Moon* in 1928. He had not entirely given up on a law degree, for when *The New Moon* went on the road, he enrolled at Northwestern during extended runs in Chicago and Milwaukee in 1930; however, he left school again just short of exams when the run in Milwaukee closed, and though he wrote to his professor that "I hope to re-enter in the summer," he never did.[14]

That summer he won a role in *Green Grow the Lilacs,* Lynn Riggs's "folk play in six scenes," which would be extensively revamped and be reincarnated as *Oklahoma!* a decade later. The original play was a simpler affair. Woodward Ritter portrayed Cord Elam, sang four songs, and understudied the star, Franchot Tone. He spent the fall of 1930 in rehearsals and test runs in Boston before the play opened on Broadway on January 26, 1931. The play brimmed with cowboy folk music: Franchot Tone sang the title song and "Sam Hall"; Ritter sang "Get Along Little Dogies," "The Old Chisholm Trail," "Goodbye, Old Paint," and "Oh Bury Me Not on the Lone Prairie"; and Everett Cheetham, billed only as "banjo player," sang "The Strawberry Roan" and his own "Blood on the Saddle."

New York was a vital area for cowboy music at the time; it attracted the interest of the urban intelligentsia, who were becoming enthralled with folk music. But New York was also the commercial music capital of America—the home of the record labels, booking agencies, radio networks, and music-publishing houses, and the headquarters, or at least offices, of most motion picture studios.

*Green Grow the Lilacs* was only a moderate success, lasting a few weeks on Broadway before touring Chicago, St. Louis, Philadelphia, and Minneapolis. But record executive Arthur Satherley and film executive Edward Finney both attended performances, and both remembered Ritter's performance, his easy, comfortable stage presence, and the unique, sonorous quality of his singing and speaking voice. Both men would play major roles in his life in months to come.

With the end of the play's run, Ritter returned to New York, where he began to obtain parts in radio and in commercials. He appeared on *Lone Star Rangers* (1932), *Maverick Jim, Gang Busters, Bobbie Benson,* and the daily *Cowboy Tom's Roundup* (1933–1936), in which he played the singing sidekick, Tex. The name stuck and would remain with him for the remainder of his career. In short order Tex obtained his own program, *Tex Ritter's Campfire* (1933), and began cohosting (with Ray Whitley) the *WHN Barn Dance.* There were dramatic roles in nonwesterns on radio, and commercials as well. He starred in a short-lived revival of a play called *The Roundup* (1932) but appeared in only two other short-lived Broadway plays before his career on radio and film took him in other directions. Although professionally this was a heady time for Woodward (which his family had always pronounced Wood'ard), it was difficult personally. He lost his parents within months of each other in the winter of 1934–1935.

Ritter had first recorded for Art Satherley and the American Record Corporation in 1932 and 1933, and in the early thirties quickly became the leading figure in cowboy music and the cowboy image on the New York scene. On October 31 he recorded "The Cowboy's Christmas Ball," which was never to be released. He returned to Art Satherley's studios the following March 15, where he recorded "A-Riding Old Paint" and "Everyday in the Saddle" (both deemed unacceptable for release and re-recorded on April 14), as well as "Goodbye Old Paint" and "Rye Whiskey, Rye Whiskey." There was a deep traditional character to Ritter's work, and while the records were widely released on the ARC family of labels (Banner, Conqueror, Melotone, Oriole, Perfect, Romeo, and Vocalion), they were not particularly successful. Ritter did not return to the studio until January 1935, when he signed with the new Decca label. His four pre-Hollywood sessions in 1935 and 1936 reflect the changing times. While the first included the ultratraditional songs he loved and with which he had built his reputation, "Sam Hall," and "Get Along Little Dogies," the next three featured not only contemporary country music like "Answer to Nobody's Darling but Mine," but also contemporary western songs written by professional songwriters— "(Take Me Back to My) Boots and Saddle," "The Oregon Trail," "A Melody from the Sky," "The Hills of Old Wyomin'," and "We'll Rest at the End of the Trail."

By December 1936 Ritter was in Hollywood, and the remainder of his recording for Decca consisted primarily of songs from his films. In contrast to the mammoth record-selling success of Gene Autry, Ritter's sales were modest, though he was one of the most popular western movie stars in the country and was second only to Autry in being identified as a cowboy singer. After January 1939 Ritter was without a recording contract at all. It was not until he was signed by the newly created Capitol label and started recording straight contemporary country music that he became a chart-topping record seller. But for all his success with country love songs like "Jealous Heart," "You Two Timed Me One Time Too Often," "There's a New Moon over My Shoulder," and "Have I Stayed Away Too Long," a good half of his recorded output, though not his hits, remained thoroughly western. In the 1950s the spectrum broadened, and like many popular recording artists with long careers, he recorded a wide variety of material: patriotic, religious, spoken-word (including an entire set of readings of the Psalms), and experimental albums, like one with the Stan Kenton Orchestra and another, in Spanish, with a mariachi orchestra. Tex Ritter charted a great many records and had a few western successes with western themes: "High Noon" in 1952, "The Wayward Wind" in 1956, and "I Dreamed of a Hill-Billy Heaven" in 1961.

As a record seller Tex was topped only by Autry among the singing cowboys. His output was far more varied than Autry's, and his recording career was far longer—his last recording session in December 1973 came less than two weeks before his death. His commitment to traditional cowboy music remained strong to the end. He recorded an album of wholly traditional cowboy songs in 1969, and "Green Grow the Lilacs" one last time in 1972.

In the mid-1930s, at the height of his success in New York, Ritter found time to unwind and to work on his horsemanship on the weekends at a friend's dude ranch in New Jersey: "It wasn't a terribly authentic dude ranch but they had horseback riding and things like that and it was a nice place to get outdoors. I used to go out there just about every week to . . . sing a few songs for the guests, and I'd help with the horses and so on. Then, too, there were a few pretty little unattached girls who were always coming out there."[15] It was there that film executive Edward Finney approached Ritter with the proposal that he make films like the Autry pictures that were sweeping the nation. Ritter quickly signed with Finney and left for Hollywood to become Grand National's entry in the singing-cowboy sweepstakes.

Grand National's story is somewhat typical of the Gower Gulch or Poverty Row film studios. The company was formed in the spring of 1936 by Edward L. Alperson, a former film exchange manager, and three other executives, including Edward Finney, who was in charge of advertising and publicity. It was Finney who discovered Tex Ritter and produced his films as well, and they were steady profit makers for the company—in fact, they were often the only profit makers. Grand National hoped to step right into the big time—or at least to compete with Republic and Monogram—when it managed to sign James Cagney, who had walked out of Warner Bros. in a contract dispute. Grand National made two big films with this major star. The first, *Great Guy,* was a reasonable success, although critics rate it a notch or two below Cagney's Warner Bros. efforts. For the second, they passed on *Angels with Dirty Faces,* to which they had the rights (it later was a landmark film for Cagney at Warner Bros.), to do a musical, *Something to Sing About.* The musical flopped, and it had gone so far over budget the company was left reeling for the rest of its short existence. Cagney returned to Warner Bros. at the price he wanted, Finney took Tex Ritter with him to Monogram, company president Alperson left the sinking ship in 1939, and Grand National was liquidated in 1940. The studio itself became the property of Producer's Releasing Corporation, which, as PRC, made a number of musical westerns in the following decade.

In the boom-or-bust tradition of Hollywood, Grand National made a splash—it released more than seventy films in its four brief years and along

Tex Ritter sets villain Charles King straight. (Author's collection)

the way brought several singing cowboys to the screen: George Houston, Ark Jarrett, James Newill, Tex Fletcher, Dorothy Page, and its only true success, Tex Ritter.

Finney, a New York–born publicist, had been hired as advertising director at Grand National when it was founded. Canny fellow that he was, Finney had Tex Ritter signed to him personally, not to the studio, and as producer-agent worked out the financing and distribution deal with Grand National. Tex's films had budgets of between $8,000 and $12,000, and he made $2,400 per film as the star.

Ritter's first film for Alperson's Grand National company was *Song of the Gringo,* released on November 22, 1936, and quickly followed by *Headin' for the Rio Grande,* released on December 20. The first of the Grand National series showed great promise: Tex had a unique voice, conservative outfits, and a beautiful horse called White Flash. He could handle both the riding and the action scenes and, as a trained actor, could display steely determination or be genuinely likable as the situation demanded. Ritter was thirty when the series began, old enough to carry the weight of authority a hero needs, young enough to be believable in action sequences. The series provided action, authenticity in the singing, and an extremely interesting new star.

Grand National was ecstatic. A bulletin to distributors fairly crowed with delight: "*Starlight Over Texas* with Tex Ritter compares favorably as a singing western with any of the most important stars on the market today. Tex has a western singing voice which is superb and . . . has a tremendous amount of personality. I prophesize that we have a real sensation in Tex Ritter. . . . Gentlemen, I assure you that everything we hoped for in Tex Ritter is a reality." A longer letter to exchanges says of the same film: "Tex Ritter and Ed Finney have certainly given you a swell picture and this one should definitely put Ritter over in your territory. Get back of it fast, because this is the type of Western they are waiting for."[16]

Although the Tex Ritter series had a great deal going for it, the small studio's cheap production values showed, a flaw that unfortunately became more apparent as the series progressed. More and more obvious stock footage padded out these little dramas, some (in *Tex Rides with the Boy Scouts*) from as far back as 1912. When Edward Finney deserted the sinking ship to go to Monogram in 1938, he took his protégé with him.

Monogram, hoping to rival Republic as the best of the B studios, put a lot of energy into its twenty films with Ritter, and these are some of the best, and best remembered, of his career. He finally broke with Finney and moved over to Columbia, which was without a singing-cowboy star. For reasons unknown, Columbia chose to costar and co-bill Ritter with action star Wild Bill Elliott, something of a surprise since Tex was one of the best of the singers at handling his own action.

In 1942 Elliott moved to Republic, and Tex moved to Universal the following year, again in a costarring role, this time with Johnny Mack Brown. When Brown took a hike in 1943, Ritter took over the roles intended for Brown, and he was in turn supported by up-and-coming nonsingers Dennis Moore and, later, Russell Hayden. Although in later years Ritter would make a few more brief appearances on-screen, he ended his film career in 1945 at low-rent PRC, which was making a series of westerns about a trio called the Texas Rangers, in which he replaced singer James Newill to join Dave O'Brien and Guy Wilkerson. Ritter felt that his film career was not going anywhere in these cheapies, and after his eighth in the series, *Flaming Bullets* in 1945, he bowed out of singing-cowboy films with the grace and dignity that marked his entire career.

By the time he left PRC, he probably didn't have much time for making films anyway, for shortly after signing with Capitol Records in 1942 he began an astonishing string of hit records that made him one of the most popular recording artists in the nation. The first hit, "Jingle Jangle Jingle," was western, but the rest were country, with titles like "You Two Timed Me One Time Too Often," "Jealous Heart," and "There's a New Moon over My Shoulder." It was a fertile time for Tex, and he exploited it to the hilt, touring constantly, recording, and, in the 1950s, cohosting a local country television show called *Town Hall Party* with his good friend and business partner, Johnny Bond. In 1952, producers of the film *High Noon* (United Artists, 1952), faced with unfavorable responses at prescreenings, asked classically trained composer Dmitri Tiomkin to compose a theme song to both complement and enliven the stark morality play starring Gary Cooper and Grace Kelly. A fan of country and cowboy music despite his classical training (he and lyricist Ned Washington also composed "Rawhide" and several other western songs), Tiomkin looked to Tex Ritter to provide a sound and feel that summed up much of what the film embodied. Tex's performance is all that and more—grim, determined, lonely, authentic. Tiomkin won two Oscars (best score, and, with Washington, best theme song) for *High Noon*.

Although Ritter's recording and touring slowed as he grew older, he stayed active to the end. He remained popular on record and had major and minor hits with "High Noon" in 1952, "The Wayward Wind" in 1956, and "I Dreamed of a Hillbilly Heaven" in 1961, and many other charted records. In addition he did a bit of film score work, but primarily he toured, endlessly crisscrossing America. Although Tex Ritter was the cowboy performer with the most authentic background in the song and music of the cowboy, he was also the cowboy singer who was most identified with country music, and eventually he left California to move to Nashville, to work on radio, on the Grand Ole Opry, and to continue to tour. He served on the boards of the Country Music Foundation and the Country Music Association, and he and his wife, Dorothy, were active supporters of the United Cerebral Palsy Association. Late in his life Ritter exhibited political ambitions, making an unsuccessful bid for the Republican nomination to the U.S. Senate in 1970. He remained active until his death, of a sudden heart attack, on January 2, 1974.

With the success of Tex Ritter's movie debut at Grand National in 1936, at last another studio had found someone who had what Autry had: an instantly recognizable voice, likable and unpretentious, a voice that evoked the warmth and authenticity of the West. The appeal seems obvious in retrospect, yet many in Hollywood scratched their heads in bewilderment over the successes of Autry and Ritter at the box office, while finer, more polished singers in cowboy clothes failed to draw patrons to the theater. The studios still had a lot to learn, and 1937 was to see the introduction of yet another wave of young singers and actors and studios hoping to grab a slice of the pie that Nat Levine, Gene Autry, and Republic Pictures had created.

It has been a theory for years that one of the reasons that studios rushed to make singing-cowboy films was that they were so cheap to make, and this is a reasonable argument. As Buck Jones noted, using up an entire reel of film in song saved on horses, ammunition, and extras. Not only were singing scenes cheaper to stage, but also studios could save money by hiring unknown radio and stage stars who were eager to work in films for relative peanuts. Only Gene Autry, ever sharp about finances, was able to get paid a per-film salary commensurate with his worth. Even Roy Rogers at his peak was only making $400 a week from Republic and had to tour to make a serious income. He finally moved up rapidly in the late 1940s, having been bumped from a $1,000-a-week salary to a per-film fee of $21,000, which was raised to $25,000 for his final two films. Eddie Dean made only $1,750 per film for his all-color westerns, and while Tex Ritter's $2,400 was a great deal of money in the Depression, it was a far cry from the huge salaries Ken Maynard and Buck Jones had commanded just a few years earlier.

While pressure was building at Republic due to Autry's walkout, other studios had begun full-scale attempts to enter the fray. Nearly every studio, major and minor, was by this time mounting its own series of singing-cowboy films in earnest, and consequently a wide variety of new performers found its way to the screen that year.

Twentieth Century-Fox's entry was a series of five films starring very tall, suavely handsome, big-band singer Smith Ballew, who had broken into movies the year before costarring with Frances Langford in Paramount's high-society film *Palm Springs*. Ballew was born in Palestine, Texas, on January 21, 1902, but he was far from a cowboy. He headed his own band while attending the University of Texas and began appearing on radio in Austin, and then later in Chicago. He had played banjo, sung, and recorded prolifically with a number of swing and pop bands led by the likes of Joe Venuti, Ben Pollack, Red Nichols, the Dorsey brothers, Benny Goodman, and Glenn Miller, and with his own orchestra on OKeh and Columbia. He and his orchestra were also featured on NBC's *Shell Chateau* on radio, and he was considered one of the premier popular vocalists of his day.

Based on Ballew's capable performance in *Palm Springs,* producer Sol Lesser signed him and sold a western series to Twentieth Century-Fox. It turned out that Ballew could ride as well as act and sing, but his westerns were hobbled by second-rate production. The writing, however, was at times interesting, or at least took trails off the beaten path. *Hawaiian Buckaroo* (1938) took place on pineapple plantations and cattle ranches in what was to become the Aloha State, while *Rawhide* (1938) featured—in a role somewhere between costar and sidekick—New York Yankees great Lou Gehrig in his only screen appearance.

Although Ballew made the list of top ten cowboys among theater exhibitors in 1938, he starred in no more films after *Panamint's Bad Man* in 1938. He appeared in supporting roles, sometimes singing and sometimes not, with Gene Autry (*Gaucho Serenade,* 1940) and Johnny Mack Brown (*Drifting Along* and *Under Arizona Skies,* both 1946). In *Drifting Along,* he dubbed Brown's singing voice, while in *Under Arizona Skies* he was billed as Smith Ballew & the Sons of the Sage. He also appeared as a supporting actor with James Ellison (*I Killed Geronimo,* 1950) and Audie Murphy (*The Red Badge of Courage,* 1951). As for his starring roles, despite his tall (6' 6") Gary Cooperesque good looks and his warm, smooth voice, Ballew never caught the public's fancy. He went right back to singing and leading big bands, which he did successfully into the early 1950s, and also made appearances with both the Riders of the Purple Sage and the Beverly Hillbillies in person

Smith Ballew. (Author's collection)

and on radio. Having done defense work during the war, he eventually gave up both film and music to become an executive with the Howard Hughes organization in Tucson in 1950, then moved to General Dynamics in Fort Worth in 1952. He remained there until his retirement in 1967 and died in Longview, Texas, on May 2, 1984.

Smith Ballew's films were fair, his screen presence good but not outstanding, his voice lovely but clearly that of a pop singer. Twentieth Century-Fox, Sol Lesser, or both had misjudged what the Gene Autry phenomenon was all about, and neither would mount a singing-cowboy series again.

The next singing cowboy to ride onto the screen was Bob Baker. Like Ray Whitley before him, he had the makings but not the breaks, and he did not become a major star in this style. He had come to the attention of Universal Pictures, which mounted a national search for their singing cowboy, and over all the cowboys in Hollywood who applied—including young Leonard Slye of the Sons of the Pioneers, whom they considered too young looking and too slender for the part—they chose a radio singer who went by the name of Tumble Weed.

He was born November 8, 1910, in Forest City, Iowa, and had been christened Stanley Leland Weed. When he was fourteen, his family pulled up stakes and moved to Wheat Ridge, Colorado, then to Phoenix, Arizona, when he was sixteen, where he dropped the name Stanley and took up the logical nickname "Tumble." A dude-ranch guide and rodeo performer, Weed was as close to an authentic cowboy as could be found in those latter days.

While serving a couple of hitches in the cavalry at Fort Bliss, Texas, beginning in 1929, Weed learned to play guitar and got a job on radio at KTSM in El Paso. After his release from the army in 1934, he became a guide at the Grand Canyon, but performing was in his blood. He auditioned for WLS—which had just lost its singing cowboy, Gene Autry—and moved to Chicago in the winter of 1935, appearing on an early-morning variety show *(Smile a While),* on his own daily program, and on the *National Barn Dance* every Saturday night. For reasons that are unclear, his time in Chicago was relatively brief; within a year he was back at the Grand Canyon. If his ambition for a performing career had cooled, it apparently still burned strong in his mother's heart: "My mother . . . had read in the Sunday Arizona Republic newspaper that Universal was looking for a singing cowboy, so she wrote a letter and enclosed some snapshots of me."[17] Against all odds, Universal contacted him, and the young radio singer won the role. As authentic a cowboy as ever sang on-screen, he was in addition a handsome fellow and a fine horseman, with a pleasant, natural style that was not quite as relaxed as Autry's or Ritter's but was far closer to their approach than it was to the mellow pop sound of Smith Ballew or the light-opera tenor of Fred Scott.

Universal's instincts were correct: They went after someone very much

Bob Baker serenades Dorothy Fay—who soon would marry Tex Ritter—and a bunch of cowpokes in *Prairie Justice* (1938). (Author's collection)

Bob Baker, born Stanley Leland Weed, on guitar, backed by Hi Busse, *left,* and Bill Benner in *Honor of the West* (1939). (Author's collection)

like Gene Autry, a radio singer who sang in an authentic, unaffected style, and whose roots were in folk music and in the West. Tumble Weed seemed to have everything going except acting experience, but he proved capable if not fluid in his first starring role, *Courage of the West,* in 1937. Universal had changed his name to Tex Baker by this time, to which he objected strongly, and for the rest of his film career they reached a compromise with the name Bob Baker. His short film career was an active one. He made no fewer than ten singing-cowboy films in 1938. The series skidded to a halt with only two releases in 1939, when the studio demoted him to second-banana roles in Johnny Mack Brown films.

Bob Baker returned briefly to the army in 1940 as the storm clouds of war gathered on the horizon, worked as a police officer in Flagstaff, Arizona, then returned to Hollywood in 1942, where he made a handful of films, hoping for another break. He did bit parts and stunt work, and appeared as a bus driver in Abbot and Costello's *Ride 'Em Cowboy* (Universal, 1942). His final chance at the brass ring was a secondary role in the first Monogram Trail Blazers film, *Wild Horse Stampede* (1943), in which he supported aging Hoot Gibson and Ken Maynard, who reportedly ragged him unmercifully. Monogram dropped him from the series and indeed did away with the trio format in the Trail Blazers films—the studio left it to the two aging former stars to carry the short series into oblivion. Baker's last screen appearance was as an unbilled member of the posse in a 1944 Hopalong Cassidy film called *Mystery Man* (United Artists, 1944).

Disenchanted with Hollywood and the business of films, Bob Baker sold his horse, Apache, to Montie Montana, moved back to Flagstaff to rejoin the police force, served in the Korean War, opened a saddle shop in Wickenburg, Arizona, in 1954, ran a dude ranch, and opened another saddle shop in Camp Verde in 1959. By 1970 he had suffered three heart attacks, and he succumbed to heart trouble on August 30, 1975.

Universal's instincts had been astute in casting Baker, but according to most film historians the studio botched the job badly. Baker's series had started out with a splash; the first four films were bolstered by the excellent direction of Joseph Lewis. But a new and less innovative director, the ever-tightening purse strings, and the strain of putting out all those 1938 releases led to shoddier and less interesting films as the series progressed. As historian Jon Tuska—who has written extensively on what he calls "the Autry fantasy"—points out: "Universal discovered to their dismay, as did the others, that singing Westerns weren't the answer to Autry. Baker, like most of his peers, ignored the Autry Fantasy, and his writers weren't even conscious that there was such a thing." In other words, Bob Baker was another cowboy who sang from time to time, not a cowboy singer who solved problems and lived in the sunny musical fantasy world that Gene Autry inhabited. The essence of "the Autry fantasy," to Tuska, is a dream world in which an unassuming fellow like Gene Autry can take on all manner of villains, crooks, bushwhackers, thieves, and killers with just a smile and a song (and yes, usually in the modern West). Baker, Scott, and the others were often too rooted in the historical past; their music was not central to the plot. Of the early singing cowboys, only Ray Whitley, in his musical shorts for RKO, approached the level of Autry fantasy that Tuska posits—"a dream of . . . comfort, solace, and reassurance"—but Whitley never got the chance to play out the fantasy in full-length westerns of his own.[18]

In any event, there are indications that Baker may have been the source of at least some of his own problems, hurting his chances for further employment. As Tuska goes on to say, "After his third Universal picture Bob Baker thought himself an expert, and was continually fighting with the producers and the various technicians as to how his films should be made."[19] A longtime Baker champion retorted: "Tumble was a man who believed in Western lore, history, fact, and realism. From the beginning at Universal, he wanted his films to be realistic and not a fantasy or dream world. Many times Bob stepped on a lot of his boss's toes at Universal to prove his point, and nine times out of ten he got his way. Not so much as trying to be a big shot, but for REALISM."[20] Apparently all the friction was self-defeating; neither Bob Baker nor Universal seemed to comprehend that fantasy, not realism, was exactly what the public wanted in singing-cowboy films.

A couple of final notes about Bob Baker. He was encouraged and coached in screen acting by Max Terhune, a comedian on the *National Barn Dance* in Chicago who himself appeared in many musical and nonmusical Westerns. The *National Barn Dance* seems to have been a breeding ground for aspiring singing cowboys; not only had Gene Autry risen to prominence there, but Patsy Montana & the Prairie Ramblers were the hit performers of the show when Tumble Weed was there, and Rex Allen would later move from the *National Barn Dance* to Hollywood's sound stages. It gave the movies not only three of its finest singing cowboys, but also other musical acts that appeared on film, including Montana, Tex Atchison, Bob Atcher, Pee Wee King & His Golden West Cowboys, and the Hoosier Hot Shots. In addition, Max Terhune, Pat Buttram, and Smiley Burnette were but three of several supporting players, sidekicks, and comedians from *National Barn Dance* who would grace the silver screen.

An inexplicable aspect of Baker's career was his failure ever to have been recorded, even for Universal's own record labels, which released a whole series of records by some of its screen vocalizers—including Dick Foran—in the 1940s. It is remarkable that a radio and film star of that era would be without a record contract, especially with his *National Barn Dance* contacts.

Jack Randall was another talented young man who met with a lack of smashing success in somewhat the same way as Baker: His studio lost faith in him. Though less a cowboy and more a trained singer, he was good looking in an unusual vulpine way, athletic though slender, and a fine vocalist. Born Addison Owen Randall on May 12, 1906, in Quincy, Illinois, he was the brother of B-western star Robert Livingston (born Robert Randall), who encouraged Addison to join him in the film business. Randall had some success as a vocalist on the stage and began appearing in RKO films in 1934 in nonwestern roles, *His Family Tree* being his first feature in 1935. He played romantic leads until Monogram signed him as their great shining hope in the singing-cowboy sweepstakes. At the very least Monogram anticipated that Randall would equal the success of his brother, who was popular and busy doing serials and the Three Mesquiteers series at Republic.

*Riders of the Dawn* was Randall's first entry. Although he was good in action sequences, rode well, and acted capably, Monogram had made the common mistake of assuming that a better singer was a better singing cowboy. Although Randall had an excellent voice, he did not sound authentic, and as the series wore on he sang less and less. By this time, too, singing-cowboy films were beginning to be a glut on the market. One singing cowboy was a great novelty indeed; a couple provided a refreshing change of pace; but three started to be a crowd, and there appeared to be only so large a market for this type of film. By the time Jack Randall came along, he didn't stand out from the parade of cowboy vocalists who seemed to be materializing weekly.

Monogram backpedaled furiously, quickly recasting Randall as an ac-

Jack Randall in a pensive moment. (Author's collection)

tion star in 1938. A Monogram release to exhibitors reflects this: "What about Randall as a Western star? We heard a lot of complaints about his singing and Scott Dunlap listened and now won't even let Randall hum on the lot, but did you see *The Mexicali Kid*? If you don't think Randall can act, if you don't think the women will go for him, and if you don't think this is a Western picture that will fit every situation, you are just plain haywire. You have a great bet in Randall for a straight Western star." They had said a couple of months earlier that in reviewing *Gun Smoke Trail,* one thing exhibitors "do comment on is that Randall didn't sing. The inference here is we are off on the right track with Randall."[21]

Randall's conversion to nonsinging cowboy actually served him well. His features became more popular and his star began to rise again until, as one critic put it, "to show their gratitude Monogram turned Randall over to Harry S. Webb who, with low production values and lower skills, promptly did in the series. . . . Without producer trouble [Randall] might have been at Monogram without a hitch."[22]

Part of the problem, clearly, was with Monogram itself. Although it was the only studio besides Republic to have much success at all with singing cowboys, it couldn't seem to pull off what Republic could on small budgets. Though Monogram tried hard with Ritter, Randall, and Wakely, the studio could not duplicate what Republic did with Autry, Rogers, and Rex Allen.

Randall's series was finished with the release of his twenty-second starring film, *Wild Horse Range,* in 1940, and he began to take supporting roles in all sorts of features. In 1942 he enlisted in the Army Air Corps, rising to the rank of captain before his discharge in 1945. He attempted at once to get back into film work and landed a role in a cheap serial called *The Royal Mounted Rides Again,* for an independent outfit. Director William Witney recounts that the returning veteran, perhaps too eager to prove himself or perhaps because the production was too cheap to hire a double, was doing the hard riding himself in a chase scene and met with a sad and unnecessary death during the filming. Fighting for control of his horse, Randall was knocked from the saddle at full gallop by a tree limb and died within hours. The date was July 16, 1945—he was only thirty-nine years old. The obituary in the following day's *New York Times* was brief: "Addison (Jack) Randall, aged 38 *[sic]*, husband of Barbara Bennett, was killed today when he fell from his horse while making a Western Thriller at Canoga Park. He had started work on the picture this morning. While he was riding a horse at breakneck speed past the cameras, the actor's hat blew off and in attempting to grab it, he lost his balance and fell, striking a tree."

The death certificate was more terse yet: "accident. thrown from horse, hit tree, while making picture." Immediate cause of death was "lacerations of left lung with Pulmonary Hemorrhage (left). Multiple fractures of left ribs (3 to 9)."

The career of Jack Randall's brother Robert warrants a closer look as well. Born in Quincy, Illinois, on December 4, 1904, Robert Randall broke into films in 1929 in bit parts. As Bob Livingston, he had a long career as an action hero in westerns through 1944, largely with Republic, and is best remembered as Stony Brooke in the Three Mesquiteers. He also acted in films of all genres through 1950, when he left acting to concentrate on script writing. Bob Livingston deserves inclusion in this company not only because he encouraged his younger brother to enter western films but also because he sang a song or two in a couple of Republic westerns himself, *The Bold Caballero* (1936) and *Hit the Saddle* (1937). There is some debate among film scholars as to whether his voice was dubbed; Livingston himself recalled singing for the sound track but did not remember whether they used his singing voice on the finished product. Regardless, he was a cowboy who sang, albeit briefly, on screen. He died March 7, 1988, in Southern California.

One of the most fascinating entries in the singing-cowboy field trekked west in 1937: Herb Jeffries (sometimes spelled Jeffrey or Jeffreys), a deep-voiced balladeer with a bluesy style who starred in a short series of singing-cowboy films with all-black casts. He was born in Detroit on September 24, 1911, of African, Italian, Irish, French, and American Indian descent. The son of a Canadian traveling musician named Howard Jeffrey and a young Irish American widow from Port Huron, he grew up in an ethnically diverse Detroit neighborhood, with a Jewish family on one side and an African

American family on the other. He followed in his father's footsteps by breaking into singing in Detroit, then headed for New York in the early 1930s, where professional singing jobs came his way. "For some reason those people went crazy for my stuff. I thought, *boy, this is for me*—here are people who appreciate me!"[23]

From there Jeffries traveled to Chicago, where he appeared in Erskine Tate's band and appeared and recorded with Earl Hines's orchestra before heading for Hollywood in the mid 1930s. In 1937 he moved to Los Angeles and appeared as a singer and emcee at the Club Alabam. There he was contacted by Jed Buell—the same man who brought Fred Scott to the screen—of the newly formed Associated Features and was signed to do features. The first film of the series, *Harlem on the Prairie,* premiered at the Paramount Theater in Hollywood and at the Rialto Theater on Broadway in New York.

The film, widely touted as "the first 'all-colored' western musical," appeared as *Bad Man of Harlem* in its New York opening and featured such songs as "Romance in the Rain" and "There Is a New Range in Heaven."[24] Afterward, Jed Buell moved on to other projects, so the following year Jeffries found a new partner, producer-director Richard C. Kahn of Merit Pictures/ Hollywood Productions, and they ground out three more all-black singing-cowboy films: *Bronze Buckaroo, Harlem Rides the Range,* and *Two-Gun Man from Harlem,* released in 1938 and 1939. Several of the films featured Spencer Williams Jr.—later known to TV fans as Andrew H. Brown of *Amos and Andy*—who also wrote at least one of the features. (Williams's father, Spencer Williams Sr., was an accomplished pianist and composer. A longtime associate of Fats Waller, he wrote a number of jazz classics, including "Everybody Loves My Baby" and "I Found a New Baby.")

Jeffries claims his original impetus was not to star in these films, simply to get them made. Having grown up in a racially tolerant neighborhood, he was deeply offended by the segregation he found when he began traveling in pop bands, and he wanted to provide westerns for the black kids he saw flocking to all-white westerns in segregated theaters. In Hollywood, "we had trouble finding African Americans who could ride, sing, and act. We tested ten or twelve and none could do all three. But I could."[25] Tall and handsome, with a powerful and unusual voice, Jeffries as a youth had learned to ride on the farms of his mother's family in Ohio. Now in Hollywood the confident young man became Bob Blake, black singing cowboy.

Also appearing in the Jeffries films was a smooth, slick musical harmony group called the Four Tones: Lucius Brooks, bass; Ira Hardin, guitar and baritone; Rudolph Hunter; and Leon Buck, tenor. They accompanied Jeffries on a promotional tour of the South in 1939 to promote these films, the time-honored way of producing publicity for movies and bringing in some income for the star.

However, the production standards for Jeffries's films were even shod-

Poster from Herb Jeffries's first film, *Harlem on the Prairie* (1938). (Author's collection)

dier than for the standard Poverty Row productions, and while locations were sometimes excellent, the technical aspects, especially sound, were embarrassing. These dramas were played out in a totally black West—whites were not friends, enemies, or oppressors; they just didn't exist. But as film historian William K. Everson points out, the comedy sequences in these films consisted of familiar stereotypes such as "the comic pal scared of ghosts, the chicken-stealing cook, the crap-shooting, lazy roustabouts . . . which black audiences understandably objected to when [they] appeared in a more restrained form in regular Hollywood films."[26]

After the tour with the Four Tones, Jeffries dropped in at the Greystone Ballroom in Detroit to visit Duke Ellington. Their conversation, according to Jeffries, went like this: " 'So you're the Bronze Buckaroo now! . . . How are you doing?' 'Oh great. . . . Just finished my personal appearance tour. I'll probably be going back to Hollywood to make some more pictures.'

James Newill as Renfrew of the Royal Mounted. (Author's collection)

'Yeah?' said Ellington, 'Anything wrong with you that $80 a week with me wouldn't cure?' 'Just give me that contract!' "[27] Jeffries recorded a good bit of material for Victor with Duke Ellington (most notably "Flamingo") and later on his own for Columbia, Mercury, and other small labels. After his stint with Ellington he pursued a solo career before entering the service during World War II. Upon his discharge he joined the exodus of talented black performers to Europe, where jazz musicians were lionized and race was no barrier.

A 1953 article in *Life* renewed interest in Jeffries's career in the United States, and he divided his time between the States and Europe before returning for good in 1959. He appeared in one final film, *Disc Jockey,* with popular singers and bands such as Tommy Dorsey, Ginny Simms, and Sarah Vaughan. Late in his long life Jeffries returned to the studio to record an album, *The Bronze Buckaroo (Rides Again),* for the upstart Warner Western label and displayed a still vibrant suppleness and power in his singing.

The singing-cowboy movie phenomenon also embraced a related film subject in 1937: the Royal Canadian Mounted Police. Film historians have tended to link Mountie films with westerns and other such anomalies as

Gene Autry's *Yodelin' Kid from Pine Ridge* (Republic, 1937), set in Florida, and *Saginaw Trail* (Columbia, 1953), set in Michigan. The outdoorsy Mountie dramas appealed to the same audience who enjoyed cowboy films. Given the success of Nelson Eddy and Jeanette MacDonald in *Rose Marie* in 1936, it was inevitable that one of the Gower Gulch studios would come up with a series for a singing Mountie. The studio was Grand National and the singing Mountie was a popular radio singer named James Newill, with light wavy hair and a chin dimple that rivaled Kirk Douglas's, who appeared in more than a dozen films as Renfrew of the Royal Mounted.

Newill was born in Pittsburgh, Pennsylvania, on August 12, 1911, and moved to Gardena, California, as a youth. He attended the University of Southern California and in about 1930 joined the Los Angeles Opera Company. As an actor, he worked with Murphy's Comedians, and he obtained a spot as a featured singer on the *Burns and Allen* radio show. He sang with the orchestras of Eddy Duchin, Gus Arnheim, and Abe Lyman and was featured on the nightly radio show *Say It with Music* when he was tapped by Grand National to enter films. His first feature was *Something to Sing About,* the James Cagney musical, in 1937; in September his first Renfrew film, *Renfrew of the Royal Mounted,* was released. Monogram picked up the series when Grand National dropped it, and it lasted through 1940, with *Sky Bandits* the final release. Newill began a new series for PRC in 1942, when he costarred with Dave O'Brien in the Texas Rangers series, beginning with *The Rangers Take Over.* When Universal dropped Tex Ritter in 1944, PRC picked Ritter up for the Texas Ranger series, and James Newill became expendable. Apparently Ritter's authentic voice and manner was more to PRC's and the public's liking.

Newill went on to a few smaller film roles but concentrated on his first love, singing. He appeared in the revival of the musical *Rain* on Broadway and toured at home as well as abroad. He did thirteen episodes of Renfrew in the early days of television before going into business with his old costar, Dave O'Brien, in Southern California. He died July 31, 1975.

The continuing saga of the Sons of the Pioneers also brought another singing-cowboy hopeful to the screen, Donald Grayson. After the Pioneers signed exclusively with Columbia in 1937—against the advice of their manager, Ray Whitley—Columbia made a curious decision. Having just signed the group on the strength of their harmony and their songs, the studio decided it did not care for the guttural baritone of Bob Nolan. For several westerns the vocal solos were handled by a handsome young easterner named Donald Grayson, who was being groomed to take over a series of singing-cowboy westerns of his own, though as it turned out this never happened. Although his voice was lovely and, oddly enough, blended well on some songs, on others he sounded embarrassingly out of place, with inflections and mannerisms that rang of the New York nightclub scene. Boyish and slender, he had neither sufficient physical authority to play a western hero, nor a voice that seemed authentic, and after a few films Bob Nolan was promoted to second lead and returned to singing his own songs at last.

Born Carl Frederick Graub in Canton, Ohio, on July 23, 1908, Donald Grayson was the son of Swiss-German immigrants. Something of a child prodigy, he made his professional debut at the age of nineteen as a violinist and vocalist, and soon became a staff artist on WLW in Cincinnati. He caught the attention of Columbia Pictures president Harry Cohn, who quickly signed him to appear in the Starrett features, holding out the possibility of his own series if things worked out. His first western was *The Old Wyoming Trail* (Columbia, 1938), where he appeared in support of Starrett and sang with the accompaniment of the Sons of the Pioneers while Len Slye was still a member.

Grayson never clicked on-screen, and he was dropped from the series after a half dozen or so films, replaced by Bob Nolan. From there he might have drifted into obscurity, but he was gifted in reinventing himself. It turned out he was a comedian as well, and he joined a wacky new organization called Spike Jones & His City Slickers as violinist, vocalist, and front man. With Jones he recorded some of his most memorable sides, including the trademark glug-glug-glug (in time and in tune) on "Der Fuehrer's Face" and "Cocktails for Two." A fellow City Slicker, clarinetist Del Porter, recalled of Grayson: "When he joined, we didn't know he had all these attributes, of making funny sounds. Had no idea. But he was indispensable. Whenever you needed a funny sound Carl [he had gone back to his given first name] had it. Musical saw, anything."[28]

A gifted mimic and master of dialects, Grayson was an integral part of Jones's meteoric rise during the war years. The relationship could have gone on much longer, but like many musical bands of the era, the hardworking, intensely creative Jones outfit was a hard-drinking bunch, and when Jones himself got sober in 1946, he let what became known as "the drinking band" go. First on the list was Grayson, whose alcohol intake showed badly onstage and occasionally prevented him from performing at all. Though only thirty-eight years old, "Grayson never worked again," according to his biographer, "apart from an RCA session for Spike and a brief stint with [Eddie] Brandt's band. An irredeemable alcoholic, he was reduced to panhandling in his last days; at his premature death [April 16, 1958], three people attended his funeral."[29] He was forty-nine years old.

In 1937 the floodgates for singing cowboys had been thrown open by the success of Gene Autry, and a host of hopefuls streamed through. But the big story that year in the world of the singing cowboy was Gene Autry's second walkout from Republic.

When Autry hit the road with his band for a series of personal appearances and failed to show up for the shooting of his next film, *Washington Cowboy,* Yates, who had clearly been expecting such a showdown and such a result and had begun a search for a potential replacement in the early

Donald Grayson conducts the Sons of the Pioneers—*from left,* Hugh Farr, Pat Brady, Bob Nolan, and Lloyd Perryman—in a 1940s Charles Starrett western. (Author's collection)

autumn, promptly suspended him. Although these events happened just a couple of years before Johnny Bond got to Hollywood, he eventually became intimate with all the players, and he reports that among the several people Republic considered was the extremely popular *National Barn Dance* singer Red Foley. According to Bond, Republic said that "we'd rather have Tex Ritter," but Ritter was forced to turn the deal down because his contract was with Edward Finney, not Monogram, and Republic did not want or need Finney as part of the deal.[30]

Red Foley was a fine, good-looking singer and, like Autry just three years earlier, was an established regional radio star and a good record seller. Art Satherley corroborated Bond's story, claiming it was he who approached Foley, who in turn eagerly referred Satherley to his manager, John Lair, founder of the popular radio show the *Renfro Valley Barn Dance.* Satherley recalls being rebuffed by Lair, who claimed that releasing Foley to make films "would break up my outfit! Besides, I haven't any time to go to Hollywood."[31]

Although Autry didn't reflect on this particular episode, he had roomed with Foley when both were on the *National Barn Dance* and knew him well.

I always thought that Red Foley at that time had one of the greatest voices of any country singer I ever heard. He could do all types of things, he could do a hymn, he could do a song with a beat, he could do . . . well, he was always just very versatile. And I always said back in that era that if old Red had not been lazy, he'd have given me a big run for the money if he'd have come to Hollywood to make pictures. . . . He was easygoing, and he didn't care. It didn't make a bit of difference to him. . . . [I]f he'd had a little getup about him, if he'd really got out and hustled, why he could have given me a run for the money in the picture business, 'cause he was a good looking fellow, had red hair, and was just a good guy and could sing! A likable man. I was very fond of him. He was one of my good close friends.[32]

Foley in fact did appear in a western or two in secondary roles in years to come, but by that time he was a little late, and—again according to Satherley—he later in life deeply regretted not having tried earlier and harder.[33]

Ultimately, Republic's search for a new singing cowboy ended with Len Slye, who tested and signed with the studio on October 13, 1937. He was a pivotal member of the Sons of the Pioneers, and it is unclear why he was so quick to leave the outfit; he had been the spark plug for forming the group and the member who again and again held the group together during its difficult formative years. Tim Spencer had already quit the group again— he was replaced on an interim basis by Wesley Tuttle, then permanently by Lloyd Perryman. If anything, Len Slye seemed the one member most dedicated to the preservation of the successful quintet. The Pioneers were still causing a sensation, recording and appearing in films with Charles Starrett, Gene Autry, Dick Foran, and even Bing Crosby. Why did Slye leave at such a crucial time for the band? Jon Tuska maintains that "there was some friction between Roy and Bob Nolan during this period"[34]—but there is little, if any, other evidence of this. In fact, if there was conflict it would more likely have been with the notoriously cranky Hugh Farr. Ray Whitley, who managed the band during this period, stated unequivocally that there was no such conflict.[35]

Despite the Pioneers' growing popularity, Len Slye tried out first at Universal, where "I lost out to Bob Baker, who went on to make quite a few musical Westerns back then. They told me I wasn't right to be a movie cowboy hero because the camera made me look like a teenager." Next he tried Republic. Hal Spencer, Tim's son, reflected that Rogers "was just an ambitious young guy, looking for a break," and looking back on it, Rogers seemed to confirm it: "I did manage to land a few bit parts in movies that involved a little more than singing. . . . I wasn't very good at playing bad guys. I guess I wanted to be the hero, and I wanted to be the one whose name was on the movie marquee outside." Rogers's recollection of these events has the smooth patina of an oft-told tale, but it deserves retelling in his own words:

In the fall of 1937 I walked into a hat shop in Glendale to pick up my white Stetson, which I had left there to be cleaned and reblocked. While I was standing at the counter a big guy, about the size of John Wayne, came running through the door, wild-eyed and in a hurry. "What's all the excitement about?" I asked him. He said that Republic Pictures was holding auditions the next day for a new singing cowboy, and he needed a hat fast so he could look the part. Now, Republic already had Gene Autry, but Gene's contract was up for renewal and the word around town was that he was hoping to go to the mat to fight for the great big raise he thought he deserved. To put the pressure on Gene to keep his contract demands in line, Republic had set up these auditions to find another singing cowboy.

I didn't have an appointment, but I went anyway, unaware that the guard at the gate had orders to let in only those people with a gate pass. The guard told me to get lost. I walked away but didn't leave, lurking around all morning hoping to figure out a plan to see someone I knew going in. Around the end of the lunch hour, I saw a large group of studio workers heading for the gate to return to work. I slipped into their midst, collar up and Stetson hat pulled down low so the guard wouldn't recognize my face and, sure enough, I got past him. About ten yards inside, though, I heard him call out for me to stop. I froze, ready to get the bum's rush. But before the guard had a chance to turn me around, I heard a friendly voice.

"Len, Len Slye! Hello!" It was Sol Siegel, the producer, who . . . remembered me as one of the Sons of the Pioneers. "I assume you're here to try out for the singing cowboy screen test," he said. "I've tested seventeen men already, and don't feel good about any of them. If you have your guitar, come in and give it a try." . . . When I returned [with guitar] and caught my breath, I sang "Tumbling Tumbleweeds," which had been the theme song of the Sons of the Pioneers, and "Haddie [sic] Brown," which is a fast paced ol' country song with a lot of flashy yodeling.

By the smile on Mr. Siegel's face I could tell he liked my work. "Len, come back in the morning and let's do a screen test." He later told me as much as he liked the music of the Sons of the Pioneers he had never once considered me when thinking of hiring a new singing cowboy. It was only when he saw me there walking through the gate that it dawned on him that I might be right for the role. . . . On October 13, 1937, I became a contract player at Republic Pictures.[36]

The trade press covered it thus:

## Rogers: Gene Autry's Walkout
## Was Lucky Break for Cowboy Singer

The row between Gene Autry, the Western star, and Republic Pictures is following the familiar course of such feuds in Hollywood. Republic now has named a successor to Autry in Roy Rogers, a 25 year old radio singer who has worked in a couple of pictures. Exactly the same tactics that MGM used in the Freddie Bartholomew dispute. By the way, what has become of Rennie Sinclair since Freddie went back to work? . . .

Some of you movie-goers may wonder why all this bother about a western star. But there are 7500 theaters in the U. S. who play Hollywood "horse operas." Get a few miles out of a city and Autry and his competitors are big shots with the fans.[37]

Young Leonard Slye signed a seven-year contract with Republic at $75 a week and was happy to get it. (This salary was doubled in 1940. Clearly the future Roy Rogers did not make his millions as a film star; it was personal appearances and merchandising that made his fortune.) In the fall of 1937 Slye's immediate concern was replacing himself in the Sons of the Pioneers, and his suggestion was a bass-playing comedian named Robert Ellsworth O'Brady, known professionally as Pat Brady. Now that Slye was being primed for movies, the name Len Slye had to go, and after a brief stint in a couple of supporting roles as Dick Weston he became Roy Rogers.

Arthur Satherley admits that he was firmly in the camp of those who had little confidence in Roy Rogers: "Yates called me up and said 'Art, I want you to record Roy Rogers quick and get a nice bunch of numbers in by him. We're going to give it to this guy Autry.' I said, 'Herb you're not going to give it to Autry so quick. Number one, I've heard Roy Rogers sing. He's as much country as you are, and you're not! . . . I'll tell you before I record him he's not going to sell.' [Yates] said, 'So you won't record him?' I said, 'If it's your wish, I'll record him. I'm still your vice president.' "[38]

Satherley, speaking as a record man, may have had a point. Though a fine singer and an outstanding yodeler, Roy Rogers had a good but not spectacular career on record. But Satherley certainly did not foresee the screen appeal that would make Roy Rogers one of the most beloved movie cowboys in history.

# Roy Rogers

## King of the Cowboys

Although he would rise to the pantheon inhabited by the most beloved cowboy figures in history, Roy Rogers came inauspiciously into the world. Leonard Frank Sly was born to Andrew Earlin Sly and Mattie Womack Sly in a two-room tenement on Second Street in Cincinnati, Ohio, on November 5, 1911. His father was a shoemaker but had a spotty work history as a common laborer, working the docks and at carnivals; he also had worked as an acrobat and as a showboat entertainer, talents he would pass on to his son.

The Sly family moved to Portsmouth, Ohio, when Len was a year old and stayed there eight years before going farther upriver to Duck Run, then returning to Portsmouth. At about the age of twelve Len began playing the guitar and learning square-dance calls, and he excelled in music and sports in high school before leaving in his sophomore year to work with his father in a shoe factory. Seeking an easier trade, Andrew Sly moved his family to California in an old Dodge in June 1930, and the family found work driving gravel trucks for a relative, then picked fruit and did general day labor as the Depression squeezed tighter. Len began appearing with his cousin Stanley as a duo called the Slye Brothers in 1930; the two rode about on a single motorcycle, seeking day labor while the sun shone and work as entertainers at house parties at night. Stanley despaired at this hardscrabble existence and quit, but Len was long on determination, and eventually his raw talent and his rapidly developing yodeling ability were recognized by several of the popular Los Angeles cowboy and hillbilly bands of the day. In 1931 he appeared with the Rocky Mountaineers in his first professional radio appearance, over Long Beach station KGER, and there he met Bob Nolan and then Nolan's replacement, Vern Spencer. There were short stints with Benny Nawahi's International Cowboys, followed by a fateful barnstorming tour with the O-Bar-O Cowboys through Arizona, New Mexico, and Texas. Len actively recruited Spencer and Nolan to regroup as members of Jack LeFevre & His Texas Outlaws, and the three young men quickly broke off from this group to become the Pioneer Trio. They obtained their own radio spot over Hollywood's KFWB late in 1933 for $35 a week and were joined by Hugh Farr in 1934 and Karl Farr not long thereafter; together they would make history as the Sons of the Pioneers.

The Pioneers were an instant sensation. Within months they began to record and to appear in films in support of Charles Starrett at Columbia. *Gallant Defender* (1933) was their first release. But even as their film career began to flower, Len's sights were beginning to focus on a horizon farther than a group setting would allow.

It was Republic's Sol Siegel—ARC-label head Moe Siegel's brother— who gave Slye his big screen break, taking the young yodeler under his wing and auditioning him for a role as the studio's second singing cowboy. Siegel was in charge of running Republic's day-to-day operations in those days before New York–based Yates moved to Hollywood. Like Yates, Siegel (1903–1982) was born and educated in New York. After a stint at the *New York Herald Tribune,* he became a sales executive for the American Record Corporation and went to Hollywood in 1934 to organize and supervise Yates's merger and the formation of Republic. Though Yates was boss, the singing-cowboy era at Republic flowered under Siegel's aegis; when Yates finally moved to Hollywood full time, Siegel moved on, to Paramount in 1940, Twentieth Century-Fox in 1947, and MGM in 1956. His career as a producer was long and honored, and his contributions to the singing-cowboy genre, while confined to his Republic years, were substantial.

It was Siegel who spotted Len Slye trying to sneak into Republic's 1937 singing-cowboy auditions, gave the youngster a screen test, and signed him. The name Slye (with or without the *e*) had to go, and the name Roy Rogers was chosen; it was apparently Sol Siegel who came up with the alliterative screen name. Republic lost no time putting Rogers to work; he filmed a small part in a Three Mesquiteers film, *Wild Horse Rodeo,* the day he signed his contract. He was billed as Dick Weston in this film and in Autry's final prestrike film, *The Old Barn Dance,* before starring as Roy Rogers in *Under Western Stars* and all future films.

Republic's Herbert Yates instructed Art Satherley to record Slye immediately, to promote the young man and his film. As Roy Rogers (he legally adopted the name October 6, 1942), he recorded the yodeling features "Cowboy Night Herd Song" and "Hadie Brown," as well as "When a Black Sheep Gets the Blues," and Tim Spencer's "That Pioneer Mother of Mine." He recorded his final sessions as Len Slye with the Sons of the Pioneers on December 14 and 16, 1937, and remained close to the Pioneers through the years. After their contract was up with Columbia, he brought them to Republic to support him in films through 1947. Rogers returned to the ARC studios in March 1938, recording four songs that he'd performed in

Roy Rogers with Carol Hughes in his first starring role in *Under Western Stars* (1938), which he landed on the heels of Gene Autry's walkout at Republic. (Country Music Hall of Fame collections)

*Under Western Stars,* two of them co-written by Johnny Marvin and Gene Autry.

With the April 1938 release of *Under Western Stars* Roy Rogers became the new singing-cowboy star in the firmament. "This was what I had been shooting for, although it sure as heck wasn't how I wanted to get my first big part." However, with the return of Gene Autry to Republic the following spring, Autry once again got the big budgets, the best scripts, and the best songs, while Roy Rogers went about making solid films and surprising more than a few people with his genuine acting ability in secondary roles in major features such as 1940s *Dark Command.* As Rogers noted about his early films, they were quite different from Autry's: "Gene always played himself, and his movies were all set in modern times with cars and radios and bad guys in business suits. Most of my early pictures after *Under Western Stars* were set in the past and I played someone else, not Roy Rogers. I was Billy the Kid, Wild Bill Hickock, or Buffalo Bill; and we tried to give each picture an historical flavor."[1]

The first of these was *Billy the Kid Returns,* released in September, in which Roy played the legendary bandit in the prologue, and then himself as a lookalike who is mistaken for the Kid. He found time while straightening

Roy Rogers plays for a packed arena in the 1940s with the Sons of the Pioneers. *From left:* Pat Brady, Bob Nolan, Tim Spencer, Hugh Farr, and Lloyd Perryman. Karl Farr is either hidden by the camera angle or missed that show. (Author's collection)

out the case of mistaken identity to sing no less than seven songs in a film that lasted just under an hour. Typical Rogers titles were *Billy the Kid Returns* (1938), *Frontier Pony Express* (1939), *Young Bill Hickock* (1940), and *Sheriff of Tombstone* (1941). Though he was intimately associated with George "Gabby" Hayes throughout his career—Hayes acted as acting coach, father figure, mentor, and friend—Roy's first starring films did not feature the lovable geezer as sidekick. Smiley Burnette, who did not go on strike with Autry, made the first two films per his contract. Roy was then paired with the dependably crusty Raymond Hatton for two other movies before being joined by Gabby Hayes beginning with *Southward Ho!* in May 1939.

Although Rogers was perhaps not in a league with the savvy Autry as a businessman, he made two extremely shrewd decisions during these years. In 1938 he bought the palomino stallion Golden Cloud, better known to the world as Rogers's faithful screen horse Trigger, assuring a costar for life. It also assured his place on Trigger's back should Herbert Yates, realizing that Trigger was in some ways as big a draw as Rogers, try to replace the singer and keep the horse, something Yates in fact proposed to do in one of his many fits of pique. Rogers's second smart business decision was to retain control of his own endorsement rights. In exchange for Rogers's continued low salary, Yates conceded these rights to Rogers. The notoriously tightfisted Yates may have saved a few bucks at the time, but over the years Roy Rogers made untold millions from marketing his name and image on a bewildering panoply of products, from food to pajamas to lunch boxes. As the King of the Cowboys, Roy's persona became one of the most iconic images stamped on children's items nationwide.

With the release of *Red River Valley* in 1941, the setting of Roy's films shifted to Autry's modern West. By then Republic apparently felt there was plenty of room to cast both of its top cowboys in similar films and left historical singing westerns to other stars and studios.

On the recording front, Rogers had several more ARC sessions, primarily cowboy material, and was occasionally backed by Hugh and Karl Farr and Perryman and Brady of the Pioneers. He moved to Decca from 1940 to 1942, where his accompaniment was first provided by the Rough Riders and additional musicians, then by Spade Cooley's Orchestra. The releases from these sessions were typical of the West Coast country of the period—twin fiddles, steel guitar, muted trumpet, accordion, rhythm guitar, and bass—while the songs were primarily country love songs or western-swing tunes like "New Worried Mind" and "Time Changes Everything," recorded with small-band accompaniment. Roy was in glorious voice for these sessions—clear, precise, charming, though with no yodeling. The records were well received and sold well enough, but no true hits emerged.

Roy Rogers and his son Dusty. The lessons must have stuck. Today Dusty Rogers leads his own band and oversees, with his sister Cheryl, the museum and legacy left by the King of the Cowboys. (Country Music Hall of Fame collections)

Roy Rogers and Trigger on the set, between takes. (Country Music Hall of Fame collections)

With the arrival of World War II, Rogers experienced a major power shift on the film scene. When Gene Autry enlisted in the Army Air Corps in 1942, Republic put its mighty publicity machine fully behind Roy Rogers, proclaiming him the King of the Cowboys and gracing a 1943 film with that title. In 1943 Rogers appeared astride a rearing Trigger on the cover of *Life,* and it was at this time that Trigger also received an inflated sobriquet: "The Smartest Horse in the Movies." The war years (Rogers was classified 3-A and was not called to duty) also saw the first pairing with young Dale Evans as costar, beginning with *The Cowboy and the Señorita* in 1944. Here he vaulted past Gene Autry as the top singing cowboy, a title he never really relinquished, though Gene's records were consistently more successful and his film career in singing-cowboy westerns lasted a couple of years longer.

Shortly thereafter Yates saw the stage production of *Oklahoma!* on Broadway and declared that Roy Rogers would make bigger-than-life western musicals along those lines. Beginning with *Heart of the Golden West* in December 1942, Rogers's films were upgraded from smaller dramas to big, upscale musical fantasies, supported by the Sons of the Pioneers. This approach prevailed, with the outlandish costuming that became Roy's trademark, from 1944 to 1946, until it was abruptly replaced by far starker westerns in 1947, when Republic sensed a shift in the nation's mood.

A series of tragedies in his personal life began during these years as well. After fearing they would not have their own child, Roy and his second wife, Arline Rogers, adopted a girl, Cheryl, in 1941, and then produced a daughter themselves, Linda, in April 1943. On October 28, 1946, Roy Rogers Jr.—known then and now as Dusty—was born, but the joy of this new birth was quickly tempered by grief when Arline died of a sudden embolism on November 3 while still in the hospital. Rogers found a sympathetic soul in his costar, Dale Evans, who nourished him emotionally during this agonizing time, and fourteen months later he and Dale married in Murray County, Oklahoma, on New Years Eve 1947, while filming *Home in Oklahoma.*

Even though Dale Evans never headlined a western—as Dorothy Page had five years earlier—she nonetheless is the woman most identified with the singing cowboy in film and on record, and she well deserved her sobriquet, the Queen of the West. Although Roy sang duets with other costars, Jane Frazee most notably, none had the impact of Dale Evans. In the beginning she was frequently cast as a spoiled, sassy, strong-willed young woman, often from the East, but she gradually changed her image to the more motherly, but still strong-willed, matriarch of the Roy Rogers television shows.

There is an odd bit of confusion about her birth date and name. Though she claimed October 31, 1912, and Frances Octavia Smith, her birth certificate is dated October 30 and names Lucille Wood Smith as the baby girl. Whatever these discrepancies, she grew up being called Frances, and though born in her in-laws' house in Uvalde, Texas, in the southwest part of the state, she spent her early childhood in the small farming community of Italy, south of Dallas, before the family moved to the Memphis, Tennessee, area. A gifted singer, she aspired early to a career as a pop singer on radio, and after a brief stint on Memphis radio, she landed a job on WHAS in Louisville, where her name was changed to Marion Lee, then finally to Dale Evans, a name she kept when she moved to WFAA in Dallas in 1936. A stint with the Anson Weeks Orchestra and radio work in Chicago led to a Hollywood screen test in 1940, and in 1941 she signed a one-year deal with 20th Century-Fox, which led to a contract at Republic in 1943. Though still hoping for a career in popular music, she found herself cast in hillbilly pictures (*Swing Your Partner* and *Hoosier Holiday*) and in small roles in other films. Her first appearance in a western was with John Wayne in Republic's *War of the Wildcats* (1943), also released as *In Old Oklahoma.*

The following year Herbert Yates cast her as Roy Rogers's leading lady in *The Cowboy and the Señorita,* and history was made. Rogers and Evans would make twenty-eight more films together—separated only for a time after their marriage when Republic felt it unseemly to star husband and wife in the same film—as well as one hundred television shows. They would become one of the best-known married couples in America. Evans almost left the series and the studio in 1945. Still ambitious for a career as a singer and actress more than as a costar, she stated flatly, and honestly: "A heroine in a Western is always second string. The cowboy and his horse always come first."[2] A quick check of typical Roy Rogers movie posters of the era confirms this: Roy was billed first, inevitably followed by Trigger, then Gabby

Hayes, and finally his female costar. Despite her misgivings, Evans was persuaded to stay, and as Roy's popularity exploded she became part of his road show and radio cast as well. Evans underwent a religious conversion in 1948, and as the singing-cowboy era wound down she became well-known as the author of several inspirational books, and of songs both secular ("Happy Trails") and religious ("The Bible Tells Me So"). She was also a frequent guest, with and without Roy, on religious television shows. Dale Evans Rogers died of congestive heart failure February 7, 2001.

As for Roy's recording career, it reached its peak when he signed with RCA after the recording ban of 1942–1944. The Sons of the Pioneers, who had signed with RCA at the same time, were frequent visitors on Rogers's records, although Roy's signature sound was provided by drummer Joseph "Country" Washburn & His Orchestra. His first sessions were in August 1945, and over the next several years he recorded such classics as "Along the Navajo Trail." Possibly the peak came on December 1, 1947, when Roy and the Pioneers recorded definitive versions of "Blue Shadows on the Trail," "Pecos Bill," "That Palomino Pal o' Mine," and "Home on the Range." At this point, on this session, recorded western music reached its acme, for these performances are filled with exquisite feeling, energy, sensitivity, control, expression, and dynamics.

With the filming of *Pals of the Golden West* in 1951, Roy's second seven-year contract with Republic was up, and he did not re-sign. There were a number of reasons—chief among them the personality conflict with the abrasive Yates—but more than anything, Rogers wanted to go into television, where he felt his enormous popularity with children could be put to best use. Meanwhile Yates and Republic, which was planning to sell his film catalog to television, attempted to block his entry into that medium. On October 18, 1951, the issue went to court, and Roy won, although Republic immediately appealed, and the decision was overturned in 1954.

Roy Rogers's television show, *The Roy Rogers Show,* premiered on NBC on December 30, 1951. The initial half-hour show led off with a bang, featuring Bob Hope, Dale Evans, the Whippoorwills, and Pat Brady, and highlighted a sketch in which Trigger bested Hope in a poker game. A second filmed half-hour became the basis for the series, a miniature western melodrama in which music was a minor factor. Unlike Autry's limitless West, Rogers had a ranch—the Double R Bar Ranch—located in Paradise Valley, not far from Mineral City, where Dale Evans ran the Eureka Cafe. The setting was the present, a place where horses, automobiles, airplanes, and Pat Brady's cranky jeep Nellybelle cheerfully coexisted. More than a hundred of these shows were produced before the series ended in 1957, though it was shown in rerun for a number of years. It was a popular entry in early television, but by then the singing had largely gone from the singing cowboys. With the exception of Dale Evans's "Happy Trails (to You)," which closed the show, music played a minor role. Roy and Dale also hosted an

Dale Evans and Roy Rogers. The Queen of the West and the King of the Cowboys, in a scene from *Man from Oklahoma* (1945). (Country Music Hall of Fame collections)

hour-long variety series in the fall of 1962, which prominently featured the Sons of the Pioneers.

Roy's first film project after leaving Republic was a costarring role in *Son of Paleface* (Paramount, 1952), which starred Bob Hope and Jane Russell and featured Roy in a tongue-in-cheek performance as a cowboy hero. He sang beautifully and, at forty, looked as lithe and athletic as ever. At this point, rather than reinvent himself or try to milk a little more life out of a fading genre, he simply gave up western films to concentrate on his family, on television, and on his tours. He made a cameo appearance in Bob Hope's *Alias Jesse James* (United Artists, 1959) and was lured out of film retirement to portray a middle-aged western drifter who mentors a young boy in the independent film *Mackintosh & T. J.* (Pentland Productions, 1976). Though he was still a familiar face on television even in that era, this was his last film.

As for his recordings, like most of the cowboys of that era Roy Rogers drifted away from pure western material at about that point. He recorded love songs, novelty songs, seasonal songs ("Frosty the Snowman," "Gabby the Gobbler"), and a number of religious songs, many in duet with Dale Evans. Although his magic onscreen was palpable, he never really found

In a smart business move, Roy Rogers gained the rights to merchandise his name in return for a lower salary from Republic Pictures. (Author's collection)

the magic on record, and his years with RCA wound down not with the country hits that Ritter and Wakely enjoyed, or the seasonal smashes that dominated Autry's late career, but with a series of children's records. Though he remained busy with rodeos, personal appearances, and television throughout the 1950s and 1960s, he had a long hiatus from recording before beginning a series of country albums for Capitol. There were a few charted entries but no real hits, save the nostalgic "Hoppy, Gene, and Me" in 1974 and 1975. There was a single for MCA in 1980, and then the loving but overproduced *Tribute* album on RCA in 1991, in which Rogers duets with dozens of country stars. A final project was a half-hour radio show, with Riders In The Sky, for Rabbit Ears Radio. A planned CD release was stalled when the company went under.

Despite his virtual retirement from the movies, the 1950s were a busy time for Rogers, with network radio and television shows, as well as a demanding personal appearance schedule that kept him as active as any entertainer in Hollywood. His radio show appeared through 1955, and the television show through 1957 (and in syndication through 1960). His earlier films were cut to an hour and frequently appeared on television, and he and Dale were guests of most of the popular television hosts of the early years of the medium: Perry Como, Dinah Shore, and Ed Sullivan. Though their commercial affiliations fell off with the ending of their television and radio series, their biographer Robert Phillips reports that in 1961 they still received royalties into the millions from merchandise.

The next two decades saw a slowing down in personal appearances. Life also dealt the couple several tragic personal blows, which only made the stoic twosome more beloved by the public. Roy and Dale endured extraordinary heartache with the loss of their daughter Robin—the only biological child the two had together—who was born with Down's syndrome and died in 1952. Roy and Dale subsequently adopted four children, two of whom died in tragic accidents: Debbie in 1964 and Sandy in 1965.

Roy branched out into other business arenas, activities that saw the opening of the Roy Rogers restaurants in 1969 and the Roy Rogers Museum in Apple Valley in 1967, rebuilt in Victorville in 1976. By the 1980s Roy was in semi-retirement, overseeing the museum, receiving the Pioneer Award from the Academy of Country Music in 1987, and being inducted into the Country Music Hall of Fame in 1988 (for a second time—he was earlier inducted as a member of the original Sons of the Pioneers). Despite his athletic physique and active lifestyle, he began to experience angina as early as the mid-1950s, and he underwent several heart surgeries as the years passed. It was of congestive heart failure that the King of the Cowboys died on July 6, 1998.

# High Noon

## The Musical Western at Its Zenith

Although Gene Autry was the undisputed king of the movie cowboys upon his return to Republic in 1938, and Roy Rogers was the up-and-comer, a plethora of other musical hopefuls appeared on the screen that year as well. When Autry went back to work at Republic, his first release was *Gold Mine in the Sky,* in which he was supported by Pee Wee King & His Golden West Cowboys. It was a logical move on Autry's part—cowboy bands lent atmosphere and a touch that made westerns appealing. Then, too, the star needed musical support, so why not use a cowboy band that was selling records or making waves on radio? To the delight of scholars and historians, many such bands have been captured on film in just this way.

Pee Wee King—born Julius Frank Anthony Kuczynski in Milwaukee on February 18, 1914—formed his own polka band in high school. Shortly after embarking on a professional career in 1933, he was discovered by promoter J. L. Frank, whose daughter, Lydia, King eventually married. Frank brought King and his band together with young Gene Autry over WHAS in Louisville in 1934. *Gold Mine in the Sky* was King's only film with Autry, although he appeared in others through the years, including two Charles Starrett films, *Ridin' the Outlaw Trail* (Columbia, 1951) and *The Rough, Tough West* (Columbia, 1952). He concentrated his energies on radio and television instead, appearing for a decade on the Grand Ole Opry, and he co-wrote some of the most memorable hits in popular and country music: "You Belong to Me," "Bonaparte's Retreat," "Slow-Poke," and of course "The Tennessee Waltz." This charming and accessible entertainer remained extremely active well into the 1970s and died at his Louisville home on March 7, 2000.

The best of these singing support groups was the Sons of the Pioneers in the 1937–1941 Charles Starrett films for Columbia. No other group of campfire singers approached their seemingly casual blend of harmony, their subtle

Pee Wee King & His Golden West Cowboys as they appeared with Gene Autry on Eddie Cantor's radio program, May 30, 1938. *Standing, from left:* Curly Rhodes, Milton Estes, Texas Daisy, Pee Wee King, Cowboy Jack Skaggs, and Abner Simms. *In front:* Eddie Cantor and Gene Autry. (Author's collection)

jazziness, and the depth and breadth of their original songs. Charles Starrett—who did not sing but occasionally spoke a verse as he and the boys did chores or tended the horses—replaced the Pioneers in his westerns with vaudeville performer Cliff Edwards, known as "Ukulele Ike." Starrett or Columbia or both apparently were fond of the musical interludes in his films, and in coming years he used dozens of singers and bands. Some of the more well-known were Jimmie Davis, the Jimmy Wakely Trio, Johnny Bond, Grand Ole Opry star Roy Acuff, Ernest Tubb, Elton Britt, Foy Willing & the Riders of the Purple Sage, Spade Cooley, Bob Wills & His Texas Playboys, the Cass County Boys, Smiley Burnette, Pee Wee King & His Golden West Cowboys, and Merle Travis. Some of the more obscure were Curt Barrett & the Trailsmen, Walt Shrum & His Colorado Hillbillies, Hank Penny & His Plantation Boys, Ozie Waters & His Colorado Rangers, Donald Grayson, Hank Newman & His Georgia Crackers, Texas Jim Lewis, Curly Williams, Curly Clements & His Rodeo Rangers, Doye O'Dell & His Radio Rangers, the Sunshine Boys, Red Arnall & the Western Aces, Shorty Thompson &

His Saddle Rockin' Rhythm, T. Texas Tyler, and Eddie Cletro & His Roundup Boys. Only after 1952, when the novelty of music had long worn off and Starrett's career was nearly at trail's end, did music cease to become so much a factor in his films.

Although many of these names have been forgotten, and many more are perhaps historically important but known these days largely to scholars of country and folk music, it is an impressive list. Acuff, Wills, Travis, Davis, Tubb, and Wakely were—or were about to become—the brightest stars of their time; many would star in their own films, though their musical careers are far better remembered. Regardless, in many ways the long series of films Starrett made for Columbia (1935–1952) probably contained the best selection of western music of any series.

While several of these musical support players were cowboy in image and style, many others reflected western swing (Wills, Cooley), honky-tonk (Tubb), current country music (Davis, Atcher, Britt), and even the emotional Appalachian sound (Acuff). This is precisely because these acts were top record sellers during the war years, when jukeboxes helped increase country music's popularity nationwide. In certain areas of the country a song or two by a Tubb or an Acuff or a Wills boosted ticket sales enormously. Given the fact that many, even most, country music acts of this era were donning western wear for a dashing and flashy and glamorous look onstage, many of these performers looked right at home in the West, if not necessarily on a horse.

It was a trend that had been a long time coming, at least since radio star Gene Autry had appeared in *In Old Santa Fe*. Ken Maynard used Frank Yaconelli and Charles King as musicians in *The Strawberry Roan* as early as 1933, and there was an overabundance of cowboy hillbilly string bands on the radio in Los Angeles, providing a deep talent pool to choose from.

Although *The Old Homestead* (Liberty, 1935) was ostensibly a hillbilly picture, the three songs the Sons of the Pioneers sang in it seem to be the first appearance of an organized western musical group on film. That start was followed closely by the Arizona Wranglers in Universal's *Stormy,* starring Noah Beery Jr., released in October. Later that year Chill Wills & His Avalon Boys appeared in their first Hopalong Cassidy film, *The Bar 20 Rides Again*. This same group would make an indelible impression in Laurel and Hardy's *Way Out West* (MGM) in 1937, with the then tall and unrecognizably skinny Wills doing what can only be described as bass yodeling in counterpoint. Already the idea of cowpokes leaning around the corral or saloon, singing in harmony, was firmly entrenched. Other long-forgotten acts of the era soon followed: the Five Radio Buckaroos in *Five Bad Men* (starring Noah Beery Jr., for Sunset, 1935), Johnny Luther's Cowboy Band in *Rough Riding Ranger* (starring Rex Lease, for Merrick/Superior, 1935), and the Singing Buckaroos in *The Singing Buckaroo* (starring Fred Scott, for Spectrum, 1937). Famous acts appeared as well: the Sons of the Pioneers

Jimmie LeFevre & His Saddle Pals were an extremely influential Southern California cowboy band, not so much for their radio and film appearances as for the many musicians who gained experience with the Saddle Pals before moving on to better-known groups. (Country Music Hall of Fame collections)

with Starrett, Foran, and Autry; Autry's own core group of Smiley Burnette and Frank Marvin; Chill Wills & His Avalon Boys; Ray Whitley & His Range Ramblers (Ken Card and the Phelps brothers) in Hopalong Cassidy, Jack Randall, and Tex Ritter films; Ezra Paulette of the Beverly Hillbillies in Buck Jones's films; Jimmy LeFevre's Saddle Pals with Tex Ritter; the Colorado Hillbillies with Jack Randall; Louise Massey's Westerners with Tex Ritter; Art Davis popping up with Bill Elliott, Jack Luden, and his boss Gene Autry. Perhaps the most interesting in the realm of might have been was the one-time appearance (obviously assembled for this film alone) of a group called the Singing Cowboys—Lloyd Perryman, Rudy Sooter, and Curley Hoag—in an obscure Bob Custer western called *Santa Fe Rides* (Reliable/William Steiner, 1937).

Autry himself, after a year or two of filming, began using regionally popular groups in his own films. Western-swing pioneers the Light Crust Doughboys appeared in *Oh, Susanna!* (Republic, 1936), and the Tennessee Ramblers appeared in *Ride, Ranger, Ride* (title song by Tim Spencer) the same year. Autry traveled to Dallas for the Texas Centennial to film the musical extravaganza *The Big Show,* released in 1936; besides starring Autry in two roles (as egotistical movie star Tom Ford and as his good-natured singing stand-in, Gene Autry), it featured musical performances by the Sons of the Pioneers, the Light Crust Doughboys, the Beverly Hillbillies, the Jones Boys, and even showgirl Sally Rand and the SMU 50, a college choir. He used the Maple City Four and the Cabin Kids the following year in *Git Along Little Dogies,* and Oklahoma's finest, Al Clauser & His Oklahoma Outlaws (as well as Art Davis), in *Rootin' Tootin' Rhythm* (Republic, 1937). In coming years he would use the Tennessee Ramblers, the Maple City Four, and Al Clauser again, Walt Shrum & His Colorado Hillbillies, Polly Jenkins & Her Plowboys, Eddie Dean, the CBS-KMBC Texas Rangers, the Hoosier Hot Shots, the Ranch Boys, and an act called Nora Lou Martin & the Pals of the Golden West. Autry also enlisted the Stafford Sisters, whose youngest member was future pop singing star Jo Stafford. The Stafford Sisters had appeared on a radio transcription with the Sons of the Pioneers as the Sons and Daughters of the Pioneers at about this time.

As the years went by, Autry's films grew slicker, and more often than not an orchestra, not a string band, provided accompaniment. Autry's band on radio, the Rough Riders (Johnny Bond, Jimmy Wakely, and Dick Reinhart), appeared in only one of his films, much to their disappointment. As the Jimmy Wakely Trio they appeared in quite a few films starring other cowboys. It wasn't until the Cass County Boys appeared in *Sioux City Sue*

A 1939 songbook for Al Clauser & His Oklahoma Outlaws. *Clockwise from bottom:* Curly Bray, Bud Roberts, Speed Foreman, Al Clauser, and Tex Hoeptner. (Country Music Hall of Fame collections)

The Jimmy Wakely Trio when they first came to Hollywood around 1940. *From left:* Johnny Bond, Jimmy Wakely, and Dick Reinhart. (Country Music Hall of Fame collections)

(Republic, 1946) that Autry finally had a more or less permanent cowboy harmony trio associated with him on film and on stage.

Along with these groups, a flood of singing cowboys came to the screen in 1938. The sheer numbers are dizzying. Westerns themselves were hot, whether they included singing or not. More than 700 were released from 1938 to 1941, an average of almost three and a half a week![1] Of the roughly 110 released in 1938, 47 were singing-cowboy features, and another 12 featured significant music: the Sons of the Pioneers in Charles Starrett's films, Ray Whitley in George O'Brien's. The trend continued in 1939: approximately 118 westerns, 45 by singing cowboys, and 11 others with significant music—some, a *lot* of music—and it was starting to create a glut on the market. In terms of popularity the musical western had achieved its apex in the prewar years, an era of excitement and freshness.

Several new singers joined the fray in 1938, the first of whom was George Houston, who starred in Grand National's *Frontier Scout*. Houston was no youth when he entered the singing-cowboy sweepstakes. Born in Hampton, New Jersey, in 1896, George Fleming Houston was the son of a clergyman and had attended Blair Academy and then studied voice at the Institute of Musical Arts (which became Juilliard), graduating with two degrees before serving with the U. S. Army Ambulance Division in France in World War I.

George Houston, as the Lone Rider, serenades the lady, the law, and the mob.
(Author's collection)

He began a career in opera upon his return and by 1927 appeared in lead roles, first in Mozart's *Abduction from the Seraglio,* then in *Faust* and *Carmen* the following year. Feeling his career in opera was going nowhere (although he appeared in *Faust* in a performance for President Calvin Coolidge), Houston moved to Broadway, appearing in *Shooting Star, Thumbs Up,* and *Casanova,* and in the starring role in *The New Moon.* He moved to Hollywood to star in *The Melody Lingers On* in 1934 and became a veteran of films, only occasionally in singing roles. His career actually seemed to be winding down in such action adventures as *Wallaby Jim of the Islands* (1937), when he took the role of Wild Bill Hickock in his first western, *Frontier Scout* (Grand National, 1938). His costar was Dorothy Fay, soon to become Mrs. Tex Ritter.

George Houston was by this time forty-two years old. What he lacked in youthful athleticism he made up for in authority and command (although some critics have termed it stolidity), and though his operatic voice was a magnificent instrument, it was far from at home on the range. Grand National was tottering on its last legs at this point, and this was Houston's only release for the studio. This role, however, and a well-received appearance in an A picture called *The Howards of Virginia* (Columbia, 1940) convinced Henry Briggs of PRC studio to sign him to a series of singing westerns in which he appeared as the Lone Rider, which some skeptical film critics have suggested was an attempt to lure kids into the theater thinking they were about to see a Lone Ranger film.

Houston made eleven of these musical Lone Rider films in 1941 and 1942, beginning with *The Lone Rider Rides On* (PRC, 1941). The series was continued thereafter with Robert Livingston as a nonsinging Lone Rider. It seems odd that Grand National and PRC, both of which employed the authentic-sounding Tex Ritter, would go to the opposite extreme with an operatic baritone like George Houston; perhaps they simply wanted to cover the bases. At any rate, Houston was a trained actor, capable as an aging action hero but thoroughly unbelievable as a singing cowboy.

His end was a sad one. After his final Lone Rider film Houston returned to the stage, heading the American Music Theater of Pasadena, a group that presented opera in English. He was preparing to take this troupe on a national tour when felled by a heart attack on Franklin Avenue in Hollywood while out for his evening walk. Mistakenly thinking he was intoxicated, the police hauled him into the drunk tank, where he died, in police custody, November 12, 1944.

Producer Jed Buell had made a mark in both Fred Scott's and Herb Jeffries's careers, and in 1938 he also had a hand in what was surely one of the most bizarre westerns in film history. He produced *The Terror of Tiny Town* (Columbia, 1938), a novelty western that employed an all-midget cast. Its hero was Billy Curtis, who had appeared in films with John Wayne and others, and who sang a fine version of "Down the Sunset Trail." It was an experiment that was never repeated and remains a curiosity that has as its sole appeal its uniqueness.

The final new cowboy singer introduced in 1938 was not new at all: Gene Austin (born July 24, 1900, in Gainesville, Texas) had been a popular 1920s recording star with hits such as "How Come You Do Me Like You Do?" (1924), "When My Sugar Walks Down the Street" (1924), and his signature song, "My Blue Heaven" (1927). Though he still sang sweetly, by this time Austin was past his prime and did not give the impression of being an outdoorsman. *Songs and Saddles* (Roadshow Pictures/Colony, 1938) was, in the words of one critic, "a haphazard indie that encouraged no followup and merited none."[2] In fact, the same critic suggests that, just as the producers of Lone Rider may have hoped to lure folks into theaters thinking they were to see the Lone Ranger, so this little independent film company may have hoped not only to attract Austin's remaining fans, but also to draw in careless ticket purchasers who thought they'd be seeing Gene Autry.

Gene Austin's career continued for a number of years. He had recorded a western song, "Under a Texas Moon," as early as 1930 and recorded at least two cowboy sides for the Universal label (for whom Dick Foran also recorded), "I'm Coming Home" and "Give Me a Home in Oklahoma." In addition, he took four jazzy mountain boys called the Fidgety Four (Douglas Dalton, Roy Lanham, Gene Monbeck, and Dusty Rhodes) and

Multimillion-record-selling pop star Gene Austin ("My Blue Heaven") in his only appearance as a singing cowboy in films, in *Songs and Saddles* (1938). (Author's collection)

renamed them the Whippoorwills after the opening line of "My Blue Heaven": "When whippoorwills call and evening is nigh." These four men, with the later addition of Juanita Vastine (billed onstage as Sweet Georgia Brown), would become one of the classiest and most exciting of country/ swing/jazz bands in the late 1940s and early 1950s; it achieved great artistic but little commercial success. Gene Austin died in retirement in Palm Springs, California, January 24, 1972.

As 1939 dawned, the wolves were nipping at Grand National's heels, but the little studio was still gamely trying to stay afloat. Having quickly lost Cagney and more recently Tex Ritter, the studio, desperate for a new star and a new gimmick, came up with the idea of a singing cowgirl.

Singing cowgirls on record were nothing new: Patsy Montana, the Girls of the Golden West, and others sold well to their largely rural constituents. But the idea of taking a singing feminine hero to the screen was entirely new. Grand National turned to radio for a singer to play the role and chose Dorothy Page, a popular singer and aspiring actor. She was born Dorothy Lillian Stofflett in Northampton, Pennsylvania, on March 4, 1904, and majored in music at Cedar Crest College. In the mid-1920s she was the subject of a *Saturday Evening Post* cover, portrayed as "one of America's ten most beautiful women," but she gave up a modeling career for marriage to a Detroit doctor. As the Depression deepened, the young mother of two auditioned for Paul Whiteman's radio program *Youth in America,* and her surprise win launched a career on radio, where she appeared as a singer and actress on *Paducah Plantation* on the NBC Red network.

Movies were the logical next step, and she was signed by Universal in 1935, where her first films were starring roles in the decidedly nonwestern *Manhattan Moon* and *King Solomon of Broadway* (1935). Her late start began to hurt her, for at thirty-one she was no longer an ingenue and was still learning film acting. But she was a beautiful woman with a lovely if trained voice, and an experienced rider and comfortable on a horse. Although she was in many ways a logical choice for the experiment, Page may have had a bit too much polish to be fully convincing as a singing cowgirl.

Her first release in the singing-cowgirl series was *Water Rustlers* on January 6, 1939, followed rapidly by *Ride 'Em, Cowgirl* on January 19. The former, unfortunately, did not do good business, and the second fared even worse at the box office. Although Wonder Woman would become extremely popular with young women just a few years later, the public was seemingly not ready for a proactive, self-actualized singing cowgirl. And it is possible to

Dorothy Page leaves the gunplay to Dave O'Brien *(second from right)* in *The Singing Cowgirl* (1939), the last of her three musical westerns for Grand National Pictures. (Author's collection)

speculate that although studio executives may have hoped to draw a whole new audience, they apparently misjudged the appeal of a sagebrush chanteuse to the preadolescent boys who were a significant part of the audience for action westerns. With the release of *The Singing Cowgirl* in June, this fascinating experiment in film and music came to an end.

Grand National had been in deep trouble since the financial disaster of the 1937 James Cagney musical *Something to Sing About.* The studio had been flying on a wing and a prayer ever since, and though it released a few foreign-made films over the next year or two, *The Singing Cowgirl* was the final full production under its aegis. It is not surprising that the studio failed to give this film, or this series, much time, attention, publicity, or push. *Variety* summed it up crisply in the March 15 issue: "*Water Rustlers* is a western cheapie whose only redeeming feature is Dorothy Page."[3]

As for Page, this was her show business swan song. She remarried in 1939 but was widowed in 1941; she then married a rancher and oversaw operations on ranches near Fresno and in Pecos, Texas. She died after a long battle with cancer on March 26, 1961, in Fort Meyers, Florida.

Dorothy Page was but one of three last gasps for Grand National, which saved its dying energy for singing-cowboy films. Another of the studio's January releases was *Trigger Pals,* starring Art Jarrett, who provided by-the-book pop vocalizing. Even the comic talents of Al St. John and the lovely Dorothy Fay could not raise this entry above the very ordinary, and it was to be Jarrett's only singing-cowboy film. A big-band vocalist, guitarist, and trombonist with Phil Harris, Red Nichols, and Ted Weems, Jarrett had recorded on his own for Columbia, Victor, and Brunswick as a pop artist. He had been in films since playing opposite Joan Crawford in *Dancing Lady* (1933) and went back to leading his big band until entering the navy as a lieutenant commander during World War II. He left entertainment after the war, prospered as a business executive, and died July 23, 1987.

Tex Fletcher, who began his recording career during the short-lived but extremely influential heyday of western music in New York City, was a darkly handsome tenor who played guitar left-handed. He was born Germino "Jerry" Bisceglia in Harrison, New York, on January 17, 1909. Because of his popularity in New York, he was beckoned by Grand National to make *Six Gun Rhythm,* but, unfortunately for Fletcher, Grand National went under just as production wrapped up on the movie. With gritty determination Fletcher bought the film and toured the country with it. Although he did not distinguish himself from the ordinary, Fletcher might have had a future in films had not Grand National folded. As it was, he went back to his successful career in New York, where he eventually appeared for fifteen years as "The Lonely Cowboy" on WOR radio and served two years on the Mutual network as the singing sidekick on *Songs of the B-Bar-B* (1952–1954) and on early television as well. Tex Fletcher drifted out of show business and died in upstate New York on March 14, 1987.

Though he starred in only one singing-cowboy movie, Tex Fletcher had a fifteen-year career on New York's WOR radio as "the Lonely Cowboy." This songbook dates from 1940. (Country Music Hall of Fame collections)

In 1940 popular bandleader Bob Wills made his first western film. He and his Texas Playboys were one of the most popular dance bands of the era, and given their snappy western image it is no surprise he was cast in films. Although he tended to stoutness, Wills had a million-dollar smile and a charismatic stage personality, and he was cresting the wave of a huge national hit, "San Antonio Rose," when he accepted an offer from Monogram to provide musical support for Tex Ritter in *Take Me Back to Oklahoma* (1940). Though he was forced to use only a few members of his normally large dance band (Wayne Johnson, Son Lansford, Leon McAuliffe, Eldon Shamblin, and Johnny Lee Wills), the response from exhibitors and from the public was good. Columbia, having scored with the Pioneers in the Starrett films, signed Wills & His Texas Playboys to appear in *Go West, Young Lady* (1941), a comedy starring Penny Singleton. They then appeared in musical support of the studio's new western star, Russell Hayden, who had recently been promoted from action sidekick roles in the Hopalong Cassidy series. They made eight films with Hayden, and Wills, though somewhat stiff, did a surprisingly good job in dramatic scenes. The Texas Playboys who appeared in these films generally were Joe Holly or Jesse Ashlock, Leon McAuliffe, Harley Huggins, Luke Wills, and Cotton Thompson. However,

Bob Wills made his first film appearance with Tex Ritter in *Take Me Back to Oklahoma* (1940). (Country Music Hall of Fame collections)

other than a couple of small appearances in Columbia's Starrett series, a few musical shorts, and several Snader Telescriptions (soundies for video jukeboxes, an idea that seemed good in 1951 but never really caught on), this was the extent of Wills's career in films. His movie appearances seem to have been just an exciting break, and he doubtless had his hands full leading the most popular country dance band of that era. Born in Kosse, Texas, on March 6, 1905, he died of complications of a stroke on May 13, 1975.

A brief look at *Go West, Young Lady* is appropriate, if only because Penny Singleton won top billing in the film, outsmarted and outshot not only the villain but her male costar Glenn Ford, and even sang a fine western song on horseback ("Don't Get Along, Dogies," by Sammy Cahn and Saul Chaplin) to the cattle. It was one of the rare westerns that featured a singing female star; as the headliner Singleton joins Dorothy Page and Jane Frazee in the elite company of top-billed singing-cowgirl stars. It was, however, the only western in which Penny Singleton starred. Born Mariana Dorothy McNulty on September 15, 1908, in Philadelphia, the singer, acrobat, and comedian was far better known for her role as Blondie in more than a dozen films from 1938 to 1950, and to a later generation as the voice of Jane Jetson in the television cartoon series *The Jetsons*. Her long career included many other films, television, and Broadway, and she now lives in retirement.

Penny Singleton in a scene from *Go West Young Lady* (1941), the only western in which she starred. (Author's collection)

John "Dusty" King broke into singing westerns in 1940 as well. A former radio announcer and big-band singer, he was given a costarring role in Monogram's answer to Republic's popular Three Mesquiteers. Monogram called its version the Range Busters and lured away two disaffected Republic stars, Max Terhune (who had been denied a raise by Yates) and Ray "Crash" Corrigan, for the new trio. These trio adventures followed a formula used by several of the studios of the time. There was a heroic type (Corrigan in this case), a sidekick (Terhune), and often a singer to provide breaks in the action and to handle guns and fists when necessary. The latter job fell to Dusty King, who was born Miller McCleod Everson in Cincinnati, Ohio, on July 11, 1909. He sang and announced over WCKY and WKRC in his hometown and joined the popular Ben Bernie Orchestra as a vocalist in 1934. Paramount signed the band to appear in the film *Stolen Harmony* (1935), and King both acted and sang in the film, fueling a desire to go into pictures. As John King he had leads in serials like *The Adventures of Frank Merriwell* (1934) and *Ace Drummond* (1936), singing roles in several musical comedies, and romantic leads in such films as *Charlie Chan in Honolulu* (1939).

It is hard to know whether Dusty King considered his move into the singing-cowboy field a step up or a step down in his career; on the one hand

Monogram's Range Busters—*from left,* Ray Corrigan, Dusty King, and Max Terhune—starred in a series of twenty-four films for the studio. (Author's collection)

he was costarring in his own series for a legitimate studio, while on the other his career was not particularly going anywhere at the time. Perhaps he thought a western look and feel and sound would give his career a shot in the arm. The first of the series, appropriately titled *The Range Busters,* was released in August 1940, and though the trio eventually made some twenty-four films, they never really approached Republic's Three Mesquiteers series in popularity.

King made twenty of the twenty-four Range Busters films; after *Haunted Ranch* (1943) he was called into the Army Air Corps and was replaced by nonsinger Dennis Moore. Upon his return from the service he appeared in a few more pictures but found film work hard to get, and he went back to a successful career announcing on radio and singing commercial jingles. After many years in radio King opened a waffle restaurant in La Jolla, California; he retired in La Jolla and died there on November 11, 1987.

A new stampede of the hopeful thundered onscreen in 1941, all in supporting roles that never developed into singing-cowboy careers. Most of these appearances by these singing cowboys were mere detours or side excursions on the highway of their own successful careers. First was Red Foley (1910–1968), who at last made his film debut singing and playing guitar in support of Tex Ritter in Monogram's *The Pioneers,* released May 10, 1941.

Although he continued to appear in films from time to time and even had roles in both dramatic and musical television series in years to come, this film proved to be his only foray as a singing cowboy. Foley's long and exemplary career as a country and gospel singer was keeping him active enough and indeed would explode in the 1950s.

The Pioneers also introduced a young Texan named Doye O'Dell to the screen. Born Allen Doye O'Dell in Gustine, Texas, on November 22, 1912, the strapping young man had begun a career in radio in Amarillo in 1931. He then went across the border to XEPN, then to New York as vocalist for Doc Schneider's Texans on the NBC Red Network. After several years with Schneider he obtained his own show over the Red network in 1938, based out of WTIC in Hartford, Connecticut. As with all aspiring singers of the era, the next step seemed to be Hollywood, and The Pioneers was O'Dell's first role in films, followed shortly by an appearance in a Range Busters film, Fugitive Valley (Monogram, 1941). His career was stopped in its tracks by World War II, and he spent three years as a Marine before returning to Hollywood, where Bill Elliott got him signed to a contract at Republic.

The Pioneers (1941) marked the film debut of both Red Foley and Doye O'Dell. In this still from the film, *from left,* Doye O'Dell, Arkansas Slim Andrews, Red Foley, Wanda McKay, and Tex Ritter. (Author's collection)

Whatever plans the studio may have had for O'Dell, they did not develop into starring roles. He appeared in *Man from Rainbow Valley* (1946) with Monte Hale and *Heldorado* (1946) with Roy Rogers, then in another Monte Hale, *Last Frontier Uprising* (1947). He popped up in a couple of Charles Starrett westerns with his Radio Rangers and closed out his film career in 1949 with small roles in Roy Acuff's *Home in San Antone* (Columbia) and Lash LaRue's *Son of a Badman* (Western Adventure/Screen Guild).

O'Dell spent quite a bit of time with the Sons of the Pioneers, and he filmed several movies with them when Tim Spencer was attending to other business. He toured in Spencer's place from time to time as well; in fact, a 1947 Pioneers souvenir program features him with a short bio and photo (along with Ken Carson, Shug Fisher, and Deuce Spriggins) as one of the "artists [who] have been capable Sons of the Pioneers alternates in the past." For whatever reason, chance or timing or luck, O'Dell never landed a starring role, and he drifted into several successful television shows (hosting his own *Western Varieties*) and character roles in series (including *Maverick, Sugarfoot, The Tall Men, Bronco,* and *Empire*) before retiring. His recording career was fitful; he recorded (using Texas Jim Lewis's band) for Exclusive beginning in 1947 and scored a Top Twenty hit in 1948 with a novelty song called "Dear Oakie." He also cut sides for Odeon, Mercury, Intro, Sage and Sand, Liberty, and Era, where he was joined in the studio in 1956 by the Cass County Boys. Doye O'Dell died in quiet retirement on January 3, 2001.

The Sons of the Pioneers' departure from the Charles Starrett films at Columbia left a serious gap in that series. Though Starrett would go on making popular B westerns into the 1950s, part of the appeal of his films was the music as counterpoint to the heroics, and Columbia decided to continue the process. The studio experimented with the gentle presence of Cliff Edwards (1895–1971) rather than use a harmony group—it would have been awfully difficult to replace the Pioneers; the Jimmy Wakely Trio was under contract elsewhere; and the other top-flight western harmony groups were yet to form. Better known as Ukulele Ike, Edwards played a character called Harmony in several Starrett westerns before heading over to RKO and similar roles with Tim Holt in 1943. He is best remembered as the voice of Jiminy Cricket in Walt Disney's *Pinocchio*, where he made a lasting impression on the national consciousness with his breathy falsetto rendition of "When You Wish upon a Star." He even starred in his own singing-cowboy film around this time: *Cliff Edwards and his Buckaroos* (Warner Bros., 1941), a ten-minute musical short with only a skeletal plot between songs.

Warner Bros. also made similar shorts featuring Bob Wills and with Spade Cooley. One of the most fascinating of these shorts was *Ride, Cowboy, Ride* (1939), an all-color short that starred Irish tenor Dennis Morgan. Born Stanley Morner, Morgan (December 20, 1908–September 1994) was soon to become a major star for Warner Bros. The music was completely recycled from Dick Foran's *Land beyond the Law* (1937), including Foran's theme

A 1941 Texas Jim Lewis songbook. Lewis and his band appeared in the films of Gene Autry, Eddie Dean, and Charles Starrett. (Country Music Hall of Fame collections)

song, "The Prairie Is My Home." Though Morgan did many subsequent westerns, this little short and its follow-up, *The Singing Dude* (1940), were his only singing-cowboy roles, as he was being groomed for A-picture stardom.

With the Starrett features, Columbia hit upon the scheme of trying to recreate the Autry magic by grabbing a top young record seller or radio star on the way up, perhaps with the thought of developing him into starring roles while he provided the music for the Starrett features. Texas Jim Lewis made his film debut in *Pardon My Gun* (1942) and returned five years later in *Law of the Canyon* and *Stranger from Ponca City*. Lewis was born October 15, 1909, in Meigs, Georgia; the family soon moved to Florida, then Texas, where he picked up his stage name. He worked in and out of music in Detroit, then Houston (with the Swift Jewel Cowboys), then Detroit again before moving to New York with his Lone Star Cowboys, who included a couple of musicians who would become a part of the West Coast scene with the Spade Cooley organization—Smoky Rogers and Cactus Soldi. They spent five years in New York before moving to the West Coast in 1940, where they began recording country and novelty songs for Decca, played western swing in the nascent ballroom scene, and appeared in films.

Even honky-tonker Ernest Tubb showed up in a couple of Columbia westerns in the 1940s. (Author's collection)

Lewis was drafted late in 1942 and turned his band over to up-and-comer Spade Cooley, who took it to spectacular heights. Lewis returned to performing upon his release from the service in 1944 and led one of the popular western-swing dance bands of that time and place; he even scored a Top Ten hit with a cover version of Al Dexter's "Too Late to Worry, Too Blue to Cry" in 1944. Lewis moved his base of operations to Seattle in 1950, where he first appeared on radio and in a television variety show, then became a children's show host with the long-running *Sheriff Tex's Safety Junction* on KING. His performances were limited to local club work after his TV days were over, and he died January 23, 1990.

During the 1940s Columbia's Charles Starrett films feature a broad spectrum of country singers in western clothes, most notably Ernest Tubb (with Johnny Luther's Ranch Boys) in *The Fighting Buckaroo* (1943). The Texas Troubadour, born in Crisp, Texas, on February 9, 1914, was enjoying his first wave of national success with "Walking the Floor over You," after a decade in the music business. His screen debut was not auspicious—he seemed self-conscious and uncomfortable before the camera, though he sang well—and he appeared in only one other Starrett western, *Riding West,* in 1944. Tubb did not actively pursue a film career after joining the Grand Ole Opry in February 1943, although he did star in Republic's *Jamboree* (1944) and a musical extravaganza called *Hollywood Barn Dance* for cheapie independent Screen Guild in 1947. Tubb doubtless felt that his energies were better spent on his recording and touring career, and he became a major country star, eventually easing into a grand old man role in the industry while maintaining a vigorous touring schedule. Though slowed by emphysema, he was still active as a performer until just months before his death on September 6, 1984.

Tubb was replaced in the Starrett series by Jimmie Davis & His Singing Buckaroos. At this point in his career the future two-term governor of Louisiana was a major record seller with a decade of hits behind him: "Beautiful Texas" (1933), "Nobody's Darling but Mine" (1934), "It Makes No Difference Now" (1938), the national sensation "You Are My Sunshine," and "Too Late" (both 1940), and "Sweethearts or Strangers" (also 1940). His first Starrett feature was *Frontier Fury* in 1943; his laid-back, laconic singing style and easygoing country-swing feel was pleasant, but he did not generate much charisma on screen. His only starring role came in 1947, when he played himself in his own life story, *Louisiana,* the rags-to-riches tale of a poor country boy who becomes a top recording artist and vaults to the governorship of Louisiana in 1944. He served a second term from 1960 to 1964. Born in Beech Springs, Louisiana, on September 11, 1899, Jimmie Davis died November 5, 2000.

The next singer through the revolving doors at Columbia was Bob Atcher, a popular radio singer who had carefully crafted an image of part cowboy singer, part folk singer, part country singer, and part comedy singer.

WLS radio star Bob Atcher made an appearance in a Charles Starrett western. (Author's collection)

His "crying" version of "Thinking Tonight of My Blue Eyes" had been a national hit early in the 1940s. He was born in Hardin County, Kentucky, on May 11, 1914, moved to the North Dakota prairies at the age of five, and returned to the Bluegrass State in 1926. He and his brother Randy (born 1918), who would become a popular cowboy on radio and television in Louisville in the 1950s, began a musical career in the early 1930s, and by the time the call came from Columbia Pictures, Atcher was a popular OKeh Records recording artist and a star at WGBM in Chicago, with a network radio show to boot. He and his wife, Loeta (known on stage and record as Bonnie Blue Eyes), both had featured roles in Starrett's *Hail to the Rangers* (1943). Atcher's career in Chicago was in full swing, and he joined the *National Barn Dance* over WLS in 1949, presided over it until its demise in 1960, then hosted its successor, the televised *WGN Barn Dance,* until it ended in 1971. He commuted from a rural village on the outskirts of Chicago called Schaumburg and served as its mayor from 1959 to 1975, guiding its growth into a major Windy City suburb. Bob Atcher left Illinois and retired to Kentucky, where he died in Prospect, near Louisville, on October 30, 1993.

Next up at Columbia was Jimmy Wakely, who had been peering out from the curtains at the side of the stage for awhile. He had been recording and appearing on radio and had played in films as a solo singer and with the Jimmy Wakely trio for a number of years. The half-dozen or so singing second-lead roles in Starrett films, beginning with *Cowboy from Lonesome River* (1944), were the last step before Wakely began his own series for Monogram; in fact, a couple of the Starretts in which he appeared were released after he had begun starring in his own series at Monogram. As Columbia ground out the Starrett series in between Wakely appearances, Ernest Tubb returned for *Robin Hood of the Range* and *Riding West* (with Johnny Bond), and Jimmie Davis was back for *Cyclone Prairie Rangers* (1944).

Starrett had starred in a film called *The Durango Kid* in 1940, supported by Bob Nolan & the Sons of the Pioneers. In 1945 Columbia decided to make this a series character, and the genial Starrett often remarked, in his later years, how ironic it was for a film star, whose face is often his fortune, to have built the second half of his career on a character with a mask. With *The Return of the Durango Kid* in 1945, Starrett was to spend the next several years of his life behind that mask in a popular and profitable series of films for Columbia, all of which featured music to some degree.

Having lost Wakely to his own starring series, and tired of one- and two-shot musical guest stars from the world of country music radio and records, Columbia put a big publicity buildup behind an unknown singer in the hopes of developing him into a singing-cowboy star. The *Return of the Durango Kid* prominently billed Tex Harding, who appeared in the first eight of the Durango Kid series in the following two years, supported musically by Bob Wills & His Texas Playboys a couple of times. Harding was born John Thye on January 4, 1918, and followed his sister Dorothy Dix to Hollywood after

Tex Harding provided the songs in the first eight installments of Columbia's "Durango Kid" series. (Author's collection)

serving in the Marines during World War II—Dix had appeared in musical westerns with Ken Maynard in *Wheels of Destiny* (Universal, 1934) and Gene Autry in *Guns and Guitars* (Republic, 1936), as well as other films. Boyishly handsome, tall and broad-shouldered, with a smooth baritone, Tex Harding did not have the desired effect on the public, despite the studio's buildup, and was reportedly difficult on the set as well. After eight films his contract was not renewed; he appeared in but one other Starrett film (*Desert Vigilante,* 1949) before drifting into obscurity. Harding died in Tacoma, Washington, in 1981.

After the failure with Harding, Columbia tried a different tack, bringing on Smiley Burnette to provide both musical and comic relief, although in many of the pictures other groups or singers were trotted on for a song or two. The first of these was Merle Travis & His Bronco Busters, who were in two 1946 Durango Kid releases.

Merle Travis was one of the most versatile men in American musical history; a groundbreaking and widely influential guitarist, he was also a popular vocalist, a hit-record maker, a hit songwriter, and a talented cartoonist, impressionist, and author of prose. Born in Rosewood, Kentucky, on November 29, 1917, he became obsessed with the guitar as a youth and developed his syncopated finger-picking guitar style as a teenager. He turned pro at the age of twenty, playing first with fiddler Clayton McMichen & His Georgia Wildcats, then with the Drifting Pioneers over WLW in Cincinnati. At the suggestion of Wesley Tuttle, who spent a season in Cincinnati, Travis moved to Hollywood in 1944. There he began doing occasional film work before signing with Capitol Records in 1946 and beginning a series of clever country hits, including "No Vacancy," "So Round, So Firm, So Fully Packed," and "Fat Gal." He also wrote "Smoke! Smoke! Smoke! (That Cigarette)" and "Sixteen Tons," both million sellers (in 1947 and 1955 respectively). Although Travis's film career was inconsistent and a small part of his oeuvre, he may be best remembered as the guitar-picking southern soldier who sang "Re-Enlistment Blues" in *From Here to Eternity* in 1953. He also appeared in several of the Snader Telescriptions, a series in which several other western artists appeared, including Bob Wills, Elton Britt, and Tex Ritter. Though thoroughly associated as friend and co-worker with most of the singing-cowboy entertainers throughout his life, Travis from this point on in his career was in mainstream country and, later, folk, during the folk revival. He was rediscovered more than once during the 1960s and 1970s, despite changing national musical tastes. In the 1970s he moved to eastern Oklahoma, where he died of a massive heart attack on October 20, 1983.

Zeke Clements, "the Alabama Cowboy" from the Grand Ole Opry, got a shot in *Two Fisted Stranger* (1946), as did country-swing string bands like Hank Penny (1918–1992) & His Plantation Boys (Penny, Slim Duncan, Frank Buckley, and Bob Morgan). Penny enjoyed a long and somewhat fractured career as a western-swing bandleader, disc jockey, recording artist (for OKeh, Columbia, King, RCA, and others), songwriter ("Little Red Wagon" and "Bloodshot Eyes," a #5 hit in 1950, memorably revived by Asleep at the Wheel), and nurturer of talent (Noel Boggs, Thom Bresh). After 1950, though he continued to record in the country jazz style, Penny was best known as the comedian on Spade Cooley's TV show, then on his own.

There were other acts and artists who got their shot on the silver screen in Starrett's Columbia westerns: Ozie Waters & His Colorado Rangers, Hank Newman & the Georgia Crackers (actually brothers Hank, Slim, and Bob Newman with accordionist Johnny Sipes), Tommy Duncan & His Western All Stars (*South of Death Valley*, 1949), and Curly Williams & His Georgia Peach Pickers (*Riders of the Lone Star*, 1947). Williams (1913–1970), best known as writer of "Half as Much," was a former Grand Ole Opry entertainer swimming in the teeming western-swing waters of wartime Southern California. Gene Autry's crack trio the Cass County Boys appeared in a couple of Starrett's movies in 1947 and 1948, and several now-forgotten western bands did as well: Doye O'Dell led his Radio Rangers in *Whirlwind Raiders* (1948), and there were one-shot film appearances by bands with such names as the Sunshine Boys, Shorty Thompson & His Saddle Rockin' Rhythm, Red Arnall & the Western Aces, and Eddie Cletro & His Roundup Boys. Yodeler deluxe Elton Britt appeared in *Laramie* (1949); regionally popular country singer T. Texas Tyler made a film; novelty acts Harmonica Bill, and Mustard and Gravy, each made a couple; and Pee Wee King & His Golden West Cowboys appeared in *Riding the Outlaw Trail* (1951) and *The Rough Tough West* (1952).

But by this time tastes were changing, the Durango Kid series was seven years old, and Starrett, who had been making very similar films for Columbia for fifteen years, was himself was no longer a young man. With no need to work—he was heir to the Starrett Tool fortune—he retired from the screen. No singer, he nevertheless ought to be awarded an honorary singing-cowboy title for the fifteen years of quality western music he and Columbia presented on film.

A singing-cowboy hopeful who greatly benefited from his association with Gene Autry was western-swing fiddler Oathar "Art" Davis, who was born May 31, 1913, in Paradise, Texas. He moved to Oklahoma, then to East Texas, before settling in Dallas for his high school years, where he was befriended by young Jim Boyd and his older brother, Bill. He then enrolled at Jefferson University, a Dallas law school. His father, Philip, an avid amateur musician, encouraged Art's musical career, and in the early days of the Depression he began playing with several of the Dallas-area western-swing bands that the region produced in such abundance: Milton Brown & His Musical Brownies, the Light Crust Doughboys, and most importantly Bill Boyd & His Cowboy Ramblers, with whom he recorded several of the tunes for which Boyd became famous, including "Under the Double Eagle" and "Lone Star Rag."

Art Davis had the good fortune to run into Gene Autry, who was in Dallas prior to filming *The Big Show* (Republic, 1936) at the 1936 Texas Centennial. Autry liked the young man's fiddling, brought him in to record "Nobody's Darling but Mine" and several other county songs in September 1935, and offered him a job on the road. Young Davis, a strapping ex–high school football star, was a visual and musical addition to the Autry show, and he remained with Gene through the period of Autry's explosive popularity. Davis appeared in several Autry movies, became an integral part of the touring show, and recorded with Gene until mid-1941, when Autry slid from a string band sound to that of a small, smooth band, led by violinist Carl Cotner. Although raised in towns and cities, Davis enlisted in the 112th Cavalry unit of the Texas National Guard, and the training he received there with horses stood him well in Hollywood; he rode as an extra in many films, when time allowed.

Davis left the Autry show at about this time to lead his own band in Oklahoma, although he recalls Autry recommending him for a starring role at Republic. "Gene wrote back later," he said, "and said that Republic finally decided on a fellow named Don [Red] Barry." In time he did get an offer to support now-forgotten Monte Rawlins in *The Adventures of the Masked Phantom* (1939) for the shoestring Equity studio, but a contract with independent producer-director Cliff Sanforth that went nowhere prevented him from making a film for another two years.

I signed a personal contract with [Sanforth] and he changed my name to Larry Mason. . . . Later [producer] Phil Krasne came to me and offered me a contract to work in a series [at Grand National] with Art Jarrett and Al St.

Art Davis, a superb
western fiddler, had
a short career as a
singing cowboy.
(Author's collection)

John. Sanforth wouldn't release me to make the picture unless they took him as director. No dice. Krasne wouldn't hear of that. I received no salary from Sanforth, but I couldn't work for anyone else and he wouldn't or couldn't make another picture. All I could do was take my band back to Texas and wait out my contract, which I did.[4]

Eventually Davis and his band, the Rhythm Riders, were free to work in films, and Davis was delighted to support his boyhood idol Tim McCoy in *The Texas Marshal* (1941) at Producers Releasing Corporation, where the aging McCoy wound up his film career. Davis's work was noticed favorably, and PRC chose him to be one of the three stars of their entry in the trio western format, teaming him with granite-jawed action star Lee Powell and a third yet to be named as the Frontier Marshals. Rather than choose a sidekick type, Davis suggested his old boss and friend Bill Boyd, whose popularity in Texas and the Southwest was exceeded only by Bob Wills's. The powers that be at PRC decided to give Boyd a try, dubbing him Bill "Cowboy Rambler" Boyd to avoid confusion with William "Hopalong Cassidy" Boyd and stage actor William "Stage" Boyd, whose drunken escapades once nearly scuttled Hoppy's career simply by mistaken name association. Pulling no punches, western critic Buck Rainey wrote of the Frontier Marshals series that "Boyd was a terrible actor and unconvincing as a cowboy, yet he had a name in the country music world that gave him some pulling power in rural areas. Davis was the highest paid of the trio though Powell was admittedly the only actor among the three."[5]

Acting skills or not, Bill Boyd was the only one of the Frontier Marshals with a national reputation, and he received top billing. The series opened with *Texas Man Hunt,* released in January 1942. These three actors made only six films before PRC decided the trio was not working out. The studio planned next to pair Art Davis, who they hoped would emerge as a star, with Dave O'Brien in a series called *The Texas Rangers.* However, as so often happened during World War II, military service broke up the trio for good. Art Davis joined the navy, while James Newill took his spot as one of the Texas Rangers. Davis served in the South Pacific and survived uninjured when his ship was hit by a kamikaze pilot near Okinawa. Lee Powell was not so lucky; he was killed in the Marine assault on Japanese-held Tinian Island in 1944.

Davis returned to Oklahoma and the life of a dance bandleader after the war, appearing in but one more film, a ten-minute short filmed in Dallas called *A Cowboy's Holiday* (1949). He opened a music school in the 1950s, continued to perform on a regional level, fought and won a long battle with alcohol, appeared at several western film festivals in the 1970s and 1980s, and even recorded a couple of albums. Davis passed away on January 16, 1987.

As for Bill "Cowboy Rambler" Boyd, he returned to his successful musical career upon completion of the Frontier Marshal series. Born William Lemuel Boyd in Fannin County, Texas, on September 29, 1910, he grew up on a farm. Inspired by records and radio, he and his younger brother, Jim—who for decades would be associated with his brother's band and with the Light Crust Doughboys—landed a radio show over KFPM in Greenville, Texas, in 1926. The Boyds moved to Dallas in 1929, and while Bill got a job on radio station WFAA, his brother befriended a fellow high school musician, fiddler, and clarinetist Art Davis. By the time the two school pals, Jim

Lobby card for
*Rolling down the
Great Divide* (1942).
(Author's collection)

Boyd and Art Davis, graduated, they teamed up in Bill's fledgling band and called themselves the Cowboy Ramblers, mixing their musical inspirations: the songs of the West and of Jimmie Rodgers.

The Cowboy Ramblers mined the same musical vein as Bob Wills & His Texas Playboys and the other early western-swing bands: jazz, big band, folk, fiddle tunes, and cowboy songs. Although their most successful records were fiddle instrumentals, Bill Boyd's outfit had the strongest cowboy image and flavor of all the western-swing bands.

Boyd's year in Hollywood was surely an adventure, but it was clearly just a small detour on the trail he blazed as a western-swing bandleader and radio star. With a total of 229 sides cut for Victor, and at least two major hits before the war and two Top Ten hits after it ("Shame on You" in 1945 and "New Steel Guitar Rag" in 1946), he had an outstanding career in western swing, overshadowed only by Bob Wills. Boyd continued to perform until his career was ended by a stroke in 1973. He died on Pearl Harbor Day, 1977.

A final new face in 1942 was that of Jimmie Dodd, a talented singer and songwriter who had worked his way up from playing talented juveniles in such B comedies as *Snuffy Smith* to becoming the singing Lullaby Joslin character in Republic's Three Mesquiteers series, beginning with *Shadows of the Sage,* released in September. The other two Mesquiteers then were Bob

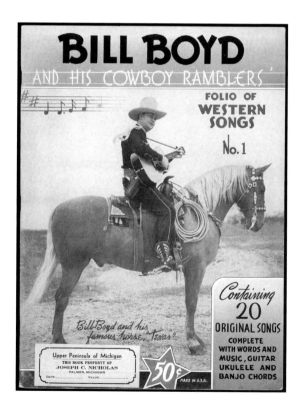

Western-swing bandleader Bill "Cowboy Rambler" Boyd took his turn in westerns with Producers Releasing Corporation. This song folio was published in 1939. (Country Music Hall of Fame collections)

A late version of Republic's Three Mesquiteers. *From left:* Tom Tyler, Jimmie Dodd (future Mouseketeer), and Bob Steele. (Author's collection)

Steele and Tom Tyler, and these three filmed the final six entries in the series. At this point the idea was no longer fresh, and Republic let it drop after *Riders of the Rio Grande* (1943). Jimmie Dodd, slight and boyish, was born in Cincinnati, Ohio, in 1910. After the demise of the Mesquiteers series he bounced around in small roles in such films as *Keep 'Em Sluggin'* with the East Side Kids and *Buck Privates Come Home* with Abbott and Costello. He is best remembered as the ultracheery tenor guitar–playing host of more than three hundred episodes of Walt Disney's *Mickey Mouse Club* on television. When he was finished impressing the minds of a generation, he drifted off to Hawaii, where he hosted a local television show until his death on November 10, 1964, in Honolulu.

In the annals of western music, the most memorable moment of 1942 was the swearing in of Sgt. Gene Autry to the Army Air Corps in July. World War II changed the face of America, and no business, including the entertainment business, remained untouched. Whatever course the singing-cowboy sensation might have taken, it was altered for good with the coming of war and the evolving national mindset. Battles in the Old West would soon seem like so much gossamer fantasy in the face of real battles all over the planet. An innocent world in which evil could be turned back with sweet reason and a couple of happy songs died in those years, never to return.

# 10

# Riding into
# the Celluloid Sunset

World War II touched every aspect of American life. Everyone was affected, from farmers and mechanics to major league baseball players and even singing cowboys. Many careers put on hold while the nation went to war would never be the same. However, a number of promising young film players got their chance during the war years; some joined the most memorable of the singing cowboys.

No one made a more surprising career move than Gene Autry, who enlisted and was officially inducted into the Army Air Corps in 1942.

With Autry's departure, Republic was left with the task of filling the enormous gap in its production schedule. Bob Steele was rumored as a replacement for a time, even though he had dropped the singing part of his career after *Oklahoma Cyclone* nearly a decade earlier. Then a contingent within Republic pushed hard for a female star, hoping to succeed with a cowgirl heroine where Grand National could not with Dorothy Page. Republic chose Kay Aldridge ("the Serial Queen," late of *Perils of Nyoka*), who starred with Alan Lane in *Daredevils of the West,* a serial meant to test her appeal to the western audience, but the studio never opted to let her star in her own series. Republic did boost the careers of several nonsinging cowboys during these years—Bill Elliott, Alan Lane, and Red Barry—but the ever cost-conscious studio found a most cost-effective and efficient alternative for musical westerns: not to develop a new singing star at all, but simply to re-release eight older Autry pictures per year while Autry was away at war.

With Republic's top singing star out of the picture, it was now up to Roy Rogers, and Yates's studio brought its considerable publicity muscle to bear in turning Rogers into the screen's reigning singing cowboy. Rogers, who had already connected with the public, quickly rose to even greater national stardom, often accompanied on-screen by his frequent costar and future wife, Dale Evans.

The war years also brought four new singing cowboys to the screen; actually, only Monte Hale and Ken Curtis were new, for Jimmy Wakely and Eddie Dean had been appearing in films in small acting and singing roles since the late 1930s, and in some ways were familiar faces.

James Clarence Wakely was born in Mineola, Arkansas, on February 16, 1914, and was raised dirt-poor in the red clay hills of eastern Oklahoma until the age of ten, when his family moved to western Oklahoma to raise cotton. An early fan both of Jimmie Rodgers and of seminal western-swing pioneer Milton Brown & His Musical Brownies on radio, Wakely learned to play guitar and piano, and by 1937 he and his wife were touring with Little Doc Roberts's Medicine Show. While with that troupe he was discovered by the owner of the Bell Clothing Stores, who teamed Wakely with young singer, guitarist, and composer Johnny Bond and with bassist and tenor Scotty Harrell. The new threesome appeared as the Bell Boys over radio, a dynamic trio in the tradition of the Sons of the Pioneers. Combining excellent musicianship, vocals, and new songs by Bond and Wakely, they quickly built a local reputation.

As Gene Autry was reputedly encouraged by Will Rogers, he in turn encouraged this trio to head to California to further their career. After an exploratory 1939 trip, during which they played small parts in Roy Rogers's *Saga of Death Valley,* the Bell Boys made the move west on June 4, 1940. They arrived, however, without Scotty Harrell, who, according to Johnny Bond, chose to remain in Oklahoma "for reasons of his own." He was replaced—inconveniently and at the last minute—with a relatively older fellow, Dick Reinhart, formerly of the Light Crust Doughboys. Bond recalls the intense frustration of showing up in Hollywood with a new bassist, and having to start all over to recover the smooth blend the trio had worked so

Jimmy Wakely in a still from Monogram's *Across the Rio Grande* (1949). (Author's collection)

An interesting but short-lived trio who performed on Gene Autry's *Melody Ranch* after Jimmy Wakely's departure. *From left:* Wesley Tuttle, Jimmy Dean, and Merle Travis. (Author's collection)

hard to develop in Oklahoma City: "The only rehearsals that we had were in the automobile as we drove from Oklahoma to California. Even though Dick was an accomplished musician and fine tenor singer, time and time alone builds a singing trio."[1]

The switch may have been awkward, but it turned out well. By November, Wakely had signed with Decca Records, and Bond and Reinhart were recording for Columbia, and within months they had become Gene Autry's backup trio on the *Melody Ranch* radio program. Wakely recalled those exciting early days with enthusiasm and passion: "I guess that was the height of my pleasure in show business. By the time I got to be a star, I was rather blasé. There'd been so much happening to me that it wasn't anything new, you know. I had come straight from Oklahoma onto the CBS network with Gene Autry. I had gotten a picture contract and a record contract almost immediately. . . . Everything just went bingo! I had the records, the Autry radio show, and I was working in the Hoppy Pictures. That was a happy position to be in!"[2]

Wakely and Reinhart left *Melody Ranch* after a couple of years, replaced by Eddie and Jimmy Dean. Johnny Bond stayed on and remained with the Autry organization for years, though he had an active recording and songwriting career of his own. Wakely had been picking up more and more film roles (with and without Bond) in Starrett, Hopalong Cassidy, and Johnny

Jimmy Wakely, *right,* in *Oklahoma Blues* (1948), with legendary Grand Ole Opry fiddler Arthur Smith and Dick Reinhart on bass. (Author's collection)

Mack Brown/Tex Ritter films, and by 1942 he scored his first recording hit, "Too Late," for Decca. As Wakely's film roles as an actor and singer grew, and as his record successes increased, it was only natural that some studio would give him a shot in the singing-cowboy sweepstakes. After a successful third billing in *I'm from Arkansas* for PRC, he was signed to Monogram for a series of four pictures, beginning with *Song of the Range* in 1944. The four-film deal eventually led to twenty-eight starring films for the studio, a streak that lasted until 1949.

Among his strengths, Wakely could count a melodious voice, a charming smile, and good looks; going against him was his slight build, which made heroics look a little improbable. Perhaps Monogram hoped they'd found another Gene Autry, an average-sized guy who beat all odds with a song and a good heart. Regardless, the films were successful, though in the postwar period Wakely's outfits were toned down to jeans and dressy shirts, no costuming frills, and the action was increased while the number of songs was decreased. It was an industrywide trend.

*Song of the Sierras* (1946), filmed in that glorious mountain country, remained Wakely's favorite, and *Lawless Code* ended the Monogram series in 1949. Though Wakely was far from the burliest western hero, his series was on the whole enjoyable—he was a natural and unpretentious singer, and his screen appeal rested on his charm, not his muscle or gunplay. He was supported by fine musicians, often including his lifelong buddy Johnny Bond, the Sunshine Girls, Wesley Tuttle, and Foy Willing & the Riders of the Purple Sage. With his superb gift for harmony, Wakely frequently sang memorable duets with his leading ladies, including a young Polly Bergen in her film debut in *Across the Rio Grande* (1949).

The postwar emphasis on action and the move away from song probably doomed Wakely's series more than anything, though he made more singing-cowboy films than anyone else outside the "big three" of Autry, Rogers, and Ritter. Although the whole industry was moving awkwardly to a more realistic presentation, Wakely had made a personal decision about the direction he wanted to take: "I had wanted to be a cowboy star when I came [to Hollywood] but about halfway through the series I decided it really wasn't what I wanted. When you're working for a studio like Monogram Pictures, you are not going to get any place, not really. . . . I don't care how good you were, you were not going to get anywhere at Monogram."[3]

Wakely had not given up the recording side of his career, and he had a national hit in 1948 with a song written by Eddie Dean, "One Has My Name, the Other Has My Heart," for the blooming Capitol label. It featured the uncredited harmony vocals of Colleen Summers, who had appeared as one of the Sunshine Girls with her sisters in several Wakely films, and who would later achieve fame as Mary Ford of the team of Les Paul & Mary Ford. Her vocals with Wakely blended beautifully on this national pop and country hit, and he and Capitol conceived the idea of further duets. He was then paired with popular singer Margaret Whiting, and this seemingly unlikely duo was successful in the biggest way in 1949. Their recording of Floyd Tillman's cheating song "Slipping Around" became a national sensation on the pop and country charts, on jukeboxes, and in record stores, where it sold well over a million copies.

Wakely and Whiting recorded together frequently in ensuing years, though they never equaled the heights of "Slipping Around." Wakely also continued to record solo records for Capitol, Decca, and then Coral (a division of Decca, now MCA). He dabbled in record production as well, appeared in a few more movies (most notably as the singing sidekick to Sterling Hayden in *Arrow in the Dust* in 1954), wrote music for several films, toured with Bob Hope and with his own band, had a short-lived musical variety television show (*Jimmy Wakely's Western Theater* in 1949), and had a network radio show on CBS from 1952 to 1958. In the years that followed, he became a pioneer in opening the Nevada showrooms to western music.

Wakely, who had a reputation for stubbornness and ego, nevertheless became one of the most passionate preservers of western music in the 1960s and 1970s. He created a largely mail-order label called Shasta that both repackaged old recordings of his and his contemporaries and featured new recordings of his old saddle pals Eddie Dean and Johnny Bond and the like. As did Tex Ritter, he became one of the country's foremost advocates of the singing-cowboy genre, and he gave generously of his time and energy to keep the sound alive. Wakely continued to work actively with his family band, although his health, occasionally frail, began to fail him. A lifelong smoker, he died of complications of emphysema on September 23, 1982.

The immediate postwar era brought a starring role at last to Cal Shrum. Born in Mountain Home, Arkansas, on July 4, 1910, Shrum moved to Colorado in 1919; he and musical brother Walt—who was also a hayseed comedian—eventually made dozens of films both together and separately. Cal had appeared in musical support roles in films as early as 1938, when he and his band, the Colorado Hillbillies, appeared in Gene Autry's *Old Barn Dance*. He split amicably with Walt, who continued with the Colorado Hillbillies, and formed his own outfit, the Rhythm Rangers, with whom he appeared in films with Tex Ritter, Johnny Mack Brown, Dave O'Brien, James Newill, and Charles Starrett. By 1944 Cal had put together a band that included Spade Cooley on fiddle, Deuce Spriggins on bass, and his wife, Alta Lee, on vocals, and he was cast as the singing star of *Swing, Cowboy, Swing* (Wells-Shrum Productions/Westernair Pictures, 1946). Though a cheapie, the film could afford the affable Max Terhune as a sidekick and uber-villain I. Stanford Jolley. Music was provided by Shrum's Rhythm Wranglers and brother Walt's Colorado Hillbillies. This film was re-released by Astor in 1949 as *Bad Man from Big Bend,* a move that led to a second starring feature, *Trouble at Melody Mesa,* which had been filmed along with *Swing, Cowboy, Swing* and likewise not released until July 1949. Shrum claimed in his autobiography that he starred in six more films for Three Crown productions after 1948, but their existence is suspect. He died of a sudden heart attack on March 11, 1996, in Springfield, Illinois.

Some singing cowboys never became heroes on-screen but nevertheless had quietly influential careers. Wesley Tuttle began appearing with Jimmy Wakely in his early Monogram years, and though Tuttle never starred in films, he had a long career in and out of cowboy music; while firmly associated with it, he also made hit country records. Born in Lamar, Colorado, on December 30, 1917, Tuttle grew up in the San Fernando Valley. He became starstruck by the Beverly Hillbillies and began hanging around their broadcasts as a teenager. He soon became part of the band, where his powerful voice, fine yodeling, gift for harmony, and strong rhythm-guitar playing were major assets. He was briefly a member of the Sons of the Pioneers, and he played for Stuart Hamblen as well, before starting a solo career at WLW in Cincinnati. He then retreated from those frigid Ohio winters back to California.

Tuttle became the second country artist—after Tex Ritter—signed by the new Capitol label, and his second release, "With Tears in My Eyes," topped the charts for four weeks in 1945. He had three Top Ten records in

Johnny Bond & His Red River Valley Boys—*left to right,* Jimmy Dean, Wesley Tuttle, Paul Sells, and Bond—serenade Fuzzy Knight and Tex Ritter in *Arizona Trail* (1943). (Author's collection)

1946—"I Wish I Had Never Met Sunshine," "Tho' I Tried (I Can't Forget You)," and "Detour"—and after that recorded steadily for Capitol and Coral but produced no more hits.[4] Though Tuttle's stage repertoire was laced with western music, and he looked every inch the cowboy, his recorded output and his successful records were straight-ahead West Coast country. He and his wife, former Sunshine Girl Marilyn Myers, became fixtures of Los Angeles television on *Town Hall Party, Ranch Party, Hometown Jamboree,* and *The Foreman Phillips Show* in the fifties.

But increasingly the West Coast music scene became dances and nightclubs, not theaters, and with the coming of rock & roll Tuttle left his career as a country singer with cowboy style and entered the ministry. He and Marilyn recorded a fair bit of religious material from that point on, toured churches for a number of years, raised their children, and retired. Today the genial couple is a welcome fixture at western music gatherings. Merle Travis once remarked of the tall and powerfully built Tuttle: "I don't believe anybody could ride a horse better than big Wesley Tuttle in those days."[5] Although a hand damaged in a childhood accident was doubtless a factor in keeping Tuttle from starring roles, it is a little surprising that he was never tried as a series lead. But such are the mysteries of the world of the singing cowboy.

With his lanky, gangly frame and his dry, self-deprecating humor, Johnny Bond was friend, band mate, and business partner to Autry, Wakely, and Ritter and contributed substantially to western music's sound and style. Not only was he an active participant in film, radio, recording, television, and stage work during western music's heyday, but in his later years he became one of its first historians. Bond was in the planning stages of a book that was to cover much of the territory this volume addresses when he was felled by a stroke; he died June 22, 1978.

Bond wrote "Cimarron" in 1938; it was the first of hundreds of compositions. Although many of them were western, the most popular were country love songs, including "Tomorrow Never Comes," "Gone and Left Me Blues," and "I Wonder Where You Are Tonight." After Jimmy Wakely left *Melody Ranch* to pursue his own career, Johnny Bond remained, providing instantly recognizable guitar runs that became an Autry trademark. He continued to perform on *Melody Ranch* in a trio with Jimmy and Eddie Dean, and he was elevated to singing sidekick when the Cass County Boys were brought in as a permanent replacement trio. Bond's dry byplay with Autry became one of the delightful features of the show. In addition Bond continued to record for Columbia—on his own and on all Autry's records— and appeared in many films as a bit player and musician with Wakely and others.

In the 1950s Bond and Tex Ritter cohosted the extremely popular *Town Hall Party* on Los Angeles television, and while the emphasis of the show was decidedly country music, Bond and Ritter kept the cowboy image alive in those years of tumultuous change in the music business. Bond also went into music publishing with Ritter, and in the 1970s he began writing his recollections of his Autry years (titled *Champion* and still unpublished), biographies of Tex Ritter and Jimmie Rodgers, and his brief autobiography, *Reflections*. A western preservationist like Wakely and Ritter, Johnny Bond left a rich legacy for the historians who followed, all of whom remain deeply in his debt.

Eddie Dean snagged his first starring roles in 1945, after toiling for years in bit parts for half a dozen studios. Born Edgar Dean Glosup in Posey, Texas, on July 9, 1907, he was the seventh son of a seventh son. His exceptional voice became evident from his early years, and he initially set out to become a gospel singer, moving to Chicago in 1926, intent on pursuing a career. He appeared on radio stations in Shenandoah, Iowa, and Yankton, South Dakota, before he and his older brother, Jimmy (who went by the stage name of Jimmy Dean, not to be confused with the country singer and sausage magnate), joined the cast of the *National Barn Dance* from 1933 through 1936. Jimmy (August 31, 1903–February 7, 1970) frequently appeared and recorded with his brother and was an early member of Foy

Willing's Riders of the Purple Sage. He retired from the music business after World War II and spent the remainder of his career working at Lockheed.

As for Eddie Dean, he won the role of Larry Burton on the radio soap opera *Modern Cinderella* and acted and sang in that series for a year. "When the show left the air, I had to go somewhere, so I flipped a coin to see whether it would be New York or Hollywood. The man who wrote the radio show wanted me to go to New York and get into musical comedy. Well, I couldn't see myself doing that, but anyway I flipped a coin and it came up heads so I went to Hollywood. Mainly, I wanted to get into radio as a singer."[6] He spent the better part of a year appearing in clubs and looking for work. By 1938 he began a string of small appearances in Republic films, which led to singing roles in the Hopalong Cassidy films at Paramount, much like Ray Whitley's roles at RKO. Eddie and his brother Jimmy joined Johnny Bond as Autry's backup trio on *Melody Ranch* in 1942; they were replaced by the Cass County Boys when Eddie landed a spot as featured singer on Judy Canova's radio show. In addition, Eddie began recording in Los Angeles in 1941 and 1942, cutting his own songs—among them, "On the Banks of the Sunny San Juan" and "Where the Silvery Colorado Wends Its Way"—and covering many of Gene Autry's then current hits, including "Back in the Saddle Again." He would, through the years, record extensively for Decca, Capitol, Majestic, Mercury, Crystal, Sage and Sand, and Jimmy Wakely's Shasta label.

Dean ascribed his entry into starring roles largely to luck. He recalled a chance meeting—through Pete Canova, Judy's brother and manager—with film inventor Bill Crespinell, who had come up with an inexpensive though complicated color film process, a rival to the expensive Technicolor process:

> What they had to do, they had to run two films through at the same time . . . so you had one a sort of grey-blue and the other a sort of orange, and through that process they got this beautiful color, called it Cinecolor. . . . [Canova and I] went to Monogram, and Monogram turned us down. And then we went out to PRC, and PRC took the series. . . . I [had run into Bob Tansey at a Judy Canova rehearsal] and I said, "You're just the guy I'm looking for!" He said "What have you got?" I said, "Well, I want to do a series of pictures!" He says, "Come on now, Eddie, you know I've been trying to sell you out here for five years. They just won't buy you." I said, "They're going to buy me now!" He says, "Why?" I said, "Well, I've got a color process." "You have? Well come on in! Let's talk about it!"[7]

The color process, and a strong appearance in Ken Maynard's final picture, *Harmony Trail* (Astor, 1944; re-released as *The White Stallion,* with Eddie given top billing, in 1947), led producer Bob Tansey and the executives at the cheapie PRC studios to give Eddie Dean a chance at a starring series. With *Song of Old Wyoming* (1945), he began a series of eighteen west-

Part of the sidekick's job description is to cast admiring glances at the star when he sings. Here, Roscoe Ates fulfills that duty with Eddie Dean. (Author's collection)

erns for PRC, ending with *The Tioga Kid* in 1948. Only the first four were shot in Cinecolor; although the color was lovely, its complexity never allowed it to threaten Technicolor.

Eddie Dean on-screen was tall, handsome, and broad-shouldered, though slender. A good rider who appeared capable in the fight scenes, he never seemed to fully relax as an actor in the comfortable way Gene Autry learned to. Nonetheless, he had a good run as a singing cowboy. "I got started a little late . . . as far as what you call the picture cowboy, 'cause I only had three years. But I made the top ten moneymakers their first year! For the next three years I was in the top ten moneymakers. That was '46, '47, and '48."[8] What every critic agreed on was the quality of his voice. Dean could sing intimately and with feeling, and he had operatic range and power. Despite all these gifts, times were changing for singing cowboys, and Eagle-Lion (J. Arthur Rank's studio, which had bought out unstable PRC) let the series drop in 1948.

Dean was a gifted songwriter, having composed or co-composed many of the songs in his films, and he went on to co-write two huge country hits. These, ironically, were major records not for him but for his fellow singing cowboys: "One Has My Name, the Other Has My Heart" for Jimmy Wakely in 1948, and "I Dreamed of a Hill-Billy Heaven" for Tex Ritter in 1961. Dean continued a performing career with typical ups and downs. He was even managed for a time by Colonel Tom Parker, who dressed him in gold lamé and called him "the Golden Cowboy," predating Elvis Presley's similar costume by some years. As he continued to perform in clubs well into his seventies, his voice seemed scarcely touched by time. Dean was a graphic artist as well, and throughout his career spent countless hours in his home studio drawing, painting, making jewelry and stone work, and crafting golf clubs and guitars. This delightful man finally succumbed to the effects of emphysema on March 4, 1999, at the age of ninety-one. He was immortalized in Jack Kerouac's beat bible *On the Road:* "I rode and sang with Eddie Dean and shot up the rustlers innumerable times."[9]

Eddie Dean's sidekick—every hero had one or even two—was frequently Soapy Jones, played by jittery, rubber-faced Roscoe Ates. Many actors plucked from the local pool to play western sidekicks were musical; they had come up through medicine shows or vaudeville as singers, musicians,

Eddie Dean *(center, black hat)* sings while Roscoe Ates blows a jug. Around them are Andy Parker & the Plainsmen. *From left:* Charlie Morgan, George Bamby, Clem Smith, Joaquin Murphey, and Andy Parker. (Country Music Hall of Fame collections)

Ray Whitley, *left*, and Lee "Lasses" White pay close attention to Tim Holt. (Author's collection)

comedians, or acrobats. Ates, who sang frequently in Dean's films though his voice was not especially melodious, was no exception. He was born in Mississippi in 1892 and moved from vaudeville to silent films and into soundies. He sidekicked for Tex Ritter, Tom Keene, Gene Autry, Roy Rogers, and George O'Brien and worked in films until 1961. He died March 1, 1962.

The epitome of the musical western sidekick was Smiley Burnette— multi-instrumentalist, songwriter, recording artist, and film, radio, and television performer. He began as a musician but developed a bumbling stage and screen character called Frog Millhouse made famous in the Gene Autry films, a persona he carried right up through his role as Charlie the railroad engineer on the CBS-TV series *Petticoat Junction*. His partner in the cab of the Hooterville Cannonball was Floyd the engineer, played by Rufe Davis. Born Rufus Davidson in Oklahoma on December 2, 1914, Davis took over the role of Lullaby, the musical comedic sidekick of the Three Mesquiteers in 1940; a former vaudevillian, he had been a member of the *National Barn Dance* and first appeared in films in 1937. He died December 13, 1974.

Rufe Davis had taken the role of Lullaby relinquished by Max Terhune (1891–1973), another former *National Barn Dance* member who was a musician and singer as well, though Terhune was best known as a comedian and ventriloquist. Terhune left Republic unhappily, another instance of a falling-out over salary with the tightfisted Yates. He made twenty-one films as a Mesquiteer and essentially reprised the role, right along with his dummy Elmer, as Alibi in twenty-four Range Buster films at Monogram.

Although Chill Wills (1902–1978) was not primarily known as a singer or musician, it was with the Avalon Boys that he broke into films in a couple of Hopalong Cassidy vehicles—*Bar 20 Rides Again* (Paramount, 1935) and *Call of the Prairie* (Paramount, 1936)—and in Laurel and Hardy's immortal *Way Out West* (MGM, 1937) before becoming a celebrated character actor. On a lesser scale, ex–medicine show comic and singer Arkansas Slim Andrews made films and toured with Tex Ritter and also appeared in films with nonsingers Tom Keene, Clayton Moore, and Don "Red" Barry.

Two singing sidekicks stood above the rest: John Forrest "Fuzzy" Knight, and Lee "Lasses" White. Knight was born May 9, 1901, in Fairmont, West Virginia, and worked his way up through minstrel shows to vaudeville and musical comedies. A law student at the University of West Virginia, he was a musician, singer, and bandleader before he started in movies. Though talented, he was not leading-man handsome, and he turned to comedy, appearing on Broadway before heading to Hollywood to appear in *She Done Him Wrong* (1933) with Mae West. His finest hour was singing the title song in the A picture *Trail of the Lonesome Pine* (1936), in which he played a singing mountaineer. He became firmly entrenched as a lovable sidekick beginning in Kermit Maynard films and went on, through the years, to appear with Bob Baker, Jack Randall, Johnny Mack Brown (twenty-eight films at Universal), Tex Ritter, Russell Hayden, Rod Cameron, Eddie Dew, Kirby Grant, Whip Wilson, and finally Bill Elliott. He is remembered on television as Buster Crabbe's sidekick on *The Adventures of Captain Gallant,* and he worked well into the 1960s. Fuzzy Knight died February 23, 1976.

Lee "Lasses" White was born in Wills Point, Texas, on August 28, 1888, and spent twenty years in tent shows, vaudeville, and radio before he ever made a movie. He came up through blackface comedy as a member of the Lasses & Honey duo on the Grand Ole Opry and broke into films in 1938. He became Tim Holt's sidekick in 1941, then joined Jimmy Wakely for a dozen films at Monogram in 1944 through 1947. Lasses toured with Wakely as well and in addition wrote fine western songs, including "Casting My Lasso to the Sky." He died December 16, 1949.

Musical sidekicks Shug Fisher and Pat Brady also spent time as members of the Sons of the Pioneers. George Clinton Fisher was born in Chickasha, Oklahoma, on September 26, 1907, and was profoundly affected by a tent show comedian; the performer's life called to him from then on. He migrated to California in 1925, was appearing in Los Angeles by 1931, and joined the San Francisco version of the Beverly Hillbillies in 1933. He toured with Roy Faulkner—"the Lonesome Cowboy" of Dr. Brinkley's infamous border station XER—and then began recording, appearing on radio, and touring with hillbilly singer Hugh Cross (who had recorded "Red River

Valley" with blind country blues guitarist Riley Puckett for Columbia in 1927) at WWVA in Wheeling and WLW in Cincinnati. Fisher joined the Sons of the Pioneers as bassist and comedian when Pat Brady left for the service during the war. He rejoined the Pioneers in 1949 when Brady took over as Roy Rogers's sidekick in films and on television, left again in 1953, and did another stint from 1955 to 1959. Often associated with Ken Curtis on various film and television projects, the stuttering, poker-faced Fisher landed the role of Shorty Kellums on nineteen episodes of the popular *Beverly Hillbillies* television series and worked occasionally until his death on March 16, 1984.

Pat Brady was born Robert Ellsworth O'Brady in Toledo, Ohio, in 1914 to a vaudeville family—his father, John, was a dancer and comedian, his mother, Lucille, a dancer and singer—and he began performing at the age of four. He befriended the Sons of the Pioneers during their nascent years in Southern California, and when Len Slye left the group, Brady was chosen to replace him, for he had a good voice, could play the bass, and could handle the comedic load of the act that Slye had carried. Because the Pioneers already had a Bob in the group—Bob Nolan—Robert Brady was christened Pat Brady. His voice, though solid, did not blend well in the trio, and upon the hiring of Lloyd Perryman and the return of Tim Spencer, Brady's singing was limited to the score of brilliant novelty numbers written for him by Nolan and Spencer, songs like "No Good Son of a Gun," "Graveyard Filler of the West," "Come and Get It," and "Biscuit Blues," which he performed with unforgettable élan, his rubberized body a joy to behold. He and Perryman left the Pioneers to serve overseas during the war years. Brady returned to the outfit and remained until 1949, when he took over the side-kick role in Roy Rogers's final five films of that year, and on the Roy Rogers television show until 1957. He rejoined the Sons of the Pioneers in 1959, leaving in 1967 to operate a guest ranch near Colorado Springs, Colorado, where he died February 27, 1972.

It was also during the war years that Monte Hale began to work his way up through the ranks; he eventually gained his own series directly after the war. Born in Ada, Oklahoma, on June 8, 1919, he was raised in San Angelo, Texas, and became a professional singer at the age of twelve. Discovered on a USO tour in 1944 by Phil Isley, father of screen actress Jennifer Jones, Hale was brought to the attention of Herbert Yates, who may have envisioned him as a fallback should Roy Rogers press for a better contract, just as Yates had developed Rogers as a fallback in case of contract squabbles with Autry. For whatever reason, Republic felt it could once again make money with two singing cowboys; even a decade after the sensation had begun, the studio felt there was enough life left in the genre to continue to develop new performers. Evidently the studio just did not see the end coming.

Monte Hale was given the chance to practice his craft in small roles in

Monte Hale serenades his horse, Pardner, during Hale's Republic years. (Author's collection)

such films as *Steppin' in Society* and *The Big Bonanza* in 1945, in a couple of westerns supporting Sunset Carson and in a couple supporting Bill Elliott, and in the serial *The Purple Monster Strikes*. With Roy Rogers moving into big color westerns in 1946, Hale starred in *Home on the Range* (1946), supported by the Sons of the Pioneers—the first of his nineteen starring roles. Despite his fresh face, fine voice, and powerful physique, despite the studio buildup and the presence of the Sons of the Pioneers and the vivid Magnacolor cinematography, the film was not a moneymaker. Neither was its follow-up, *Man from Rainbow Valley,* in which Hale was supported by Foy Willing & the Riders of the Purple Sage.

Hale's 1947 films fared better, but his second film in 1948, *The Timber Trail,* was to be his last in color (Magnacolor had become Trucolor by then), and as Hale was creating no great excitement as a singing cowboy, the music was cut way back as well. Black-and-white films could be produced far more quickly, and several more were ground out in 1948 and 1949, ending with *The Vanishing Westerner* in 1950. "When they started shooting them in black and white I knew it was just about over."[10]

Although he was no longer under contract to Republic, Hale still had enough star power to get called back to make a guest appearance with a number of other western all-stars in Roy Rogers's *Trail of Robin Hood* in 1950. This was Hale's last screen appearance as a singing cowboy. He had started at Republic at $150 a week and ended his career with the studio at $300 a week. Hale had a small role as a bad guy in *Yukon Vengeance* (Allied Artists, 1954) and played the role of a rancher, Bale Cinch, in *Giant* (Warner Bros., 1956), a film that also featured Ray Whitley's last screen appearance. Hale did some television and had a couple of small film roles in the decades that followed, but he was not really active as an actor.

He did continue a singing career for a time, recording a number of pleasant sides for MGM in a style that was part country, part western swing, not atypical of the era. His voice was a supple Autryesque baritone, but none of the sides became hits. Hale and Ray Whitley toured extensively together in the early 1950s, often appearing in conjunction with screenings of their movies (Whitley's by this time were a decade or more old, but this mattered little—the two concentrated on small towns where they were still

Monte Hale claimed he made more from comic book royalties than he ever did as an actor. (Author's collection)

Ken Curtis *(in the hat)* with the Hoosier Hot Shots in *Song of the Prairie* (1945). (Author's collection)

movie stars). Like many movie cowboys of the era, Hale also had a series of comic books, which Fawcett published from 1950 to 1955, and he remarked with some irony that over time he made far more money from these comics than he ever did as an actor. Hale became active in real estate and joined the small circle of Gene Autry's close friends; in fact he relates that it was he who suggested that Autry, an inveterate collector of western memorabilia, create a museum to display his treasures. This suggestion became the basis for the superb Autry Museum of Western Heritage that now graces Griffith Park in Los Angeles. Hale's wife, Joanne, was executive director of the multi-million-dollar facility for the first fifteen years of its existence.

Monte Hale, now an octogenarian, remains gracious and genial, the epitome of a western gentleman. With a hearty laugh, he passes out stickers that read, "Shoot low! They may be crawlin'," commemorating what he fondly recalls as one of the most ludicrous lines of dialogue he was made to speak in his career. Unpretentious and unaffected by his film career, he says simply: "I always said I was born to plow. That's why, as I said before, I was lucky. When I was making those movies I felt like I was blessed by the Lord."[11]

"Western gentleman" also aptly describes Ken Curtis, whose long ca-

Ken Curtis, later better known as Festus of TV's *Gunsmoke*, in his singing-cowboy days. (Author's collection)

reer was a study in reinvention: from pop singer to cowboy star to character actor to film producer to television action star to beloved sidekick Festus Haggan on *Gunsmoke*.

Curtis was born Curtis Wain Gates on July 2, 1916, near Lamar in the plains of southeastern Colorado, the youngest son of a rancher and farmer who became sheriff of Las Animas when Ken was around twelve. Both parents were musical (his father, Daniel, a fiddler; his mother, Nellie, an organist), and young Curtis became a vocalist and saxophonist in high school before attending Colorado College. Short on neither ambition nor talent, young Curtis Gates made his way to New York, where a series of breaks landed him a job with the Tommy Dorsey orchestra, after Frank Sinatra had turned in his notice. It was Dorsey who suggested he become Ken Curtis, and under his new name he cut at least one session with the Dorsey orchestra ("Love Sends a Little Gift of Roses" and "The Anniversary Waltz"). Curtis also recorded and performed with Shep Fields's popular orchestra. His ascent as a pop singer was interrupted by World War II, and he enlisted in June 1942, serving a frustrating couple of years: "I trained the entire time and they kept breaking up outfits and transferring me . . . there was nothing distinguished about it for sure."[12] Upon his release Ken drifted westward, and he was soon on radio once again. A chance opportunity to sing "Tumbling Tumbleweeds" with Johnny Mercer and the Pied Pipers on Jo Stafford's radio show brought him to the attention of Columbia pictures, and he was signed up to become their newest singing cowboy.

Music had played a significant role in many of the films in the Charles Starrett series at Columbia, and the success of one, *Cowboy Canteen* (1944), decided Columbia on trying a series that leaned more toward music than toward action. *Cowboy Canteen* had been a kind of musical vaudeville of almost nonstop performances with a western theme, and Ken Curtis starred in a series of such films beginning with *Rhythm Round-Up* in 1945. Among the many singers and groups featured were the Hoosier Hot Shots, Foy Willing & the Riders of the Purple Sage, Carolina Cotton, the DeCastro Sisters, Bob Wills & His Texas Playboys, the Dinning Sisters, and Merle Travis. These pleasant musical vehicles gave Curtis a little time for horsemanship, gun twirling, and fisticuffs, but the emphasis was music until the final entry in the series, *Over the Santa Fe Trail* (1947), which was less a musical jamboree and more an action western.

In 1947 Gene Autry broke with Republic, formed his own filmmaking corporation, and moved over to Columbia. With the Autry star power and emphasis on music, and with music still a part of the Starrett westerns, Columbia had no room for another singing cowboy. Though Ken Curtis was a fine actor and singer, and a capable action hero and rider, his contract was not picked up. He starred in two independent westerns, *Riders of the Pony Express* (Kayson/Screencraft, 1949) and *Stallion Canyon* (Astor, 1949), the latter reuniting him with singing cowgirl and yodeler deluxe Carolina Cotton. He also appeared in a supporting role in *Call of the Forest* (Lippert, 1949).

It was at about this time that Tim Spencer retired from the Sons of the Pioneers, and Ken Curtis was asked to join the trio in his place. This trio (Bob Nolan, Lloyd Perryman, and Curtis) made some of the most extraordinary of the Pioneers' recordings, although Bob Nolan was soon replaced by Tommy Doss. With the Sons of the Pioneers, Curtis appeared in several John Ford movies, including *Wagonmaster,* and most notably in *Rio Grande* (Republic, 1950), wherein Ken and the rest of the Regimental Singers (the Sons of the Pioneers plus Stan Jones) sing "I'll Take You Home Again, Kathleen" to Maureen O'Hara. Curtis went on to appear in featured roles in a number of other classic westerns, such as *The Searchers* (Warner Bros., 1956); as Captain Dickinson in *The Alamo* (United Artists, 1960); in unflattering roles in John Ford's revisionist westerns *Two Rode Together* (Columbia, 1961) and *Cheyenne Autumn* (Warner Bros., 1964); and in nonwesterns like *Mr. Roberts* and *The Quiet Man.*

Curtis spent 1948 through 1953 with the Sons of the Pioneers (and recorded with them through 1957) and appeared on the Pioneers' daily radio show, *The Lucky U Ranch,* which he took over as a solo artist after he left the group. He also starred in a nonsinging role in one of Republic's last serials, *Don Daredevil Rides Again,* in 1951.

After leaving the Pioneers, Curtis concentrated on his acting career once again, reborn as a character actor in and out of cowboy clothes, and even produced and appeared in three ultra-low-budget cheapies filmed in Dallas: *The Killer Shrews* (which famously featured poorly disguised dogs in the title roles), *My Dog Buddy,* and *The Giant Gila Monster.* In 1961 and 1962 he starred in the nonwestern TV series *Ripcord* and did a wide variety of parts in any number of television shows, often westerns like *Have Gun, Will Travel* and *How the West Was Won.* He was, for a time, very much a part of John Ford's stock company—as Ford's son-in-law he had an inside track, and he often appeared with veteran western character actors Ben Johnson, Ward Bond, and Harry Carey Jr.

Carey (born May 16, 1921) was the son of silent film star Harry Carey. He tried to break into show business as a singer and sang a bit in several films—most notably in his first starring role as one of the *Three Godfathers* (Argosy-MGM, 1948). But though his career was long and his voice fine, he never sang more than a snatch or two of a song in any given film, and he never had anything remotely close to a singing-cowboy role. He, Ben Johnson, Stan Jones, and Ken Curtis apparently did a fair bit of harmonizing on desert locations while making several of these Ford films, though it was all just for recreation and pastime—perhaps it was an extension of the way the cowboys they portrayed on the screen might have whiled away the empty hours in similar remote and lonely locations many decades before. The campfire music of these participating players never made it to record or screen.

Curtis had developed a slow-talking hillbilly character called Dink Swink, "from down at the crossroads," on the *Lucky U* radio shows. (There is actually a tiny community called Swink near Las Animas, Colorado, and Curtis wrote at least five songs used in the Columbia films with Dink Rogers.) This character was called Monk on *Have Gun, Will Travel* and transmogrified into Festus Haggen when Dennis Weaver left *Gunsmoke* in 1964. Curtis is best remembered for this role, which lasted twelve years. Although Festus sang occasionally on *Gunsmoke* in the early years, few who remember the series would imagine that the grizzled old codger had one of the most beautiful voices in the singing-cowboy genre. Curtis continued to take occasional television and film roles after *Gunsmoke* left the air in 1975, appearing at fairs and rodeos all over the country. He died in his sleep on April 28, 1991, at his home in Fresno, California.

Curtis's occasional singing costar was Carolina Cotton, and although women singers had been featured in cowboy films for years, few besides Dale Evans brought such spunk and fire to the screen as Cotton, with her twinkling eyes, curly blonde hair, and superb yodeling ability. She was born Helen Hagstrom in Cash, Arkansas, on October 20, 1925. Like many Depression-era Okies and Arkies, the Hagstroms headed for a better life in California, where young Helen studied dancing. She landed a singing job

Carolina Cotton appeared in several musical westerns during the 1940s and early 1950s. (Author's collection)

with Dude Martin on KYA in San Francisco, where Martin created her memorable stage name, and then a chance meeting with Johnny Marvin at a costume fitting in Hollywood led to an audition at Republic, where she landed a small yodeling role in a Roy Acuff film, *Sing Neighbor Sing* (1944). After two more films in 1944 she was signed by Columbia, where she appeared in Charles Starrett's *Texas Panhandle* and *Outlaws of the Rockies* in 1945, in five Ken Curtis films for Columbia in 1946, in two Gene Autry films for Columbia in 1952 (*Apache Country* and *Blue Canadian Rockies,* her final film), in one of Roy Acuff's and both of Eddy Arnold's Columbia films, and in a final Starrett film, *The Rough Tough West* (Columbia, 1952), in which she moved up from featured singer to costar.

Carolina Cotton also found time to record telescriptions or soundies—the forerunner of today's music videos—with Bob Wills & His Texas Playboys for Snader in the early 1950s and with her husband, Deuce Spriggins. She toured extensively with Wills, the Sons of the Pioneers, Spade Cooley, and Eddy Arnold and appeared frequently on the *Hollywood Barn Dance.* Her recording career was not extensive, but she cut sessions for Mercury, King, Crystal, and Mastertown and was with MGM from 1950 to 1952, recording several sides on her own as well as some with Bob Wills. As her performing career wound down, she became increasingly interested in education and raising her family. Inspired by her sister, she wound up attending San Francisco City College and San Francisco State, where she eventually earned a master's degree in education. She taught in Bakersfield, California, and in Central America until months before her death, of cancer, on June 10, 1997.

Three of the finest organizations to appear in films—Foy Willing & the Riders of the Purple Sage, the Cass County Boys, and Andy Parker & the Plainsmen—also came to the screen during the war years. The Sons of the Pioneers had proved to be a major asset, first to the Starrett and then to the Rogers films; the Pioneers sang beautifully and did comedy, and Bob Nolan was a handsome and effective second lead. The notion of singing trail hands was far from new, but other studios saw the need to develop and use western harmony groups in a consistent manner, rather than simply recruiting one or another locally popular singer or group as Autry tended to do. The war years saw the creation and development of three of the best of these.

The vivid title of Zane Grey's most popular western novel, *Riders of the Purple Sage,* was an obvious choice for the name of a western band—so obvious, in fact, that at least three separate Riders of the Purple Sage bands appeared in the early years of western music. The conflicting claims of the many musicians who passed through them—most now long dead—make unraveling the tangled skein of their history a daunting challenge. A band by that name made radio appearances as early as 1933 in the Los Angeles area, and guitarist, singer, and trick roper Jack Dalton made the trek over to Catalina Island to secure legal permission from Zane Grey himself to use the name. Dalton—who died young in an auto accident—had this group up and running for the opening of border station XEBC in Tijuana; among the early members were accordionist Hi Busse, later of the Frontiersmen. Dalton's Riders of the Purple Sage did well on radio at KFI in Los Angeles, but things crumbled when they went on tour. Musicians came and went, Dalton among them—reputedly fired from his own group for chronic inebriation—and the short-term members included young Tumble Weed, later to become Bob Baker. Though they had a splashy start, the group appears to have existed only from about July 1933 through June 1934.

Meanwhile, a Pennsylvania guitarist and singer named Don Duffy (born June 18, 1922, in Pittsburgh) had the same inspiration on the East Coast. Going professionally by the rugged name of Buck Page, he and his brother Bob brought the Riders of the Purple Sage to prominence first over KDKA in Pittsburgh in 1936, then in the thriving New York music scene in 1939, where they appeared on the WOR *Village Barn Dance* and had a Mutual radio network show. Jimmy Wakely later claimed to have put together an organization called Riders of the Purple Sage in 1944, by which time the *Hollywood Barn Dance* had gone network, recruiting Jimmy Dean from the Autry organization. Tex Atchison also claimed to have had a hand in putting this band together, and indeed he, Al Sloey, and Foy Willing appeared as a trio (billed only as "singing cowboys") in a Charles Starrett film, *Cowboy in the Clouds* (Columbia), filmed in 1943 and released in 1944.

At about this time, singer, songwriter, and guitarist Foy Willing (born Foy Willingham in Bosque County, Texas, in 1915) stepped into the picture. Buck Page claimed in one interview that he turned over the reins of his Riders to Willing when he went into the service: "When I left I thought I was going to get my rear end shot off, so I turned the group over to Foy."[13] In another interview he tells an entirely different story: "When I got out in 1945 I found that there was a group in Los Angeles also known as the Riders of the Purple Sage. I had hoped I could join up with them, but they didn't need a guitarist."[14] However it happened, Foy Willing got control of the West Coast group, which by this time included Iowa-born tenor Al Sloey (1912–1975) and ever busy bassist and harmony singer Jimmy Dean. Joining the group later would be sensational jazz fiddler Johnny Paul (John Paul Gerardi), clarinetists Neely Plumb and Darol Rice, accordionists Bud Sievert and Fred Traveras, rhythm guitarist Jerry Vaughn, vocalist Dale Warren, and tenors/bassists Dick Reinhart and Scotty Harrell.

At this juncture, the major fan magazine of the day, the *Mountain Broadcast and Prairie Recorder,* ran prominent photo ads at the back of at least two 1940 issues featuring a group called the Sons of the Purple Sage endorsing Gretsch Guitars; clearly this is Buck Page's outfit. Page claims NBC made them change the name for broadcast use, fearing a lawsuit from the Zane Grey estate. A column in a 1944 issue of the same magazine remarks: "A brand new band out of Hollywood, Foy Willing and the Riders of the Purple Sage, was organized by Jimmy Wakely to appear with him in the Starrett pictures at Columbia. Then it was the Foy Willing Trio. Now since Jimmy has signed to star, they've trailed out on their own and I'd say they're definitely on their way up."[15]

It was this group led by Foy Willing, beginning in 1944, that made an impact in the movies, appearing first in films like *Saddle Serenade* (Monogram, 1945) with Jimmy Wakely and *Throw a Saddle on a Star* (Columbia,

Buck Page's Riders of the Purple Sage. *From top:* Buck Page, Hal McCoy, Bob Parker, and Kenny Cooper). (Author's collection)

1946), one of Ken Curtis's musical extravaganzas. The Sons of the Pioneers had supported Monte Hale in his first film, *Home on the Range* (Republic, 1946); Republic then signed Foy and the boys, who became Hale's musical support and trail hands for the course of several films. In 1948 they moved up to the Roy Rogers series. According to Willing, it was simple economics that caused them to replace the Sons of the Pioneers in the Rogers westerns: "There were six of them and they had no wardrobe [coordinated for TruColor films] around them. And besides that, they were making two thousand more a picture than we were, and their option was coming up which raised them another two thousand. It was cheaper for [Yates] . . . that's all."[16] It simply cost far less to use the four Riders (by this time Willing, Sloey, Harrell, and Paul) than the six Pioneers, so the decision was in perfect character for Herbert Yates.

Foy Willing got his show business start singing with a gospel group, though he had been profoundly influenced as a teen by the music of Carson Robison and the folk music of Bradley Kincaid, Doc Hopkins, and Hugh Cross, whom he heard over his crystal radio set from Chicago. He then sang with the Three Tall Texans in Nebraska and Ohio before heading for New York to appear on the Crazy Waters Crystals show, replacing Carson J. Robison. "In those days I did mostly folk songs . . . very few real solid so-called western songs. . . . Oh, I did 'Little Joe, the Wrangler,' but the big songs were the mountain songs."[17]

Willing returned to Texas to learn the fundamentals of radio, hoping to become an executive and owner, and worked in that field until the early 1940s, though he never stopped performing on the air as a folk singer and announcer. He was contacted in 1943 by Cottonseed Clark, who was putting together the *Hollywood Barn Dance,* which included Paul Sells (Gene Autry's accordionist) to lead the small orchestra and featured the talents of Johnny Bond, Colleen Summers (later Mary Ford), the Sunshine Girls trio, Kirby Grant, and later Ken Curtis. (Grant was a singer and bandleader who had a long career as a B-western hero, but who, for whatever reasons, never sang in his pictures; a later generation remembers him as the avuncular Sky King of television fame.) Foy Willing had a lovely baritone voice and was a gifted songwriter, and the trio was excellent, with an airier sound than the Pioneers'; all were excellent soloists as well. As western actors they were never fully convincing, for they looked like just what they were, somewhat sedentary musicians. As musicians, however, they were a delight, recording western and pop-country sides for Capitol, Majestic, and other labels, and doing a superb series of transcriptions for Teleways. Their harmony remained pristine, and at least one of Willing's many fine songs, "No One to Cry To," became a standard.

Roy Rogers went with a new group in 1951, first called the Roy Rogers Riders, and from this point on the Riders of the Purple Sage (humorously referred to as the Riders of the Sunset Bus by several contemporaries) drifted in and out of show business. Willing disbanded the group in 1952 and went back to his early love, radio. He managed a number of radio stations for many years and recorded a pop-country album in the early 1960s. He re-formed the band from time to time for tours, and they continued to record as Foy Willing & the Riders of the Purple Sage into the 1960s. Willing even regrouped to support Gene Autry on his final road tour in 1959, but without film or radio work, the band had no raison d'être; unlike the Pioneers, they had never made the grueling round of personal appearances, nor did they have the Pioneers' record sales and exposure. Willing made a final folk album, featuring Mary Ford, in the mid-1960s, and a partly new, partly reissued album in the 1970s on his own label. Foy Willing returned to Texas in the early 1970s and was in Nashville, planning a new recording project, when he died of a sudden heart attack on July 24, 1978.

Don Duffy (Buck Page), meanwhile, had revived the band and its name

Foy Willing's Riders of the Purple Sage. *Clockwise from bottom:* Foy Willing, Jerry Vaughn, Al Sloey, Bud Sievert, Scotty Harrell, and Johnny Paul. (Author's collection)

on his own in the early 1970s. Part-time recording-session musician (that's his guitar you hear opening *Bonanza*), film musician (he's the bassist in the *Glenn Miller Story* and other films), representative for various musical instrument firms, and horse trainer, he also began appearing in the 1970s and 1980s with a re-formed Riders of the Purple Sage, and he appears with them still. A vigorous, energetic man, he is a vivid presence at western music gatherings.

Andy Parker, of Andy Parker & the Plainsmen, was born in Mangum, Oklahoma, on March 17, 1913, and spent his early years as a singer and radio announcer in the Midwest. He came to prominence in San Francisco in 1938 as the voice of the singing cowboy on NBC's *Death Valley Days,* and he appeared on *Dude Martin's Roundup,* a popular barn dance program over KGO. Parker moved to Los Angeles in 1944, where he teamed up with bassist and baritone singer Hank Caldwell and Charlie Morgan (brother of pop singer Jaye P. Morgan) to form the Plainsmen. Their ultrasmooth and somewhat jazzy style, Parker's gifts as a songwriter, and Morgan's melodious solo voice caught the attention of Columbia, and the Plainsmen began appearing in the Ken Curtis musical westerns in 1945.

Parker was one of western music's finest songwriters, and many of his songs live on in the western music canon: "Trail Dust," "Serenade to a Coyote," "The West Is As Wild As Ever," "Throw a Saddle on a Star," and "A Calico Apron and a Gingham Gown." The Plainsmen began recording for Coast Records in 1946, augmented by fiddler Harry Simms, steel-guitar legend Joaquin Murphey, and accordionist and bass singer George Bamby (who appeared, through the years, with groups as diverse as the Sons of the Pioneers, the Spade Cooley Orchestra, and the Roy Rogers Riders/Republic Rhythm Riders). They became regulars on the *Hollywood Barn Dance* on the CBS radio network. Caldwell left the Plainsmen late that year and was replaced by baritone Paul "Clem" Smith. It was at this point that the group officially became Andy Parker & the Plainsmen, their billing when they signed to appear in eight PRC westerns with Eddie Dean in 1947. They signed with Capitol Records the same year, where they cut some of their finest records, as well as a number of excellent transcriptions of the Capitol transcription library.

Andy Parker & the Plainsmen did a good bit of television in the Los Angeles area in the early 1950s (primarily the *Leo Carillo Show*), appeared on the *Hawk Laribee* radio show on CBS, continued to record on smaller labels like Intro, and appeared in a couple of A films as well: *The Beautiful Blonde from Bashful Bend* (20th Century-Fox, 1949) with Betty Grable and Cesar Romero, and *River of No Return* (20th Century-Fox, 1954) with Marilyn Monroe and Robert Mitchum. In addition they played most of the popular night spots of that time and worked often in television and radio, but as with the Riders of the Purple Sage, it was hard to keep a band together without film work or hit records. Their Capitol contract expired in 1951; Murphey, then Bamby left the group; and when Charlie Morgan rejoined his three brothers and sister Jaye P. to form a nightclub act, Andy folded the band. The Plainsmen made their final appearance in 1957. Andy Parker died October 2, 1977, just a few years before the small but significant western music revival got off the ground. As with Tim Spencer, Bob Nolan, and others, he did not live to see their vivid, memorable songs embraced by a new generation.

The Cass County Boys formed at radio station WFAA in Dallas about 1935, where, as staff musicians, they spent time between programs harmonizing. They were first called the Early Birds, then the Cass County Kids— Cass County was the home of accordion player Fred Martin (born June 22, 1916 in Linden, Texas). The group consisted of Martin; guitarist and baritone singer Jerry Scoggins (born September 30, 1911, in Mount Pleasant, Texas); and bassist and tenor singer Bert Dodson (May 27, 1915–October 3, 1994). The Cass County Boys began recording for Bluebird in the early 1940s, but World War II sundered the band and their plans to join Gene Autry as his replacement for the Rough Riders on *Melody Ranch*. Autry did not forget them, however, and they joined the cast of *Melody Ranch* when it

Andy Parker & the Plainsmen. *Clockwise from bottom left:* Joaquin Murphey, Hank Caldwell, Andy Parker, George Bamby, and Charlie Morgan. (Author's collection)

The Cass County Boys—*from left,* Bert Dodson, Fred Martin, and Jerry Scoggins—support Carolina Cotton in *Blue Canadian Rockies* (1952). (Author's collection)

The Roy Rogers Riders—*from left,* Buddy Dooley, George Bamby, Michael Barton, Darol Rice, and Jimmy Bryant—stand behind Pat Brady, Bullet, and Rogers. (Author's collection)

The Republic Rhythm Riders with Rex Allen. (Author's collection)

returned to the air at the end of 1945, toured with the Autry road show for years to come, and appeared in Autry's final Republic films in 1946 and 1947.

The Cass County Boys were absent from the first couple of years of Autry's Columbia features (which began with *The Last Roundup* in 1947), then began appearing sporadically, first in *Rim of the Canyon* (1949). Autry's Columbia features contained plenty of music, but Autry did not consistently surround himself with harmonizing cowhands the way Roy Rogers did with the Sons of the Pioneers. In fact, reversing the formula that had made him a star at Republic, Autry's Columbia films were often set in the historical West and did not feature either regionally popular bands or a steady band of singing sidekicks like the Cass County Boys, who returned to the screen for most of the late 1952 and early 1953 releases, save the final four. The band recorded a bit, both commercially and on transcription, but did not develop a career outside of the Autry tours. As Autry moved into television and business in the late 1950s, the Cass County Boys went into businesses of their own. Scoggins, though he became a stockbroker, kept a hand in music and sang the theme song for the *Beverly Hillbillies* television show, among many other projects. At ninety his baritone is still strong, and he continues to perform at nursing homes.

The Roy Rogers Riders and the Republic Rhythm Riders were created from the ample supply of western musical talent wandering around Hollywood for the express purpose of appearing in films. The groups did not record nor, it is presumed, did they tour. (Rogers usually used the Sons of the Pioneers or the Whippoorwills on tour.) The Roy Rogers Riders were created after the Riders of the Purple Sage were not renewed at Republic; the apocryphal story circulated that an inebriated Foy Willing slowed production by being unable to remain seated on his horse. The Roy Rogers Riders, who made the final three Roy Rogers features at Republic, consisted of Pat Brady, Jimmy Bryant on guitar, George Bamby on accordion, Buddy Dooley on rhythm guitar, Michael Barton on bass, and Darol Rice on clarinet. Bamby, Dooley, and Rice were rehired to appear as the Republic Rhythm Riders in six of Rex Allen's films, augmented by bassist H. Michael Behan Jr. and fiddler Slim Duncan.

Although these years marked the beginning of the decline of the singing cowboy, many more fascinating characters came to the screen as the studios strove to bring new life to a time-tested genre that was only then beginning to tire. Tito Guizar appeared as an ultraromantic singer in two Rogers films of the postwar years: *On the Old Spanish Trail* (1947) and *The Gay Ranchero* (1948). Guizar had been in U.S. films since 1938, often in stereotypical Latin roles, as in *Brazil* (1944) and *Mexicana* (1945) for Republic, and *Blondie Goes Latin* and *The Thrill of Brazil* for other studios, and had even starred in a semi-singing cowboy feature, *The Llano Kid*, for Paramount in 1939, which featured Eddie Dean in a small singing role. Guizar had come to stardom in his native Mexico in 1936 with a film, like so many of Autry's, named for a currently popular song; *Alla En El Rancho Grande* marked the beginning of Guizar's career as the star of a series of very successful singing-*charro* films.[18]

Federico Arturo Guizar Tolentino was born April 8, 1908, in Guadalajara and, despite the objections of his upper-middle-class family, entered show business, moving to New York City at the age of twenty-one. He appeared on radio, in clubs, and even at Carnegie Hall, where his program consisted of opera before the intermission, and traditional *corridas* and *rancheras* (folk songs of the border country and ranches), sung in full charro costume, to conclude the concert. He returned to Mexico to star in *Alla En El Rancho Grande,* and the huge success of this film on both sides of the border brought him to Hollywood's attention. His first U.S. film appearance was in *The Big Broadcast of 1938.*

Guizar returned to years of concert success and film work in Mexico after bowing out of U. S. films in 1948. He composed and recorded for film and television and appeared in a regular role as a silver-haired grandfather in a Mexican television soap opera well into the 1990s. He died of the complications of old age on December 24, 1999.

The war years were tumultuous ones for the film industry in general, and the singing cowboys in particular. There was change in the air, and it was hard to spot and identify trends with everyone's attention so intensely focused on the news from overseas. When the soldiers and sailors returned, they returned as different people to a different America, and their altered perspectives led to a taste for a different kind of western, far removed from the bright, sunny, song-filled fantasies of Gene Autry and Roy Rogers.

Time was running out on the singing cowboys, though few then may have seen it, busy as they must have been in the hustle and bustle of their careers. Stars were rising and falling; films were being scheduled, shot, and released; personal appearances were as tightly scheduled as ever; radio was still a pervasive part of American life; records were being cut and released; and television, though it loomed as a threat to studios, looked like just another set of opportunities to the performers.

Still, the cracks were showing. Television was indeed a threat to film studios and film careers. Country songs about broken promises and broken hearts, not western songs about open ranges, were what customers now bought at the record stores; only one major western star, Rex Allen, was developed after this date. Indeed, World War II had drastically changed America, physically as well as spiritually. Dreamy films about the Old West and fantasy movies about a new West where telephones and convertibles mixed with six-guns and posses were no long terribly attractive to a public that had experienced four years of world war and now faced the new, pervasive threat of atomic attack.

A trend away from the dreamy, song-filled extravaganzas of the 1930s and toward a more realistic western became more evident, and this era saw

Tito Guizar *(at right)* and Jane Frazee *(at left)* singing with Andy Devine, Estelita Rodriguez, and the Sons of the Pioneers in *On the Old Spanish Trail* (1946). (Author's collection)

the release of some of the finest, most mature westerns of all time—John Ford's legendary cavalry trilogy with John Wayne: *Fort Apache* (RKO, 1948), *She Wore a Yellow Ribbon* (RKO, 1949), and *Rio Grande* (Republic, 1950). There were many others: *Red River* (United Artists, 1948), *Duel in the Sun* (Selznick, 1948), *Broken Arrow* (Fox, 1950), and *High Noon* (United Artists, 1952).

This industrywide trend extended to the singing-cowboy westerns. Roy Rogers's films changed dramatically in mid-1946 when serial director William Witney took over, creating darker, more serious westerns. Gone were the floral shirts with lavish trim and fringe, and gone were the huge musical production numbers. While Roy still sang a bit, the stories were more serious and more violent, with brutal whippings and fistfights—which Roy sometimes even lost—not uncommon. Ken Curtis's musical revues were dropped by Columbia, while songs and colorful outfits were increasingly de-emphasized in Jimmy Wakely's, Monte Hale's, and even Gene Autry's films. As always, the singing-cowboy films reflected their times, in their ways. They could not change enough, however, to save the genre.

But before the singing cowboys and their vivid characters rode into the sunset, a few final characters emerged on film. Universal had not featured music in a western since Ray Whitley bowed out of the Rod Cameron se-

How'd you like to give Jane Frazee lessons?

Tex Ritter and Jane Frazee in Columbia's western music variety show *Cowboy Canteen* (1944). (Author's collection)

ries. It tried again in 1948 with a series of musical shorts starring Red River Dave, filmed in New York. Red River Dave McEnery had made an appearance in one of the few musical westerns with a woman headliner, Jane Frazee's *Swing in the Saddle* (Columbia, 1944), and on this basis he was cast in *Hidden Valley Days* and *Echo Ranch,* both 1948 releases. He returned once again to Texas after this adventure and continued his long and colorful career as a radio singer, local television star, recording artist, rope spinner, whip artist, and songwriter.

Jane Frazee was a pop singer through and through, but her credentials as a singing cowgirl are solid. She was born Mary Jane Freshe in Duluth, Minnesota, on July 18, 1918, and began singing and dancing professionally with her sister Ruth at the age of six. The two moved to Hollywood in 1939, but where Ruth failed her screen tests, Jane became a promising young star. She began appearing in musicals in 1940, in Republic's *Moonlight and Melody.* She played costarring roles for Universal, often supporting comedians like Abbott and Costello, Olsen and Johnson, and the Ritz Brothers. Her musical western at Columbia, *Swing in the Saddle,* made her one of the very few singing cowgirls to headline a feature, but this film was much more a musical than a western.

After Roy Rogers married Dale Evans in 1946, Republic felt it unwise to pair a married couple as costars and brought in Jane Frazee for several of Rogers's 1947 and 1948 features. Although she acquitted herself well in these features, singing solos and duets with Rogers, she herself felt that it was "the beginning of the end" of her career.[19] With *Rhythm Inn* (Monogram, 1951), Frazee bowed out of feature films, although she appeared on television and played Joe McDoakes's wife in a popular series of comedy shorts until the series ended in 1956. Like Fred Scott before her, she enjoyed a very successful career as a realtor after her retirement from films. She died in Newport Beach, California, September 6, 1985.

Another new face in westerns, Elton Britt, made his feature film debut in 1948 as well, appearing in the Charles Starrett film *Laramie* (Columbia, 1949). He had played in short films as a member of the Beverly Hillbillies fifteen years earlier, but this was to be his only venture into B westerns.

And 1948 also saw the introduction of Whip Wilson, who replaced Jimmy Wakely as a star of B westerns at Monogram. His specialty was whip artistry, and although Monogram was through with singing cowboys, the studio apparently felt a little music in a series designed to emulate the surprising success of Lash LaRue at PRC would not be a bad thing. Not really a singing cowboy, Whip Wilson rarely burst into song in his films, but he did sing the closing theme in his twenty-two Monogram films over the closing credits. Born Roland Charles Meyers in Granite, Illinois, on June 16, 1911, he acted and sang as a youth, tended bar and sang in St. Louis, and served in the army. Spotted by Scotty Dunlap of Monogram—who saw Wilson as the studio's answer to Lash LaRue—he got his first screen credit in Jimmy Wakely's *Silver Trails* (1948) before beginning his starring series with *Crashing Thru* in 1949. After his final film, *Wyoming Roundup* (1952), Wilson did a great deal of touring, with his wife and a musical group, then opened a construction business in 1958. He died on October 24, 1964, of a heart attack.

The western films story was virtually unchanged in 1949: Autry and Rogers ruled the roost, Wakely made good westerns, and few newcomers were introduced into the fading genre. Universal moved their Red River Dave series west and replaced McEnery with vocalist-bandleader Tex Williams, who made a series of fifteen musical shorts known as *Tales of the West*. These minidramas were between nineteen and twenty-seven minutes long and went by titles like *Rustler's Ransom, Thundering Rails,* and *Western Courage* (all 1950). Williams was a good-looking man with a speaker-shaking bass voice, but a childhood bout with polio made him an unlikely action hero— he walked with a slight but noticeable limp. Doubtless the producers were trying to capitalize on Williams's record "Smoke! Smoke! Smoke!" which had been a major hit in 1947. Williams, whose given name was Sollie Paul Williams, was the tenth child of a blacksmith and grist mill operator in Ramsey, Illinois, where he was born August 23, 1917. He began playing music with his siblings as a child, and by 1934 he had found work on radio in Decatur and Tuscola, in central Illinois. He moved to Washington with a brother in 1938 and joined his first really professional band (Cliff Goddard & his Reno Racketeers) in 1940. Months later he joined Walt Shrum's Colorado Hillbillies, who were fixtures of the Los Angeles music and film scene. He then defected to Cal Shrum's Rhythm Wranglers, with whom he first appeared in film, in Tex Ritter's *Rollin' Home to Texas* (Monogram, 1940).

Tex Williams became a pioneer in the exploding wartime western-swing scene in the Los Angeles area. Western-oriented swing bands were in huge demand for the enormous wartime work force in Southern California, and even Bob Wills's relocating there did little to meet the demand. A promoter named Foreman Phillips opened several ballrooms and venues for swing bands, and many of the movie cowboys whose stories appear here threw together dance bands, including Ray Whitley, Hank Penny, Merle Travis, Deuce Spriggins, Happy Perryman (the older brother of Lloyd Perryman), and Ole Rasmussen. Perhaps the most popular of all was Spade Cooley, who hired Tex Williams as his vocalist. The charismatic Cooley was hugely popular in person and on record, and crowds in the thousands came to see the big, swinging ensemble that is credited with coining the term "western swing"—Spade dubbed himself the King of Western Swing. It is Williams's voice that is featured on the Cooley megahits "Shame on You" (#1 in 1945) and "Detour" (#2 in 1946), as part of the humorously named trio Oakie, Arkie, & Tex.

Williams stayed with Cooley five years before forming his own band, the Western Caravan, and signed with Capitol records in July 1946. His films were but a brief excursion in a long career as a singer and bandleader, which continued with charted records well into the 1970s, with stints at RCA, Decca, Capitol (again), Liberty, Monument, and smaller labels. The coming of rock & roll forced him to disband the Caravan and end his ten-year run at Los Angeles's Riverside Rancho in 1957, but Williams continued to perform, on an increasingly limited basis, in country music situations and venues up until his death on October 11, 1985.

The fifteen musical shorts were later cobbled together into four somewhat incoherent full-length features, beginning with *Tales of the West* (Universal-International, 1950), padding out the music with action sequences and stock footage from the Bob Baker westerns of a dozen years before. The three additional films, all similar, were released in 1951. Though his career in western film was small, Tex Williams's career in western swing and country music was large indeed, and he was universally regarded as one of the most genuine performers in the business.

Also in 1949, the tiny Astor Studios, a fringe player in films since the middle 1930s, released a series of musical one-reelers, including *Mountain Rhythm* with Georgia Slim & the Texas Roundup Boys, *Saturday Night Square Dance* with Jim Boyd & the Men of the West, *A Cowboy's Holiday* with Art Davis & His Rhythm Riders, *Dude Ranch Harmony* with Dewey Groom & His Texans, and *The Talented Tramps* with Billy Gray & the Sons of Texas. All were Texas acts, presumably filmed in Texas, and they must have seen some limited distribution, for Astor did continue with this one-reel series. Red River Dave chimed in with one last short, *Pretty Women* (Sack Amusement Enterprises), in 1949 as well.

Tex Williams's old boss Spade Cooley starred in a couple of musical shorts for Universal-International that year—*King of Western Swing* and *Spade Cooley and His Orchestra*—and in three low-budget films. Two were filmed for an ultracheapie called Friedgen Productions some time in the late 1940s but were not seen until 1950, when they were released by Astor: *The Kid from Gower Gulch* and *The Silver Bandit*. Cooley made one film for Eagle-Lion in 1950 called *Border Outlaws*. Although he was the snappiest of dressers and a charismatic, riveting performer as a fiddler and bandleader, his films left little mark on the genre.

Born Donnell Clyde Cooley in Pack Saddle, Oklahoma, on December 17, 1910, he moved with his family to Oregon at the age of four, then to Southern California in 1934, where he began making his living as a musician immediately, fiddling for any number of regional bands. He drifted into film work, occasionally working as Roy Rogers's stand-in, and he can be seen as a skinny and thoroughly unbelievable Indian in Ray Whitley's *Redskins and Redheads* (RKO, 1941), along with Jimmy Wakely, even skinnier and less believable; Cooley had at least some claim to actual Native

Tex Williams with Linda Romay in *Six Gun Music* (1949). (Author's collection)

Poster advertising one of Eddy Arnold's two starring westerns, *Feudin' Rhythm* (1949). (Author's collection)

American ancestry. He appeared in musical roles in Starrett's *Texas Panhandle* (Columbia, 1945) and was a part of a couple of the Ken Curtis musical extravaganzas at Columbia. Cooley's rise to the King of Western Swing was meteoric, but it came to a tragic end. First a heart attack, then changing musical tastes, brought his career to a standstill; in 1961 he brutally killed his wife during a violent argument and was sentenced to an extended prison stay, where he suffered a second heart attack. While being considered for parole, he played a law enforcement benefit in Oakland, California, where he suffered a third and final heart attack and died backstage on November 23, 1969.

At about the same time, the late forties, Eddy Arnold made a couple of what might loosely be called westerns, though they might more accurately be called "southeasterns," not too dissimilar from the eight films Roy Acuff had starred in for Republic and Columbia from 1940 to 1949. Both the Weaver Brothers & Elviry series (1938–1943) of hillbilly music and broad comedy, and the Judy Canova series (1940–1955), which was a more sophisticated version of the same formula, had been profitable for Republic for a number of years. These quickly made vehicles for singing stars were, in fact, the precursors of the formulaic Elvis Presley films of the 1960s. Columbia had a history of similar musical pictures meant for a limited market, and Arnold was a logical choice: A fine singer and a handsome man, he was hot as a firecracker, with staggering record sales. The films, however, didn't do much, and Columbia did not try to further Arnold as an actor or a film star. *Feudin' Rhythm* (Columbia, 1949) and *Hoedown* (Columbia, 1950) sum up his career in musical films. Born near Henderson, Tennessee, on May 15, 1918, Arnold has flirted with western music from time to time, and in fact the song with which he is most identified, "The Cattle Call," is one of the standards of the genre. He has long declared Gene Autry to be his musical hero and inspiration, and he even spent a formative period with Pee Wee King's Golden West Cowboys, from 1940 to 1943, before launching his successful solo career.

Helping to provide musical backup in these films were the Oklahoma Wranglers, who later became longtime members of the Grand Ole Opry as the Willis Brothers—Guy (1915–1981), Skeeter (1917–1976), and Vic (1922–

The Willis Brothers, then known as the Oklahoma Wranglers. *From left:* Skeeter Willis, bassist Chuck "the Indian" Wright, and Guy Willis stand behind Vic Willis. (Country Music Hall of Fame collections)

Poster for pop bandleader Vaughn Monroe's 1952 Republic western, *Toughest Man in Arizona*. (Author's collection)

1995) Willis. They began a career in Oklahoma in the 1930s, rising to star on the *Brush Creek Follies* in Kansas City before disbanding to enter the service. They regrouped after the war and joined the Grand Ole Opry in 1946, and it was in Nashville that they began their recording career on Sterling Records and backed Hank Williams on his first recordings. Their film appearances with Eddy Arnold, with whom they toured for a number of years, were their only ventures into cinema, and so little did Arnold think of the future of western music that it was he who suggested they call themselves the Willis Brothers to avoid being typecast as a cowboy band. Having left the Opry in 1949 to tour with Arnold, they appeared on the *Ozark Jubilee* and the *Midwestern Hayride* before rejoining the Opry cast in 1960, where they remained an active and popular group for two decades.

Republic tried an interesting and uncharacteristic experiment at about this time. Diverging wildly from its proven strategy of developing young western singing stars who were firmly in the rural mold, the studio tried casting an established pop singer as a singing cowboy. Other studios had tried this again and again and failed, and it didn't really work this time either. However, the two films that big-bandleader Vaughn Monroe made for Republic were interesting in their own right, for they were big-budget Technicolor releases that were serious stories in the late 1940s mold. There were no fringe, glitter, and stage shows in *Singing Guns* (1950) and *The Toughest Man in Arizona* (1952), somber stories of righting injustice in the West in which music takes a mostly incidental role. Republic must have considered the investment worthy: The $87,500 base salary Monroe received for *Singing Guns* was far more than Autry or Rogers ever got from the studio.

Vaughn Monroe was born October 7, 1911, in Akron, Ohio, and was something of a child prodigy; he won the Wisconsin state trumpet championship at the age of fifteen. He began playing in professional bands as early as 1933, but realizing that his real gift was his powerful, distinctive voice, he studied at the Northeast Conservatory of Music in Boston. He formed his own big band in 1940 and had several popular records, including "Racing with the Moon," the wartime classic "There! I've Said It Again," "Ballerina," and "Let It Snow! Let It Snow! Let It Snow!" In 1949 he had another #1 record with a song his producers pitched him after it was turned down by the Sons of the Pioneers, fellow RCA artists, who felt it was too derivative of "When Johnny Comes Marching Home." The song was "(Ghost) Riders in the Sky," written by a Death Valley park ranger named Stan Jones. The compelling big-band arrangement, with dramatic horns, a driving guitar rhythm, and Monroe's baritone, was a huge record in 1949 and doubtless led to his starring film roles, though he and his orchestra had previously appeared in *Meet the People* (1944) and *Carnegie Hall* (1947).

Although Monroe was handsome and popular, he was no horseman, and at forty a little old to be starting out in the genre, which was on its last legs anyway. The films are better than one might expect, but they left no

Rex Allen with two sidekicks, Fuzzy Knight and Roscoe Ates, who sing harmony and provide comic relief. (Author's collection)

lasting impact. When changing musical tastes rendered big swing bands obsolete, Monroe disbanded his outfit in the late 1950s, only to return from time to time to appear on nostalgia tours and television specials. He eventually retired to Stuart, Florida, where he died May 21, 1973. He recorded one western album, *Vaughn Monroe Sings New Songs of the Old West* for Victor, cut a couple of sides with the Sons of the Pioneers, and had a handful of single western-oriented releases, but with the exception of "(Ghost) Riders in the Sky" and these two films, he was a popular bandleader first and foremost.

In 1948 Monte Hale's contract was allowed to run out, and he was replaced by the last of the singing cowboys, Rex Allen. Perhaps Herbert Yates had hoped to keep Roy Rogers in line by developing an exciting new talent, as he had probably tried to do with Monte Hale. If so, it didn't work. Rogers, as disgusted with Yates as Autry had been, was already looking forward to leaving films and entering the new medium of television.

Rex Allen was a strapping, likable young westerner with a powerful voice free of operatic affectations and inflections. He was the real deal. His only drawback was his crossed eyes, which were corrected after several surgeries while he was a star on the *National Barn Dance* in Chicago. Born in Willcox, Arizona, on December 31, 1920, Rex Elvie Allen came by his horsemanship naturally, growing up on a ranch. After he won a statewide talent contest in 1939, he began a career on radio that took him to WTTM in

Trenton, New Jersey. While doing summer shows at various country music parks in the East, Allen became acquainted with stars of both the *National Barn Dance* and the Grand Ole Opry. Several, including Roy Acuff, suggested he try out for a spot on the popular barn dances.

He tried the Opry first in 1944, only to be told that they had just filled a spot for a new soloist with a young singer from Pee Wee King's band named Eddy Arnold. It was suggested to Allen that he might try out for Bill Monroe's Blue Grass Boys, as the Father of Bluegrass was then looking for a new guitarist. Allen had no desire to be a sideman and went to Chicago instead, while Bill Monroe found Lester Flatt, and musical history was made in another style.

Allen appeared from 1945 to 1949 on the *National Barn Dance* and helped fledgling Mercury records get off the ground as well. He was auditioned by Herbert Yates himself. "Not much love in him," according to Allen. "Just a pretty solid old businessman." Offered a contract, he was at first hesitant because he was making $75,000 a year as the major star of the *National Barn Dance,* and, in his words: "It wasn't like I needed Hollywood. I had very serious doubts as to whether I could make it as an actor. But I got there and found out I didn't have to be an actor anyway. Anybody could have done it."[20]

Rex Allen was well received by Republic and by moviegoers as well. He starred in nineteen Republic films, beginning with *The Arizona Cowboy* in 1950 and ending with the final singing-cowboy film, *Phantom Stallion,* in 1954. His sidekicks were Gordon Jones, Fuzzy Knight, Buddy Ebsen, and, most notably and memorably, Slim Pickens. His horse was Koko, and musical support was often provided by the Republic Rhythm Riders, although his own band, featuring fiddler Wade Ray (1913–1998), appeared in several of his films. Allen was one of the few with good things to say about Herbert Yates: "He didn't have a whole lot of friends, especially among actors. [But he] did everything he promised to do for me, even gave me raises that weren't in my contract. He was a good guy, and I'll always have nice things to say about Mr. Yates."[21]

Despite his many strengths, Rex Allen came too late to the singing-cowboy game. Dwindling budgets were cut further and further, the same action footage was repeated again and again, and his series was allowed to die with two films in 1954, without fanfare or farewell. Allen went from B westerns into a television series called *Frontier Doctor* and pursued his singing career; "Crying in the Chapel" became his biggest hit, in 1953. He did as much country as pure western through the years but continued to record memorable western songs, including a lush and lovely symphonic album with the Victor Young Orchestra called *Under Western Skies* on Decca. His singing voice was a phenomenal instrument of tone, expressiveness, power, and believability. Of it, he said: "I've had a bass voice since I was 12 years old, and a three octave range. I could sing tenor or bass, it didn't make any difference, particularly. Just something God gave me. Thank you, God."[22]

In the course of his long career, Zeke Clements spent time on children's television. Here, he and Topper appear on WUSU in New Orleans in 1964. (Country Music Hall of Fame collections)

Allen's speaking voice was deep, folksy, and avuncular, and he forged a third career as a narrator and announcer in commercials and in dozens of Disney productions, though he worked for other studios as well; for example, he narrated *Charlotte's Web* for Hanna-Barbera. A founding member and passionate advocate of the Western Music Association, he lived in semi-retirement in his native Arizona before a heart attack took his life on December 17, 1999, just short of his seventy-ninth birthday.

With the release of Allen's *Phantom Stallion* in 1954, singing-cowboy films ground to a quiet halt, outmoded by changing American tastes and the advent of the exciting new medium, television. The light-opera baritones had been tried, tested, and rejected by the public by the early 1940s; Tex Ritter had made his last film in 1945, Eddie Dean in 1948, Jimmy Wakely in 1949, Roy Rogers in 1951, Gene Autry in 1953. Just a few months after Rex Allen's swan song, Wayne Morris made his last film, *Two Guns and a Badge*. Although not a singing-cowboy film, it is considered by critics to be the last of the B westerns.

There were other musical westerns, of a sort, but they couldn't really be called singing-cowboy films. Howard Keel posed in gambler's duds as Doris Day donned buckskin in *Calamity Jane* (Warner Bros., 1953). Clint Eastwood even sang in *Paint Your Wagon* (Paramount, 1969). But these and others like them were not singing-cowboy films. They were Broadway shows brought to the big screen, and they fall well outside the scope of this book. Sterling Hayden pawed the guitar and croaked a tune in the title role in *Johnny Guitar* (Republic, 1954), in one of the few quiet moments when Joan Crawford and Mercedes McCambridge were not chewing the scenery. A tongue-in-cheek version of the classic singing-cowboy hero, part nostalgia and part spoof, was attempted in *Rustler's Rhapsody* (Paramount, 1985). A few television films touched on the theme, such as Kenny Rogers in *Wild Horses,* which featured songs by R. W. Hampton and Riders In The Sky, and Michael Martin Murphey's role as an Irish cowboy in the miniseries *Lonesome Dove.* George Strait starred as a western-oriented country singer in *Pure Country* (1992), and Don Edwards won a role as the singing ranch hand in Robert Redford's *The Horse Whisperer* (Touchstone, 1998)—shades of those singing second-banana roles Ray Whitley toiled in all those years.

Disney/Pixar's *Toy Story 2* (1999) included the computer-animated singing hero Sheriff Woody, his sidekick, Jessie the Yodeling Cowgirl, and Randy Newman's theme song "Woody's Roundup," performed by Riders In The Sky. The accompanying album, *"Woody's Roundup" Featuring Riders In The Sky,* won a Grammy award for Best Musical Recording for Children in 2001, the first Grammy won by a pure-western artist or group (though "El Paso" won for best song in 1959).

Although many in the film industry were threatened by the coming of television, many of the original singing-cowboy movies found new life, at least for a time, in reruns on the small screen, although when the films were edited to hour length to fit television's time format, often music was the first thing cut. These films provided cheap programming, and although their release to TV was mightily resisted by some in the film industry, they became a staple of early television, introducing Gene Autry and Roy Rogers and the rest to a whole new generation.

Frequently, cowboy films were introduced by a genial, kid-friendly singing-cowboy host who was a little Roy Rogers and a little Fred Rogers, evoking the likes of "Cowboy Bob" in Dennis the Menace cartoons and epitomized by Buffalo Bob on national television's *Howdy Doody.* On more than a hundred local stations, these cowboy hosts became heroes and stars in their broadcast areas: Kenny Roberts in Dayton and Saginaw; Buck Berry in Grand Rapids; Curley Meyers in Indianapolis; Fred Kirby in Charlotte; Jesse Rodgers (Jimmie Rodgers's cousin) in Philadelphia; Texas Jim Lewis (as Sheriff Tex) in Seattle and later Vancouver, B.C.; Heck Harper in Portland, Oregon; Rusty Draper in San Francisco; Yodeling Slim Clark in Bangor; Famous Lashua in Duluth; and Sheriff John in Los Angeles. Sheriff John even recorded a series of children's records ("Smile and Be Happy," "Put Another Candle in the Birthday Cake") for Imperial, the independent label that kicked off the careers of such diverse performers as Fats Domino and Slim Whitman.

Some of these westerns returned to national television when The Nash-

Children's television of the 1950s was the last bastion of the singing cowboy for a number of years. Here, Kenny Roberts, "the Jumping Cowboy," entertains some of his Jumping Pals. (Country Music Hall of Fame collections)

Kenny Roberts hosted several children's shows over Michigan and Ohio TV stations. (Country Music Hall of Fame collections)

Every region had its children's cowboy hero. In Charlotte, North Carolina, it was Fred Kirby over WBT. (Country Music Hall of Fame collections)

Buck Barry and Thunder entertain children in Grand Rapids, Michigan. (Photo courtesy of Fred LaBour)

Sheriff John, an
Imperial recording artist,
was a children's idol
in Los Angeles.
(Author's collection)

ville Network (TNN) premiered in 1983; Riders In The Sky hosted *Tumbleweed Theater*, interspersing songs and skits, along with a little biographical and historical information during commercial breaks, for three years. Knoxville producer Ross Bagwell convinced the fledgling network that since the two greatest singing cowboys were still very much alive, TNN should do similar shows with the stars and guests who were there during the original filming. In 1986 *Happy Trails Theater*, with Roy Rogers and Dale Evans, went on the air, and in 1987 *Melody Ranch Theater*, with Gene Autry and Pat Buttram, debuted, presenting excellent prints of favorite westerns and unparalleled insight into their making. Both were off the air by 1989. Very nice prints of singing-cowboy movies occasionally pop up on cable movie channels, particularly the Western Channel; this is currently virtually the only outlet for these films. The Nashville Network—before its buyout and makeover into The National Network in 2000—remained committed to an occasional western presence, and besides frequent guest appearances by most of the current favorites in western music, both Riders In The Sky and Michael Martin Murphey hosted several TNN specials devoted to the West and its music.

Western music returned all too briefly to network television when CBS ran *Riders In The Sky* as a replacement for *Pee Wee's Playhouse* on Saturday mornings from 1991 to 1992. A surrealistic half-hour filled with cliffhanger adventures and a broad cast of stock characters (geezer cook, schoolmarm, villain and henchman, and Indian princess), it also featured two western songs per show. But animated superheroes ruled Saturday morning in those days, and this bit of the Old West lasted but a year.

Roy Rogers and Dale Evans on the set of their NBC television show, which ran from 1951 to 1964. (Country Music Hall of Fame collections)

Gene Autry on the set of the CBS Saturday morning television show *Riders In The Sky*.
*From left:* Ranger Doug, Gene Autry, Woody Paul, and Too Slim. It must have been a familiar
setting for Autry, as the CBS lot in North Hollywood is the site of the old Republic Studios;
many of the buildings that appear in old Republic films are still standing. (Author's collection)

Despite the fact that television reruns resuscitated some of the old
singing-cowboy films on the small screen for a new generation, as a bona
fide movie phenomenon the singing-cowboy films ended in 1954. Gene
Autry, reflecting on their quiet demise, offered this poignant recollection:
"There were no farewell toasts, no retirement dinner with someone hand-
ing out a pocket watch for twenty years of faithful service. Actually, nineteen years between the release in November of 1934 of *[In] Old Santa Fe*,
when I made my first appearance with Ken Maynard, for Mascot, until
Columbia released my last *[Last of the Pony Riders]* in November of 1953. It
just kind of slipped up on us. I don't recall ever saying that I had quit, or that
I would never make another motion picture."[23]

# 11

# In the Ether

## Radio, Records, and Television from 1935

The vast influence of the Sons of the Pioneers, as well as the pervasive songs of Billy Hill, markedly changed the sensibility of the cowboy song. As those two musical forces ascended in the 1930s, recordings by other artists reflected their influence, and songs about the West increasingly left behind the standard cowpoke themes and shifted toward a deeper lyricism over the next two decades.

In the early 1930s, familiar sidekick Smiley Burnette—in between sessions with Gene Autry and Autry and Long—began a solo recording career for the American Record Corporation. In May 1934 he recorded his classic versions of "Mama Don't Like Music" and "The Lonely Cowboy." Although the bulk of his material was novelty, the occasional cowboy song ("The Lone Cowboy," "Ten Gallon Hat") did come up.

The rotund multi-instrumentalist, songwriter, and comedian was born Lester Burnette on March 18, 1911, in Summum, Illinois. The son of a preacher, he made his way into local radio after graduating from high school. Although Burnette is best remembered as an accordionist, he played almost anything that could be plucked, tooted, bowed, honked, squeezed, or fingered. According to his family he was mercilessly teased as "Lester the Pester" in school, and he had his name legally changed in the mid-thirties to Smiley. His grandchildren report he frequently said, "If you want to stay friends please don't call me Lester."[1]

After joining Autry's band in Chicago, Burnette accompanied Gene on his first trips to Hollywood and played the sidekick in all Autry's early movies, often in the character of Frog Millhouse. He built a long career as a western personality in other stars' films as well. In some of these he was given top billing, though he left the action to his younger, fitter costar. Eddie Dew, Bob Livingston, Roy Rogers, Charles Starrett, and Sunset Carson were just a few who used his services. In addition he had his own Mutual network radio show (with musical support by the Whippoorwills) and was the first supporting actor to appear regularly on the yearly list of top ten moneymaking Western stars. Burnette was a compulsive songwriter, and while the majority of his songs were forgettable novelties such as "Minnie the Moocher's Ghost" and "Peg Leg Jack," his "Riding down the Canyon"—written in Gene Autry's Buick on their first exploratory trip to Hollywood—remains in the pantheon of all-time western classics. He left films in 1953 but was extremely popular at fairs, rodeos, and theaters; in fact, he led a life of nonstop touring and declared in the late 1950s that he had made more than ten thousand personal appearances up to that point. Burnette wound up his career appearing on television in *Petticoat Junction* from 1964 to 1967 as the roly-poly railroad engineer Charley Pratt. He died suddenly after a brief illness (acute leukemia) on February 17, 1967.

Like Burnette, Bill Boyd, who enjoyed a brief career as a film star, began his long recording career in 1934, recording "The Strawberry Roan," "Texas Plains," and "Ridin' Old Paint and Leadin' Old Ball" in San Antonio on August 7 for the fledgling Bluebird label. He came out of that fertile nexus of Fort Worth musicians such as Bob Wills and Milton Brown who would create western swing in the coming years. Bill Boyd & His Cowboy Ramblers began as a cowboy string band, but the special demands of the Texas audience pulled him into the realm of western swing early on. Nevertheless, he remained the most cowboy of all the western-swing bands, recording songs like "Tumbling Tumbleweeds," "Way Out There," "Wah-Hoo," and "The Yellow Rose of Texas" in the course of his long recording career. In 1935, with fellow future singing cowboy Art Davis on fiddle, he recorded his signature instrumental, "Under the Double Eagle," and his long career as a swing bandleader began. Despite his brief foray in Hollywood he remained, for the most part, a fixture of the Dallas–Fort Worth radio and dance hall scene for decades.

Another Texan who cut his first record in 1934, Tex Owens, was forty-two years old when he began recording for Decca in Chicago on August 28. The strapping ex-lawman had spent his life as a rancher, an auto mechanic, and a deputy sheriff before taking on music as a full-time profession. Born Doie Owens on June 15, 1892, in Killeen, Texas, he came from a musical family. His sister went on to fame as Texas Ruby of the Grand Ole Opry duo Curly Fox & Texas Ruby, and his daughters Laura Lee and Dolpha Jane both had musical careers as well, Laura Lee's most prominently as a featured singer with Bob Wills.

Owens adapted an old fiddle tune, which he retitled "The Cattle Call," and despite his rather rough performance, the song created a sensation and assured his career in music. He became a fixture on radio at KMBC in Kansas City under the moniker Tex Owens, "the Original Texas Ranger," and was backed by a quartet called the Texas Rangers (with whom he had

Tex Owens plays rhythm for daughters Laura Lee and Dolpha Jane on the *Brush Creek Follies,* broadcast over KMBC in Kansas City in the 1930s. (Country Music Hall of Fame collections)

recorded on August 27, 1934). Owens even appeared in 1931 on one of the earliest experiments in television broadcasting.

Perhaps because he was not as smooth and accomplished as the cowboy singers sweeping the country at the same time, Owens's recording career was short. He cut just one other song for Decca on that session, the standard "Pride of the Prairie," and did not return to the studio for two years, this time for Bluebird. Of the ten songs he recorded on September 23, 1936—including his signature "The Cattle Call"—none were released. Regardless, Owens enjoyed a lengthy performance career that was halted only when he broke his shoulder in a horse spill. He lived for many years in California before returning to Texas in 1960, and it was in New Baden that he died of a heart attack on September 9, 1962.

Ray Whitley, *seated, left,* with the Phelps Brothers and Ken Card. (Author's collection)

As national interest in romantic western music grew, another recurring figure in the singing-cowboy saga, Ray Whitley, recorded several songs for the American Record Corporation in New York on September 17, 1934. They were a typical pair of songs of the day: a sentimental mother ballad ("Have You Written Mother Lately?"), and a topical-event song about the sinking of a passenger ship ("The Morro Castle Disaster"). Whitley was a recording partner during this era with both Frank Luther and Buck Nation.

Ray Otis Whitley was born in Atlanta, Georgia, on December 5, 1901; after the death of his mother in 1906 his father remarried and the family relocated to Clay County in northern Alabama. Although it was a musical family, Whitley recalled that he had been particularly inspired by "a colored fellow that used to come through the county about once a month. They called him Banjo Bill, and he was about the finest that any of us had ever seen or heard . . . he would come by for whatever donations anyone would offer, and he played the blues type things . . . similar to 'John Henry.' . . . I enjoyed it because he used to really make those strings talk!"[2] Eager to leave the sharecropper life, Whitley joined the navy at the close of World War I and became an electrician. He continued in that trade when he left the service in 1923, when he settled in Philadelphia with his new bride, Kay.

Jumping at the opportunity to learn steel work, he moved to New York in 1928. He worked on bridges and construction projects all over New England and was involved in building such major structural works as New York's subway system, the Empire State Building, the West Side Highway, and the George Washington Bridge. His musicmaking was confined to ukulele playing and singing duets with his wife (who would frequently tour with him in later years) at parties. When the Depression deepened and construction work became scarce, his wife urged him to learn guitar and concentrate seriously on his singing. He learned "five or six chords" and took his original songs, strong baritone voice, and spectacular yodeling ability down to WMCA and auditioned. There he was accepted and placed with a group that included Dwight Butcher, Buck and Tex Ann Nation, and Otis Elder; they were sponsored by Crazy Water Crystals. Butcher wrote the dramas, the entire cast performed the music, and Ray Whitley's musical career was born. "I hadn't had any previous show business experience, but being a ham as I am I just loved it. I loved the work and had no fear of anything. I just stepped out on the stage like I'd been doing it all my life."[3]

Whitley then moved to the *WHN Barn Dance* (which he cohosted with another young up-and-comer, Tex Ritter), performed at numerous theaters

Buck and Tex Ann Nation, East Coast pioneers of the western sound. (Country Music Hall of Fame collections)

and clubs in the thriving New York western scene (including the Roxy and the Stork Club), and played the theater circuit up and down the East Coast. He recorded frequently with this loose band of New York–based performers, and though the material was often country and current-events songs, his image on stage and in his mind was strictly western. By February 1936 he was recording cowboy songs for the fledgling Decca label: "Saddle Your Blues to a Wild Mustang," and "Wah-Hoo," featuring his crisp yodeling and the skills of his Range Ramblers, the Virginia string band that consisted of Earl, Willie, and Norman Phelps, along with Ken Card and his dazzling plectrum-banjo work. The same group, known by this time as the Six Bar Cowboys, recorded several times in the coming years; the material, mostly western, included the original version of "Back in the Saddle Again."

Buoyed by his rapid success in New York, Whitley set his sights on Hollywood. Determined to hone his cowboy skills, he spent months on Col. W. T. Johnson's sprawling Six-Bar Ranch in West Texas—he'd met Johnson, a rodeo promoter, at the annual New York rodeo. Finally, convinced that a career awaited him in California, Whitley, along with Card and the Phelps brothers, loaded up a Buick with a huge coffin case on the roof for the bass and headed into the sunset. Whitley & His Six Bar Cowboys (by this time with Spade Cooley on fiddle and Ken Carson on guitar) recorded only one more major-label session, an August 1941 date in Hollywood for OKeh that featured country songs with yodeling. Despite his success on-screen in Hollywood, Whitley's only records after this point were on small regional labels such as Cowboy, Apollo, and Veejay.

The final significant western act to record in 1934, the Ranch Boys, is probably the most overlooked western band in western music's history, most likely because two of its three members—Curley Bradley and Ken "Shorty" Carson—went on to significant careers after the trio split up. For a few brief years, however, the Ranch Boys stood as the only harmony group that rivaled the Sons of the Pioneers, in execution of material if not in songwriting, though Carson composed several enduring songs in his long career, including "Cowboy Jubilee" and "Wondrous Word of the Lord." The three men met as members of the Beverly Hillbillies and moved to Chicago in July 1934 to strike out on their own. The young trio recorded for the fledgling Decca label as it struggled to its feet during the Depression, recording first in Chicago on September 7. Their material was familiar: "The Last Round-Up," "The Old Spinning Wheel," "Tumbling Tumbleweeds," and "When It's Springtime in the Rockies." On September 11 they recorded "Utah Trail" and "Ragtime Cowboy Joe," and on September 28, "The Cowboy's Lament," "The Strawberry Roan," "Home on the Range," and "Red River Valley." If the material was predictable—Decca was likely trying to build up an instant library of classics to offer consumers at its discount price of thirty-five cents—the performances were not. The trio was superb.

The Ranch Boys' recording of "Tumbling Tumbleweeds" came just one

A 1939 songbook for the Ranch Boys, the first serious rivals of the Sons of the Pioneers for title of best western harmony group. *From left:* Ken Carson, Jack Ross, and Curley Bradley. (Country Music Hall of Fame collections)

month after the Sons of the Pioneers had recorded the song for the same label. Indeed, Decca managed to release the Ranch Boys' record first, on October 9, a full seven weeks before the November 26 Pioneers' version appeared; clearly the song was already considered a classic. Through their final session in 1941, the Ranch Boys continued to record cowboy music almost exclusively. By 1939 they were well-known fixtures on radio in the Windy City, and they even landed parts as singers and actors on the *Tom Mix* radio show. Mix, who died in 1940, had simply lent his name to the show and never appeared on it; when the opportunity came to portray Mix, Curley Bradley—who had been playing the part of Pecos Williams—took over the role, in which he continued until 1950.

Bradley (1914–1985) was born Raymond Courtney in Oklahoma and emigrated to California in 1923. Jack Ross, who apparently came up with the idea of putting the group together, is the mystery member of the trio.

Born in Mexico about 1904 and raised in Arizona, he silently departed from the annals of history after the breakup of the Ranch Boys.

Ken Carson was born Hubert Flatt in southeastern Oklahoma on November 14, 1914, and joined the Ranch Boys after brief stints with Stuart Hamblen, and then the Beverly Hillbillies. He sang over WGN in Chicago after the Ranch Boys dissolved in 1941 (after a seven-year run on NBC Radio) and replaced Lloyd Perryman with the Sons of the Pioneers during the war. After leaving the Pioneers in 1947, Carson became a radio and commercial-jingle singer in Los Angeles, then joined Tom Brennan's *Breakfast in Hollywood,* after which he moved to New York and was featured on *The Garry Moore Show,* where he remained until 1958. He appeared on television, radio, and as a jingle singer for a number of years and performed for both Tricia and Julie Nixon at their weddings. He continued to appear with small groups in clubs in New York and, after 1979, in Florida, performing "society music: Cole Porter, Gershwin, Rodgers and Hammerstein and things like that," until his death, in Delray Beach, on April 7, 1994.[4]

According to Carson, it was Ross who came up with one of the great publicity stunts of all time. He recalls that in 1938, Jack Ross

> suggested to [sponsor] Miles Laboratories that as long as we were singing cowboys we could prove our mettle by going to California, buying three horses, and [riding them] from Los Angeles to Chicago. We could be picked up by remote radio and broadcasted *[sic]* every Saturday night over WLS. Which we did. We started out on May 10, 1938, [rode] clear through to Chicago, got a big reception there, and we said, "Oh shucks, why stop now? We might as well do the whole thing." We rode from Chicago into New York, right up on the steps of City Hall, and got a big plaque [from] Mayor LaGuardia. I always tell everybody it's 3,975 miles on horseback, and I've got the calluses to prove it![5]

Carson appeared in a number of Roy Rogers pictures as a member of the Sons of the Pioneers, but the Ranch Boys appeared in only one film, Gene Autry's *In Old Monterey* (Republic, 1939). Although they have been largely forgotten today, the Ranch Boys were definitely players in the 1930s, and while they lacked the Pioneers' visionary original material, they did much to spread the music of the West across the nation, on record and radio.

There were others in 1934. A young yodeler named Margaret West recorded "Chime Bells" and three other cowboy songs for Decca on December 17, but although she had a lovely voice, she was not heard from again. The Texas Rangers (Tex Owens on guitar, Herb Kratuska on banjo and guitar, and future Autry sideman Paul Sells on accordion) recorded in Chicago in August and in the following April. They did not cut another side until a 1941 Hollywood session, when they recorded patriotic songs. They appeared on radio as well and, billed as the CBS-KMBC Texas Rangers, made their only film appearance—in Gene Autry's *Colorado Sunset* (Republic) in 1939. Sells began recording with Autry in 1940 and was a fixture of the West Coast recording scene for many years.

Eddie and Jimmy Dean had made an unreleased test record as far back as 1928, but they spent six years playing deep in America's heartland before they recorded again. Though they were native Texans, they bounced between radio stations in Shenandoah, Iowa, and Yankton, South Dakota, before landing with WLS in Chicago. They recorded "My Last Moving Day" and seven other songs, two of them cowboy ("When I Move to That New Range," "End of a Bandit's Trail"), for the American Record Corporation, November 2–5, 1934. Through the next year they recorded sixteen songs in five different sessions, a mixture of sentimental hillbilly and cowboy songs. Though Eddie poses with a fiddle in a WNAX publicity shot of a slightly earlier period, the instrumentation is simple guitar and vocals on all these tracks. In 1936 the brothers split up. Jimmy joined Chicago radio station WJJD when Eddie won the role of Larry Burton on a daily network soap opera called *Modern Cinderella,* where he played, in a part that mirrored his own life, a Texas cowboy who encounters the trials and perils of the big city. During the program's year and a half run, he studied voice under Forrest Lamont of the Chicago Civic Opera, and when *Modern Cinderella* came to an end he went to Hollywood.

Although there was plenty of film activity in Hollywood in 1935 and 1936, it was not a fertile time for the recording of new western artists. Bob Miller, however, had been recording variety, novelty, and hillbilly songs as far back as 1928; his career is intimately entwined with Elton Britt's as composer ("There's a Star Spangled Banner Waving Somewhere" and dozens of others), manager, musician, and producer. Miller's February 21, 1935, session with the Prairie Ramblers marked his only billed appearance on western records, though he appeared as a staff musician on hundreds. Miller was born in Memphis on September 20, 1895, and was an active musician and songwriter even as a young man. He relocated to New York in 1922 and became a professional songwriter for the Irving Berlin Publishing Company. Inspired by the success of Dalhart and Robison, he began writing country songs; his best-known numbers included "Twenty One Years," and "Seven Years with the Wrong Woman." Miller opened his own publishing company in 1933 and was also a producer, talent scout, and record executive for Columbia and OKeh records in the late 1920s and early 1930s. He died August 26, 1955.

The Phelps brothers also first recorded in 1936. The talented young Virginians (Earl, Norman, and Willie) had already recorded as members of Ray Whitley's recording, touring, and filmmaking troupe, but their small recorded output on Decca was all hillbilly. According to Whitley they came from a prosperous mercantile family in the Tidewater and, tiring of show business, returned to Virginia to pursue a variety of business interests. In addition, they had long-running radio and later television shows in Norfolk, where they maintained a cowboy look but where their material tended toward gospel and country.

The Tune Wranglers, featuring Buster Coward, also began recording in 1936; their song "Texas Sand" has become a western classic. Formed in 1935, the San Antonio band (Coward, Tom Dickey on fiddle, Charlie Gregg on bass and banjo, and Joe Barnes on banjo and vocals) was primarily a western-swing organization but did record and perform cowboy music from time to time, including Coward's musical adaptation of the poem "Chopo." They claimed to be true cowboys and were the first western-swing group to wear flashy cowboy outfits. Longtime radio stars at WOAI in San Antonio, they moved to KFJZ in Fort Worth in 1939 and apparently disbanded in 1940.

On February 2, 1937, two of the more vivid characters in country music history began their recording careers for Decca Records in Dallas with a solo, a woman's version of "T for Texas," and a duet, "Pride of the Prairie." The couple, billed on the label as Texas Ruby & Zeke, consisted of a tough, salty Texas girl with a lush contralto voice named Ruby Agnes Owens and Zeke Clements, "the Alabama Cowboy." The sister of Tex Owens, Ruby was born June 4, 1910, in Wise County, Texas. Following in her brother's footsteps, she had broken into radio as early as 1930 and teamed up with Zeke, late of Otto Gray's pioneering group, as a western duo. They appeared on both WHO and WSM, but the duo broke up when Clements was invited to stay on at WBAP in Fort Worth, and Owens was pointedly not invited, after having directed some particularly earthy language at their show's sponsors. She went on to marry fiddler Antrim LeRoy "Curly" Fox, and Curly Fox & Texas Ruby became a mainstay on several shows, including the Grand Ole Opry from 1937 to 1939, the *Boone County Jamboree* over WLW in Cincinnati, and the Opry again from 1944 to 1948. After a stint on NBC-TV in New York, they became radio and television fixtures in Houston for a decade, then returned to Nashville in 1962, where they continued to perform until Ruby's death, in a trailer home fire, on March 19, 1963. Though her repertoire consisted largely of love songs—often fittingly rowdy and raucous—her image was pure cowgirl from start to finish.

Zeke Clements was born September 6, 1911, in Warrior, Alabama. He got a shot on the *National Barn Dance* at the age of eighteen and toured for a time with Otto Gray as musician, yodeler, and comedian. After radio stints in Detroit, Cincinnati, and Philadelphia he joined the Grand Ole Opry in 1933; Zeke Clements & His Bronco Busters, who included Texas Ruby, were among the first performers to wear cowboy outfits on the Opry stage and were the first cast members with a western, not southeastern, image. Their travels took them later to New York, Fort Worth (where Owens infamously left the band), and California, where Zeke obtained the part of Bashful, the yodeling dwarf, in *Snow White and the Seven Dwarfs* (Disney, 1937).

After a bit of film work he returned to Nashville and the Grand Ole Opry in 1939.

Clements had his first national hit as a songwriter when several artists (Red Foley and Bob Wills, among others) recorded a patriotic song called "Smoke on the Water," and another when Eddy Arnold recorded "Just a Little Lovin' (Will Go a Long Way)," which was also a pop hit for Eddie Fisher. He became a respected songwriter, with numerous cuts over two decades, but only one of them, "Blue Mexico Skies," was western. Clements had modest success as a recording artist himself, and in the 1950s he did radio and television throughout the Southeast before settling into a decade-long career as a tenor banjoist in Dixieland bands on cruise ships based in Miami. Ever a charming hustler, Clements found a final job operating a curio booth in flea markets across the Southeast. He died June 4, 1994.

March 17 saw a set of five excellent pure-western sides cut in Los Angeles by Al Clauser & His Oklahoma Outlaws (Slim Phillips on fiddle, Larry Brandt on accordion, Don Austin on banjo, Tex Hoeptner on bass, and Clauser on guitar and vocals): "The West, a Nest, and You," "The Death of Jesse James," "Rocky Mountain Express," "I'm Riding down the Trail to Albuquerque" (Fred Scott's movie theme song), and "Little Black Bronc." Clauser was born on February 23, 1911, in Manito, Illinois, and by 1934 he and his band were radio stars over WHO in Des Moines. He met Gene Autry during Autry's premovie days on WLS, and once Autry had become a movie star, Clauser boldly telegraphed him. Autry remembered him, and Clauser & the Oklahoma Outlaws were brought out to appear in *Rootin' Tootin' Rhythm* (Republic, 1937), in which they performed "Little Black Bronc." Clauser recalls their disappointment that, having brought their white hats and flashy western wardrobe, they were issued the drab outfits of background players: "Autry is the only one who wears a white hat," they were told in no uncertain terms.[6] At this time they cut their sides for the American Record Corporation. Film work did not prove consistent, and they returned to WHO, then moved to WCKY in Cincinnati, then WHBF in Rock Island, Illinois, before settling at KTUL in Tulsa in 1942, where they became a western-swing dance band and worked days building B-24s at Spartan Aircraft. After the war Al Clauser kept the swing band, adding young Oklahoma vocalist Clara Ann Fowler, who as Patti Page soon became a national recording star. He appeared as Tulsa's first all-night disc jockey on radio and produced and performed on television in its emerging years. Later he was a supervisor, set designer, director, and actor—playing Uncle Zeb—on the *Uncle Zeke* children's program on KTUL. Clauser retired in 1976 after thirty-four years at the same station, and he was semi-active in music publishing and custom recording until his death on March 3, 1989.

A half-cowboy, half-western-swing act, the Saddle Tramps, began recording for Art Satherley and ARC's Vocalion imprint in Dallas on June 23 and 24, 1937. The Saddle Tramps recorded some fine cowboy sides—"Away

The DeZurik Sisters, stars of the *National Barn Dance* and the Grand Ole Opry. (Author's collection)

out There," "There's a Blue Sky Way out Yonder," "Rolling Herd," "Texas Home," "Rocky Mountain Express," and "Hold Them Critters Down"—but were better known for the sizzling western-swing version of "Hot As I Am," featuring the fiddle talents of western-swing pioneer J. R. Chatwell. The group had its beginnings with Bob and Buster Fite (rhythm guitar and harmonica) and Jimmy Carroll on mandolin. Formed in San Angelo they toured with Jimmie Rodgers before heading west and becoming part of the Texas Ramblers. The Fites fell out, and Carroll, Bob Fite, fiddler Shorty Scott, and accordionist Hi Busse formed the Saddle Tramps in 1935 and made a series of western transcriptions for Radio Producer's Sales. Hired to play at the Texas Centennial in 1936, they added Chatwell and became a popular and influential band.

Enright August ("Highpockets") Busse was born in Warroad, Minnesota, on August 6, 1914. He joined Jack Dalton's Riders of the Purple Sage at the age of nineteen, and in about 1938 he formed his first version of the Frontiersmen, a group that would be an integral part of western music for years to come. After the group dissolved, Busse worked variously as an accordionist and comedian with numerous West Coast bands. The Frontiersmen re-formed in 1947 with Busse, Eddie Martin, Andy Hokum, Don Poole, Shorty Scott, and George Morris; this is the group that recorded on their own and with Eddie Dean on Crystal Records and cut some superb transcriptions. Through the years, several important individuals passed through the organization, including Hal Southern (co-writer of "I Dreamed of a Hill-Billy Heaven"), Wayne West, Joanie Hall, and fiddler Billy Armstrong and world-class yodeler and tenor Rusty Richards—both of whom would also serve long stints with the Sons of the Pioneers.

The Frontiersmen & Joanie developed into a lounge act in the 1950s and 1960s, although they performed many a rodeo and fair backing western singers Rex Allen, Ken Curtis, and nonsinging cowboys Dale Robertson, Milburn Stone, and Hugh O'Brien. Hi Busse retired to Tome, New Mexico, and died on July 13, 1997. He lived long enough to see his election to the Western Music Hall of Fame in 1993.

Late in the fall of 1937, Len Slye of the Sons of the Pioneers made his transition to Roy Rogers, movie cowboy. Backed frequently in the recording studio by the Pioneers, Rogers recorded some of his finest sides throughout the 1940s and, at the end of his career, had the distinction of cutting a record in every decade from the 1930s through the 1990s. (The recording careers of Rogers and the Sons of the Pioneers are covered in depth in their respective chapters.)

Closing out the memorable year 1937, Jimmie Davis recorded "There's a Gold Mine in the Sky" in Dallas in December. Though he flirted with the music of the West from time to time and appeared in several Charles Starrett films, his involvement in the field was small.

Despite the overwhelming success of Gene Autry on record, singing cowboys on radio, and the mad scramble to introduce new singing cowboys to the screen, 1938 proved a rather unimpressive year for new cowboy acts on record. A fine trio called the Twilight Trail Boys recorded in San Antonio on October 30, cutting an all-western set of traditional songs that included "Press along to the Big Corral," then were heard from no more.

Mary Jane (1917–1981) and Carolyn (born 1919) DeZurik had a western image on the *National Barn Dance* (1936–1941), the *Midwestern Hayride* (1941–1944) and the Grand Ole Opry (1944–1947) and were renowned for their intricate yodels that could hit the upper reaches of the auditory capacity of the human ear. Despite their popularity, they recorded only six sides in their career—under their own name and as the Cackle Sisters on the Mutual network's *Opry House Matinee* radio show from Nashville. Their only western entry was, predictably, a yodeling extravaganza, "The Arizona Yodeler," cut on December 16 for the American Record Corporation. A younger sister, Lorraine, replaced Mary Jane when she retired in 1948, and their youngest sister, Eva, filled in for any of the other three throughout the years. After the act dissolved in the early 1950s, Carolyn performed in a duet with her husband, Rusty Gill, sometime member of the Prairie Ramblers and sometime solo singer on the *National Barn Dance*. They appeared in one film, *Barnyard Follies* (Republic, 1940) as the Cackle Sisters.

Texas Jim Robertson began recording for RCA Victor—with Elton Britt supporting him—in New York in May 1939. Like most country performers of that time and place, he had a strong western image but recorded a mixture of country songs and cowboy tunes. Born in the mill town of Gastonia, North Carolina, on February 27, 1914, Robertson broke into radio in nearby Charlotte, where he was heard by an NBC executive who brought him to New York as a cowboy singer and character actor. Robertson's deep, powerful voice worked well not only in music, but also on radio, and he included *Death Valley Days, Against the Storm, Lone Journey,* and a long-running villain role on *Dick Tracy* among his on-air acting credits. Robertson served with the Marines during World War II, then resumed recording for RCA and broadcasting over ABC. He scored four Top Twenty records in the late 1940s and 1950s for RCA, all covers of other artists' hits: "Filipino Baby," "Rainbow at Midnight," "Signed, Sealed, and Delivered," and "Slipping Around." He also appeared on television in New York and Baltimore and in at least one Broadway production.

As rock & roll began to dominate the musical landscape, Robertson played more and more taverns and recorded for progressively smaller and smaller labels (including smaller majors like MGM, then lesser lights like Strand, Design, and Grand Prix) before slipping out of performing and into disc jockeying. He eventually left show business for factory work in the 1960s. Traumatic incidents in his personal life took a toll. As his career faded, Robertson was also devastated by the death of his young daughter in a hit-and-run accident, and an injury he suffered at work. He died November 11, 1966, in Newton, New Jersey, by his own hand.

One of the most vivid acts to embark on a recording career in 1939 was the Swift Jewel Cowboys, so called because of their sponsor, Swift and Company, maker of Jewel oil and Jewel shortening. Their material (recorded by Art Satherley for Columbia's OKeh and Vocalion imprints) was dance band blues and swing, but their image was cowboy to the core. The band's posters trumpeted "The Swift Jewel Cowboys—Only Mounted Cowboy Band in America. Every Man Owns His Horse and Equipment. Now Doing Ten Fast Acts." The act's live show depended more on horsemanship than on music—though the members were accomplished players—but it was odd that they were based out of Memphis, a southern city not known for its interest in cowboy music. Regardless, the Swift Jewel Cowboys began broadcasting in 1934 and lasted until World War II split them up in 1942. The band's three July 1939 sessions contained no cowboy songs at all.

Texas Jim Robertson.
(Author's collection)

As singing cowboys continued to record in the studio and ride across the nation's movie screens in 1940, radio also remained a powerful force in spreading western music. That year the Sons of the Pioneers left Columbia Pictures and the Charles Starrett films and moved to Chicago to appear on *Station EZRA,* a comedy starring *National Barn Dance* favorite Pat Barrett as Uncle Ezra, the loveable owner of a "powerful little five watter down in Roseville." The Pioneers and the Hoosier Hot Shots provided music, and the Pioneers were busy recording a superb set of radio transcriptions, which were syndicated all across the country. These represented some of their finest work and include hundreds of songs the group never got around to recording commercially, among them many of the Nolan and Spencer classics these two gifted composers had created for the Charles Starrett films.

But the big network radio news of 1940 was the debut of Gene Autry's *Melody Ranch.* Unquestionably the most successful and influential of the singing-cowboy radio shows, it was a nationwide success and rated several times in the top five most popular radio shows, regardless of genre. The year after *Melody Ranch* debuted, Louise Massey & the Westerners, on the strength of their hit recording of "My Adobe Hacienda," began the first of their several network radio shows, a fifteen-minute program on NBC called *Reveille Round-Up.* With their smooth and sophisticated sound, their act was a natural for radio, and Louise was a gifted singer in a variety of styles, while her brother

Cottonseed Clark *(center)* host of the *Hollywood Barn Dance,* waxes philosophical or poetic as Tex Ritter *(behind Clark)* and the Riders of the Purple Sage (Al Sloey, Foy Willing, and Jimmy Dean) look on. (Author's collection)

Curt was a superb announcer. He later hosted a pop radio show called *Curt Massey Time* over CBS, beginning in 1943. Pop artists like the Dinning Sisters and Martha Tilton were the staples of the show, but an interesting footnote was that the orchestra leader, Billy Liebert, thirty years later would play accordion with the Sons of the Pioneers. Back with the family band, Curt began a fifteen-minute syndicated show, *Louise Massey and the Westerners,* in 1945, while at the same time he appeared on ABC's *Sunday on the N. K. Ranch,* a musical variety show sponsored by Nash-Kelvinator. And Carson Robison was back on network radio by 1943, a regular on the NBC variety show *Hook 'n' Ladder Follies,* and the following year a kid's show with a musical western theme appeared. Called *Friendship Ranch,* it was a thirty-minute show on NBC.

On the West Coast, the well-established *Hollywood Barn Dance* had gone network on the CBS West Coast affiliates by September 1944. Hosted by Cottonseed Clark, the show initially featured fiddler Charlie Linville, perky yodeler Carolina Cotton, Johnny Bond, and the Riders of the Purple Sage. Clark was born Sim Clark Fulks in Reno, Texas, on April 12, 1909, and got into radio early as an announcer and actor. After a time in New York, he moved to Los Angeles in 1943 as a producer, director, and writer. The

The Sunshine Girls—*left to right,* June Weidner, Colleen Summers, and Vivian Earls—with Wesley Tuttle at the microphone of KFWB-Hollywood. (Author's collection)

*Hollywood Barn Dance* was a project close to his heart, and he served as host, emcee, and resident poet. Clark died January 1, 1992.

The *Hollywood Barn Dance* was considered for a time the Grand Ole Opry of the West. It featured virtually every West Coast country and cowboy singer of the era; Ken Curtis and Andy Parker & the Plainsmen were cast members toward the end of its run in 1948. Also, it was while singing with the Sunshine Girls on this show that Iris Colleen Summers met guitar wizard Les Paul, who changed her name to Mary Ford; Eddie Dean introduced them.

One of the interesting stories of the *Hollywood Barn Dance,* the Sunshine Girls were representative of several excellent groups who became stars of radio and even appeared in a film or two (with Jimmy Wakely, in the case of the Sunshine Girls) but never recorded and are little remembered. The Sunshine Girls (Summers, Vivian Earls, and June Weidner) were notable for their excellent harmony and Summers's strong guitar work. They toured frequently with Gene Autry, and when Colleen Summers left she was replaced by Marilyn Myers, who went on to sing with, record with, and marry Wesley Tuttle. Summers, born in Pasadena on July 7, 1924, went on to sing in Jimmy Wakely's band and on records ("One Has My Name, the Other Has My Heart") and to sell millions of records as Mary Ford with Les Paul before their split-up in 1963. She died in 1977.

In 1944 the Andrews Sisters, fresh off their string of successful cowboy records with Bing Crosby, began a somewhat tongue-in-cheek radio show on the NBC Blue network called *The Andrews Sisters Eight-to-the-Bar Ranch,* which costarred veteran character actor Gabby Hayes and featured the Riders of the Purple Sage. The Andrews Sisters, cresting a big wave of success, were not about to be confined to the ranch, however, and their show became simply *The Andrews Sisters Show* the following year. The only tenuous connection with the West was the presence of Curt Massey as a regular.

Roy Rogers made the inevitable move to radio in 1944 as well, starring

The Whippoorwills prepare to take off for London on tour with Roy Rogers in the late 1940s. *Clockwise from top left:* Roy Lanham, Dusty Rhodes, Gene Monbeck, Sweet Georgia Brown, and Douglas Dalton. (Country Music Hall of Fame collections)

on the Mutual network and the NBC network into 1955. *The Roy Rogers Show* featured a dramatic sketch on every program and variously included the music of the Sons of the Pioneers, and later the jazzy vocals and stunning instrumentals from the Whippoorwills. Over time, cast members included Dale Evans, Gabby Hayes, and Pat Brady. Along the way, the sponsors numbered such well-known companies as Goodyear Tire and Rubber, Quaker Oats, and the Dodge Motors Division of the Chrysler Corporation.

In 1945 a short-lived magazine called *Cowboy Music World* published a radio listing of all cowboy shows on all radio stations in the United States. The list of more than 260 programs seems impressive at first, but a cursory look indicates that the magazine's definition of cowboy music was liberal indeed. The list included country music shows that might contain western music, the Grand Ole Opry and *National Barn Dance* among them; any shows with a rural theme; and shows that featured such varied artists as old-time blind duet singers Mac & Bob over WLS in Chicago, rising country star Eddy Arnold & His Plowboys on WSM in Nashville, Deep South singer-comedian Lew Childre on WSM, and the Rambling Hillbillies on WMBG in Richmond. In addition there was a little gospel (the Chuck Wagon Gang on KGKO in Fort Worth), a little pop (the Andrews Sisters on WJZ in New York), a little folk (Woody Guthrie on WNEW in New York), and some western that was really western swing—Bob Wills's brother Johnny Lee Wills on KVOO in Tulsa, and Bill Boyd & His Cowboy Ramblers on WRR in Dallas.

Yet despite its liberal parameters, the listing reveals an abundance of western music, with somewhere between fifty and sixty daily, tri-weekly, or weekly shows. There are familiar names: Roy Rogers and the Sons of the Pioneers from WOR in New York (where the network feed originated), Stuart Hamblen on KFWB in Los Angeles, Red River Dave over WOAI in San Antonio, Elton Britt over WAAT in Newark, and Foy Willing & the Riders of the Purple Sage on the Andrews Sisters show. More telling is the variety of local and regional acts, most long forgotten now, that spread from border to border and coast to coast: the Sons of the Range over KVOO; Big Slim "the Lone Cowboy" over WWVA in Wheeling; Famous Lashua over KDAL in Duluth; *The Bar Nothing Ranch* over WIBW in Topeka; Rodeo Roy over KSFO in San Francisco; Cowboy Paul Groves over WDZ in Tuscola, Illinois; Ranch House Jim over WHO in Des Moines; Slim Wilson's Trail Riders over KWTO in Springfield, Missouri; the Westerners over WOMI in Owensboro, Kentucky; Chuck Harding & the Colorado Cowhands over WJOB in Hammond, Indiana; and the Texas Rangers over KMBC in Kansas City. These are just a sample of the names listed, a testament to the widespread appeal of western music in those years, surely its radio heyday.

A country musical variety network radio show called *Oklahoma Roundup* ran on CBS beginning in 1946 and featured Dick Reinhart as its resident western singer. Another former cowboy singer, Ken Carson, recently re-signed from the Sons of the Pioneers, was the featured vocalist for *Summerfield Bandstand,* the summer replacement for *The Great Gildersleeve,* in 1947. A couple of years later Curley Bradley—who had come to Chicago with Carson as a member of the Ranch Boys, and had taken over the role of Tom Mix on radio—eventually obtained his own variety show on the Mutual network. The fifteen-minute *Curley Bradley Show* was expanded to thirty minutes in 1950, and the name changed to *Curley Bradley—The Singing Marshal.* As Rex Allen noted in his autobiography: "Curley Bradley at that time was doing Tom Mix on the radio and singing on everything in town. He also sang with [the Ranch Boys] for many years, and I have the idea during that period that Curley Bradley's annual income was one of the biggest in Chicago."[7]

Though his time as a singing cowboy on film was but a brief fling in his long career, as we shall see, dance bandleader Spade Cooley had an hour-long network show on CBS beginning in 1950. This was oriented to lovers of slick country and western swing, but the cowboy image was very much a part of this network presentation. If anything, it probably tended to blur the already fuzzy line between country and cowboy music in the public's mind.

As the 1950s marched on, network radio became less and less a factor in the popularity of western music, with entire shows and casts moving directly to television. Radio concentrated on playing records, and live broadcasts, whether network or local, became rarer and rarer. Jimmy Wakely enjoyed a run from 1952 to 1958 on CBS with a radio show that was not particularly cowboy oriented, although he was still closely associated with the genre. Pat Buttram, Gene Autry's radio and television sidekick, had a brief fling as a radio host over CBS with the fifteen-minute variety show *Just Entertainment* in 1956, but that was more or less the end. *Melody Ranch* left the air that year, and *The Roy Rogers Show* was gone by 1955.

Rex Allen hosted *Country Hoedown* in syndication for several years, and the Sons of the Pioneers did several years of local radio on *The Lucky U Ranch,* as well as a three-year set of transcriptions (1955–1957) for the U.S. Department of the Interior called *The Smoky the Bear Show.* Featuring Billy Johnson, "the Singing Woodsman," it highlighted many Pioneer songs, along with urgings by guest stars like Barbara Stanwyck to protect America's wilderness.

Not for more than two decades would live studio cowboy music return to radio, with the rise of public radio in the 1970s and the surprising national popularity of *A Prairie Home Companion.* The acceptance of that show opened the door for *Riders Radio Theater,* which was regularly produced and syndicated on public radio from 1988 to 1995, and which still provides sporadic fresh episodes and specials. Many public stations still air reruns of the show. The brainchild of Riders In The Sky, the show was co-written by the band and the host, Texas Bix Bender. It featured a cliffhanger adventure, songs, and guests from the world of contemporary country, folk, and western music.

Red River Dave McEnery at the 1939 World's Fair in New York, with Bill Benner on fiddle and Roy Horton on bass. (Author's collection)

As radio further spread cowboy music through the late 1930s and early 1940s, the flood of cowboy recordings continued unabated. In 1940, Red River Dave began recording for Decca in New York on January 18. Backed by Roy Horton on bass and Vaughn Horton on steel guitar, his first sessions display the strong, sweet voice that had made him a radio favorite in his native San Antonio, where he was born David Largus McEnery on December 15, 1914. He moved to rural Simmons City, Texas, at the age of fourteen, then back to San Antonio to take his first radio job in 1932. After striking out in Hollywood the following year, he tried New York, where "I was a real freak—I mean they'd never seen nothing like me. I was so country they couldn't believe it !"[8] He moved back to Texas, then hopped from radio station to radio station: Grand Forks, Richmond, Miami, and San Antonio once again. After his third trip to New York, in 1938 he became an integral part of the Manhattan cowboy scene, replacing Tex Fletcher on WOR (when Fletcher left to make his single western for Grand National), and he appeared not only on radio but experimental television during the 1939 World's Fair.

A champion rope artist and excellent yodeler, Dave McEnery was also a compulsive songwriter, known for his publicity stunt of chaining himself to the piano at WOAI in San Antonio in 1946 and writing fifty-two songs in twelve hours. Though he wrote good cowboy and country songs, he became best known for his current-events sagas such as "Amelia Earhart's Last Flight." His early recordings were a typical mixture of contemporary love songs and western tunes, including his lovely radio theme song, "Is the Range Still the Same Back Home?" He recorded on Deluxe, Savoy, MGM, Continental, Sonora, Musicraft, and other labels after serving in World War II, tried films (both soundies and features), and wound up back in Texas doing television and radio from 1949 to 1956. As his career tapered off, Red River Dave drifted into real estate after 1957, though he continued to record an astonishing set of topical songs on his own label, covering virtually all the events and people who made major newspaper headlines, including Vietnam, Watergate, Patty Hearst, Emmett Till, Francis Gary Powers, and Don Larson's perfect game with the New York Yankees in the 1956 World Series. After the death of his wife in a house fire, he revived his performing career in the mid-1970s, and, dressed as a sort of Buffalo Bill with gold boots, he entertained passersby at Knott's Berry Farm in California with his strong yodel and rope tricks. He returned to his native San Antonio in the 1990s, and died there January 15, 2002. Sadly, little of his large recorded output is currently available in reissue.

When the Rough Riders (Jimmy Wakely, Johnny Bond, and Dick Reinhart) got to Hollywood in 1939, they sought out Gene Autry, who had befriended them in Oklahoma and invited them west. Although Autry welcomed them warmly, he was not forthcoming with employment, and the band scrambled, looking for work in films and on records. They returned for good in 1940 and soon joined the cast of Autry's *Melody Ranch* radio show. In one of the odder moves in recording history, each member of the Rough Riders obtained a solo recording contract with the other two providing backup music and harmony; thus the same band was recording various material under three different names.

These three versions of the Rough Riders recorded as Jimmy Wakely & His Rough Riders on Decca, Johnny Bond & His Red River Boys on Columbia, and—the first to record—Dick Reinhart & His Universal Cowboys on OKeh. Wakely later recalled those heady early recording days:

> If we were doing a record session and if it was a Johnny Bond date, Dick and I would shut up and do as Johnny told us, and on Dick's date—Dick used a drum; Johnny and I didn't use a drum, but Dick used Spike Jones on drums—Dick would give us the orders and we'd do as we were told. And if it was my session, well, I'd tell them what I wanted and I'd run the session, and we found it very workable that way. Never had a battle of any kind. I sang the lead on all of our stuff, but when Johnny Bond recorded he'd use a duet, and he and Dick would sing a duet, so we wouldn't sound like the Wakely group, and on Reinhart's records he sang solos.[9]

Reinhart cut a set of honky-tonk sides for OKeh in Fort Worth on April 21, 1940, then did several more sessions up through March 1942 (billed later as Dick Reinhart & His Lone Star Boys) featuring Bond on guitar, Carl Cotner on fiddle, and Spike Jones on drums. In a sense, Reinhart had preceded the others by an even wider margin, having first recorded some bluesy sides in Dallas for Brunswick back in 1929. A sometime member of the Light Crust Doughboys (with whom he took lead vocals on "Ding Dong Daddy," "Sittin' on Top of the World," and others) and other early western-swing outfits, Reinhart had replaced Scotty Harrell at the last moment when the Rough Riders were called to Hollywood. Born in Tishomingo, Oklahoma, on February 17, 1907, he worked and recorded with Bond and Wakely after moving with them to California, appeared for a brief time with the Riders of the Purple Sage, and made several more solo recordings in a more contemporary, less bluesy style than in his western-swing days, right up through his 1947 sessions for Columbia. Dick Reinhart died young, and suddenly, of a heart attack on December 3, 1948.

The next version of the Rough Riders to record was Jimmy Wakely's, on August 29, 1940. Backed by Bond, Cotner, Reinhart, and Frank Marvin on steel guitar, Wakely cut his first hit, "Too Late," as well as "Marie Elena" and Bond's classic "Cimarron." With that lineup the sound was Autryesque, and it propelled him to the top ranks of the industry. "Too Late" was a country love song, and Wakely later recalled its original inspiration: "I had a brother-in-law that was always knocking his wife around and drank a lot . . . so I wrote . . . 'Too Late.' . . . I went back to Oklahoma City and I ran into my brother-in-law . . . [a]nd he said, 'Man, you never wrote anything as pretty as "Too Late" in your life.' I said, 'You should like it, you son of a bitch, it's the story of your life.' " [10] The success of the song probably steered his recording career away from western and into mainstream country, although he did record "The Cattle Call" and "Rocky Mountain Lullaby" in September 1940, also for Decca. But the bulk of his prewar recording was love songs. These were to be his bread and butter in later years, as "One Has My Name, the Other Has My Heart" became a #1 hit in 1948 and "Slipping Around" sold more than a million in 1949. Wakely returned to western recording later in his career, doing occasional sides for both Capitol (including "Song of the Sierras" and "Moon over Montana") and Coral, and he later began his own western label, Shasta, probably the first label devoted exclusively to cowboy and western music.

August 12 and 19 brought Johnny Bond, the final member of the Rough Riders, to the Columbia recording studio in Los Angeles, where he recorded fourteen country love songs, mostly his own compositions; this was typical of his prewar recorded output, which did not feature any of his western songs. Born Cyrus Whitfield Bond in Enville, Oklahoma, on June 1, 1915, Bond continued to record for Columbia after the war and landed three Top Five hits, including the Merle Travis songs "Divorce Me C.O.D." and "So

Round, So Firm, So Fully Packed." Though he wrote many western classics, "Cimarron" chief among them, he found—as did most of the postwar recording artists—that country love and novelty songs far outsold cowboy material.

Johnny Bond was a busy man in the 1940s, touring and doing radio on *Melody Ranch* and on the *Hollywood Barn Dance,* and though he appeared in only one of Autry's films, he was in dozens of other movies, making music for Charles Starrett, Johnny Mack Brown, his old singing partner Jimmy Wakely, and his business partner-to-be Tex Ritter. He was not invited on the cast of Autry's TV show (Pat Buttram became the sidekick, and musicians were not seen on-screen), so he and Tex Ritter cohosted the long-running and influential television show *Town Hall Party* in the 1950s. He remained a fixture on the Autry tours and *Melody Ranch* as well until the coming of rock & roll. But even rock & roll did not slow him down: he shocked country purists with a hit version of "Hot Rod Lincoln" in 1960.

Bond continued working and recording, though less frequently, through the 1960s and early 1970s, and his novelty record, "10 Little Bottles," became a #2 hit for Starday in 1965. In later years he turned his abundant energy to prose and wrote biographies of Autry, Ritter, Jimmie Rodgers, and his own autobiography, *Reflections.* One of the very few singing cowboys to put history on paper, this dryly humorous man, a gentleman and a scholar, suffered a stroke in 1977 and died of its consequences on June 22, 1978.

For his part, in 1940 Gene Autry was still king cowboy on screen. (His reemergence on record, as well as his musical makeover during this period, is covered at length in the Autry chapter.) The slick-singing trio that later became intimately associated with him first recorded for Bluebird in Dallas on April 3, 1941. Called the Cass County Boys, they were sophisticated musicians who presented a straightforward cowboy image: Fred Martin on accordion, John "Bert" Dodson on bass, and Jerry Scoggins on guitar. Tenor singer and bassist Dodson had been a member of western-swing groups like the Wanderers and the Light Crust Doughboys; Martin was the all-around musician of the group; and Scoggins used his rich baritone and strong rhythm guitar to anchor their sound. Their only Bluebird session consisted of three standard cowboy songs done with slick arrangements and ultrasmooth harmony—"Great Grand Dad," "Riding down the Canyon," and "Trail to Mexico"—and one novelty number, "Since I Put a Radio out in the Hen House." Their trio sound was hot, swingy, and vocally sophisticated, and who knows what might have happened had not the draft gotten in the way. They regrouped after each member spent time in the service and moved to Hollywood to take over the trio spot on *Melody Ranch* and on Gene Autry's road shows, and they appeared in some Autry films but, other than some MacGregor Transcriptions, did very little recording after the war

Eddie Dean began his solo recording career in earnest on September 4,

Denver Darling, a leading light of New York's singing-cowboy scene, with Smilin' Eddie Smith on accordion and Slim Duncan on bass. (Author's collection)

1941, entering the Decca studios to record such western classics as "On the Banks of the Sunny San Juan" (his signature song), "Little Grey Home in the West," and "Where the Silvery Colorado Wends Its Way." Subsequent Decca sessions included covers of Gene Autry hits like "Back in the Saddle Again," featuring Autry musicians Frank Marvin and Paul Sells. Like other budget record firms, Decca often had one or another of its artists cover an established or breaking hit by an artist on another label. So even though Eddie Dean was a fine songwriter, he was often put in the unenviable position of covering other western singers' hits in his Decca years. He moved to Capitol after the war and also recorded for Sage and Sand, Crystal, and other smaller West Coast labels. Though possessed of a beautiful voice, Dean never had a major hit on records, and his biggest successes came with songs he had recorded to limited acclaim that went on to become million sellers for other artists. Though his chart record success was minimal, he had a long recording career that lasted well into the 1970s.

On November 6, 1941, Denver Darling made the first of many recordings for Decca in New York. Born April 6, 1909, in Whopock, Illinois, and raised in nearby Jewett, he became one of the most popular and influential of the New York cowboy set after radio stints in various Midwestern cities like Terre Haute, South Bend, Des Moines, Chicago, Wheeling (on the *WWVA*

*Jamboree*), and Pittsburgh. He arrived in New York in the fall of 1937, where he broadcast first from WOR, then WNEW. His image was pure cowboy—his band was called his Texas Cowhands—but his songs at first were pop-country love songs. His material took a patriotic turn during the war years—"Cowards over Pearl Harbor" and "The Devil and Mr. Hitler" were typical. A composer as well, he wrote "Silver Stars, Purple Sage, Eyes of Blue," which was a successful record for Roy Rogers; he also worked in radio as an announcer, as well as a vocalist. Darling cut twelve sides for MGM in 1947, but, increasingly plagued by throat problems and unhappy with the urban environment in which he was raising his three children, he retired to the life of gentleman farming in Jewett, Illinois. There he died on April 27, 1981.

John "Dusty" King (1909–1987) found success on the screen as the costar of Monogram's popular Range Busters trio series and recorded shortly before the American Federation of Musicians' strike cut off recording for a year and a half between 1942 and 1944. King was an accomplished big-band singer who was believable singing western ballads, though his single recording date, for Bluebird on January 22, 1942, yielded but four sides, and just one of those ("Deep in the Heart of Texas") was western. The other three were country songs of love and wartime separation, like "Promise to Be True While I'm Away." Although the label billed King and his four-piece band as John (Dusty) King & His Range Busters, his supporting musicians were not the same Range Busters who appeared as his screen costars, Ray "Crash" Corrigan and Max Terhune. His backup band was instead a fine western ensemble that included Jesse Ashlock on fiddle, Fred "Tony" Travers on accordion, longtime Tex Ritter sideman Rudy Sooter on guitar, and Rufus Cline on bass. Although the sides were fine, the musician's strike and the wartime shortage of shellac, along with King's own sputtering film career, did nothing to enhance his recording success, and this Bluebird session was Dusty King's only solo outing.

Once the musicians' union and the record labels had come to terms and ended the de facto recording ban, no one was more eager to get into the studio than young Eddy Arnold, who had left Pee Wee King's Golden West Cowboys to begin a solo career. WSM had great faith in him, and he was a well-known radio star before he ever approached the Victor microphones. It was at the WSM studios that he finally recorded, on December 4, 1944. The four songs included "A Mother's Prayer," a standard wartime ballad; "Mommy Please Stay Home with Me," a lachrymose tale of a dying child that would not have been out of place in Roy Acuff's repertoire; "Each Minute Seems a Million Years," a catchy country love song of the type he would make so popular in coming years; and "The Cattle Call," the song that justifies his inclusion in this volume. Tex Owens's classic from a decade before, spruced up with a new chorus from the pen of the prolific Fred Rose, was a sensation. Buoyed by Arnold's plaintive delivery and dreamy yodel, "The Cattle Call" became a signature tune for him, and a western classic.

In the long run, western music played but a small part in Arnold's career. He became country music's biggest star at midcentury, and for a crossover countrypolitan pop singer of the 1960s and 1970s, there was little room for western songs other than "The Cattle Call." Along the way, however, he recorded "Tennessee Stud," "Riders in the Sky," and "The Red Headed Stranger" on his popular 1959 folk album *Thereby Hangs a Tale*. Arnold also cut an entire album of western standards in 1963, predictably titled *The Cattle Call*, possibly in response to the renewed interest in western music engendered by Marty Robbins's recent gunfighter ballad hits. Although Arnold's western cuts were profoundly important to the development of the style, they played but a small part in a career that lies, for the most part, outside the range of this work.

Walt Shrum and his brother Cal show up repeatedly in the singing-cowboy saga as members and leaders of steady but unspectacular West Coast bands who appeared in a number of films. Walt Shrum & His Colorado Hillbillies recorded on the upstart Coast label and scored a Top Ten hit in 1945. Predictably, it was a country novelty tune, "Triflin' Gal," and it reached #3 on the *Billboard* charts; it would be Walt's only chart appearance. Cal Shrum appeared in, and starred in, more films but left little mark on the recording industry. (Record charts first appeared in *Billboard* magazine in 1944; any estimates of Top Five or Top Ten records before that date are pretty much guesswork.)

Wesley Tuttle & His Texas Stars went into the recording studio in 1945, with spectacular results. Tuttle's first Capitol single, "With Tears in My Eyes," went straight to the #1 spot. Tuttle had three more Top Ten hits the next year—"Detour," "I Wish I Had Never Met Sunshine," and "Tho' I Tried (I Can't Forget You)"—and though his image was thoroughly western, his recording successes were all with straightforward country songs.

Though his sound and voice were a bit rougher around the edges, Jack Guthrie likewise presented a country sound with a cowboy look. Born Leon Jerry Guthrie in Olive, Oklahoma, on November 13, 1915, he moved to Los Angeles with his cousin Woody Guthrie in 1937, where he and the legendary folk singer (three years his senior) wrote "Oklahoma Hills" and appeared as Oke & Woody on KFVD in Hollywood. Capitol Records recorded Jack's solo version of "Oklahoma Hills" in 1944, and it became a #1 record in the summer of 1945. Two quick follow-ups also became Top Five records ("I'm Brandin' My Darlin' with My Heart" in 1945 and "Oakie Boogie" in 1947), but Jack Guthrie was diagnosed with tuberculosis in 1946, and the disease advanced rapidly. He appeared in one film, *Hollywood Barn Dance* (Screen Guild, 1947), but died in the Veteran's Administration Hospital in Livermore, California, January 15, 1948.

One of the brightest new postwar stars was Julie Marlene Bedra, professionally known as Rosalie Allen, who began recording for RCA in 1946. Born one of eleven children in Old Forge, Pennsylvania, on June 27, 1924, she moved to New York in the late 1930s and worked with Denver Darling on his *Swing Billies* radio show, then with Zeke Manners. An outstanding yodeler with an infectious, merry voice, she scored a #5 hit with her first release, a remake of Patsy Montana's decade-old "I Want to Be a Cowboy's Sweetheart." Allen recorded extensively with Elton Britt, although only two of their collaborations became hits, neither of them western: the inspirational "Beyond the Sunset," a #7 record in 1950, and the clever pop-country love song "Quicksilver," released the same year. The most spectacular of the Britt-Allen duets were yodeling extravaganzas like "Yodel Blues" (written by Johnny Mercer), "Tennessee Yodel Polka," and "Prairieland Polka."

Though Rosalie Allen recorded a fair bit with and without Elton Britt, her recording career never caught fire, and she turned to television and later to radio as an influential disc jockey over WOV in New Jersey for a number of years before marrying and retiring to rural Alabama. Though she is in frail health, her voice is still delightful, and she now lives in Southern California.

Another Allen, unrelated to Rosalie, began his recording career in this postwar era as well: Rex Allen, of Willcox, Arizona. His recordings for the fledgling Mercury label were immediately successful, and strongly cowboy in sound and style, and both "Arizona Waltz" and "Teardrops in My Heart" became hits. In his precinema days as the star of the *National Barn Dance,* Allen recorded a number of humorous songs with a western theme: "Hawaiian Cowboy," "Texas Tornado," and "Who Shot the Hole in My Sombrero?" His greatest recording success during his singing-cowboy years was his commanding version of the old warhorse "The Streets of Laredo" (which he retitled "I'm a Young Cowboy"); in this version Allen sang the verse in a powerful tenor and the chorus in a thundering bass. He gained seven chart makers on Mercury and Decca in the 1950s and 1960s, recorded a symphonic album with the Victor Young Orchestra, and last made a mark with a western song with the satirical "Don't Go Near the Indians" in 1962. In his twilight years he recorded a fine album with western revivalist Don Edwards, released in 1999 on the Western Jubilee label, and despite advancing age and failing health his voice was in excellent form.

Another important western music act that began to record in these postwar years was Andy Parker & the Plainsmen, who cut several sides for Coast Records before moving to Capitol and made some fine MacGregor Transcriptions along the way. The Plainsmen's blend was airy and beautiful, and Parker's songwriting was distinctive and occasionally brilliant, but they did not enjoy any chart success. The era of the singing cowboy, and the vogue of western music, was passing.

The first recordings of New England legend Yodeling Slim Clark also came out in 1946, for the New York–based Continental Records, which re-

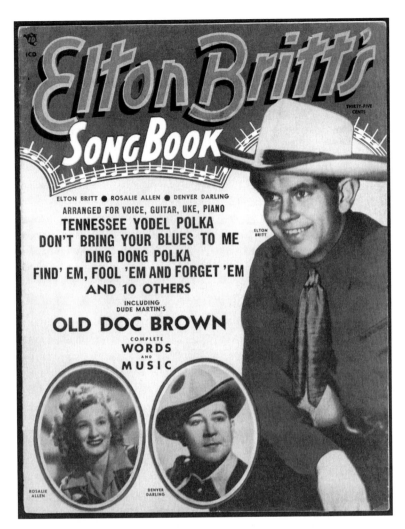

This 1950 Elton Britt songbook featured the current triumvirate of East
Coast stars of western music: Rosalie Allen, Denver Darling, and Britt.
(Country Music Hall of Fame collections)

corded several other western artists, most notably Red River Dave. Born
Raymond LeRoy Clark in Springfield, Massachusetts, on December 11, 1917,
Slim Clark had a largely regional appeal; his delivery was earnest and old-
fashioned, not unlike a tenor Montana Slim, and his yodeling precise. He
had a long career on radio in Massachusetts and New Hampshire, and on
radio and television in Bangor, Maine. A gifted painter as well as a singer,
he died July 5, 2000.

One of the finest yodelers, Kenny Roberts, made his first recordings in
1946 as well. He cut "Out Where the West Winds Blow" on Vogue Picture
Records when he was still a featured member of the Down Homers, a group
of Indiana singing cowboys regionally popular over Fort Wayne radio sta-

tion WOWO. Born George Kingsbury in Lenoir City, Tennessee, on October 14, 1926, Roberts grew up near Athol, Massachusetts, and after winning a talent show (hosted by Yodeling Slim Clark) in 1942, he left school to join the Down Homers. Following a stint in the navy, he returned to the Down Homers but landed his own ABC radio show in 1946. He had a long and successful career as a recording artist (with postwar hits like "I Never See Maggie Alone" and "Choc'lit Ice Cream Cone"), a radio star (with a short stint on the *National Barn Dance,* stays at WOWO in Fort Wayne, KMOX in St. Louis, and WLW in Cincinnati, and a fifteen-year stay on the *WWVA Jamboree*), and a star of children's television in Dayton from 1952 to 1957 and in Saginaw and Cadillac, Michigan, after 1957. He recorded for Dot, Starday, King, and Vocalion, and a fine Bear Family reissue covers the broad spectrum of his work. Roberts is now in his mid-seventies, his appearance and voice still youthful, and he is still working dates. Though his greatest record success has been with country music, his image in person and on television was strictly cowboy, and he remains one of the relatively unsung heroes of the genre.

Although there was a constant infusion of new cowboy and cowgirl singing talent from the mid-1930s on, by the early 1950s the air had all but gone out of the cowboy music balloon. With the exception of Tex Ritter's theme-song hit "High Noon" and a handful of others, the top-selling western records belonged to the 1930s and early 1940s. By the early 1950s only country love songs and children's songs were selling for singing cowboys. The minirevival started by Marty Robbins at the end of the 1950s was one of the few bright lights that shone during the fallow years.

# 12

# *The Fallow Years*

The swan song of the singing cowboys on film came with Rex Allen's *Phantom Stallion* in 1954, but the end had been in sight for some time. Western music increasingly took a back seat in recording sessions, even in sessions by cowboy stars. The heyday of cowboy songs had been the 1930s; by the middle 1940s relatively few were being recorded at all. Fewer still became hits, with notable exceptions being Vaughn Monroe's "(Ghost) Riders in the Sky" (1949) and Tex Ritter's "High Noon" (1952). But even Ritter—who of all the singing cowboys hewed closest to a western repertoire from start to finish of his career—had the vast majority of his recording successes with country songs in country style. As early as 1946 Gene Autry wrote aspiring songwriter Jack Howard: "I have made it a practice not to fool with cowboy songs unless they are the type of a standard number or have been popular in the past, simply because they do not sell on phonograph recordings. I have tried many of them but find that a good hillbilly song sells about ten to one the number of recordings and copies as a cowboy song. . . . You will note that I use only cowboy songs that have been hits in the past."[1]

Perhaps the only man of that era who bucked that trend was a poet named Stanley David Jones, born June 5, 1914, in Douglas, Arizona. After receiving a degree in zoology, he worked as a park ranger in Death Valley and acted as a guide for the cast and crew of the classic John Wayne western *Three Godfathers* (Argosy/MGM, 1948). In periods of after-hours relaxation during the shooting of the film, he introduced to the cast and crew his haunting musical cowboy ghost story, "(Ghost) Riders in the Sky." Then things happened fast. Jones was whisked to Hollywood, where his song became a huge hit for Vaughn Monroe and the title of a 1949 Gene Autry film, one of several title songs Jones would write for film and television in years to come, including "Whirlwind," "The Searchers," and "Cheyenne." Like Bob Nolan, he had a boundary-stretching approach to both lyrics and music and wrote many classics of the West, including "The Lilies Grow High," "Cowpoke," and "Song of the Trail." A homespun singer, he recorded five sides with the Sons of the Pioneers for Disney in 1957 and 1958, and he cut a couple of Disney albums of his own songs, *Creakin' Leather* and *This Was the West*. He also appeared with the Pioneers as one of the cavalry in *Rio Grande*, a film that featured three of his compositions. Stan Jones died on December 13, 1963.

Despite these occasional western-music successes, the handwriting had been on the wall for some time. As long as marginal profit could be squeezed from the dying genre, the film industry continued to make singing-cowboy movies, but the recording industry was quick to abandon the style when its fad value wore off and the public's taste shifted.

A look at the Top Ten records of the era tells the tale. Every one of Tex Ritter's chart records, save "High Noon," was country. Ritter went a decade without a hit before "I Dreamed of a Hill-Billy Heaven" in 1961, which, though it was written by Eddie Dean and mentions a number of cowboy stars, cannot be considered western music. As for Dean, his only chart appearance in the 1950s was when he hit #10 with his own recording of that song on the obscure Sage and Sand label in 1955. Gene Autry's biggest record of the 1940s was "Rudolph the Red-Nosed Reindeer," and his biggest nonholiday hit during that time was the wartime love song "At Mail Call Today." He was not a factor on the charts at all after 1950. Nor was Jimmy Wakely, who sold millions by himself and in duet with Margaret Whiting from 1944 to 1951, but who was off the charts entirely after 1952. Rex Allen maintained a chart presence, but the only western record among his country hits was the novelty "Don't Go Near the Indians," which peaked at #4 in 1962.

Roy Rogers was the only singing cowboy to enjoy postwar record success with pure-western music: "My Chickashay Gal" rose to #4 in 1947, while the two songs from the Walt Disney film *Melody Time* (Disney, 1948)— "(There'll Never Be Another) Pecos Bill" and "Blue Shadows on the Trail"— rose to #13 and #6 respectively in 1948. Rogers's "Stampede" (which found him again backed by the Sons of the Pioneers) was a #8 song in the spring of 1950, but from that point on he did not chart another western song until the nostalgic country song "Hoppy, Gene, and Me" in 1974.

Of the groups, the Sons of the Pioneers charted western music in the 1940s ("Cool Water" in 1947 and again in 1948, and "Tumbling Tumbleweeds" in 1948), but more than half of their charted successes came with country songs like "Room Full of Roses," pop songs like "My Best to You" (both in 1949), and the novelty "Cigareetes, Whusky, and Wild, Wild Women" in 1947. The Pioneers' lovely "Room Full of Roses," featuring Ken Curtis's solo voice, was the outfit's last chart record. Similarly, Foy Willing & the Riders of the Purple Sage had a #3 hit in 1944 with a western song, a

Impromptu sing-alongs—even among those not known as singers—were apparently not uncommon on the remote locations John Ford frequently chose for his films. Here, *left to right,* composer Stan Jones teams up with actors Harry Carey Jr. and Ben Johnson for a bit of musical fun. (Photo courtesy of Lida Rose Maze)

Willing composition called "Texas Blues," but their other Top Twenty hits were covers of others' country hits: "Detour" and "Have I Told You Lately (That I Love You)," both in 1946, and "Anytime" in 1948.

Bassist, emcee, record producer, disc jockey, and longtime West Coast figure Cliffie Stone hit the charts in 1947 with a remake of Denver Darling's "Silver Stars, Purple Sage, Eyes of Blue," which peaked at #4. Stone, born Clifford Gilpin Snyder on March 1, 1917, had worked as a bassist with big bands led by Anson Weeks and Freddie Slack in the 1930s, but he turned to country music in the 1940s. His multifaceted output was prodigious. He recorded prolifically for Capitol; wrote hit songs; discovered Tennessee Ernie Ford and Molly Bee and managed those two, as well as other artists; hosted television and radio shows; worked as an executive and producer with Capitol; and even started his own independent label, Granite, in the 1970s, for which the Sons of the Pioneers, Tex Williams, and Molly Bee recorded. Though the bulk of his career was more country than western, he was a friend and associate of most of the cowboy singers of the day. His long and honor-filled career was still perking along when he died January 17, 1998.

A number of country performers occasionally turned to cowboy material. The second most successful was Slim Whitman, the Florida-born yodeler with a distinctive fluid falsetto. Whitman tackled a number of musical styles: cowboy songs such as "Love Song of the Waterfall" (1952), "The Singing Hills" (1954), and "Cattle Call" (1955); pop songs like "Secret Love" (1954) and "My Happiness"(1960); and light opera, including "Indian Love Call" (1952) and "Rose-Marie" (1954). Joining him in this group—in the wake of interest in roots music during the folk boom—was Johnny Cash, the one-time rockabilly whose gritty records "Don't Take Your Guns to Town" in 1959, "The Rebel—Johnny Yuma" in 1961, and "The Sons of Katie Elder" in 1965 all charted well.

There was for a short time a fascination with Davy Crockett, which became nothing short of a national mania. Walt Disney's three-part series, which premiered on the *Disneyland* ABC television series December 15, 1954, ushered in a marketing craze that topped even the merchandizing success of Hopalong Cassidy and Roy Rogers. Coonskin caps and Kentucky rifles were ubiquitous among the children of America for a time, and "The Ballad of Davy Crockett" was recorded dozens of times and hummed all across the country. Fess Parker's laconic portrayal of Crockett did not much resemble the real-life garrulous and bonhomie-filled Tennessean, but like the real Crockett, he both sang and played the fiddle in the Disney series, which was later cobbled together into a full-length movie released in the summer of 1955 (*Davy Crockett, King of the Wild Frontier,* Buena Vista). Though not a cowboy, Crockett was a frontiersman, a musician and singer, and a genuine hero. Thus he appealed to the same audience that the singing cowboys did, in much the same way.

The undisputed king of western music of this era was Marty Robbins. Born Martin David Robinson in Glendale, Arizona, on September 26, 1925, he loved cowboy music from his youth and idolized Gene Autry. His first professional band was the K-Bar Cowboys on radio, and he had his own TV show, *Western Caravan,* in KPHO in Phoenix before beginning a recording career in 1952 and joining the Grand Ole Opry in 1953. Robbins's expressive voice was perfect for cowboy music, but the times were not, and his initial success was in singing country love songs, which garnered him the early professional nickname "Mr. Teardrop."

He apparently never lost his fascination with the West, however; indeed, the versatile Robbins even wrote a western paperback novel, *The Small Man.* Though the times for singing-cowboy westerns were long over, he appeared in *The Badge of Marshal Brennan* (Allied Artists, 1957), which also featured fellow Opry star Carl Smith and starred veteran western actor Jim Davis. In *Raiders of Old California* (Republic, 1957), Robbins again appeared in singing support of Davis, this time with Opry star Faron Young in attendance. Robbins, Smith, and country record–seller Webb Pierce made another musical western the following year, though *Buffalo Gun* (Globe) was not released until 1961. All were produced or directed by independent producer Albert Gannaway, who had made a series of color television shows for the Grand Ole Opry in 1954 and 1955. Neither Smith nor Pierce made any future appearances in western films, nor did either record any significant western material. For all their flashy spangled cowboy outfits designed by Nudie, they were pure country singers and left no other mark on the western genre. Young, for his part, fancied himself "the Singing Sheriff" for a time but did not record western material.[2] Marty Robbins had the starring role in one other full-fledged western, another cheap independent called *Ballad of a Gunfighter* (Parade, 1964), in which he sang a couple of his notable gunfighter ballads, "El Paso" and "San Angelo." He appeared in a few more drive-in specials such as the country music spectacular *The Road to Nashville* (1966) but in no more westerns.

After filming the three Gannaway westerns, however, Robbins became convinced it was time for a resurgence in cowboy music. In 1959, he had a successful record, "The Hanging Tree," the theme song of the Gary Cooper

Country music superstars play cowboy in *Buffalo Gun* (1961). Attempting to look heroic are, *left to right,* Webb Pierce, Carl Smith, and Marty Robbins. (Author's collection)

Not long after joining the Autry road show in 1956, Johnny Western brought his parents, John and Dolly Westerlund, backstage to meet Autry *(left)* and costar Gail Davis (TV's Annie Oakley) at a Chicago performance. (Photo courtesy of Johnny Western)

film of the same name, and his phenomenally successful "El Paso" was released first on the album *Gunfighter Ballads and Trail Songs,* then as a single in the fall of that year. Featuring the sinuous lead guitar of Grady Martin and the exquisite vocal harmony of Jim Glaser and Bobby Sykes, the record was an overwhelming national success both in country and in pop and led to a series of successful singles in the same style: "Big Iron" (#5 in 1960), "Five Brothers" (#26 in 1960), and a rewrite of "Zebra Dun" called "The Cowboy in the Continental Suit" (#3 in 1964), as well as three successful western albums.

Although his love for cowboy music was genuine, Robbins was well aware that variety was the spice of a career. He did not settle for long in the cowboy style (though he forever remained associated with it) but moved on immediately to a huge #1 country-pop hit, "Don't Worry," in 1961. He recorded calypso ("Devil Woman," #1 in 1962), folk ("Ribbon of Darkness," #1 in 1965), and pop ("My Woman, My Woman, My Wife," #1 in 1970); and he had consistent country chart successes as well. He charted "Mr. Shorty" (#16 in 1966), "Tonight Carmen" (#1 in 1967), and "El Paso City" (#1 in 1976), all in the western style, before his untimely death from heart failure on December 8, 1982. Bear Family Records has released a four-CD set called *Under Western Skies,* which includes most of Robbins's western recordings on Columbia.

Another keeper of the flame was Johnny Western, born John Westerlund III in Two Harbors, Minnesota, on October 28, 1934. Profoundly inspired by seeing Gene Autry's *Guns and Guitars* at the age of five, Johnny became a radio entertainer and disc jockey while still in high school. He headed for Hollywood, as all aspiring cowboy singers seemed to do, but by then it was just a little too late. Even though the singing-cowboy era was winding to a close in 1956, the starry-eyed youngster was spotted at a party by Gene Autry, who recruited Western to replace the retiring Johnny Bond in his touring show. Western was the hot young hunk for a time, touring with Autry, recording for Columbia, appearing on television, and writing "The Ballad of Paladin" for the television show *Have Gun, Will Travel.* He became part of Johnny Cash's road show from the late 1950s to the mid-1960s, recorded for Phillips after his Columbia contract ran out, then became established as a Nevada showroom headliner.

Johnny Western's career was in decline for awhile, but he jumped at the chance to join KFDI in Wichita as a disc jockey in 1986. He is currently playing records and charming audiences on the air while still appearing on the road on weekends, his voice as strong and distinctive as ever. An avid supporter of the Western Music Association and a tireless devotee of the singing cowboy, he is a familiar face at western gatherings and festivals and has become an elder statesman for the revival of the style. A gifted storyteller, he is reportedly busy collecting his thousands of reminiscences of cowboy and country stars for publication.

Eddy Arnold did his part to keep western music on the record charts, though the style was not his usual province: "The Cattle Call" was a #1 record in 1955. Like several other country singers of the time, Arnold sought to cash in on the folk revival, and his version of Jimmy Driftwood's frontier folk song "The Tennessee Stud" rose to #5 in 1959.

One of the delights the folk revival brought to mainstream music was the collection of quirky historical ballads of an Arkansas schoolteacher named

James Corbett Morris, who went by the professional name Jimmy Drift-wood. In the wake of the folk boom, Driftwood's songs were authentic enough to sound genuinely folk, and clever and catchy enough to be commercial, and a great many of them were set in the West or on the frontier. Though he never had another record like "The Battle of New Orleans" (a #1 hit for Johnny Horton in 1959, and a #24 chart hit for Driftwood himself that year), he recorded a great many haunting folk numbers for RCA in the late 1950s and early 1960s. Driftwood became a member of the Grand Ole Opry and toured actively for a time, but he tired of commercial musicmaking and took his songwriting gains and returned to Arkansas, where he developed and ran the Ozark Folk Center in Mountain View, the community in which he had been born June 20, 1907. He passed away on July 12, 1998.

Other country singers who chipped in with western songs during these years include Tennessee Ernie Ford with "River of No Return" in 1954; Claude King with "The Comancheros" in 1961; Jim Reeves with "The Blizzard" in 1961; Hank Snow with "The Man Who Robbed the Bank at Santa Fe" in 1963; the Statler Brothers with "Whatever Happened to Randolph Scott" in 1974; Stu Phillips (who had begun his career in Edmonton, Alberta, as a cowboy singer) with "Bracero" and "The Great El Tigre," both in 1966; Hank Thompson with a remake of "Oklahoma Hills" in 1961; Ernest Tubb with "The Yellow Rose of Texas" in 1955; and Billy Walker with "Cross the Brazos at Waco" in 1964. Walker, a native Texan (born in Ralls on January 14, 1929) who began his career singing cowboy songs, has begun recording original western music on his own Tall Texan label. His lilting voice is still strong, and songs like "Coffee Brown Eyes" are continuing the tradition to this day.

Despite the chart successes of the occasional western song, the years that stretched between 1955 and 1975 were bittersweet, as year by year the successes grew more scant: fewer and fewer western popular songs, no more films, the end of the Autry television series in 1955, the end of the *Melody Ranch* radio show in 1956, the end of the Roy Rogers television series in 1957 (though it was rerun for several years), the steady decline of even the television kiddie cowboy shows. Rock & roll seemed to finish off what was left of the genre's vitality, and public interest showed a steady and sure decline.

There were remaining points of light, to be sure. Knott's Berry Farm, the little picnic grove in Orange County, California, that has now become a major amusement park, hired a young group of musicians to provide western singing around a campfire. The Wagonmasters introduced thousands (including me) to the joys of live western harmony singing through the thirteen years they played there.

Bassist, songwriter, and emcee Dick Goodman (born 1932) spun off from the group and formed the Reinsmen in 1962 with Jerry Compton (born 1935) and Don Richardson (born 1935). While they played music only part-

The Reinsmen. *From left:* Doc Denning, Dick Goodman, Jerry Compton, and Don Richardson. (Country Music Hall of Fame collections)

time through these years, they were the classiest of the harmony groups, appearing all over the West, and frequently toured with Rex Allen. Later members included guitarist, songwriter, vocalist, and outstanding western painter Bob Wagoner (born 1928) and fiddler and vocalist Max "Doc" Denning (born 1921), who had recorded for Four Star back in 1946. Although their appearances and recordings were relatively infrequent, the Reinsmen kept the flame alive with impeccable harmony in the tradition of the Sons of the Pioneers.

In Colorado an enterprising group of young singers and businessmen began the Flying W Chuck Wagon in the resort town of Colorado Springs, and for more than four decades now the Flying W Wranglers have dispensed beef and beans, applesauce, and cornbread on tin plates along with

The early Flying W Wranglers. *From left:* Buck Teeter, Cy Scarborough, Babe Humphrey, Chuck Camp, and Bob Minser. (Photo courtesy of Cy Scarborough)

an hour of western music and humor for tourists from all over the world. The idea spread, and indeed some of the early members of the Wranglers (Cy Scarborough, Chuck Camp, and Babe Humphrey) began their own such operations in Durango, Colorado, Tucson, Arizona, and Jackson Hole, Wyoming, respectively, while others sprang up in such scenic locations as Estes Park, Colorado, Carlsbad, New Mexico (where Sons of the Pioneers fiddler Hugh Farr finished up his career), and Mesa, Arizona. It's true that the scale was fairly small, and the shows seasonal, but through the years, hundreds of thousands have been introduced to and become familiar with western music through visits to these and other chuck wagons, which have an active professional association and continue profitably to this day.

Although the folk boom of the late 1950s and early to middle 1960s had introduced such genres as bluegrass music—and such iconic musical figures as Bill Monroe—to a devoted new audience, western music on the whole was not embraced by the folk revival. While a few western-oriented performers like Katy Lee, Glenn Ohrlin, Harry Jackson, and Jimmy Driftwood were part of the folk movement, there was no folk boom "rediscovery" of the Sons of the Pioneers and western music. The style was caught in an odd limbo, considered too quaint and dated for any niche in popular music, and too slick and not quaint enough to fit any niche in folk.

It was also during the lean years that small groups of nostalgia-oriented film buffs and collectors began organizing western film festivals. Though these were a national phenomenon to a small degree, the main focus was in the Southeast, with leading festivals in Charlotte, Knoxville, Raleigh, and Memphis. Amid nonstop showings of old films on dozens of small screens, these festivals also provided workshops and panels featuring stars, costars, heavies, and character actors of the B western's golden age. Many singing cowboys became fixtures of these events, endearing themselves to their loyal fans and a new generation as well. Eddie Dean, Ray Whitley, Johnny Bond, Cal Shrum, Art Davis, Monte Hale, and many others entertained the hundreds who attended the yearly events. Western film festivals seemed to reach a peak in the 1970s and 1980s, when many of the stars of yesteryear were aging but still active. With the passing of most of these performers, the festivals have become smaller and fewer, but they still exist, to the delight of film fans and traders of western movie art and memorabilia.

For the most part, the fallow years showed that mainstream popular culture had moved on, leaving the singing cowboys behind. Although they remained figures in the national consciousness, they were figures with little relevance beyond a nostalgia for what many perceived as a more innocent and morally unambiguous time. It looked for a time as though the story had been written, wrapped up, and put away, leaving few if any loose ends.

It had been a great ride, but to the surprise of many, it was not over yet.

# 13

# Revival

By the early 1970s cowboy music was largely a historical curiosity, a piece of nostalgia, an antique music redolent of another time. Except in the collective memory of an earlier generation, it was not a part of the experience of many music-loving Americans, even those primed to appreciate acoustic music at folk and bluegrass festivals. Western music was off the radar screen.

Even so, some of the original singing cowboys were at least somewhat active. Roy Rogers, Rex Allen, Eddie Dean, and Tex Ritter still made limited personal and television appearances, as did the Sons of the Pioneers, although after the death of Lloyd Perryman in 1977, even their existence seemed in jeopardy. As it turned out, longtime Pioneer Dale Warren refused to let the outfit die and brought in veteran country singer Rome Johnson (1916–1993), then Luther Nallie, and has continued the grand tradition of the Sons of the Pioneers to the present day.

Still, by the middle of the decade came signs that the tide might be turning. While embarking on a successful career as a country singer, Rex Allen's eldest son, Rex Jr. (born in Chicago on August 23, 1947), released a nostalgic tribute to the singing cowboys, "Can You Hear Those Pioneers." It featured Rex Sr. and the Sons of the Pioneers on backing vocals and emphasized the refrain, "I think it's time that we put Western back in the country sound." It was a fine sentiment, but it came just a little too early. Although the song hit the Top Twenty in 1976, as did Rex Jr.'s remake of his father's classic cowboy love song "Teardrops in My Heart," western music was not ready for a resurgence. An album of original and classic western songs, *The Singing Cowboy,* followed in 1982, but by then Rex Allen Jr. was back in the country music mainstream, where he has forged a career that continues today. For a while he reportedly felt his foray into western music had deflected and perhaps even damaged his mainstream career, but in recent years he accompanied his father at western music festivals and gatherings, where both men acted as gracious spokesmen for the genre.

For a moment it looked like Willie Nelson might make a difference. Born in Abbott, Texas, on April 30, 1933, Nelson enjoyed an early career as a top Nashville songwriter and performer, though not a big record seller on his own. This all changed when he left Nashville's Music Row and returned to Texas in 1970, when he began recording personal and quirky albums for Atlantic. *Phases and Stages* and *Shotgun Willie* were critically acclaimed, but the breakthrough came with his 1975 Columbia concept album *The Red Headed Stranger,* based on the song that had been a minor hit for Eddy Arnold nearly two decades before. The album was sparse to the point of starkness and intensely emotional, unlike anything being produced in Nashville, and the record yielded a huge single, a remake of the Fred Rose classic "Blue Eyes Crying in the Rain."

Willie Nelson's version of the West was not the sunny landscape painted by Autry and Rogers; it hearkened back to the darker "adult westerns" of the 1950s and Marty Robbins's gunfighter ballads. Still, cowboys were back on the charts. But Nelson, Waylon Jennings, and the boys became icons of the "outlaw" movement, playing up their image as societal misfits, pool hall denizens, outsiders, and drifters. A number of pretenders and poseurs climbed on the outlaw bandwagon, and the movement, though it made a brief bright impact on the country music charts, collapsed of its own weight as the ever-evolving Willie Nelson went on to record "Star Dust" and other great pop standards.

Nelson himself never lost his love of western music or his desire to see "The Red Headed Stranger" translated to film. As an actor he was featured in several films with a western outlook, including *The Electric Horseman* (Wildwood Productions/Columbia/Universal, 1979) and *Barbarossa* (ITCI, 1982). His concept album eventually made it to film as well—with Morgan Fairchild as "the yellow-haired woman"—when he starred as *The Red Headed Stranger* (Alive Films), which was filmed in 1984 but not released until 1987.

An entirely different tack was taken by Chris LeDoux, born in Biloxi, Mississippi, on October 2, 1948. A champion rodeo rider, he began releasing a series of self-produced albums featuring many of his own songs on his own Lucky Man label out of Mount Juliet, Tennessee, around 1976. His sensibility was his own; instead of singing about the cinematic West or the rancher and cowman, LeDoux concentrated on his own experiences as a rodeo cowboy. Combining lyrics about the rodeo life with an increasing rock orientation in his music, he built a devoted following among contestants.

LeDoux eventually landed a deal with Capitol in 1991 and had several chart records, including a duet with Garth Brooks called "What You Going to Do with a Cowboy?" a raucous paean to the swaggering rodeo lifestyle. LeDoux's career continues to thrive. His high-energy live shows encore with

Rodeo star and recording artist Chris LeDoux sings of the rodeo cowboy from hard experience—he's been there! (Country Music Hall of Fame collections)

him singing from the back of a bucking mechanical bull, which never fails to rouse his audience. Despite health problems that culminated in a successful liver transplant in 2000, he has carved out a unique niche in contemporary country music that is evocative of the modern West.

On other fronts, mainstream West Coast country music producer Snuff Garrett coaxed long-retired Bob Nolan into the recording studios in 1979 to cut a brand-new album, *The Sound of a Pioneer*. It was the striking last stand of one of the legends of western music, and amid the classics, fans were able to hear two new vivid original songs from Nolan's prolific pen. It became a moving tribute after Nolan's death the following year.

It was into this relative void that three young Nashville musicians stepped, when Riders In The Sky was formed on a whim late in 1977. Members included me, Douglas "Ranger Doug" Green, born in Great Lakes, Illinois, on March 20, 1946; Fred "Too Slim" LaBour, born in Grand Rapids on June 3, 1948; and Bill "Windy Bill" Collins, born in 1948, who was replaced within months by Paul W. "Woody Paul" Chrisman, born in Nashville on August 23, 1949. They combined historical and musical sensibilities and a love of the music of the West and, with a free-reigning sense of humor, began to play the Nashville club scene in the 1970s. They recorded extensively for Rounder, then MCA, then Columbia, then Rounder again, and

Riders In The Sky at Melody Ranch for the filming of *Twang. From left:* Woody Paul, Joey the Cowpolka King, Ranger Doug, and Too Slim. (Author's collection)

most recently for Disney. The act appeared on *Austin City Limits,* hosted *Tumbleweed Theater* on The Nashville Network, and became members of the Grand Ole Opry in 1982.

As the 1980s rolled on, Riders In The Sky and the resurgence of western music began to build. The Riders appeared in the 1985 film *Sweet Dreams* and the 1984 TV film *Wild Horses,* then obtained a syndicated public radio program, *Riders' Radio Theater* (1988–1996), which led to a CBS Saturday morning network television series in 1991 and 1992. These major media appearances were followed by a series of Christmas specials and the *Riders' Radio Theater: The Television Show* specials on The Nashville Network in the 1990s. They added Joey "the Cowpolka King" Miskulin (born in Chicago, Illinois, on January 6, 1949) in the late 1980s, which solidified their sound and provided a sympathetic and experienced record producer as well.

The success of Riders In The Sky was a harbinger that the time was right for a revival of interest in the music of the cowboy and the heritage of the West. The early 1980s saw Gene Autry planning the development of his Western Heritage Museum, which covered not only film and music history but the history of the settling the West, the Native American, and in turn the Spanish and the Anglo resettling of the entire region. The museum was founded in 1984 and opened, to great acclaim, in 1988.

Another sign of the times came with a full album of cowboy songs by Gary McMahan (born in Greely, Colorado, on August 28, 1948). Released on the independent Tomato Records, with major-label distribution, the album was full of original songs (a couple of which have become contemporary western standards) and yodeling. While the 1980 release was not the commercial success the label hoped for, it helped McMahan forge a successful career as a cowboy poet and singer. At about the same time, Ian Tyson (born in Victoria, British Columbia, on September 25, 1933) returned to his cowboy roots. This folk legend (as half of Ian & Sylvia) turned country rocker (Great Speckled Bird) turned horse trainer began recording a series of commercially and artistically successful Canadian albums of cowboy music, much of it original. The man knows the craft of songwriting, and a great many of his compositions—among them, "Someday Soon," "The Gift," and "Navajo Rug"—have become standards in contemporary western music. A frequent visitor to western events, festivals, and gatherings, Tyson remains at the forefront of the western-music revival as one of its most creative and popular major figures.

Add to this the love of a few folklorists for the authentic poetry of the cowboy—the basis, we will recall, of many of the earliest songs westerners sang—which is, to the surprise of many, still being composed today. Hal Cannon, Jim Griffith, and others set up a gathering of contemporary cowboy and ranch poets in the obscure gold-mining and gambling town of Elko, Nevada, in 1985, and the Cowboy Poetry Gathering has since become a nationally celebrated event, giving regional favorites like Baxter Black and

Michael Martin Murphey backstage. No figure has been more influential in the rebirth of western music. (Country Music Hall of Fame collections)

Waddie Mitchell national exposure. The music of the cowboy and the West was not emphasized as heavily as was the poetry, but it was always an integral part of the gatherings, and this in turn exposed thousands of attendees to western music. New talents were recognized in a field that had been considered commercially dead.

This renewal of interest in all things western won over talents who were successful in other fields, including Russell "Red" Steagall, born in Gainesville, Texas, on December 22, 1937. After a successful career as a country singer and songwriter—often with a western-swing flair and orientation—Steagall turned his energies and talents to cowboy poetry and music. Besides making some of the finest contemporary cowboy music, he has also has become a premier cowboy poet.

No one has played a more pivotal role in the revival of western music than Michael Martin Murphey, born in Oak Cliff, Texas, on March 14, 1945. As adept as Gene Autry at reinventing himself, Murphey became a successful pop songwriter and folk-rock performer (with the Lewis and Clark Expedition) in the late 1960s. He then transformed himself into the epitome of the cosmic cowboy in the early 1970s during that phase of Austin, Texas's musical development, writing and performing such classics as "Geronimo's Cadillac" and "Cosmic Cowboy." After charting mainstream pop hits "Wildfire" and "Carolina in the Pines" in the middle 1970s, Murphey moved into a successful mainstream country music career in the early 1980s, but even as he was doing so, he fell deeply under the spell of western music. Using his influence in the business, he began a series of festivals called West Fests in 1986, which featured a wide variety of western and country singers, and western arts and crafts as well. He also persuaded his label, Warner Bros., to record and promote heavily his 1990 album of traditional and contemporary western material, *Cowboy Songs*. The album was a commercial success and led to three follow-up albums and the creation of the Warner Western label in 1992, a division of Warner Bros. devoted to western singers and the poetry of Waddie Mitchell and Red Steagall.

On this label two other emerging stars began to shine. Don Edwards (born on March 20, 1939, in Boonton, New Jersey) had been working in semi-obscurity as a cowboy and western-swing singer since moving to Texas in 1958. He suddenly became a hot property and began an active touring and recording schedule as the western revival began in earnest in the late 1980s. His forty-year career reached a peak when he was cast as Smokey, Robert Redford's singing sidekick, in the 1997 Buena Vista film *The Horse Whisperer*.

Warner Western also showcased the powerful vocal talents of the Sons of the San Joaquin, an act that consisted of brothers Joe (born in 1932) and Jack (born in 1933) Hannah, and Joe's son Lon (born in 1956). Schoolteachers and coaches by trade, they were "discovered" at the Cowboy Poetry Gathering in 1989, where their astonishing voices and their collection of under-recorded Bob Nolan and Tim Spencer songs—compositions that had been collecting dust for decades—made them a sensation. After cutting two albums filled with these undiscovered classics, they began writing distinctive western songs of their own, and their career remains in full bloom.

The Warner Western experiment was an exciting one, though the label has not been able to repeat its earliest successes. However, other artists such as Red Steagall, myself, Tim Ryan, and Joni Harms, as well as silver-screen cowboys Herb Jeffries and Rex Allen, have released albums of original cowboy music on the label.

On the other hand, as with a number of genres like bluegrass and polka that are out of the commercial mainstream, a lot of western music exists on self-produced CDs and tapes. Many of the finest current artists of the genre, like R. W. Hampton, Gary McMahan, Liz Masterson & Sean Blackburn, Sourdough Slim (Rick Crowder), Andy Wilkinson, and Craig Chambers, can be found only on their own labels or on microlabel independents. Some of the big names in western music—Murphey, Edwards, and the Sons of the San Joaquin—have now gone to independent labels as well.

Don Edwards's long career as a western singer reached a peak when he appeared as Robert Redford's sidekick, Smokey, in *The Horse Whisperer* (1998). (Author's collection)

Specialty labels like Rounder, Rhino, and Life, Times, and Music have produced handsome and informative anthologies of western music, from the earliest recordings to the singing-cowboy heyday. Bear Family Records, a German label, has produced lavish boxed sets of the Sons of the Pioneers, Johnny Western, Rex Allen, Tex Ritter, and Eddy Arnold (among many others) and has released smaller sets of Kenny Roberts, Eddy Arnold (his cowboy and folk records), and other related performers. Smaller labels have also produced a plethora of reissues, including Varese Sarabande (a silver-screen collection with several sets of film soundtracks by Autry, Rogers, and the Sons of the Pioneers) and ASV (a fine Carson Robison set), as have Yazoo (*When I Was a Cowboy,* volumes 1 and 2, collections of pre-singing-cowboy western folk music) and Simitar (collections of film-era cowboys Rex Allen, Eddie Dean, Jimmy Wakely, Smiley Burnette, and the mislabeled Foy Willing & the Riders of the Purple Sage—actually a couple of Willing cuts in a collection of various artists that include Red River Dave). Most of the major labels carry a vintage or historical series as a public service, and some of the major label recordings of most of the singing cowboys covered in this book are currently available: Wakely and Ritter on Capitol, Rogers and the Pioneers on RCA, and Autry on Sony. In addition, Boston-based Rounder Records maintains a small but distinct cowboy presence with Riders In The Sky (twelve albums), Wylie & the Wild West, and Skip Gorman.

In other areas of the business, the Western Music Association is moving into its second decade of existence, with a yearly festival and showcase in Tucson. A hall of fame to celebrate the careers of the leaders in the field is also planned. There are currently West Fests, poetry gatherings, and festivals dotted throughout the West, and yodeling and western harmony have shown up repeatedly in film and television, including commercials for Levi's,

The Sons of the San Joaquin. *From left:* Lon Hannah, Jack Hannah, and Joe Hannah. (Author's collection)

HBO, Cheer, Budweiser, and Yahoo. A number of artists make full-time livings touring, and the chuck wagons that sustained the music in the 1950s and 1960s are more popular than ever. There are several magazines that cover cowboy or western life, and western folk art is trendy.

Although no one expects western music to have the broad-based commercial impact it had in the 1930s, it has, over the last twenty-five years, come back from near extinction to a rightful place alongside such diverse musical styles as Cajun, bluegrass, polka, and zydeco. Most recently there has been the success of the animated films *Toy Story* and *Toy Story 2* (Disney/ Pixar, 1999); the latter features singing-cowboy puppet hero Sheriff Woody, his sidekick, Jessie the Yodeling Cowgirl, and theme music written by Randy Newman and performed by Riders In The Sky. The film's director, John Lasseter, expressed the feelings and hopes of all who love the musical culture of the singing cowboy when he triumphantly exclaimed at the film's premier, "Cowboys are back!"

# Time Line

1822 — "The Hunters of Kentucky" becomes popular, the first known song about the frontier and frontiersmen.

1831 — "The Lion of the West" becomes a popular stage play.

1844 — "The Blue Juniata" becomes a popular song, celebrating the Native American and the West, part of which was western Pennsylvania.

1872 — Dr. Brewster Higley writes "Home on the Range."

1874 — Joseph G. McCoy, one of the early organizers of trail drives, documents the dawning days of the era with the first book on the subject: *Historic Sketches of the Cattle Trade of the West and Southwest.*

1877 — Thomas Edison patents the first phonograph, which plays cylinder recordings.

1880 — Herbert J. Yates is born in Brooklyn, August 24.

1882 — Show business reinvents the West with Buffalo Bill Cody's first Western Exposition. Within three years he adds Annie Oakley, Chief Sitting Bull, and the first national cowboy hero, Buck Taylor, to his Wild West Show.

— *Parson Jim, King of the Cowboys,* the first novel featuring a cowboy hero, is published by Erastus Beadle.

— Harry "Haywire Mac" McClintock is born in Knoxville, October 8.

1883 — Jules Verne Allen is born in Waxahatchie, Texas, April 1.

— Vernon Dalhart is born in Jefferson, Texas, April 6.

1884 — Otto Gray is born in South Dakota, March 2.

1888 — Emile Berliner patents the first phonograph to play flat, two-sided discs.

1889 — Thomas Edison invents the kinescope, with sound in mind.

— The Dodge City Cowboy Band plays at the inauguration of U.S. president Benjamin Harrison.

— Arthur E. Satherley is born in Bristol, England, October 19.

1890 — Carson J. Robison is born in Oswego, Kansas, August 4.

1892 — Tex Owens is born in Killeen, Texas, June 15.

1893 — D. J. O'Malley publishes "When the Work Is Done Next Fall."

— Historian Frederick Jackson Turner marks this year as the closing of the frontier.

1895 — Carl T. Sprague is born near Houston, May 10.

— Ken Maynard is born in Vevay, Indiana, July 21.

1896 — George Houston is born in Hampton, New Jersey.

1897 — Johnny Marvin is born in Oklahoma, July 11.

— Jimmie Rodgers is born in Meridian, Mississippi, September 8.

1898 — Jack Thorpe writes "Little Joe the Wrangler."

1899 — Billy Hill is born in Boston, July 14.
— Frank Luther is born near Lakin, Kansas, August 4.
— Jimmie Davis is born in Beech Springs, Louisiana, September 11.
1900 — Nat Levine is born in New York, July 26.
1901 — *The Journal of American Folklore* publishes the words to "Bury Me Not on the Lone Prairie," the first academic interest paid to the songs of the cowboy.
— Ray Whitley is born in Atlanta, December 5.
1902 — *The Virginian* by Owen Wister is published.
— Smith Ballew is born in Palestine, Texas, January 21.
— Fred Scott is born in Fresno, California, February 14.
— John I. White is born April 12.
— Louise Massey is born in Hunt County, Texas, August 2.
1903 — The birth of the Western film: *The Great Train Robbery* and *Kit Carson* are released.
1904 — Frank Marvin is born in Butler, Oklahoma, January 27.
— Dorothy Page is born in Northampton, Pennsylvania, March 4.
— Bing Crosby is born in Tacoma, Washington, May 2.
— Wilf Carter is born in Guysboro, Nova Scotia, December 18.
1905 — Tex Ritter is born in Murvaul, Texas, January 12.
— Bob Wills is born in Kosse, Texas, March 6.
1906 — Billy Murray's recording of "Cheyenne" becomes a minor pop hit.
— Jack Randall is born in Quincy, Illinois, May 12.
1907 — Songs about the West abound on Broadway: "San Antonio," "In the Land of the Buffalo," and "Ida-Ho" are featured on stage and recorded.
— Arkie the Woodchopper is born near Knob Noster, Missouri, March 2.
— Jimmy Driftwood is born near Mountain View, Arkansas, June 20.
— Eddie Dean is born in Posey, Texas, July 9.
— Gene Autry is born in Tioga, Texas, September 29.
1908 — Jack Thorpe's *Songs of the Cowboy,* the first collection of cowboy songs, is published.

— "Pride of the Prairie" and "My Pony Boy" are popular on Broadway and on record.
— Bob Nolan is born in Winnipeg, Manitoba, Canada, April 13.
— Tito Guizar is born in Guadalajara, Jalisco, Mexico, April 8.
— Tim Spencer is born in Webb City, Missouri, July 13.
— Donald Grayson is born in Canton, Ohio, July 23.
— Penny Singleton is born in Philadelphia, September 15.
— Stuart Hamblen is born in Kellyville, Texas, October 20.
— Patsy Montana is born in Hope, Arkansas, October 30.
— Rufe Davis is born in Oklahoma, December 2.
1909 — *The Journal of American Folklore* publishes "Songs of the Western Cowboy."
— Tex Fletcher is born in Harrison, New York, January 17.
— Texas Ruby is born in Wise County, Texas, June 4.
— John "Dusty" King is born in Cincinnati, July 11.
— Texas Jim Lewis is born in Meigs, Georgia, October 15.
1910 — *Cowboy Songs and Other Frontier Ballads* by John Lomax is published.
— Curt Massey is born in Midland, Texas, May 3.
— Dick Foran is born in Flemington, New Jersey, June 18.
— Cal Shrum is born in Mountain Home, Arkansas, July 4.
— Bill Boyd is born in Ladonia, Texas, September 29.
— Bob Baker is born in Forest City, Iowa, November 8.
— Spade Cooley is born in Pack Saddle, Oklahoma, December 17.
1911 — Cowboy Slim Rinehart is born near Gustine, Texas, March 11.
— Smiley Burnette is born in Summum, Illinois, March 18.
— James Newill is born in Pittsburgh, August 12.
— Zeke Clements is born in Warrior, Alabama, September 6.
— Herb Jeffries is born in Detroit, September 24.
— Vaughn Monroe is born in Akron, October 7.

— Roy Rogers is born in Cincinnati, November 5.

1912 — "Ragtime Cowboy Joe" becomes a national hit.
— Dale Evans is born in Uvalde, Texas, October 30.
— Doye O'Dell is born in Gustine, Texas, November 22.

1913 — Andy Parker is born in Mangum, Oklahoma, March 17.
— Art Davis is born in Paradise, Texas, May 31.
— Elton Britt is born in Marshall, Arkansas, June 27.

1914 — Nineteen-year-old Ken Maynard is a star of the Kit Carson Show.
— Ernest Tubb is born in Crisp, Texas, February 9.
— Jimmy Wakely is born in Mineola, Arkansas, February 16.
— Pee Wee King is born in Milwaukee, February 18.
— Texas Jim Robertson is born in Gastonia, North Carolina, February 27.
— Bob Atcher is born in Hardin County, Kentucky, May 11.
— Foy Willing is born in Bosque County, Texas, May 14.
— Stan Jones is born in Douglas, Arizona, June 5.
— Hi Busse is born in Warroad, Minnesota, August 6.
— Red River Dave McEnery is born in San Antonio, December 15.
— Pat Brady is born in Toledo, December 31.

1915 — Johnny Bond is born in Enville, Oklahoma, June 1.

1916 — Carl Cotner is born in Lake Cicotte, Indiana, April 8.
— Ken Curtis is born in Las Animas, Colorado, July 2.

1917 — Vernon Dalhart begins recording light opera and classics for Edison.
— Lloyd Perryman is born in Ruth, Arkansas, January 29.
— Tex Williams is born in Ramsey, Illinois, August 23.
— Merle Travis is born in Rosewood, Kentucky, November 29.
— Wesley Tuttle is born in Lamar, Colorado, December 30.

1918 — Tex Harding is born in New York, January 4.

— Herbert J. Yates leaves a successful career in the tobacco industry and buys Republic Film Laboratories, beginning his career as a movie mogul.
— Eddy Arnold is born in Henderson, Tennessee, May 15.
— Jane Frazee is born in Duluth, Minnesota, July 18.

1919 — Bentley Ball records "Jesse James" and "The Dying Cowboy," the first recording of cowboy folk songs.
— *The Song Companion of a Lone Star Cowboy* by Charles Siringo is published.
— Monte Hale is born in Ada, Oklahoma, June 8.

1920 — *Songs of the Cattle Trail and Cow Camp* by John Lomax is published .
— Tommy Doss is born in Weiser, Idaho, September 26.
— Rex Allen is born in Willcox, Arizona, December 31.

1921 — Ken Maynard joins the Ringling Brothers Circus.
— Nat Levine, who will bring the first singing cowboy to the screen, moves to Hollywood.

1922 — Motion Picture Producers and Distributors of America is organized. Will H. Hays, as president, is given broad powers to regulate morality in movies and in the movie industry.
— Carson J. Robison begins broadcasting over WDAF in Kansas City.
— Buck Page is born in Pittsburgh, June 18.

1923 — "Cowboy Song—Whoopee Ti Yi Yo" is recorded by the Glenn and Shannon Quartet.

1924 — Carson J. Robison teams with Vernon Dalhart.
— The *WLS Barn Dance* begins broadcasting over WLS-Chicago in April.
— Rosalie Allen is born in Old Forge, Pennsylvania, June 27.
— Vernon Dalhart records "Way Out West in Kansas," his first western recording, August 13.
— Charles Nabell, the first truly folk cowboy performer to make a record, records for OKeh Records in St. Louis.
— Herbert J. Yates forms Consolidated Film Industries, a conglomerate of film-related businesses.

1925 — Gene Autry finds employment on the St. Louis & Frisco Railroad.

— Dale Warren is born in Rockford, Illinois, June 1.
— Carl T. Sprague records the first cowboy hit record, "When the Work's All Done This Fall," August 5.
— Marty Robbins is born near Glendale, Arizona, September 26.
— The *WSM Barn Dance* begins broadcasting over WSM in Nashville, Tennessee, October 5.
— Carolina Cotton is born in Cash, Arkansas, October 20.
— Otto Gray & His Oklahoma Cowboys begin broadcasting over KFRU in Bristow, Oklahoma.

1926 — Otto Gray records for OKeh in St. Louis.
— Kenny Roberts is born in Lenoir City, Tennessee, October 14.

1927 — Jimmie Rodgers first records in Bristol, Tennessee, August 4.
— Will Rogers encourages Gene Autry to pursue a career in music.
— Gene Autry makes his first trip to New York. On the way (September 22) he stops to see the second Dempsey-Tunney fight and meets Jack Kapp at Soldier Field in Chicago, who recommends him to OKeh Records's Tommy Rockwell.
— *The Jazz Singer,* the first full-length sound film and sound musical, premiers October 6.
— The *WSM Barn Dance* becomes the Grand Ole Opry.

1928 — Haywire Mac begins recording traditional cowboy songs, March 1.
— Marc Williams records a series of traditional cowboy songs, March 22–24.
— Jules Verne Allen begins recording for RCA in El Paso, April 21.
— Tex Ritter leaves the University of Texas law school to tour in the production of "Maryland, My Maryland."
— Frank Luther begins recording with Carson Robison in New York.
— Ray Whitley moves to New York to work construction and teaches himself to play guitar.
— Silent film star William S. Hart records the poems "Lasca" and "Pinto Ben" for Victor on October 18, becoming the first movie cowboy to record (though these were recitations, not songs).
— Arkie the Woodchopper records for Columbia in Dallas, December 6.

— Lloyd Perryman migrates to California.
— Gene Autry appears as "Oklahoma's Yodeling Cowboy" on KVOO in Tulsa.
— Sears, Roebuck sells WLS to the *Prairie Farmer* magazine.

1929 — *In Old Arizona,* the first all-sound western and the first to feature a singing cowboy and western music, is released in January.
— Bob Nolan moves to California.
— Billie Maxwell becomes the first woman to record cowboy songs; Adelyne Hood quickly becomes the second.
— Jimmie Rodgers records his first cowboy song, "The Desert Blues," February 21.
— John I. White begins his recording career.
— Tim McCoy sings in a short film, *A Night on the Range,* as does Everett Cheetham in *Cow Camp Ballads.* Ken Maynard sings in *The Wagon Masters,* released October 6.
— Otto Gray & His Oklahoma Cowboys bring their stage show to film.
— Gene Autry returns to New York and begins recording, October 9.
— The stock market crashes, ushering in the Great Depression.

1930 — Warner Baxter wins an Oscar for his singing role as the Cisco Kid in *In Old Arizona.*
— Roy Rogers moves with his family to California.
— Ken Maynard records cowboy songs for Columbia Records, April 14.
— John I. White joins the cast of *Death Valley Days* on NBC Radio as the Lonesome Cowboy.
— The Beverly Hillbillies begin recording in Los Angeles, April 25.
— Ken Maynard sings in several of his films, beginning with *The Fighting Legion* and including *Mountain Justice, Song of the Caballero,* and *Sons of the Saddle*
— Bob Steele sings on film as well in *Oklahoma Cyclone,* released August 8.
— Comedian Joe E. Brown appears with a guitar in *Song of the West.*

1931 — Tex Ritter appears in *Green Grow the Lilacs,* which opens on Broadway on January 26.
— *Singing Cowboy* by Margaret Larkin is published.
— Tim Spencer moves to California and meets Bob Nolan and Roy Rogers.
— Gene Autry moves away from blue yodels and begins recording mountain

ballads; he and Jimmy Long record "That Silver Haired Daddy of Mine" in October, which becomes a major hit in 1932.

— Ray Whitley, laid off because of the worsening Depression, auditions and is accepted as a radio performer over WMCA in New York.

— Dr. John R. Brinkley's border station XER goes on the air.

— Roy Rogers joins the Rocky Mountaineers.

— Bob Nolan answers an ad for a yodeler in the *Los Angeles Examiner* placed by Roy Rogers for the Rocky Mountaineers.

1932 — Tex Ritter is the toast of New York, dominating the cowboy scene there by regularly appearing on four radio shows; he makes his first records, but they are unreleased.

— Roy Rogers's horse, Trigger, is born near San Diego, California.

— Bob Nolan leaves the Rocky Mountaineers and is replaced by Tim Spencer. Nolan writes "Tumbling Leaves," the basis for "Tumbling Tumbleweeds."

— Carson J. Robison splits with Frank Luther and moves to a flashy cowboy image as a composer and performer. Robison's Pioneers become the first country or western group to tour overseas, visiting England, Australia, and New Zealand.

— Tex Owens becomes the first cowboy singer on television, appearing with newscaster John Cameron Swayze over experimental station W9XAL in Kansas City.

1933 — Gene Autry's recordings continue to shift toward cowboy and country music, January 27.

— Nolan, Spencer, and Rogers form the Pioneer Trio and are hired on KFWB in Los Angeles.

— Bob Wills leaves the Light Crust Doughboys, forms his Playboys band, and works on radio in Waco.

— Billy Hill's "The Last Roundup" becomes a national hit, introduced on Broadway by Joe Morrison.

— Tex Ritter makes his first released recordings, "Goodbye Old Paint" and "Rye Whiskey, Rye Whiskey," in New York, March 15.

— Jimmie Rodgers dies, May 26.

— The Kentucky Ramblers become the Prairie Ramblers and add Patsy Montana to the group.

— The Girls of the Golden West join the *WLS Barn Dance.*

— Ian Tyson is born in Victoria, British Columbia, September 25.

— The *WLS Barn Dance* becomes the *National Barn Dance* with an NBC affiliation, September 30.

— Louise Massey & the Westerners join the *National Barn Dance* in October and begin their recording career with ARC/Columbia.

— Jack Dalton forms the first band called the Riders of the Purple Sage and plays at the opening of XEBC in Tijuana.

— John Wayne, in the role of Singin' Sandy, sings in *Riders of Destiny,* his voice dubbed by Bill Bradbury.

— Ken Maynard re-signs with Universal and makes several musical westerns, including *The Strawberry Roan.*

— Jules Verne Allen's *Cowboy Lore* is published.

— Gene Autry hires Smiley Burnette in December.

— Wilf Carter first records, December 30.

1934 — The Catholic League of Decency imposes the notorious Production Code on the motion picture industry.

— Hugh Farr joins the Pioneer Trio, which becomes the Sons of the Pioneers.

— The Ranch Boys move to Chicago in July.

— Decca jumps into the singing-cowboy field in a big way and begins recording Stuart Hamblen and the Sons of the Pioneers in August, and the Ranch Boys in September.

— Smiley Burnette begins recording.

— Bill Boyd & His Cowboy Ramblers begin recording.

— Eddie and Jimmy Dean join the *National Barn Dance* and begin recording.

— Johnny Western is born in Two Harbors, Minnesota, October 28.

— Ken Maynard and Gene Autry appear in *In Old Santa Fe,* released November 15.

1935 — Gene Autry and Smiley Burnette star in the western/science fiction serial *The Phantom Empire,* then in *Tumbling Tumbleweeds,* Autry's first starring feature and the first true singing-cowboy film, in September.

— Dick Foran and Warner Bros. follow closely with the release of *Moonlight on the Prairie* in November.

— "I Want to Be a Cowboy's Sweetheart" by Patsy Montana & the Prairie Ramblers becomes a national hit.

— Tex Ritter and Ray Whitley begin hosting the *WHN Barn Dance.*

— Tex Ritter begins recording for Decca.

— The Sons of the Pioneers appear in their first films: *Radio Scout (*Warner-Vitagraph), *The Old Homestead* (Liberty), *Slightly Static* (MGM), *Gallant Defender* (Columbia), and the short *Way Up Thar* (Mack Sennett).

— Bob Baker joins the *National Barn Dance.*

— The Cass County Kids form in Dallas.

— Herbert Yates reorganizes Consolidated Film Industries and forms Republic by merging Mascot and Monogram, then buying Liberty, Majestic, and Chesterfield. John Wayne's *Westward Ho* is the first release.

1936 — The title of an early Gene Autry film, *The Singing Cowboy,* defines the genre.

— Bing Crosby stars (with the Sons of the Pioneers in a musical role) in *Rhythm on the Range.*

— Tex Ritter's first film, *Song of the Gringo,* is released by Grand National.

— Fred Scott makes his first film, *Romance Rides the Range,* for Spectrum.

— Ray Whitley makes his first screen appearance.

— Lloyd Perryman joins the Sons of the Pioneers in September.

— Buck Page and his brother Bob form an East Coast version of the Riders of the Purple Sage.

— Ray Johnston leaves Republic and re-forms Monogram as a direct competitor.

— Gene Autry goes on strike at Republic, the first of four lawsuits the litigious star would bring against the studio.

1937 — Gene Autry is ranked the #1 moneymaking western star. He again walks off the set during a contract dispute.

— Texas Ruby and Zeke Clements begin recording.

— Ray Whitley begins making musical shorts for RKO; Smith Ballew begins a

singing-cowboy series with *Roll along Cowboy* for 20th Century-Fox, as does Bob Baker with *Courage of the West* for Universal, Jack Randall with *Riders of the Dawn* for Monogram, Herb Jeffries with *Harlem on the Prairie* for Sack Amusement, and James Newill with *Renfrew of the Royal Mounted* for Grand National.

— The Sons of the Pioneers are signed by Columbia Pictures to provide musical support for the Charles Starrett movie series.

— Len Slye (Roy Rogers) auditions for Republic and signs on as a contract player, October 13; he appears in small roles in *Wild Horse Rodeo* and *The Old Barn Dance* (as Dick Weston) before being thrust into a starring role, replacing the striking Gene Autry in *Under Western Stars.*

— Red Steagall is born in Gainesville, Texas, December 22.

— Nat Levine leaves Republic and is replaced by Moe Siegel, whose brother Sol C. Siegel is brought in to oversee serials and the Gene Autry westerns.

1938 — Tex Ritter moves to Monogram.

— Roy Rogers buys Trigger, and Rogers's first starring film is released.

— The Ranch Boys ride horseback from Los Angeles to New York (3,975 miles), stopping along the way to broadcast remote over WLS.

— Hi Busse forms the first version of the Frontiersmen.

— Red River Dave McEnery moves to New York.

— *Carson Robison's Buckaroos* national radio show airs over NBC.

— Universal releases nine Bob Baker films.

— Gene Autry tours constantly and scores the three biggest western hits of his career: "There's a Gold Mine in the Sky," "Take Me Back to My Boots and Saddles," and "Springtime in the Rockies." He and Yates resolve their differences, and he becomes Republic's singing-cowboy star again.

— More singing cowboys enter films, including George Houston in *Frontier Scout* and Gene Austin in *Songs and Saddles.*

1939 — Red River Dave McEnery appears on

experimental television in New York at the World's Fair.

— The Rough Riders, encouraged by Gene Autry, visit Hollywood.

— Gene Autry continues his string of hits with "Back in the Saddle Again" and "South of the Border."

— Grand National struggles and goes under but releases several new singing-cowboy films: *Trigger Pals* starring Art Jarrett; *Water Rustlers* starring Dorothy Page, the Singing Cowgirl; and two others.

— Buck Page's Riders of the Purple Sage move to New York.

— Dennis Morgan appears in the short *Sing Cowboy Sing,* followed by *The Singing Dude,* the first singing-cowboy films in color.

— Don Edwards is born in Boonton, New Jersey, March 20.

— Gene Autry tours England and Ireland to tumultuous acclaim.

1940 — Gene Autry's *Melody Ranch* goes on CBS Radio, January 7.

— The Rough Riders move to Hollywood for good, join the cast of *Melody Ranch,* and eventually record as three separate acts: Jimmy Wakely, Johnny Bond, and Dick Reinhart.

— Red River Dave McEnery begins his recording career for Decca, January 18.

— The Sons of the Pioneers leave Columbia Pictures and relocate to Chicago for radio work.

— Bob Wills makes his film debut in Tex Ritter's *Take Me Back to Oklahoma.*

— Dusty King enters singing-cowboy films as a Range Buster at Monogram.

— Billy Hill dies, December 24.

1941 — The breakup of the Ranch Boys: Curley Bradley sings the theme song and takes over the role of Pecos Williams on the *Tom Mix Show;* Ken Carson obtains his own show on WGN before joining the Sons of the Pioneers; Jack Ross recedes into the mists of time.

— The Cass County Boys begin recording for Bluebird in Dallas, April 3.

— Eddie Dean begins recording for Decca, September 4.

— The Sons of the Pioneers join Roy Rogers at Republic with *Red River Valley* in September.

— Gene Autry's "Be Honest with Me" is nominated for an Academy Award.

— Red Foley and Doye O'Dell make film debuts in Tex Ritter's *The Pioneers.*

— Tex Ritter moves to Columbia Pictures.

— Comedian Penny Singleton headlines *Go West Young Lady;* Bob Wills & His Texas Playboys are the band.

— Berwyn, Oklahoma (near Autry's boyhood home of Ravia) officially changes its name to Gene Autry, Oklahoma, in November. (Ravia would have been the town to get the name change, but on the Ravia town council sat the physician who had delivered Gene in 1907. He vetoed the plan, still resentful that Delbert Autry had never paid his bill!)

1942 — Dusty King has his only recording session, January 22.

— Tex Ritter moves to Universal.

— Gene Autry enlists and is inducted into the Army Air Corps on the July 26 broadcast of *Melody Ranch.*

— Len Slye legally changes his name to Roy Rogers, October 6.

— James Newill slips out of his Mountie outfit and joins the Texas Rangers in the Producers Releasing Corporation (PRC) film *Rangers Take Over.*

— PRC debuts the Frontier Marshals series with Bill Boyd, Art Davis, and Lee Powell.

— Future Mouseketeer leader Jimmie Dodd joins the Three Mesquiteers at Republic.

— Abbott & Costello star in two comedy western musicals, *Private Buckaroo* and *Ride 'Em Cowboy.*

1943 — Republic dubs Roy Rogers "King of the Cowboys," and Trigger "the Smartest Horse in the Movies."

— NBC sells off its Blue network, which becomes ABC.

1944 — Roy Rogers obtains a radio show on the Mutual network.

— Roy Rogers introduces "Don't Fence Me In" in *Hollywood Canteen.*

— Eddy Arnold records "The Cattle Call" for the first time.

— The Andrews Sisters' *Eight to the Bar Ranch* airs on NBC.

— Tex Ritter has three of the Top Ten records on the hillbilly jukebox charts.

— Jane Frazee stars in a western musical, *Swing in the Saddle.*
— Dale Evans first appears with Roy Rogers, in *The Cowboy and the Señorita.*
— Jimmy Wakely begins starring in films for Monogram with *Song of the Range.*
— Andy Parker forms the Plainsmen with Hank Caldwell and Charlie Morgan.
— The *Hollywood Barn Dance* airs on the CBS Radio network; Foy Willing re-forms the Riders of the Purple Sage for the show.
— George Houston dies, November 12.

1945 — Roy Rogers begins recording for RCA.
— Rex Allen joins the *National Barn Dance.*
— Eddie Dean appears in *Song of Old Wyoming,* his first starring role and the first full-length color singing-cowboy film.
— Ken Curtis begins starring roles with *Rhythm Round-Up* for Columbia Pictures.
— *Melody Ranch* returns to the air with the return of Gene Autry from the service.
— Tex Ritter makes his final films as a B-western star for PRC studios.
— Curley Bradley takes over the role of Tom Mix on radio.
— Michael Martin Murphey is born in Oak Cliff, Texas, March 14.
— Jack Randall is killed, July 16.

1946 — Rosalie Allen begins recording for RCA.
— Red River Dave McEnery chains himself to a piano and writes fifty-two songs in twelve hours over the air at WOAI in San Antonio.
— Kenny Roberts begins recording for Vogue, featured on segment of the *Hoosier Hop* from WOWO, Fort Wayne, Indiana.
— Monte Hale begins starring in singing-cowboy films, with *Home on the Range,* in color, for Republic.
— The Willis Brothers, a.k.a. the Oklahoma Wranglers, join the Grand Ole Opry.
— Ranger Doug is born in Great Lakes, Illinois, March 20.
— Gene Autry and Republic go to court over Autry's contract.
— Roy Rogers Jr. (Dusty) is born October 28; his mother, Arline, dies suddenly, November 3.

1947 — Gene Autry moves to Columbia Pictures, and *The Last Roundup* is released on November 5; he adds the Cass County Boys to his films as well as radio and stage shows.

— Andy Parker & the Plainsmen begin recording for Capitol.
— Roy Rogers and Dale Evans wed on December 31.

1948 — The Sons of the Pioneers leave Republic Pictures, replaced by the Riders of the Purple Sage.
— Eddie Dean makes his last starring film, *The Tioga Kid.*
— Roy Rogers and the Sons of the Pioneers sing "Pecos Bill" and "Blue Shadows on the Trail" in the Disney animation feature *Melody Time.*
— Too Slim is born in Grand Rapids, Michigan, June 3.
— Vernon Dalhart dies, September 15.
— Cowboy Slim Rinehart dies, October 28.

1949 — Joey the Cowpolka King is born in Chicago, January 6.
— Tim Spencer leaves the Sons of the Pioneers and is replaced by Ken Curtis; within months Bob Nolan retires as well, replaced by Tommy Doss.
— *The Curley Bradley Show* debuts on the Mutual Radio network.
— Jimmy Wakely makes his last western, *Lawless Code.*
— Universal continues its series of low-budget singing westerns, replacing Red River Dave McEnery with Tex Williams.
— Vaughn Monroe's "Riders in the Sky" becomes a major popular hit.
— Woody Paul is born in Nashville, August 23.
— Rex Allen leaves WLS.

1950 — *The Curley Bradley Show* becomes *Curley Bradley—The Singing Marshal* on Mutual Radio.
— Spade Cooley obtains a CBS Radio network show.
— *The Gene Autry Show* debuts on CBS Television, July 23.
— Monte Hale makes his last western, *The Vanishing Westerner.*
— Rex Allen makes his first starring western, *The Arizona Cowboy.*
— Vaughn Monroe makes his first starring western, *Singing Guns.*

1951 — Roy Rogers makes his last starring singing-cowboy film, *Pals of the Golden West.*
— *The Roy Rogers Show* debuts on NBC Television, December 30.
— Roy Rogers, then Gene Autry, take

Republic to court in separate lawsuits over the sale of their older films to television. (The court found for Rogers—overturned in 1954—and against Autry.)

1952 — Tex Ritter sings the memorable theme to *High Noon.*
— Roy Rogers guests in an A film, *Son of Paleface,* with Bob Hope.
— The Riders of the Purple Sage disband.

1953 — Gene Autry makes his final starring singing cowboy film, *Last of the Pony Riders,* released in November.

1954 — Rex Allen's final starring singing cowboy film, *Phantom Stallion,* is released, marking the end of the singing-cowboy film era.

1955 — Roy Rogers's radio show ends its run.
— *The Gene Autry Show*'s final episode airs on CBS-TV, December 24.
— The Davy Crockett craze sweeps the country.

1956 — Tex Ritter scores a national hit with "The Wayward Wind."
— Gene Autry's *Melody Ranch* leaves the air, May 13.

1957 — Andy Parker & the Plainsmen disband.
— Carson J. Robison dies, March 24.
— Marty Robbins appears in two films, one of them, *Raiders of Old California,* for Republic.
— Roy Rogers's TV show ends.

1958 — Donald Grayson dies, April 16.

1959 — Herbert Yates sells Republic Pictures Corporation, turning over controls to Victor Carter, July 1.
— Marty Robbins begins a mini western revival—almost single-handedly—with the million-selling "El Paso" in November.

1960 — Marty Robbins's western streak continues with the popular "Big Iron" and "Five Brothers."
— WLS drops the *National Barn Dance,* which moves to WGN for another ten years.

1961 — Dorothy Page dies, March 26.

1962 — The Reinsmen are formed.
— Tex Owens dies, September 9.

1963 — Stan Jones dies, December 13.
— Eddy Arnold releases an album of western classics.

1966 — Herbert J. Yates dies, February 3.
— Texas Jim Robertson dies, November 11.

1967 — Smiley Burnette dies, February 17.

1969 — Spade Cooley dies, November 23.

1972 — Gene Austin dies, January 24.
— Pat Brady dies, February 22.
— Elton Britt dies, June 23.

1974 — Tex Ritter dies, January 2.
— Tim Spencer dies, April 26.
— Bob Wills dies, May 13.

1975 — James Newill dies, July 31.
— Bob Baker dies, August 30.

1976 — Rex Allen Jr. resuscitates interest in western music with his hit single "Can You Hear Those Pioneers" and a singing-cowboy album.

1977 — Ken Maynard dies, March 23.
— Lloyd Perryman dies, May 31.
— Andy Parker dies, October 2.
— Bing Crosby dies, October 14.
— Riders In The Sky are formed, November 11.
— Bill Boyd dies, December 7.

1978 — Johnny Bond dies, June 12.
— Foy Willing dies, July 24.

1979 — Carl T. Sprague dies, February 19.
— Ray Whitley dies, February 21.
— Dick Foran dies, August 10.
— Bob Nolan's final album, *The Sound of a Pioneer,* is released.

1980 — Bob Nolan dies, June 16.
— Frank Luther dies, November 16.

1981 — Arkie the Woodchopper dies, June 23.

1982 — Tex Harding dies.
— Jimmy Wakely dies, September 23.
— Marty Robbins dies, December 8.

1983 — Louise Massey dies, June 20.
— *Tumbleweed Theater* appears on The Nashville Network.

1984 — Smith Ballew dies, May 2.
— Ernest Tubb dies, September 6.

1985 — First Cowboy Poetry Gathering is held in Elko, Nevada.
— Curley Bradley dies, June 3.
— Jane Frazee dies, September 6.
— Tex Williams dies, October 11.
— *Rustler's Rhapsody,* a singing-cowboy spoof, is released.

1986 — Arthur Satherley dies, February 10.
— Carl Cotner dies, November 14.

1987 — Tex Fletcher dies, March 14.
— Art Davis dies, June 16.
— Dusty King dies, November 11.

1988 — Autry Museum of Western Heritage opens in Los Angeles.
— Western Music Association is founded.

— *Riders' Radio Theater* debuts on National Public Radio.

1989 — Stuart Hamblen dies, March 8.
— Nat Levine dies, August 6.

1991 — *Riders In The Sky* airs on CBS-TV.
— Cottonseed Clark dies, January 9.
— Ken Curtis dies, April 28.
— Curt Massey dies, October 20.
— Fred Scott dies, December 16.

1992 — Warner Western record label is launched.
— John White dies, November 26

1993 — Bob Atcher dies, October 30.

1994 — Zeke Clements dies, June 4.
— Aaron Spelling buys the rights to the Republic film library.

1995 — Warner Western releases Herb Jeffries's *The Bronze Buckaroo Rides Again.*

1996 — Patsy Montana dies, May 3.
— Wilf Carter dies, December 5.

1997 — Carolina Cotton dies, June 10.
— Hi Busse dies, July 13.

1998 — Roy Rogers dies, July 6.
— Gene Autry dies, October 2.

1999 — Eddie Dean dies, March 4.
— Rex Allen dies, December 17.
— Riders In The Sky are featured in the animated film *Toy Story 2.*
— Tito Guizar dies, December 24.

2000 — Pee Wee King dies, March 7.
— Yodeling Slim Clark dies, July 5.
— Cliff Bruner dies, August 25.
— Zeke Manners dies, October 14.
— Jimmie Davis dies, November 5.

2001 — Doye O'Dell dies, January 3.
— Dale Evans dies, February 7.
— *Woody's Roundup Featuring Riders In The Sky* wins a Grammy for Best Musical Album for Children, February 21.

2002 — Red River Dave dies January 15
— *For the Birds,* with music by Riders In The Sky, wins an Academy Award for best short animated film

# Notes

## Chapter 1

1. H. N. Smith, *Virgin Land,* 59.
2. Savage, *The Cowboy Hero,* 109–110
3. Slatta, *The Cowboy Encyclopedia,* 336

## Chapter 2

1. Shackford, *David Crockett,* xi, 216.
2. To be a little fairer on this point, the issue was far more complex. Santa Anna had come to power as a social liberal, but as has happened again and again in Latin American politics, the populist quickly became dictatorial once in office. He was enthusiastically supported by the Texas settlers, for he promised them generous freedoms and near autonomy as a northern Mexican state, but he came to regard them as rebels, insurrectionists, and greedy invaders (as indeed a few of them were) once he was in power. Most of the Texans were quite willing to remain under lax Mexican rule but became incensed by what they came to see as high-handed broken promises and, indeed, treachery. From our viewpoint it looks as though a settlement should have been easy to broker, but an excess of pride on both sides led to war instead, and despite the bitter defeat at the Alamo the Texans won their fight for independence in 1836. Santa Anna did not change his spots: The United States secretly brought him out of Cuban exile and restored him to Mexican leadership in the 1840s, upon his promise to sell California to our government. Once in power he reneged on the secret agreement, and a war ensued in which the territory-hungry United States took the land it could not buy. Mexico sued for peace upon the U.S. invasion of Mexico City, and upon a token payment of a multimillion-dollar bribe to Santa Anna, California and most of the modern Southwest was annexed. An opportunist who fancied himself a New World Napoleon, Santa Anna headed Mexican governments no fewer than eleven times. Many good histories tell his tale, including William C. Davis's *Three Roads to the Alamo,* Randy Roberts and James S. Olson's *A Line in the Sand: The Alamo in Blood and Memory,* and John Charles Chasteen's *Born in Blood and Fire: A Concise History of Latin America.*
3. Quoted in Dillman, *The Cow Boy Handbook,* 200.
4. Ibid., 104
5. Dobie, quoted in "Did Cowboys Really Sing?"
6. Ramon Adams, *The Old Time Cowhand,* quoted in "Did Cowboys Really Sing?"
7. E. C. Abbot, *We Pointed Them North,* quoted in "Did Cowboys Really Sing?"
8. Siringo, *A Texas Cowboy,* 59, 81.
9. Quoted in Dillman, *The Cow Boy Handbook,* 104.
10. The phrase "art song" is adapted from classical music—the "art song" (Lied or Lieder in German) was a short-form wedding of a lyric poem from the height of German Romanticism to a short piece of classical music and was "consummated with . . . artistry by Franz

Schubert and his successors, notably Robert Schumann and Johannes Brahms," according to Machlis in *The Enjoyment of Music* (70–71). It flourished largely because of the increasing popularity of the piano, which allowed such pieces to be played and sung in homes as well as concert halls. This all took place in the mid-1800s, but the concept of the art song has lived on in classical and semi-classical music. "Home on the Range," with its sweeping melody and its self-consciously poetic lyrics, certainly qualifies as an example that has passed into folk and popular music.

11. Logsdon, "The Cowboy's Music Not Always G Rated," *Historical Review*.
12. Peter Stanfield, "Dixie Cowboys and Blue Yodels: The Strange History of the Singing Cowboy," in Bunscombe and Pearson, eds., *Back in the Saddle Again*, 96.
13. Cohen, liner notes to JEMF LP–109.

## Chapter 3

1. Cohen, liner notes to JEMF LP–109, 14–15.
2. Quoted in Fowler and Crawford, *Border Radio*, 83.
3. Ibid., 84.
4. Coltman, "Carson Robison."
5. Logsdon, Jacobson, and Rogers, *Saddle Serenaders*, 36.
6. It would be interesting to know on what Allen based his claim to be the original singing cowboy; it would be more fascinating yet to discover who first used the phrase "singing cowboy" at all. Gene Autry's 1936 film *The Singing Cowboy* certainly solidified the meaning and the usage, but clearly the term was in use earlier. Dick Foran's publicity buildup of 1935 called him the screen's new singing cowboy, and Margaret Larkin's pioneering song collection, *Singing Cowboy*, was published in 1931.
7. Rattray, with Cartwright, 10.
8. Griffis, *Stuart Hamblen*, 4.
9. White, John I. *Old Time Music* 11, 19.
10. Ibid., 7.
11. Autry, interview by Oatman.
12. "The Siree Peaks" is Gail Gardner's "Sierry Petes," which is more commonly known as "Tying Knots in the Devil's Tail," or some variant thereof. The "Sierry Petes" is the local nickname for the Sierra Prieta Mountains of northern Arizona.

13. Dwight Butcher untitled manuscript, Country Music Foundation Library and Media Center archives, Nashville, 54.
14. Robert K. Oermann and Mary A. Bufwack, "Patsy Montana and the Development of the Cowgirl Image," in Kingsbury, ed., *The Country Reader*, 81.
15. Atchison interview.
16. Ibid.
17. Ibid.
18. Oermann and Bufwack, "Patsy Montana," 82.
19. Atchison interview.
20. Ibid.
21. Quoted in Daniel, "Ranch Romance of Louise Massey," 41.

## Chapter 4

1. Lee DeDette Hill Taylor, "Billy Hill Story," quoted in Tinsley, *Cowboy Has to Sing*, 229.
2. Griffis, *Hear My Song*, 134.
3. Ibid., 148.
4. Don Miller, *Hollywood Corral*, 147.
5. Tuska, *Filming of the West*, 404.
6. Roy Whitley, interview by author.
7. Bob Nolan, interview by author.

## Chapter 5

1. Rainey, *The Shoot-Em-Ups Ride Again*, 31.
2. Tuska, *The Vanishing Legion*, 3.
3. Tuska, *Filming of the West*, 408.
4. Ibid., 271.
5. Ibid., 292.
6. Ibid., 280.
7. Tuska, *The Vanishing Legion*, 184.
8. Ibid., vii.
9. Rothel, *The Singing Cowboys*, 141.
10. Jolley, "Interview."
11. Quoted in Hurst, *Republic Studios*, 195.
12. Fernett, *Hollywood's Poverty Row*, 81.
13. Hurst, *Republic Studios*, 17.
14. Zolotow, *Shooting Star*, 252.
15. Autry, interview by Oatman.
16. Autry, with Herskowitz, *Back in the Saddle Again*, 33.
17. Rothel, *The Singing Cowboys*, 23.
18. Arthur E. Satherley, interview by author, for the Country Music Foundation Library and Media Center Oral History Project, Los Angeles, June 27, 1974.
19. Autry, interview by Oatman.

20. Tuska, *The Vanishing Legion,* 156.
21. Ibid.
22. Autry, interview by Oatman.
23. Rothel, *The Singing Cowboys,* 23.
24. Autry, with Herskowitz, *Back in the Saddle Again,* 38.
25. Gene Autry, TCA Press Tour interview, 20, undated, author's files.
26. Autry, interview by Oatman.
27. Quoted in Stanfield, "Dixie Cowboys," 104.

## Chapter 6

1. Until a copy of his birth certificate surfaces, some confusion will remain regarding Autry's given middle name. His official story always listed Orvon Gene Autry as his full name, and this indeed is the name engraved on his tombstone. However, his high school yearbook and a long profile in the *Dallas Times Herald* indicate Grover as the middle name. To confuse things further, his personnel records at the Frisco Railroad indicate Gordon as the middle name (and 1906 as Autry's birth year!), as does Johnny Bond's unpublished manuscript "Champion." I have chosen to go with the evidence of the high school yearbook, which has been verbally confirmed by the Autry business office in Studio City, California.
2. Autry, with Herskowitz, *Back in the Saddle Again,* 167.
3. Ibid., 13.
4. Marvin interview.
5. Autry, with Herskowitz, *Back in the Saddle Again,* 13.
6. Marvin interview.
7. Autry, with Herskowitz, *Back in the Saddle Again,* 14.
8. Marvin interview.
9. Autry, with Herskowitz, *Back in the Saddle Again,* 15.
10. Autry, interview by Oatman.
11. Autry, "Three Pals."
12. Ibid.
13. Quoted in Sherman, *Legendary Singing Cowboys,* 24.
14. Adams and Rainey, *Shoot-Em-Ups,* 89.
15. Autry, with Herskowitz, *Back in the Saddle Again,* 63. Page numbers of subsequent quotes from this source are noted in parentheses in the text.
16. Tuska, *Filming of the West,* 455–456.
17. Autry, with Herskowitz, *Back in the Saddle Again,* 97.

18. Autry interview, TCA press conference, 24.
19. Autry, with Herskowitz, *Back in the Saddle Again,* 168.
20. Quoted in Rothel, *The Gene Autry Book,* 213.
21. Autry, with Herskowitz, *Back in the Saddle Again,* 102.

## Chapter 7

1. Karl Thiede, "The Bottom Line: Low Finance in the Reel West," in Smith and Hulse, eds., *Don Miller's Hollywood Corral,* 413, 420.
2. Stanfield, "Dixie Cowboys," 110.
3. Cotterman, "The Foran Accent," 42.
4. Copeland, "Jack Randall," 16.
5. Lamparski, *Whatever Became Of . . . ? Tenth Series,* 158.
6. Tucker, "Fred Scott," 20.
7. Scott, "Interview," 3–4.
8. Lamparski, *Whatever Became Of . . . ? Tenth Series,* 158.
9. Whitley, interview by author, May 10, 1974.
10. Richard W. Bann, "Cut to the Chase: Sagebrush Short Subjects," in Smith and Hulse, *Don Miller's Hollywood Corral,* 474.
11. Holland, *B Western Actors Encyclopedia,* 294.
12. O'Neal, *Tex Ritter,* 9.
13. Ibid., 18.
14. Bond, *The Tex Ritter Story,* 21.
15. Ibid., 45.
16. Monogram Bulletin #827, August 22, 1938, Edward Finney Collection, Autry Museum of Western Heritage, Los Angeles.
17. Copeland, *The Bob Baker Story,* 31.
18. Tuska, *Filming of the West,* 420, 421.
19. Ibid., 421.
20. Copeland, *The Bob Baker Story,* 15.
21. George W. Weeks, Dispatch #58, August 30, 1938, 5; and Dispatch #49, June 2, 1938, 4, Edward Finney Collection, Autry Museum of Western Heritage, Los Angeles.
22. Don Miller, in Smith and Hulse, *Don Miller's Hollywood Corral,* 155.
23. R. L. Williams, "He Wouldn't Cross the Line," 90.
24. Saimpson, *Blacks in Black and White,* 63.
25. Ibid.
26. Everson, *Pictorial History,* 148.
27. R. L. Williams, "He Wouldn't Cross the Line," 90.
28. Jordan Young, *Spike Jones off the Record,* 78.
29. Ibid., 106.
30. Bond, *The Tex Ritter Story,* 56.

31. Satherley, interview by author.
32. Autry, interview by Oatman.
33. Satherley, interview by author.
34. Tuska, *Filming of the West,* 400.
35. Whitley, interview by author, May 10, 1974.
36. Rogers and Evans, with Stowers, *Happy Trails,* 68, 68–70.
37. Griffis, *Hear My Song,* 82.
38. Satherley, interview by author.

## Chapter 8

1. Rogers and Evans, with Stowers, *Happy Trails,* 101, 105.
2. Phillips, *Roy Rogers,* 29.

## Chapter 9

1. Adams and Rainey, *Shoot-Em-Ups,* 169.
2. Don Miller, in Smith and Hulse, *Don Miller's Hollywood Corral,* 136.
3. *Variety,* March 15, 1939, 18.
4. Rainey, "Art Davis," 17.
5. Ibid., 18

## Chapter 10

1. Bond, *Champion,* 72
2. Rothel, *The Singing Cowboys,* 219.
3. Ibid., 214.
4. "Detour" brings up an interesting point: Covers, as we'll see time and again, were an established practice in the music industry of the time—in those not so personality-driven days, consumers would often come into their local record store requesting the song, not necessarily by any particular artist. If a song by an artist on one record label showed promise of breaking out into a hit, competing labels rushed their artists into the studios to record a version of the song, to "cover" it, hence the term "cover version" or "cover." So Tuttle's recording of "Detour" on Capitol hit the charts on March 9, 1946. The following week Spade Cooley's Columbia recording (probably the biggest seller of the lot) and Foy Willing's Decca version were added to the *Billboard* charts. Elton Britt recorded the tune with a big band and had it released by Victor in May of that year, and all four versions were Top Five records. These charts also heavily reflected jukebox play, which may have been even less discriminating.
5. Travis, *Recollections of Merle Travis, Part 1,* 107.
6. Rothel, *The Singing Cowboys,* 195–196.
7. Dean interview, June 24, 1975.
8. Ibid.
9. Jack Kerouac, *On the Road* (New York: Penguin Books, 1999), 233.
10. Nye, "'40s Cowboy Star."
11. Ibid.
12. J. Hall, "Ken Curtis."
13. McAlpine, "Our Own Buck Page."
14. Quoted in Dan Forte, "Pro's Reply."
15. Case, *Mountain Broadcast and Prairie Recorder,* December 1944, 17–18.
16. Willing interview.
17. Ibid.
18. The image of the singing cowboy in Mexican cinema is an interesting one, for although Guizar was a romantic singing charro very much patterned after the Autry image, the greatest charro of them all, Pedro Infante, presented a vastly different image. With *Ay, Jalisco no te rajes!* in 1941, he began a long career as an ultraromantic singing charro; large record sales matched his screen success. Another in that vein was Jorge Negrete, whose powerful, supple voice is eerily reminiscent of Eddie Dean's. But as has been noted, the lowly cowboy was not a revered figure in Mexican culture and indeed was considered an undignified day laborer, no more romantic than a truck farmer or a construction worker. The charro was a gaudily dressed aristocrat, in direct contrast to the man of the people that Autry, Rogers, and Ritter personified. Other than the recurring successes of Zorro, the image of the heroic aristocrat never played well north of the border.
19. Lamparski, *Whatever Became Of . . . ? The New Fifth Series,* 49.
20. R. Allen, *My Life,* 25, 26.
21. Ibid., 114.
22. Ibid., 10.
23. Autry, with Herskowitz, *Back in the Saddle Again,* 102–103. Autry's use of "appeared with" is interesting here, as he never literally appeared with Maynard on the set of *In Old Santa Fe.* Autry's scenes as a singer were filmed separately—probably the "screen test" he and Levine refer to—and Maynard's reaction shots were cut in to make it appear as though he was at the barn dance.

## Chapter 11

1. Elizabeth and Stephen S. Burnette to O. J. Sikes, e-mail, February 22, 1999.
2. Whitley, interview by author, March 30, 1975.
3. Ibid.
4. Jacobson, "Cowboy Camp Meetin.'"
5. Ibid., 16.
6. Staniford and Clauser, "The Story of Al Clauser," B6.
7. R. Allen, *My Life,* 13.
8. McEnery, interview by author.
9. Wakely, interview by author.
10. Horstman, *Sing Your Heart Out,* 176.

## Chapter 12

1. Autry letter to Howard.
2. Interestingly, others adopted full cowboy regalia—Hank Williams, Hank Snow, Carl Smith, Hawkshaw Hawkins, Ray Price, and others—while doing very little if any cowboy material. Snow had done a number of singing and speaking (usually to his horse) cowboy songs in the 1930s, while Williams used Bob Nolan's "Happy Cowboy" as his theme song, but their full-out thrust was contemporary country music. Lloyd "Cowboy" Copas (1913–1963) even used the name and dressed the part, but the Muskogee, Oklahoma–born entertainer recorded very little and, of his more than a dozen hits, charted none in the western style.

# Bibliography

I have listed the sources I drew on for this book in four categories: (1) books, articles, and documents; (2) record album liner notes; (3) songbooks; and (4) interviews. Many of the articles were sent to me as clippings and photocopies in my thirty years of collecting singing-cowboy materials and were from such obscure fan-generated source material that full citations of number and volume, even dates in a few cases, are now irretrievable. I hope the forgiving reader can overlook these few lapses.

## Books, Articles, and Documents

Adams, Andy. *The Log of a Cowboy: A Narrative of the Old Trail Days.* Lincoln: University of Nebraska Press, 1964.

Adams, Les, and Buck Rainey. *Shoot-Em-Ups: The Complete Reference Guide to Westerns of the Sound Era.* New Rochelle, N.Y.: Arlington House, 1978.

Allen, Bob. "Tim Spencer Helped Originate a Music Tradition." *Music City News,* February 1977, 11.

Allen, Jules Verne. *Cowboy Lore.* San Antonio: Naylor, 1933.

Allen, Rex. *My Life from Sunrise to Sunset.* Scottsdale, Ariz.: RexGarRus Press, 1989.

Amos, Jamie. "The Silvery Voiced Buckaroo." *Riders' Roundup,* November 1986, 7–9.

Anderson, W.E.A. "Roy Rogers Goes North." *Outdoor Life,* April 1966, 52–55.

Arentz, B. "Gene Autry: Businessman, Pilot." *Flying,* December 1949, 30–31, 62.

Arnold, Eddy. *It's a Long Way from Chester County.* Old Tappan, N.J.: Hewitt House, 1969.

Arnold, M. "Buckeye Buckaroo." *Photoplay,* November 1946, 45.

Asenmacher, Bob. "Fans Wonder What Happened to Duluth's Singing Cowboy." *Duluth News Tribune Herald,* February 6, 1983.

Atkins, Chet, with Bill Neely. *Country Gentleman.* Chicago: Henry Regnery, 1974.

Autry, Gene. Letter to Raymond E. Hall, September 8, 1933. Author's files.

_____. Letter to Jack Howard, February 21, 1946. Author's files.

_____. "My Partner, Champion." *TV Guide,* May 16, 1952, 4.

_____. "Sour Note." *American Magazine,* April 1947.

_____. "Three Pals." *Country Song Roundup,* June 1950, 15.

Autry, Gene, with Mickey Herskowitz. *Back in the Saddle Again.* Garden City, N.Y.: Doubleday, 1978.

Barbour, Alan. *The Thrill of It All: A Pictorial History of the B Western from the Great Train Robbery and Other Silent Classics to the Color Films of the Genre's Last Days of Glory in the 50s.* New York: Macmillan, 1971.

Becker, Joyce. "Roy Rogers, King of the Cowboys, Is Still Riding Happy Trails." *In the Know,* March 1976.

Beeman, Billy, and David Bourne. "The Wagonmasters of Knott's Berry Farm, 1955–1968." *Song of the West* 5, 3 (fall 1991): 10–12.

Berg, Charles Ramirez. *Carteles de la Epoca de Oro del Cine Mexicano.* Guadalajara: Archivo Filmico Agrasanchez, University of Guadalajara, 1998.

Bergon, Frank, and Zeese Papanikolas, eds. *Looking Far West: The Search for the American West in History, Myth, and Literature.* New York: New American Library, 1978.

Bernstein, Paul. "Happy Tales to You." *Los Angeles Magazine,* November 1979, 28–29.

Bindas, Kenneth J. "Western Mystic: Bob Nolan and His Songs." *Western Historical Quarterly* 17, 4 (October 1986): 439–456.

Birchard, Bob. "Gene Autry: Back in the Saddle Again." *Westerner,* September–October 1974, 43–46.

Bishop, Bud. "Rosalie Allen, Queen of the Yodelers." *Atmore (Ala.) Advance,* December 1, 1983, B1.

Bishop, Edwin Allen. *Memorial to Jimmie Rodgers.* Collinsville, Ill.: Dixie Publications, 1978.

Bluestone, George. "The Changing Cowboy: From Dime Novel to Dollar Film." *Western Humanities Review* 14, 3 (summer 1960): 331–337.

Bogle, Donald. *Toms, Coons, Mulattoes, Mammies, & Bucks: An Interpretive History of Blacks in American Films.* New York: Bantam Books, 1974.

Bond, Johnny. *Champion: Or, My Thirty Years with Gene Autry.* Manuscript.

———. *The Recordings of Jimmie Rodgers: An Annotated Discography.* Los Angeles: John Edwards Memorial Foundation, 1978.

———. *Reflections: The Autobiography of Johnny Bond.* Los Angeles: John Edwards Memorial Foundation, 1976.

———. *The Tex Ritter Story.* New York: Chappell Music, 1976.

———. "That's Hollywood for You." *Country Song Roundup,* February 1951, 15, 29.

Botkin, Ben. *A Treasury of Western Folklore.* New York: Crown, 1951.

Bougie-Sundin, Michelle. "Rex Allen: The Arizona Cowboy." Manuscript.

Bougie-Sundin, Michelle, and O. J. Sikes. "The Reinsmen." *Song of the West* 5, 3 (fall 1991): 6–8.

Bowen, Bill. "Meet Art Rush." *Pioneer News,* January–February 1979, 6–8.

———. "Portrait of a Pioneer: Roy Rogers." *Pioneer News,* March–April 1979, 8–10.

Boyd, Jean A. *The Jazz of the Southwest: An Oral History of Western Swing.* Austin: University of Texas Press, 1998.

Boyd, Marsha. *The Old Belleisle, Beautiful Still.* Hatfield Point, N.B.: Over the Wall Publishing, 1998.

Branson, Vickie. "Gene Autry and the Republic Records Story." *Record World,* June 4, 1977, 22, 102.

Brown, Garrett, ed. *Classic Country: The Golden Age of Country Music—The 20s through the 70s.* San Diego: Tehabi Books/Time-Life Books, 2001.

———. *Legends of Classic Country.* Richmond, Va.: Time-Life Books, 2000.

Browne, John Paddy. "Back in the Saddle Again." *Country Music Review,* January 1973, 18–19.

———. "Gene Autry, King of the Singing Cowboys." *Country Music People,* September 1979, 35–37.

Bufwack, Mary A., and Robert K. Oermann. *Finding Her Voice: The Saga of Women in Country Music.* New York: Crown, 1993.

Buscombe, Edward, and Roberta E. Pearson. *Back in the Saddle Again: New Essays on the Western.* London: BFI, 1998.

Burdo, Eleanor M. "Montana Slim Story." *Disc Collector* 12: 3–4 (n.d.).

Burton, Ozark Ed. "A Real Trouper: Tim Spencer." *Country Song Roundup,* February 1951, 24.

Butcher, Dwight. Untitled autobiography, manuscript, Country Music Foundation Library and Media Center, Nashville.

Cameron, Stella. "Wilf Carter." *Country and Western Spotlight,* July–September 1957, 8–10.

Cantwell, Robert. *When We Were Good: The Folk Revival.* Cambridge: Harvard University Press, 1996.

Canutt, Yakima, with Oliver Drake. *Stunt Man: The Autobiography of Yakima Canutt.* Norman: University of Oklahoma Press, 1979.

Cappello, Bill. "Dorothy Page: The Singing Cowgirl." *Classic Images,* June 1993, 20–22.

Carey, Harry Jr. *Company of Heroes: My Life as an Actor in the John Ford Stock Company.* Metuchen, N.J.: Scarecrow Press, 1994.

Carman, Bob, and Dan Scapperotti. *Rex Allen: The Arizona Cowboy.* N.p., 1982.

———. *The Western Films of Monte Hale.* N.p., n.d.

Carr, Jeff. "Yodeling . . . A Dead Art?" *Country Music World,* April 29–May 12, 1981, 16–17

Carr, Patrick, ed. *The Illustrated History of Country Music.* New York: Doubleday, 1979.

Carson, Gerald. *The Roguish World of Dr. Brinkley.* New York: Reinhart, 1960.

Cary, Diana Serra. *The Hollywood Posse: The Story of the Gallant Band of Horsemen Who Made Movie History.* Boston: Houghton Mifflin, 1975.

Case, Floy. "Red River Dave: Texas' Own Cowboy Star. *Mountain Broadcast and Prairie Recorder,* November 1946, 18–19.

———. "The Sons of the Pioneers." *Mountain Broadcast and Prairie Recorder,* March 1945, 18–19, 27.

Cawelti, John G. *Adventure, Mystery, and Romance: Formula Stories as Art and Popular Culture.* Chicago: University of Chicago Press, 1976.

———. *The Six-Gun Mystique.* Bowling Green, Ohio: Popular Press, 1975.

Chase, F. "Radio's Richest Cowboy." *Radio Guide* 17 (1939): 4.

Ciesla, Sunny. "Andy Parker and the Plainsmen." *National Hill-billy News,* November–December 1947, 2.

Clapham, Walter C. *The Movie Treasure: Western Movies—The Story of the West on Screen.* London: Octopus Books, 1974.

———. "Why the Western?" *Persimmon Hill* 9, 2 (1979): 9–21.

Clark, Kenneth S. *Cowboy Sings: Songs of the Ranch and Range.* New York: Paull-Pioneer Music, 1932.

Coffey, Kevin. "The Tune Wranglers: Texas Swing in the 1930's." *Journal of the American Academy for the Preservationn of Old-Time Country Music,* December 1997, 6–7.

Cole, Lillian J. "Boys 'Don't Dig' Pop's Music: Tex Ritter Visits Saginaw." *Saginaw (Mich.) News,* January 27, 1966.

Collura, Joe. "Dialogue with 'Ranger' Bob Allen." *Under Western Skies,* January 1983, 30–35.

Coltman, Robert. "Carson Robison, First of the Rural Professionals." *Old Time Music,* summer 1978, 5–13, 27.

———. "The Roots of the Country Yodel: Notes toward a Life History." *John Edwards Memorial Foundation Quarterly,* summer 1976, 91.

Cook, Elaine. *History of the Chuckwagons of the West.* N.p. (1999?).

Coolidge, Dane. *Texas Cowboys.* New York: Dutton, 1937.

Cooper, Texas Jim. "The Real Tex Ritter." *Western Film Collector,* 2, 5 (November 1974): 2–11.

———. "The Story of Tex Ritter." *Pictorial History of Country Music* 3 (1970): 56–61.

———. "Tex Ritter: Friendship Was Always His Hole Card." *Country Rambler,* March 10, 1977, 21–23.

Copeland, Bobby J. *The Bob Baker Story.* Oak Ridge, Tenn.: BoJo Enterprises, 1997.

———. *B-Western Boot Hill: A Final Tribute to the Cowboys & Cowgirls Who Rode the Saturday Matinee Movie Range.* Madison, N.C.: Empire Publishing, 1999.

———. *Five Heroes.* Oak Ridge, Tenn.: BoJo Enterprises, 1999.

———. "Jack Randall: In Retrospect." *Westerns and Serials* 34 (1995): 16–18.

———. "On the Film Festival Trail with Eddie Dean." *Under Western Skies,* 1988, 5–10.

———. "Rex." *Wrangler's Roost* 81 (1987): 1–2.

———. *Trail Talk.* Madison, N.C.: Empire Publishing, 1996.

———. "A Tribute to John 'Dusty' King." *Westerns and Serials* 47 (1987): 28–29.

———. *The Whip Wilson Story.* Oak Ridge, Tenn.: BoJo Enterprises, 1998.

Corneau, Ernest. "A Salute to Gene Autry." *Classic Film Collector* 47 (summer 1975): 28.

Cotterman, Dan. "The Foran Accent." *Horse and Rider,* May 1974, 36–37, 39–42.

"Cowboy in Clover." *Time,* August 18, 1947, 89.

"Cowboy Radio Program Guide." *Cowboy Music World,* 1945: 13–14.

"Cowboy Tycoon." *Newsweek,* January 6, 1974.

"Cowboy with Sex Appeal." *Photoplay,* November 1941, 64.

Crafton, Donald. *The Talkies: American Cinema's Transition to Sound, 1926–1931.* New York: Scribner's, 1996.

Csida, Joseph, and June Bundy. *American Entertainment: A Unique History of Popular Show Business.* New York: Watson-Guptill, 1978.

Cusic, Don. *Cowboys and the Wild West: An A–Z Guide from the Chisholm Trail to the Silver Screen.* New York: Facts on File, 1995.

———. *Eddy Arnold: I'll Hold You in My Heart.* Nashville: Rutledge Hill Press, 1997.

Daniel, Wayne. "The Ranch Romance of Louise Massey and the Westerners." *Journal of Country Music* 20, 3: 37–41.

Dary, David. *Cowboy Culture: A Saga of Five Centuries.* Lawrence: University Press of Kansas, 1989.

———. "How Cowboy Songs Came to Be." *Persimmon Hill* 26, 1 (spring 1998): 60–64.

Daugherty, Frank. "Singing Western." *Christian Science Monitor Magazine,* April 29, 1944, 89.

Davenport, Gene. "The Sons of the Pioneers: Half a Century on the Tumbleweed Trail." *Song of the West,* summer 1990, 14–17.

Davidson, M. "Are They Going to Be Headed Off at the Pass?" *TV Guide,* December 8, 1962, 10.

Davis, Paul. "Elton Britt." *Country Music People,* February 1976, 28–29.

Delehanty, T. "Cowboy in the Velvet." *Photoplay,* November 1944, 47.

Dellar, Fred, with Roy Thompson and Douglas B. Green. *The Illustrated Encyclopedia of Country Music.* London: Salamander Books, 1977.

Delmore, Alton. *Truth Is Stranger Than Publicity: Alton Delmore's Autobiography.* Nashville: Country Music Foundation Press, 1977.

Dempsey, Mary A. "The Bronze Buckaroo Rides Again." *Michigan History Magazine* 81, 2 (March–April 1997): 10–17.

Derr, Mark. *The Frontiersman: The Real Life and the Many Legends of Davy Crockett.* New York: Morrow, 1993.

DeWitt, Karen. "Cowboy Music Lives On." *USA Today,* July 23, 1983, 7A.

Dick, Bernard F. *The Merchant Prince of Poverty Row: Harry Cohn of Columbia Pictures.* Lexington: University Press of Kentucky, 1993.

"Did Cowboys Really Sing?" Program notes, "Cowboy Songs and Range Ballads," Cody, Wyo., April 5–7, 1991.

Dillman, Bruce. *The CowBoy Handbook.* Kansas City: Lone Prairie Publishing, 1994.

DiMeglio, John E. *Vaudeville U.S.A.* Bowling Green, Ohio: Popular Press, 1973.

Dimmit, Richard Bertrand. *A Title Guide to the Talkies: A Comprehensive Listing of 16,000 Feature-Length Films from October 1927 until December 1963.* London: Scarecrow Press, 1965.

Dippie, Brian W., and James H. Nottage. *West-Fever.* Los Angeles: Autry Museum of Western Heritage, 1998.

Distal, Dave. "The Good Guy in the White Hat." Gene Autry press kit material. Author's files.

Dobie, J. Frank. "Versos of the Texas Vaqueros." *Texas Folklore Society Publication* 4 (1925): 30–43.

Dodge, Tom. "Happy Trails to a Western Goddess." *Dallas Morning News,* February 18, 2001.

"Double Mint Ranch." *Time,* January 15, 1940, 47–48.

Downey, Linda, and Ron Downey. "Under Western Skies: Rex Allen." *World of Yesterday,* July 1976, 15.

Duffy, Don. "Biography of Don Duffy, PKA Buck Page." Manuscript. Author's files.

"Eddie Dean: The Golden Voiced Cowboy." *Rustic Rhythm,* August 1957.

Edwards, Don. *Classic Cowboy Songs.* Salt Lake City: Gibbs Smith, 1994.

Epstein, Dena J. *Sinful Tunes and Spirituals: Black Folk Music to the Civil War.* Urbana: University of Illinois Press, 1977.

"Ernest Tubb." *Yesterday* 7: 9–11.

Evans, James. *Prairie Farmer and W.L.S.: The Burridge D. Butler Years.* Urbana: University of Illinois Press, 1969.

Everson, William K. *A Pictorial History of the Western Film.* Secaucus, N.J.: Citadel Press, 1969.

———. "Sixty-Six-Year Saga of the Horse Opera." *New York Times Magazine,* April 14, 1963, 74–75.

Eyles, Allen. *The Western.* London: A. Zwemmer, 1967.

Fenin, George N., and William K. Everson. *The Western: From Silents to the Seventies.* New York: Grossman, 1973.

Fernett, Gene. *Hollywood's Poverty Row: 1930–1950.* Hollywood: Coral Reef Productions, 1973.

———. "Nat Levine, Founder of Mascot." *Classic Film Collector* 20 (spring 1968): 40, 63.

———. *Next Time Drive off the Cliff!* Cocoa, Fla.: Cinememories Publishing, 1968.

———. "When Republic Hit the Skids." *Classic Film Collector* 52 (fall 1976): 45–46.

Fife, Austin E., and Alta S. Fife. *Cowboy and Western Songs: A Comprehensive Anthology.* New York: Clarkson N. Potter, 1969.

———. *Heaven on Horseback: Revivalist Songs and Verse in the Cowboy Idiom.* Logan: Utah State University Press, 1970.

"The Films of the Three Mesquiteers." *Favorite Westerns* 14 (1983): 32–33.

Finger, Charles J. *Frontier Ballads.* Garden City, N.Y.: Doubleday, Page, 1927.

———. *Sailor Chanteys and Cowboy Songs.* Girard, Kans.: Haldeman-Julius, 1923.

Finney, Edward. "The Making of a Star." *Classic Film Collector* 48 (fall 1975): 11, 39.

Fitzgerald, Michael G. *Universal Pictures: A Panoramic History in Words, Pictures, & Filmographies.* New Rochelle, N.Y.: Arlington House, 1977.

Fletcher, Curley. *Songs of the Sage.* Salt Lake City: Gibbs M. Smith, 1986.

Forbis, William H. *The Old West: The Cowboys.* New York: Time-Life Books, 1973.

Forsythe, Wayne. "Gene Autry, America's Great Singing Cowboy, Part 1." *Country Song Roundup,* January 1978, 28–30.

———. "Gene Autry, America's Great Singing Cowboy, Part 2." *Country Song Roundup,* February 1978, 16–17.

Forte, Dan. "Pro's Reply: Don Duffy." *Guitar Player,* May 1978, 6.

Fowler, Gene, and Bill Crawford. *Border Radio.* Austin: Texas Monthly Press, 1987.

"Foy Willing and the Riders of the Purple Sage." *Barn Dance Magazine,* September 1947, 18.

Frantz, Joe B., and Julian Ernest Choate. *The American Cowboy: The Myth and the Reality.* Norman: University of Oklahoma Press, 1955.

Furnas, J. C. *Stormy Weather: Crosslights on the Nineteen Thirties, An Informal History of the U.S. in 1929-1941.* New York: Putnam's, 1977.

Garfield, Brian Wynne. *Western Films: A Complete Guide.* New York: Rawson Associates, 1982.

Garner, Joe. "Magazines Promote Music, Nostalgia of Cowboy Culture." *Rocky Mountain News,* December 26, 1990.

Gelatt, Roland. *The Fabulous Phonograph: From Tin Foil to High Fidelity.* Philadelphia: Lippincott, 1955.

"Gene Autry: Warrior." *Movie-Radio Guide,* October 1943, 16-17.

"Gene Autry's Story." *Disc Collector,* April-May-June 1952, 3-4.

"Gene Autry's Story." *Disc Collector,* July-August-September 1952, 20-21.

"Gene Autry's Unusual Collection." *TV Guide,* January 9, 1953.

George-Warren, Holly. "The Singing Cowboy as Everlasting Everyman." *New York Times,* January 25, 1998.

George-Warren, Holly, and Michelle Freedman. *How the West Was Worn.* New York: Abrams, 2001.

Giddins, Gary. *Bing Crosby: A Pocketful of Dreams. The Early Years 1903-1940.* Boston: Little, Brown, 2001.

Gilbert, Douglas. *American Vaudeville: Its Life and Times.* New York: Whittlesey House, 1940.

Gill, Ted. "'Hopalong Cassidy' Pictures Are Turned Out in Two Weeks." *Nashville Tennessean,* January 10, 1943.

Ginell, Cary. *Milton Brown and the Founding of Western Swing.* Urbana: University of Illinois Press, 1994.

Glenn, Wayne. "Forgotten after Twenty Years: Jimmy Long." *John Edwards Memorial Foundation Quarterly,* summer 1973, 116-117.

Goodman, Mark. "The Singing Cowboy." *Esquire,* December 1975, 154-155, 240-248.

Graham, Don. *Cowboys and Cadillacs: How Hollywood Looks at Texas.* Austin: Texas Monthly Press, 1983.

Graham, Philip. *Showboats: The History of an American Institution.* Austin: University of Texas Press, 1951.

Green, Archie. "Dobie's Cowboy Friends." *John Edwards Memorial Foundation Quarterly,* spring 1976, 21-29.

Green, Douglas B. "Gene Autry: Public Cowboy Number One." *Journal of the American Academy for the Preservationn of Old-Time Country Music* 1, 1 (1991): 20-21.

_____. "The Singing Cowboy: An American Dream." *Journal of Country Music* 7, 2 (May 1978): 4-61.

_____. "The Singing Cowboy in American Culture." *Heritage of Kansas* 9, 4: 3-9.

_____. "The Sons of the Pioneers: 45 Years on the Singing Trail." *Persimmon Hill* 8, 4 (1978): 32-41.

Greenbaum, L. "Sinatra in a Sombrero." *New York Times Magazine,* November 4, 1945.

Griffis, Ken. "The Eddie Dean Story." *John Edwards Memorial Foundation Quarterly,* summer 1972, 63-69.

_____. *Hear My Song: The Story of the Celebrated Sons of the Pioneers.* Los Angeles: John Edwards Memorial Foundation, 1977.

_____. "The Ken Maynard Story." *John Edwards Memorial Foundation Quarterly,* summer 1973, 67-69.

_____. *Reinsmen: Painters of the West in Song.* Northglenn, Colo.: Norken Publishing, 1997.

_____. *Sons of the San Joaquin: The Songs, the Music, the Men.* Northglenn, Colo.: N.p., 1999.

_____. *Stuart Hamblen: Cowboy, Poet, Songwriter, Storyteller, Evangelist, Husband, and Father.* Thornton, Colo.: N.p., 1999.

_____. "The Tex Williams Story." *John Edwards Memorial Foundation Quarterly,* spring 1979, 5-9.

Hake, Theodore L., and Robert D. Cauler. *Sixgun Heroes: A Prince Guide to Movie Cowboy Collectibles.* Des Moines: Wallace-Homestead, 1976.

Hall, Claude. "Old Cowboys Never Die." *Tune-in,* January 1984, 16-17.

Hall, John. "Ken Curtis." *Wrangler's Roost,* September 1991, 1-2.

Hall, Wade. *Hell-Bent for Music: The Life of Pee Wee King.* Lexington; University Press of Kentucky, 1996.

Hamm, Charles. *Yesterdays: Popular Song in America.* New York: Norton, 1979.

Hansen, Terrence L. "Corridos in Southern California." *Western Folklore* 18 (July 1959): 203-232.

Harper, Mr. "After Hours: Falling Idol." *Harper's,* January 1950, 99-100.

Harris, Charles W., and Buck Rainey. *The Cowboy: Six-Shooters, Songs, and Sex.* Norman: University of Oklahoma Press, 1976.

Haslam, Gerald W. *Workin' Man Blues: Country Music in California.* Berkeley and Los Angeles: University of California Press, 1999.

Hauck, Richard Boyd. *Davy Crockett: A Handbook.* Lincoln: University of Nebraska Press, 1982.

Healy, Bob. "The Beverly Hillbillies." *Country Directory* 3 (1962): 30–31.

Hearne, Will Roy. "Who's Who in Folk Music: The Sons of the Pioneers." *Disc Collector,* April–May–June 1951, 4–13.

Heide, Robert, and John Gilman. *Box Office Buckaroos: The Cowboy Hero from the Wild West Show to the Silver Screen.* New York: Abbeville Press, 1989.

"Here Comes Roy Rogers." *TV Guide,* December 28, 1951–January 3, 1952, 8.

Hersey, Harold. *Singing Rawhide: A Book of Western Ballads.* New York: George H. Doran, 1926.

Heyne, Eric, ed. *Desert, Garden, Margin, Range: Literature on the American Frontier.* New York: Twayne, 1992.

Hines, John. "Nolan Is Gone, but His Music Will Never Die." *San Antonio Express-News,* June 27, 1980.

Hoeptner, Fred G. "Country or Western—It's a Choice of Words." *Country and Western Jamboree* 4, 1 (summer 1958): 36–38.

Holland, Ted. *B Western Actors Encyclopedia: Facts, Photos, and Filmographies for More Than 250 Familiar Faces.* Jefferson, N.C.: McFarland, 1989.

Hopper, Lawrence. *Bob Nolan: A Biographical Guide & Annotations to the Lyric Archive at the University of North Carolina Chapel Hill.* Bergenfield, N.J.: N.p., 2000.

Horstman, Dorothy. *Sing Your Heart Out, Country Boy: Classic Country Songs and Their Inside Stories by the People Who Wrote Them.* New York: Dutton, 1975.

Horwitz, James. "In Search of the Original Singing Cowboy." *Rolling Stone,* October 25, 1973, 32–34, 36, 38.

———. *They Went Thataway.* New York: Dutton, 1976.

Houston, Mack A. "The Story of a Man Named Tex." *Western Trails,* July–August 1975, 6–13.

Hughes, Carol. "Gene Autry Rides Back to the Top." *Coronet,* June 1951, 89–93.

Hurst, Richard Maurice. *Republic Studios: Between Poverty Row and the Majors.* Metuchen, N.J.: Scarecrow Press, 1979.

Jacobson, William. "Bill Miller: True Singer of the West." *Song of the West* 7, 3 (fall 1993): 8–10.

———. "A Cowboy Camp Meetin' with Ken Carson." *Song of the West* 5, 1 (spring 1991): 17.

———. "Cowboy Troubadour from Texas." *Song of the West* 5, 1 (spring 1991): 6–11.

———. "Fiddling around with 'Doc' Denning." *Song of the West* 4, 1 (spring 1990): 7–9

———. "Gary McMahan: Music, Mountains, and Horses." *Song of the West* 4, 2 (summer 1990): 8–13.

———. "Hi Busse & the Riders of the Purple Sage." *Song of the West* 7, 1 (spring 1993): 20

———. "Ian Tyson: A Canadian Songwriter of Today. *Sons of the Pioneers Historical Society* 3, 3 (fall 1989): 16–17.

———. "Joey Miskulin: Accordion Player, Record Producer, and Cow-Polka King." *Song of the West* 6, 3 (fall 1992): 10.

———. "Katie Lee." *Song of the West* 6, 3 (fall 1992): 6–7.

———. "Muzzie Braun and the Boys: Sons of Idaho." *Song of the West* 6, 2 (summer 1992): 8–10.

———. "New Mexico's Michael Martin Murphey." *Song of the West* 6, 1 (spring 1992): 8–10.

———. "Rusty Richards: Singer, Songwriter, Horseman, and All Around Good Guy." *Song of the West* 7, 1 (spring 1993): 8–10.

———. "Sourdough Slim: Time Warp Cowboy." *Song of the West* 7, 1 (spring 1993): 4–5

———. "Wiley Jim Pheiffer and the Pheiffer Brothers." *Song of the West* 8, 1 (spring 1994): 9–10.

James, E. "Paradox on Horseback." *Screenbook,* September 1939, 78.

"Jimmy Wakely." *245 Well Known Songs,* winter 1947, 9, 25.

Johannsen, Albert. *The House of Beadle and Adams and Its Dime and Nickel Novels: The Story of a Vanished Literature.* Norman: University of Oklahoma Press, 1950.

Johnson, Alva. "Tenor on Horseback." *Saturday Evening Post,* September 2, 1939, 18.

Joseph, Henry. "Gene Autry: Nice Guys Finish First." *Country Gentleman,* winter 1980, 12–14, 21, 77–78.

Joseph, Tony. "Buck Page: Ventura Musician Adds Notes to a Long and Colorful Career." *Ventura County (Calif.) Star Free Press,* June 1, 1984, B1.

Kahn, Gordon. "Lay That Pistol Down." *Atlantic,* April 1944, 105–108.

Katz, Ephraim. *The Film Encyclopedia.* New York: Perigee Books, 1982.

Kelton, Elmer. "A Westerner's Point of View: In Defense of the Singing Cowboy." *Persimmon Hill* 7, 3 (1977): 70–73.

Kendall, Pete. "Smith Ballew Remembers Bix and Big Bands." *Texas Music* 1, 2 (June 1976): 36–40.

Kent, Cindy. "Foy Willing." *Music City News,* August 1976, 20.

_____. "Smokey Rogers." *Music City News,* August 1976, 18–19.

Kienzle, Rich. "Bob Wills." *Journal of the American Academy for the Preservationn of Old-Time Country Music,* February 1993, 8–11.

_____. "Merle Travis." *Journal of the American Academy for the Preservationn of Old-Time Country Music,* April 1992, 12–13.

_____. "Milton Brown." *Journal of the American Academy for the Preservationn of Old-Time Country Music,* June 1992, 16–17.

_____. "Red Foley." *Journal of the American Academy for the Preservationn of Old-Time Country Music,* December 1992, 12–16.

_____. "Spade Cooley." *Journal of the American Academy for the Preservationn of Old-Time Country Music,* April 1992, 18–19.

_____. "Tex Tells Tall Tales." *Country Music* 5, 7 (April 1977): 9, 61.

"King of the Cowboys." *Newsweek,* March 8, 1943.

Kingsbury, Paul, ed. *Country: The Music and the Musicians—Pickers, Slickers, Cheatin' Hearts & Superstars.* New York: Abbeville Press, 1988.

_____. *The Country Reader.* Nashville: Country Music Foundation Press/Vanderbilt University Press, 1996.

_____. *The Encyclopedia of Country Music: The Ultimate Guide to the Music.* New York: Oxford University Press, 1998.

Kingsley, K. "With Open Hearts." *Photoplay,* December 28, 1951, 2, 83.

Kinkle, Roger D. *The Complete Encyclopedia of Popular Music and Jazz, 1900–1950.* New Rochelle, N.Y.: Arlington House, 1974.

Kirby, Jack Temple. *Media-Made Dixie: The South in the American Imagination.* Baton Rouge: Louisiana State University Press, 1978.

Knauth, Percy. "Gene Autry, Inc." *Life,* January 28, 1948, 90ff.

Knight, Arthur. "The Decline and Fall of the Western." *TWA Ambassador,* October 1976, 12–15.

Koon, William Henry. "The Songs of Ken Maynard." *John Edwards Memorial Foundation Quarterly,* summer 1973, 70–75.

Krohn, Lewis G. "Meanwhile down in Gower Gulch." *Films of Yesteryear,* December 1977, 4–25.

LaBadie, D. W. "The Last Roundup." *Show,* September 1962, 74.

Lahue, Kalton C. *Riders of the Range: The Sagebrush Heroes of the Sound Screen.* New York: Castle Books, 1973.

Lamparski, Richard. *Whatever Became of . . . ? The New Fifth Series.* New York: Bantam Books, 1976.

_____. *Whatever Became of . . . ? Tenth Series.* New York: Crown, 1986.

Land, Dick C. "Aristocrats of the Range." *Mountain Broadcast and Prairie Recorder,* November 1946, 5–7.

_____. "A New Star Rises in the West." *Mountain Broadcast and Prairie Recorder,* September 1946, 5–7.

_____. "Texas to Tokyo with Rifle and Guitar." *Mountain Broadcast and Prairie Recorder,* December 1946, 5–9, 34.

Larkin, Margaret. *Singing Cowboy: A Book of Western Songs.* New York: Knopf, 1931.

Lee, Katie. *Ten Thousand Goddam Cattle: A History of the American Cowboy in Song, Story, and Verse.* Flagstaff, Ariz.: Northland Press, 1977.

Lingenfelter, Richard E., Richard A. Dwyer, and David Cohen. *Songs of the American West.* Berkeley and Los Angeles: University of California Press, 1968.

Lofaro, Michael A., ed. *Davy Crockett: The Man, the Legend, the Legacy, 1786–1986.* Knoxville: University of Tennessee Press, 1985.

Logsdon, Guy. "The Cowboy's Music Not Always G Rated." *Historical Review.*

_____. "*The Whorehouse Bells Were Ringing*" and *Other Songs Cowboys Sing.* Urbana: University of Illinois Press, 1989.

Logsdon, Guy, William Jacobson, and Mary Rogers. *Saddle Serenaders.* Salt Lake City: Gibbs Smith, 1995.

Lomax, John A. *Adventures of a Ballad Hunter.* New York: Macmillan, 1947.

_____. *Cowboy Songs and Other Frontier Ballads.* New York: Sturgis and Walton, 1910.

_____. *Songs of the Cattle Trail and Cow Camp.* New York: Macmillan, 1919.

Lomax, John A., and Alan Lomax. *American Ballads and Folk Songs.* New York: Macmillan, 1934.

Loppnow, Ray. "Monte Hale: The Prince of the Plains." *Under Western Skies* 11: 13, 66.

Lumpkin, Ben Gray, with Norman L. McNeil.

*Folksongs on Records.* Denver: Allen Swallow, 1950.

Machlis, Joseph. *The Enjoyment of Music: An Introduction to Perceptive Listening.* New York: Norton, 1955.

Magers, Alan Boyd. "Out of the Past and Riding High: Rex Allen." *Country Style* 5 (October 1976): 64, 65.

Magers, Boyd. "Fred Scott on Fred Scott." *Under Western Skies,* 1993, 39–41.

Mahar, William J. *Behind the Burnt Cork Mask: Early Blackface Minstrelsy and Antebellum American Popular Culture.* Urbana: University of Illinois Press, 1999.

Malone, Bill C. *Country Music U.S.A.: A Fifty-Year History.* Austin: University of Texas Press, 1969.

———. *Don't Get above Your Raisin': Country Music and the Southern Working Class.* Urbana: University of Illinois Press, 2002.

———. *Singing Cowboys and Musical Mountaineers: Southern Culture and the Roots of Country Music.* Athens: University of Georgia Press, 1993.

Malone, Bill C., and Judith McCulloh, eds. *Stars of Country Music: From Uncle Dave Macon to Johnny Rodriguez.* Urbana: University of Illinois Press, 1975.

Mare, Frank A. "Recordings of the Authentic Cowboys." *Old Time Music,* spring 1973, 20–21.

Martin, P. "Cincinnati Cowboy." *Saturday Evening Post,* January 1945, 26ff.

Mathis, Jack. *Republic Confidential: Volume 1—The Studio.* Barrington, Ill.: Jack Mathis Advertising, 1999.

———. *Republic Confidential: Volume 2—The Players.* Barrington, Ill.: Jack Mathis Advertising, 1992.

McAlpine, Ken. "It's Our Own Buck Page." *Ventura County (Calif.) and Coast Reporter,* April 24, 1986, 1, 4.

McCloud, Barry. *Definitive Country: The Ultimate Encyclopedia of Country Music and Its Performers.* New York: Berkley Publishing Group, 1994.

McClure, Arthur F., and Ken D. Jones. *Western Films: Heroes, Heavies, and Sagebrush.* Cranbury, N.J.: A. S. Barnes, 1972.

McCuen, Brad. "Bill Boyd and His Cowboy Ramblers Discography." *Country Directory* 3 (1962): 15–21.

McDonald, Archie. *Shooting Stars: Heroes and Heroines of Western Films.* Bloomington: Indiana University Press, 1987.

McDonald, Elizabeth. "Robert Clarence Nobles." Manuscript. Author's files.

McDowell, Bart. *The American Cowboy: In Life and Legend.* Washington, D.C.: National Geographic Society, 1972

McLoughlin, Denis. *Wild & Woolly: An Encyclopedia of the Old West.* New York: Doubleday, 1975

McMahan, Gary. *Gary McMahan in Poetry and Song.* Wheat Ridge, Colo.: Record Stockman Press, 1997.

McNeil, W. K. "Elton Britt, the Kid with the Fiddle." Manuscript. Author's files.

McWilliams, Carey. *North from Mexico: The Spanish-Speaking People of the United States.* Philadelphia: Lippincott, 1949.

Melaragni, Janet. "Ray Whitely: Rootin', Tootin', Singin' Star." *Pickin','* January 1979, 40–41.

Metzger, S. S. "A Day with the Round-Up." *Pacific Monthly,* June 1911.

Meyer, William R. *The Making of the Great Westerns.* New Rochelle, N.Y.: Arlington House, 1979.

Michaels, Ken. "Wait Up, Gene." *Chicago Tribune Magazine,* May 28, 1967, 18.

Miles, Eileen. "Topekan Saw TV Programs in 1932." *Topeka Daily Capitol,* April 6, 1952, 22A.

Miller, Don. *Hollywood Corral.* New York: Popular Library Press, 1976.

Miller, Douglas T., and Marion Nowak. *The Fifties: The Way We Really Were.* New York: Doubleday, 1977.

Miller, Lee O. *The Great Cowboy Stars of Movies & Television.* New Rochelle, N.Y.: Arlington House, 1979.

Mitchell, Lee Clark. *Westerns: Making the Man in Fiction and Films.* Chicago: University of Chicago Press, 1996.

Montana, Patsy, and Jane Frost. *Patsy Montana.* Jefferson: McFarland & Co., 2002.

"Monty Hale" *[sic]. Barn Dance Magazine,* September 1947, 19.

Moore, Ethel, and Chauncey O. Moore. *Ballads and Folk Songs of the Southwest: More than 600 Titles, Melodies, and Texts Collected in Oklahoma.* Norman: University of Oklahoma Press, 1964.

Moore, Thurston, ed. *Pictorial History of Country Music.* Vols. 1–4. Denver: Heather Enterprises, 1969–1971.

Mora, Carl J. *Mexican Cinema: Reflections of a Society, 1896–1988.* Berkeley: University of California Press, 1982.

Morgan, James. "Conversations with the Cowboy King." *TWA Ambassador,* October 1976, 16–18, 38, 40, 42.

Morris, Edward. "Warner Western's Jeffries Rides Again: New Hat Caps Pioneering Star's Career." *Billboard,* June 3, 1985.

Morris, Georgia, and Mark Pollard. *Roy Rogers:*

*King of the Cowboys.* San Francisco: Collins, 1994.

Munden, Kenneth. "A Contribution to the Psychological Understanding of the Cowboy and His Myth." *American Image* 15, 2 (summer 1958): 103–147.

Nareau, Bob. *The Real Bob Steele & a Man Called Brad.* Mesa, Ariz.: Da-Kine Publishing, 1991.

Nelson, William F. "The Roughriders, or the Jimmy Wakely Trio." *Song of the West* 6, 2 (summer 1992): 14–16.

Nicholls, Nick. "James Newill." *Classic Images.*

Nolan, Bob. Letter to Douglas B. Green, undated (1979).

Nye, Doug. "'40s Cowboy Star 'Giant' of Nice Guy." *Columbia (S.C.) State Record,* August 27, 1994.

_____. "The Tougher Side of Roy Rogers." *Nashville Tennessean,* July 12, 1998.

Nye, Douglas E. *Those Six-Gun Heroes.* Spartanburg: ETV Endowment of South Carolina, 1982.

Ohrlin, Glenn. "Glenn Ohrlin: Cowboy Singer." *Sing Out!* May 1975, 40–44.

_____. *The Hell Bound Train: A Cowboy Songbook.* Urbana: University of Illinois Press, 1973.

Okuda, Ted. *Grand National, Producers Releasing Corporation, and Screen Guild Lippert.* Jefferson, N.C.: McFarland, 1989.

_____. *The Monogram Checklist: The Films of Monogram Pictures Corporation, 1931–1952.* Jefferson, N.C.: McFarland, 1987.

O'Neal, Bill. *Tex Ritter: America's Most Beloved Cowboy.* Austin: Eakin Press, 1998.

O'Neal, Bill, and Fred Goodwin. *The Sons of the Pioneers.* Austin: Eakin Press, 2001.

Oney, Steve. "The Last Roundup." *Dallas Times Herald,* November 21, 1982, 1, 5–6.

Ortega, Herbert. "The Many Faces of Eddie Dean." *Western Film Collector,* March–May 1974.

Osborne, Jerry. *55 Years of Recorded Country Western Music.* Phoenix: O'Sullivan, Woodside, 1976.

Otteson, Jan. "Rodeo Star LeDoux Is 'Real' Cowboy Singer." *Music City News,* June 1977, 29B.

Owens, William A. *Tell Me a Story, Sing Me a Song: A Texas Chronicle.* Austin: University of Texas Press, 1983.

_____. *Texas Folk Songs.* Austin: Texas Folklore Society, 1950.

Paddy-Brown, John. "Happy Trails." *Country Music People,* June 1976, 37–38.

Page, Buck. Letter to Liz Masterson, March 29, 1992. Author's files.

Paredes, Americo. *A Texas-Mexican Cancionero: Folksongs of the Lower Border.* Urbana: University of Illinois Press, 1976.

_____. *"With His Pistol in His Hand": A Border Ballad and Its Hero.* Austin: University of Texas Press, 1958.

Paris, Mike. "Gene Autry, the Singing Cowboy." *Country Music People,* December 1976, 38.

_____. "The King of the Singing Cowboys: Gene Autry." *Country Music People,* October 1973, 12–13.

Paris, Mike, and Chris Comber. *Jimmie the Kid: The Life of Jimmie Rodgers.* London: Eddison Musicbooks, 1977.

Parker, Joe. "Andy Parker and the Plainsmen." *Sons of the Pioneers Historical Society,* November 10, 1987.

_____. "Trail Dust: The Passage of Andy Parker and the Plainsmen." *Song of the West* 6, 1 (spring 1992): 16–17.

Parkinson, Michael, and Clyde Jeavons. *A Pictorial History of Westerns.* London: Hamlyn, 1972.

Parks, Jack. "Hollywood's Singing Cowboys: They Packed Guitars As Well As Six Shooters." *Country Music,* July 1973, 24–32.

Parsons, Louella. "Roy Rides Alone." *Photoplay,* April 1947, 32.

Pesta, Ben. "The Original Rhinestone Cowboy." *TWA Ambassador,* October 1976, 30–32.

Phillips, Robert W. *Roy Rogers.* Jefferson, N.C.: McFarland, 1995.

_____. *Singing Cowboy Stars.* Salt Lake City: Gibbs Smith, 1994.

Pitts, Michael R. *Western Movies.* Jefferson, N.C.: McFarland, 1986.

_____. "Western Stars on Record." *Classic Images* 76 (July 1981): 30–31.

Porterfield, Nolan. *Jimmie Rodgers: The Life and Times of America's Blue Yodeler.* Urbana: University of Illinois Press, 1979.

Pound, Louise. *Folk Songs of Nebraska and the Central West.* Lincoln: Academy of Sciences Publications 9, 3, 1915.

Powel, Bob. "The Career of Jimmy Wakely." *Country Music People,* November 1976, 30–32.

_____. "Johnny Bond: 1915–1978." *Country Music People,* August 1978, 25, 39.

_____. "Thirty Years On—And Tex Still Swings with Western Sounds." *Country Music People,* August 1977, 18, 33.

_____. "The West Coast—The Dying Face of Country Music." *Country Music People,* May 1977, 28.

Price, Deborah Evans. "Roping in Western

Consumers." *Billboard,* December 20, 1997, 101–102.

_____. "Western Music Thrives as Niche Genre." *Billboard,* December 20, 1997, 1+.

Pruett, Barbara J. *Marty Robbins: Fast Cars and Country Music.* Metuchen, N.J.: Scarecrow Press, 1990.

Pugh, Ronnie. "Elton Britt." *Journal of the American Academy for the Preservationn of Old-Time Country Music,* February 1993, 16–17.

_____. *Ernest Tubb, the Texas Troubadour.* Durham, N.C.: Duke University Press, 1996.

Ragan, David. *Who's Who in Hollywood, 1900–1976.* New Rochelle, N.Y.: Arlington House, 1976.

Rainey, Buck. "Art Davis: Prairie Pal." *Favorite Westerns,* 16–20.

_____. *The Shoot-Em-Ups Ride Again: A Supplement to Shoot-Em-Ups.* Metuchen, N.J.: Scarecrow Press.

_____. "Smith Ballew." *Screen Thrills,* 1979.

Rasky, Frank. *Roy Rogers: King of the Cowboys.* New York: Julian Messner, 1955.

Ratcliff, Sam D. "The American Cowboy: A Note on the Development of a Musical Style." *John Edwards Memorial Foundation Quarterly,* spring–summer 1984, 2–7.

Rector, Lee. "Eddie Dean." *Music City News,* August 1975, 17.

Reinhart, Ted. "George Houston . . . Underrated, Unrecognized, but Unequaled." *Western Trails* 22: 8–9.

_____. "Roy Rogers Today." *Western Trails,* January–February 1976, 11–12.

Rieger, Frank. "Mr. Eddie Dean, the Golden Cowboy." *Western Music Advocate* 8, 3 (summer 1999): 28–29.

Roberts, Randy, and James S. Olson. *A Line in the Sand: The Alamo in Blood and Memory.* New York: Free Press, 2001.

Robinson, Robert J. "A Short History of Grand National Pictures." *Films of Yesteryear* 1 (July 1977): 4–86.

_____. "A Short History of Producers Releasing Corporation." *Films of Yesteryear* 2 (December 1977): 27–84.

Rogers, Roy, and Dale Evans. *Happy Trails: Our Life Story.* New York: Simon and Schuster, 1994.

Rogers, Roy, and Dale Evans, with Carlton Stowers. *Happy Trails.* Waco: Word Books, 1979.

Rogers, Roy, Jr., with Karen Ann Wojahn. *Growing Up with Roy and Dale.* Ventura, Calif.: Regal Books, 1986.

"Rosalie Allen." *245 Well Known Songs,* December–January 1948.

Rothel, David. *The Gene Autry Book.* Madison, N.C.: WOY, 1988.

_____. *The Roy Rogers Book.* Madison, N.C.: Empire Publishing, 1996.

_____. *The Singing Cowboys.* South Brunswick, N.J.: A. S. Barnes, 1978.

_____. *Those Great Cowboy Sidekicks.* Lanham, Md.: Scarecrow Press, 1984.

"Roy Rogers as Star of New York Garden Rodeo Now Official News." *Billboard,* November 12, 1942, 3.

Russell, Don. *The Wild West, or, A History of the Wild West Shows.* Fort Worth: Amon Carter Museum of Western Art, 1970.

Russell, William. *Tumbleweed: Best of the Singing Cowboys.* Fairfax, Calif.: Western Revue Publications, 1977.

Rust, Brian. *The American Record Label Book: From the 19th Century through 1942.* New Rochelle, N.Y.: Arlington House, 1978.

Rust, Brian, and Allen G. Debus. *The Complete Entertainment Discography from the Mid-1890s to 1942.* New Rochelle, N.Y.: Arlington House, 1973.

Sackett, S. J. *Cowboys and the Songs They Sang.* New York: William R. Scott, 1967.

Sampson, Henry T. *Blacks in Black and White: A Source Book on Black Films.* Metuchen, N.J.: Scarecrow Press, 1977.

Samuelson, Dave. "WLS Barn Dance." *Journal of the American Academy for the Preservation of Old-Time Country Music,* June 1994, 12–15.

Savage, William W., Jr. *The Cowboy Hero: His Image in American History and Culture.* Norman: University of Oklahoma Press, 1979.

_____. *Singing Cowboys and All That Jazz: A Short History of Popular Music in Oklahoma.* Norman: University of Oklahoma Press, 1983.

Schlappi, Elizabeth. *Roy Acuff: The Smoky Mountain Boy.* Gretna, La.: Pelican Publishing, 1978.

Schurtz, Mary Jean. "Dick Reinhart." *Mountain Broadcast and Prairie Recorder,* November 1946:, 12–13.

Seemann, Charlie. "Cowboy Singers." *Journal of the American Academy for the Preservation of Old-Time Country Music,* February 1995, 12–15.

_____. "Gene Autry." *Journal of the American Academy for the Preservation of Old-Time Country Music,* August 1994, 8–11.

Shackford, James. *David Crockett: The Man and the Legend.* Chapel Hill: University of North Carolina Press, 1956.

Shaughnessy, Mary Alice. *Les Paul: An American Original.* New York: Morrow, 1993.

Sheldon, Ruth. *Hubbin' It: The Life of Bob Wills.* Nashville: Country Music Foundation Press, 1995.

Shelton, Robert, and Burt Goldblatt. *The Country Music Story: A Picture History of Country & Western Music.* New York: Bobbs-Merrill, 1966.

Shestack, Melvin. *The Country Music Encyclopedia.* New York: Crowell, 1974.

Shively, JoEllen. "Cowboys and Indians: Perceptions of Western Films among American Indians and Anglos." *American Sociological Review* 57 (December 1992): 725–734.

Shrum, Cal, and Ray Thigpen. *Presenting Cal Shrum and Alta Lee in the Good Old Days of Western Movies.* N.p., 1986.

Sikes, O. J. "Rex Allen's Western Recording Career." *Western Music Advocate* 10, 2 (spring 2000): 11.

_____. "Tex Ritter: One of the Really Good Guys." *Western Music Advocate* 8, 4 (fall 1999): 31.

Silber, Irwin, ed. *Songs of the Great American West.* New York: Macmillan, 1967.

Simon, George T., and Friends. *The Best of the Music Makers.* Garden City, N.Y.: Doubleday, 1979.

Siringo, Charles A. *A Cowboy Detective.* Chicago: W. B. Conkey, 1912.

_____. *A Texas Cowboy, or Fifteen Years on the Hurricane Deck of a Spanish Pony.* Lincoln; University of Nebraska Press, 1966.

Slatta, Richard W. "A Century of Cowboy History." *Persimmon Hill* 27, 3 (autumn 1999): 28–29.

_____. *The Cowboy Encyclopedia.* New York: Norton, 1994.

_____. *Cowboys of the Americas.* New Haven: Yale University Press, 1990.

Slout, William Lawrence. *Theater in a Tent: The Development of a Provincial Entertainment.* Bowling Green, Ohio: Popular Press, 1972.

Smith, H. Allen. "King of the Cowboys." *Life,* July 12, 1943, 47–54.

Smith, Henry Nash. *Virgin Land: The American West as Symbol and Myth.* Cambridge: Harvard University Press, 1950.

Smith, John M., and Tim Cawkwell, eds. *The World Encyclopedia of the Film.* New York: World Publishing, 1972.

Smith, Jon. "Gene Autry's Guitar-Playing Radio Sidekick: Johnny Bond." *Gene Autry's Friends,* spring–summer 1997, 52–58.

_____. Letters to Douglas B. Green, January 3 and January 14, 1975. Author's files.

_____. "This Is Gene Autry, for Doublemint Askin' You to Keep Thinking of Us." *Gene Autry's Friends,* spring–summer 1997, 14–23.

Smith, Packy, and Ed Hulse, eds. *Don Miller's Hollywood Corral: A Comprehensive B Western Roundup.* Burbank, Calif.: Riverwood Press, 1993.

Smith, Wally. "The Golden Age of Radio." *Song of the West* 4, 2 (summer 1990): 7.

Snow, Hank, with Jack Ownbey and Bob Burris. *The Hank Snow Story.* Urbana: University of Illinois Press, 1994.

Snyder, Jean. "Elton Britt, Remembered 20 Years Later." *Fulton County (Penna.) News,* May 7, 1992, A1, A5.

"Spade Cooley." *Barn Dance Magazine,* September 1947, 20–21.

Spivey, O. D. "Smiley (Frog Millhouse) Burnette." *Under Western Skies,* January 1978, 4–25.

Squire, Harry. "Ken Maynard, Immortal Cowboy Star." *Classic Film Collector* 56 (fall 1977): 53, 63.

Stambler, Irwin, and Grelun Landon. *Encyclopedia of Folk, Country, and Western Music.* New York: St. Martin's Press, 1969.

Stanfield, Peter. "Dixie Cowboys and Blue Yodels: The Strange History of the Singing Cowboy." In *Back in the Saddle Again: New Essays on the Western,* ed. Buscombe and Pearson. London: British Film Institute, 1998.

Staniford, Mike, and Al Clauser. "The Story of Al Clauser and Oklahoma Outlaws Reads Like Fiction." *Collinsville (Okla.) News,* January 29, 1986, B6–B7.

Stevens, George. "Gene Autry's Life Story." *245 Well Known Songs,* December–January 1950, 6–7.

Streissguth, Michael. *Eddy Arnold: Pioneer of the Nashville Sound.* New York: Schirmer, 1997.

Stricklin, Al, and Jon McConal. *My Years with Bob Wills.* San Antonio: Naylor, 1976.

"Stuart Hamblen." *Yesterday* 3 (1989): 8–9.

Swann, Thomas Burnett. *The Heroine of the Horse: Leading Ladies in Republic's Films.* South Brunswick, N.J.: A. S. Barnes, 1977.

"A Tale of Two Cowboys." *San Antonio Express,* March 4, 1977.

Taylor, Hank. "Sing Now Shoot Later." *Country Music World,* April 29–May 12, 1981, 30.

Taylor, Jay. "Montana Slim: Canada's Legendary Wilf Carter." *John Edwards Memorial Foundation Quarterly,* autumn 1977, 118–121.

Taylor, Joe, and Patty Corbett. *50 Years Together:*

*The Red Birds Remember.* Fort Wayne, Ind.: N.p., 1998.

Temple, Linda. "Hollywood Tips Its Hat to Singing Cowboy Autry." *USA Today,* September 29, 1997, 6D.

Terrace, Vincent. *Radio's Golden Years: The Encyclopedia of Radio Programs, 1930–1960.* San Diego: A. S. Barnes, 1981.

"Tex Ritter: Sagebrush Vocalizer." *Country Song Roundup,* February 1951, 24.

"Tex Williams." *245 Well Known Songs,* winter 1947, 13, 26.

Thomas, Lee. "The Pride of Plainview, Texas." *Mountain Broadcast and Prairie Recorder,* October 1946.

Thorp, Howard Jack. *Songs of the Cowboys.* Estancia, N.M.: New Print Shop, 1908.

Tinsley, Jim Bob. *For a Cowboy Has to Sing.* Orlando: University Press of Florida, 1991.

_____. *He Was Singin' This Song.* Orlando: University of Central Florida Press, 1981.

Toll, Robert C. *Blacking Up: The Minstrel Show in Nineteenth-Century America.* New York: Oxford University Press, 1974.

Tomaso, Bruce. "Tip of the Hat: Oklahoma Town Changed Its Name in 1941 to Honor Autry, but Texas Birthplace Balked." *Dallas Morning News,* October 13, 1988.

Tosches, Nick. *Country: The Biggest Music in America.* New York: Stein and Day, 1977.

_____. *Where Dead Voices Gather.* New York: Little, Brown, 2001.

Townsend, Charles. "Bob Wills' Swing Was Western, Not Country." *Persimmon Hill* 7, 1 (1977): 62–71.

_____. *San Antonio Rose: The Life and Music of Bob Wills.* Urbana: University of Illinois Press, 1976.

Traver, Jerome D., and Joel M. Maring. "Stand By: Journalistic Response to a Country Music Radio Audience." *John Edwards Memorial Foundation Quarterly,* autumn 1983, 149–161.

Travis, Merle. "Recollections of Merle Travis, 1944–1955. Part 1." *John Edwards Memorial Foundation Quarterly,* summer 1979, 107–114.

_____. "Recollections of Merle Travis, 1944–1955. Part 2." *John Edwards Memorial Foundation Quarterly,* autumn 1979, 135–143.

Tribe, Ivan. "Carolina Cotton: Hollywood's Yodeling Sweetheart." *Under Western Skies* 44: 5–8.

Tucker, Rob. "Fred Scott, the Two Gun Troubadour." *Memory Lane,* November 1, 1979, 20–21.

Tully, T. "Keep Punchin.'" *Photoplay,* September 1942, 51.

Tuska, Jon. *The American West in Film: Critical Approaches to the Western.* Westport, Conn.: Greenwood Press, 1985.

_____. *The Filming of the West: The Definitive Behind-the-Scenes History of the Great Western Movies.* Garden City, N.Y.: Doubleday, 1976.

_____. *The Vanishing Legion: A History of Mascot Pictures, 1927–1935.* Jefferson, N.C.: McFarland, 1982.

Tyler, Ron. *The Cowboy.* New York: Ridge Press, 1975.

Tyson, Ian, with Colin Escott. *I Never Sold My Saddle.* Vancouver: GreyStone Books, 1995.

Valentry, D. "A Man, a Horse, and a Guitar." *American Mercury,* January 1955, 131.

Vallee, W. L. "He Took Will Rogers Advice." *Silver Screen,* November 1939, 40.

Vaughn, Gerald F. "Autry's Songs Broke Language Barriers." *Music City News,* June 1977, 19B.

_____. "Col. W. T. Johnson: Rodeo Impresario." *Rodeo News,* May 1977, 17, 31.

_____. "Early Rodeo on Radio." *Rodeo News,* February 1977, 24, 48.

_____. "NBC's Ranch Boys." *Rodeo News,* November 1978, 20.

_____. *Ray Whitley; Country-Western Musicmaster and Film Star.* Newark, Del.: Shamrock Printing, 1973.

_____. "Ray Whitley: Singing Cowboy Deluxe." *Big Reel,* October 1978, 5, 7, 9, 11.

_____. "Ray Whitley Recalls Days with the Pioneers." *Pioneer News,* November–December 1978, 20 .

_____. "Ray Whitley's Rhythm Wranglers: Chief Rivals to Wills and Cooley in 1944–1945." *Old Time Music,* autumn 1976, 9–11, 16.

_____. "Remembering Ray Whitley." *Song of the West* 8, 1 (spring 1978): 7–8.

_____. "A Singing Cowboy's Fan Club of the 1940s and Early 1950s: Reminiscences from Ray Whitley's Fan Club Presidents." *John Edwards Memorial Foundation Quarterly,* winter 1975, 197–200.

Vaughn, Gerald F., and Douglas B. Green. "A Singing Cowboy on the Road: A Look at the Performance Career of Ray Whitley." *Journal of Country Music* 5, 1 (spring 1974): 2–16.

Wakely, Jimmy. "My Early Life." *Country Music People,* November 1976, 28–29.

Wakely, Linda Lee. *See Ya up There, Baby: The Jimmy Wakely Story.* Canoga Park, Calif.: Shasta Records, 1992.

Weed, Tumble. "It's a Big Town." *Stand-By,* January 18, 1936, 5, 13.

Weill, Gus. *You Are My Sunshine: The Jimmie Davis Story. An Affectionate Biography.* Waco: Word Books, 1977.

West, Thomas, and Hall Cannon, eds. *Buckaroo: Visions and Voices of the American Cowboy.* New York: Simon and Schuster, 1993.

Weston, Jack. *The Real American Cowboy.* New York: New Amsterdam Press, 1985.

Wheeler, Keith. *The Old West: The Townsmen.* New York: Time-Life Books, 1974.

Whitburn, Joel. *The Billboard Book of Top 40 Hits.* New York: Billboard Books, 1996.

_____. *Joel Whitburn's Top Country Singles.* Menomonee Falls, Wisc.: Record Research, 1994.

Whitcomb, Ian. *Tin Pan Alley: A Pictorial History (1919–1939).* New York: Paddington Press, 1975.

White, John I. *Git Along Little Dogies: Songs and Songmakers of the American West.* Urbana: University of Illinois Press, 1975.

Whiteside, Jonny. *Ramblin' Rose: The Life and Career of Rose Maddox.* Nashville: Vanderbilt University Press/Country Music Foundation Press, 1997.

Wilder, Alec. *American Popular Song: The Great Innovators, 1900–1950.* New York: Oxford University Press, 1972.

Williams, Nick. "The Film Career of Bob Baker." *Western Film Collector* 1, 3 (July 1973): 19–27.

Williams, Richard L. "He Wouldn't Cross the Line." *Life,* September 3, 1951, 81–82, 84, 89–91, 93–94.

Williams, W. "Singing Cowboy." *Screenbook,* August 1937, 66.

Wills, Kathy Lynn. "Johnny Western." *Song of the West* 7, 2 (summer 1977): 10–11.

_____. "Sons of the Western Soil." *Song of the West* 4, 1 (spring 1974): 6–7.

Wills, Lee Roy. "Gene Autry: My Personal View." *Western Trails,* March–April 1975, 9–11.

Wilmott, Vaun. "Jimmy Wakely: Trailblazing Outlaw Rides Shotgun with Waylon and Willie." *Country Rambler,* February 10, 1977, 45–46.

Wilson, Hugh T. "Elton Britt." *International Country Music News,* September 1992, 10.

Wolfe, Charles K. *Classic Country: Legends of Country Music.* New York: Routledge, 2001.

_____. "Girls of the Golden West." *Journal of the American Academy for the Preservation of Old-Time Country Music,* December 1992, 16–17.

_____. *The Grand Ole Opry: The Early Years, 1925–1935.* London: Old Time Music, 1975.

_____. "Red River Dave McEnery." *Journal of the American Academy for the Preservation of Old-Time Country Music,* June 1993, 16–17.

_____. *Tennessee Strings: The Story of Country Music in Tennessee.* Knoxville: University of Tennessee Press, 1977.

_____. "The Willis Brothers: The RCA Years." *Devil's Box* 42: 32–35.

Wright, Herbert. "In the Best Cowboy Tradition." *American Cowboy,* November–December 1993, 38–43.

Yoggy, Gary A. *Back in the Saddle: Essays on Western Film and Television Actors.* Jefferson, N.C.: McFarland, 1998.

_____. *Riding the Video Range: The Rise and Fall of the Western on Television.* Jefferson, N.C.: McFarland, 1995.

Young, Henry. "'Haywire Mac' Wrote 'Big Rock Candy Mountain.'" *Pictorial History of Country Music* 3 (1970): 24.

Young, J. R. "Roy Rogers." *Country Music,* July 1975, 22–27, 62, 64.

_____. "West Coast Country: Cowboys and More." *Journal of the American Academy for the Preservation of Old-Time Country Music,* June 1993, 20–23.

Young, James Harvey. *The Toadstool Millionaires: A Social History of Patent Medicines in America before Federal Regulation.* Princeton: Princeton University Press, 1961.

Young, Jordan R. *Spike Jones off the Record: The Man Who Murdered Music.* Beverly Hills: Past Times Publishing, 1994.

Zinman, David H. *Saturday Afternoon at the Bijou: A Nostalgic Look at Charlie Chan, Andy Hardy, and Other Movie Heroes We Have Grown to Love.* New Rochelle, N.Y.: Arlington House, 1973.

Zolotow, Maurice. "Hillbilly Boom." *Saturday Evening Post,* February 12, 1944, 22.

_____. *Shooting Star: A Biography of John Wayne.* New York: Simon and Shuster, 1974.

Zwisohn, Lawrence J. "Johnny Bond." *Journal of the American Academy for the Preservation of Old-Time Country Music,* October 1996, 12–15.

_____. "Roy Rogers." *Journal of the American Academy for the Preservation of Old-Time Country Music,* December 1992, 8–11.

_____. "The Sons of the Pioneers, Part One—The Early Years." *Nostalgia Monthly,* March 1978, 13–16.

_____. "The Sons of the Pioneers, Part Two—The Movie Years." *Nostalgia Monthly,* April 1978, 15–20.

# Record Album Liner Notes

Ascher, Sidney H. "Texas Jim Robertson: Tales and Songs of the Old West." Strand SL1016.

Comber, Chris. "Songs of Gene Autry." CMH 114–115.

Cooper, Texas Jim. "An American Legend." Capitol SKC–11241.

Dempsey, Peter. "Carson Robison and His Pioneers: Home, Sweet Home on the Prairie." ASV AJA 5187.

Fox, Jon Hartley. "Eddy Arnold—Cattle Call: Thereby Hangs a Tale." Bear Family BCD 15441.

Fremeaux, Patrick. "Western Cowboy Ballads & Songs." Fremeaux and Associates FA 034.

_____. "Gene Autry's Melody Ranch Radio Show." Murray Hill 897296.

George-Warren, Holly. "Gene Autry: Always Your Pal." Sony Wonder 63422.

Goldstein, Kenneth S. "The Cowboy, His Songs, Ballads, and Brag Talk." Folkways FH5723.

Gordon, Alex. "Gene Autry: The Singing Cowboy, Chapter 2." Varese Sarabande VSD 5909.

Green, Douglas B. "Cattle Call: Early Cowboy Music and Its Roots." Rounder 1101.

_____. "Don't Fence Me In: Western Music's Early Golden Era." Rounder 1102.

_____. "Saddle Up! The Cowboy Renaissance." Rounder 1104.

_____. "Sing, Cowboy, Sing." Rhino R2 72630.

_____. "Stampede! Western Music's Late Golden Era." Rounder 1103.

Griffis, Ken. "The Sons of the Pioneers." John Edwards Memorial Foundation JEMF 102.

_____. "The Sons of the Pioneers: The Teleways Transcriptions." Soundies SCD 4105.

Hilmar, Jim. "The Whippoorwills: The Standard Radio Transcription Cuts." Privately pressed.

Hoeptner, Fred G. "Authentic Cowboys and Their Western Folksongs." RCA Vintage LPV–522.

Jellystone. "Eddie Dean: 'On the Banks of the Sunny San Juan.'" Soundies SCD 4116.

_____. "Rex Allen, the Last of the Great Singing Cowboys." Soundies, Bloodshot SCD 4101.

Jones, Stan. "This Was the West." Walt Disney WDL 3033.

Kienzle, Rich. "The Best of Merle Travis." Rhino R2 70993.

_____. "Jimmy Wakely." Capitol Vintage Collections 7243–8–36591–2–8.

_____. "Tex Ritter." Capitol Vintage Collections 7243–8–36903–2–9.

Laredo, Joseph F. "Eddie Dean." Simitar 55692.

_____. "Foy Willing and the Riders of the Purple Sage." Simitar 55922.

_____. "Jimmy Wakely." Simitar 55652.

_____. "Tex Ritter." Capitol Collectors Series CDP 7–95036–2.

Logsdon, Guy. "Cowboy Songs on Folkways." Smithsonian, Folkways SF 40043.

_____. "High Noon." Bear Family BCD 15634.

McNeil, W. K., and Louis Hatchett. "Elton Britt: The RCA Years." Collectors' Choice 1486.

_____. "Elton Britt: Ridin' with Elton." Soundies SCD 4121.

Ohrlin, Glenn. "The Hell-Bound Train." Puritan 5009.

Osborne, Will. "Songs of the Pioneers." Cimarron CLP–2001.

Painter, Linda L. "Original Pioneer Trio Sings Songs of the Hills and Plains." AFM 731.

Pinson, Bob. "Bill Boyd's Cowboy Ramblers." RCA Bluebird AXM2–5503.

Pugh, Ronnie. "From the Vaults: Decca Country Classics." MCA MCAD3 11069.

Ramsay, Buck. "Herb Jeffries: The Bronze Buckaroo Rides Again." Warner Western 9 45639–2.

Rumble, John. "Red Foley." MCA MCAD 10084.

_____. "Roy Rogers." MCA MCAD 10548.

"Santa Fe Trail." Decca 8409.

Seemann, Charles. "Back in the Saddle Again." New World NW 314–315.

_____. "Tex Ritter." MCA MCAD 10188.

Sherman, Samuel M. "Legendary Singing Cowboys." Sony Music Special Products A26432.

Smith, Jon Guyot. "Bud and Joe Billings." Cattle 207.

_____. "Frank Luther and Zora Layman." Cattle 103.

_____. "Gene Autry: The Last Roundup." ASV AJA 5264.

_____. "Gene Autry with the Legendary Singing Groups of the West." Varese Sarabande VSD 5841.

_____. "The Ranch Boys: Cowboy Harmony." Cattle CCD 208.

_____. "Sing, Cowboy, Sing." Rhino R2–76230.

Spencer, Tim. "Favorite Cowboy Songs." RCA LPM 1130.

Streissguth, Michael. "Eddy Arnold: The Tennessee Plowboy and His Guitar." Bear Family BCD 15726.

Vinicur, Dale. "Americana." Bear Family BCD 15465.

_____. "Johnny Western: Heroes and Cowboys." Bear Family BCD 15 552 CI.

Wakely, Jimmy. "In Person, Jimmy Wakely." Shasta 522.

_____. "Reflections." Shasta 527.

West, Jerry. "The Essential Wesley Tuttle." BGC CD 1002.

Wolfe, Charles K. "The Civil War Music Collector's Edition." Time-Life Music R103–12.

_____. "The Essential Gene Autry, 1933–1946." Columbia CK 48957.

_____. "Treasury of the West, Volume 1 & 2." Time-Life R124 06–8.

Zwisohn, Lawrence. "Happy Trails: The Roy Rogers Collection, 1937–1990." Rhino R2 75722.

_____. "Sons of the Pioneers: Songs of the Prairie—& Roy Rogers." Bear Family BCD 15 710 EI.

_____. "Sons of the Pioneers: Tumbling Tumbleweeds—The RCA Victor Years, Vol. 1." RCA 9744 2 R.

_____. "Wagons West." Bear Family BCD 15 640 DI.

## Songbooks

"100 WLS Barn Dance Favorites." Chicago: M. M. Cole, 1935.

"Andy Parker's Songs of the Plainsmen." Hollywood: Vanguard Songs, 1948.

"The Arkansas Wood-chopper's World's Greatest Collection of Cowboy Songs with Yodel Arrangement." Chicago: M. M. Cole, 1932.

"Bill Boyd and His Cowboy Ramblers' Folio of Western Songs, No. 1." Portland, Ore.: American Music, 1939.

"Bob Atcher's Home Folks Favorites." Nashville: Acuff-Rose Publications, 1943.

"Bob Nolan's Folio of Original Cowboy Classics, No. 1." Portland, Ore.: American Music, 1939.

"Bob Nolan's Folio of Original Cowboy Classics, No. 2." Portland, Ore.: American Music, 1940.

"Bob Nolan's Sons of the Pioneer's Cowboy Songs." Hollywood: Tim Spencer Music, 1947.

"Cottonseed Clark's Brushwood Poetry and Philosophy." New York: Bourne, 1950.

"Cowboy Songs by Wilf Carter." Toronto: Gordon V. Thompson, 1935.

"Denver Darling's Western Album of Home and Country Songs." New York: Bourne, 1946.

"Dick Foran's Song Folio, Number One." Hollywood: Cross Music, 1943.

"Elton Britt's Collection of Famous Recorded Songs, Book 1." New York: Bob Miller, 1943.

"Elton Britt's Songbook." Derby: Capitol Stories, 1950.

"Fleming Allan's Folio of Bob Baker Western Songs." Portland, Ore.: American Music, 1939.

"Fred Scott's Folio of Songs of the Open Trail, No. 1." Portland, Ore: American Music, 1939.

"The Gene Autry Song Book." Los Angeles: Warner Bros. Music, 1997.

"Gene Autry's Cowboy Songs and Mountain Ballads." Chicago: M. M. Cole, 1934.

"Gene Autry's Sensational Collection of Cowboy Songs and Mountain Ballads." Chicago: M. M. Cole, 1934.

"Jerry Smith's Folio of Original Home and Range Songs, No. 1." Portland, Ore.: American Music, 1939.

"Jerry Smith's Folio of Original Home and Range Songs, No. 2." Portland, Ore.: American Music, 1941.

"Jimmy Wakely Songs of the Range." Hollywood: Fairway Music, 1946.

"Ken Maynard's Songs of the Trails." Chicago: M. M. Cole, 1935.

"Original Cowboy Songs as Sung by Tex Ann and Oklahoma Buck Nation." New York: Peer International, 1942.

"Original Songs by Zeke Clements the Dixie Yodeler." Nashville: N.p., 1942.

"Original Songs of the Pioneers, Folio No. 2." Portland, Ore.: American Music, 1939.

"Powder River Jack and Kitty Lee's Songs of the Range: Cowboy Wails of Cattle Trails." Chicago: Chart Music Publishing, 1937.

"The Ranch Boys: Songs of the Plains." Chicago: M. M. Cole, 1939.

"Ranger Doug's Songs of the Sage." Fullerton, Calif.: Centerstream Publishing, 1998.

"Red River Dave's Radio Singing Lessons and Song Book." New York: American Music, 1946.

"Red River Dave's Song Book." New York: Stasny Music, 1939.

"Rex Allen, the Arizona Cowboy." Chicago: M. M. Cole, 1945.

"Rusty Gill: Cowboy Songs and Mountain Ballads." Chicago: M. M. Cole, 1941.

"Smiley Burnette: Cowboy and Western Songs." Chicago: M. M. Cole, 1935.

"Songs Gene Autry Sings." Hollywood: Western Music, 1942.

"The Sons of the Pioneers Song Folio, No. 1." Portland, Ore.: Cross and Winge, 1936.

"Stuart Hamblen and His Lucky Stars." Chicago: M. M. Cole, 1942.

"Tex Fletcher: 'The Lonely Cowboy' Song Book. New York: Stasny Music, 1940

## Interviews

Atchison, Tex. By William Lightfoot. December 31, 1980.

Autry, Gene. By Holly George-Warren. Los Angeles, March 1997.

_____. By Mike Oatman. Los Angeles, February 14, 1983.

Boyd, Jim. By Jerry West. Dallas, March 5, 1987.

Clements, Zeke. By author, for the Country Music Foundation Library and Media Center's Oral History Project [hereafter, OHP]. Nashville, March 14, 1975.

Dean, Eddie. By author, for the OHP. Hollywood, June 24, 1975, August 2, 1974; Memphis, February 17, 1976.

Jolley, I. Stanford. "An Interview with I. Stanford Jolley." By Jim Schoenberger. *Film Collectors Registry* 6 (March 1974): 4.

Marvin, Frank. By author and Johnny Bond, for the OHP. Frazier Park, Calif., April 1, 1975.

McEnery, Red River Dave. By author, for the OHP. Nashville, May 5, 1975.

Nolan, Bob. By Betty Cox Larimer and Lee Rector. Studio City, Calif., April 28, 1976.

_____. By author. Studio City, Calif., November 28, 1979.

Ritter, Tex. "An Interview with Tex Ritter, Champion of the West." By Kathy Sawyer. *Country Music* 1, 11: 25–32.

Satherley, Arthur E. By author, for the OHP. Los Angeles, June 27, 1974, April 27, 1975.

Scott, Fred. "An Interview with Fred Scott." By Frank Matheny Jr. *Film Collector's Record* 68 (September 1976): 3–5.

Spencer, Hal. By author, for the OHP. Los Angeles, June 26, 1974.

Travis, Merle. By author, for the OHP. Nashville, October 17, 1975.

Wakely, Jimmy. By author, for the OHP. Studio City, Calif., June 25, 1974.

_____. (Sound recording, no interviewer). Studio City, Calif., June 25, 1974, February 17, 1976.

Wakely, Jimmy, and Ray Whitley. (Sound recording, no interviewer). Studio City, Calif., February 1977.

Whitley, Ray. By author, for the OHP. Nashville, May 10, 1974; Mission Hills, Calif., July 1, 1974, March 30, 1975.

_____. By Jimmy Wakely. Studio City, Calif., February 1977.

_____. (Sound recording, no interviewer). Mission Hills, Calif., March 1979.

Willing, Foy. By author, for the OHP, Nashville, December 16 and 17, 1975.

# Index

Columbia Studios *(continued)*
   *Throw a Saddle on a Star*, 248
   *Two Fisted Rangers*, 80
   *Two Rode Together*, 244
Columbus, Christopher, 9
"The Comancheros," 312
"Come and Get It," 239
Como, Perry, 82, 197
Compton, Jerry, 312, **313**
Conquerer Records, 111
*Conqueror Record Time*, 128
Consolidated Film Industries,
   111
Consolidated Film Laboratories,
   110
"Cool Water," 81, 82, 306
Cooley, Spade (Donnell Clyde
   Cooley). *See also Spade*
   *Cooley and His Orchestra*
   and Autry, Gene, 136
   *Border Outlaws*, 261
   career, 261–62
   and CBS, 294
   and Cotton, Carolina, 247
   *King of Western Swing*, 261
   and Lewis, Texas Jim, 216
   and Penny, Hank, 220
   and Ray Whitley & His Six
     Bar Cowboys, 280
   records with Sons of the
     Pioneers, 82
   *Redskins and Redheads*, 261
   *Ride, Cowboy, Ride*, 214
   and Shrum's Rhythm Rangers,
     231
   and Starrett, Charles, 199
   *Texas Panhandle*, 262
   and western swing bands, 260
Cooper, Gary, 169, 309
Cooper, James Fenimore, 1–2
Cooper, Kenny, **249**
Copeland, Bobby, 153
Corrigan, Ray "Crash," 211, **212**,
   300
Cortes, Hernan, 9
"Cosmic Cowboy," 322
Cosmopolitan Studios, 102
Costello, Lou, 152
Cotner, Carl
   and Autry, Gene, 136, 221
   and Dick Reinhart & His Lone
     Star Boys, 297
   and *The Gene Autry Show*, 146
   "The Hot Canary," 141
   "Listen to the Mocking Bird,"
     141

Cotton, Carolina (Helen
   Hagstrom), 244–47, **246**,
   **253**, 290
Cottonseed Clark (Sim Clark
   Fulk), 250, **290**, 290–91
*Country Hoedown*, 294
*Courage of the West*, 173
*Cow Camp Ballads*, 96
Coward, Buster, 284
"Cowards over Pearl Harbor,"
   300
*The Cowboy and the Señorita*, 192,
   193
"Cowboy Camp Meetin," 82
*Cowboy Canteen*, 244, **258**
*Cowboy Classics*, 82
Cowboy Crooner, 38
*Cowboy from Lonesome River*, 218
*A Cowboy Holiday*, 223
*Cowboy in the Clouds*, 248
"The Cowboy in the Continental
   Suit," 310
"Cowboy Jack," 51
Cowboy Jack, 24
"Cowboy Joe," 50
Cowboy Joe. *See* Hamblen, Stuart
"Cowboy Jubilee," 280
*Cowboy Lore*, 16, 41
"Cowboy Love Song," 30
Cowboy Loye (Loye Donald
   Pack), 26
Cowboy Max, 24
Cowboy Minstrel. *See* Hall, Ewan
*Cowboy Music World* magazine,
   293
"Cowboy Night Herd Song," 188
Cowboy Paul Groves, 293
Cowboy Poetry Gathering, 320–
   21
"Cowboy Rambler." *See* Boyd,
   Bill
Cowboy Slim Nichols, 24
Cowboy Slim Rinehart. *See*
   Rinehart, Slim
"Cowboy Song—Whoopee Ti Yi
   Yo," 21
*Cowboy Songs*, 322
*Cowboy Songs and Mountain
   Ballads*, 131
*Cowboy Songs and Other Frontier
   Ballads*, 8, 15
*Cowboy Tom's Roundup*, 26, 164
"Cowboy Yodel," 124
cowboys
   defined, 9
   as Hollywood fantasy, xvi

cowboys *(continued)*
   Mexican roots, 10, 11–12
   as musicians, 13–14
   and their mythology, 5–6
   as part of the cattle industry,
     11
   as portrayed in early radio,
     22–23
   as portrayed in Hollywood, 17
   as portrayed in literature,
     12–13
   as portrayed in Wild West
     Shows, 6–7
"The Cowboy's Christmas Ball,"
   165
"The Cowboy's Dream," 36, 41
*A Cowboy's Holiday*, 260
"The Cowboy's Lament," 15, 36,
   69
"Cowboy's Lament," 104
"The Cowboy's Wife," 43
"Cowhand's Last Ride," 38
"Cowpoke," 306
CR Ranch, 34
Crabbe, Buster, 238
Crane, Edward/Crain, Edward
   L., 50
*Crashing Thru*, 259
Craver, Charlie, 41
Crawford, Joan, 208, 269
*Crazy Waters Crystals*, 250, 279
*Creakin' Leather*, 306
Crespinell, Bill, 234
Crockett, Alan, 58
Crockett, Davy, 2–3, 10–11, 308
Crockett, John, 25
Crook, Charles, 50
Crosby, Bing (Harry Lillis
   Crosby), 71, 156, **157**
Crosby, Lou, 139–40
Cross, Hugh, 238, 250
"Cross the Brazos at Waco," 312
"Crying in the Chapel," 267
Cumberland Ridge Runners, 53
*Cupid Rides the Range*, 158
*Curley Bradley Show*, 294
Curly Clements & His Rodeo
   Rangers, 199
Curly Fox & Texas Ruby, 276,
   284
Curly Williams & His Georgia
   Peach Pickers, 220
Curt Barrett & the Trailsmen, 199
*Curt Massey Time*, 290
Curtis, Billy, 205
Curtis, Ken (Curtis Wain Gates)

# H

Hackett, James, 2
"Hadie Brown," 185, 188
Hagenbeck-Wallace Circus, 101
*Hail to the Rangers*, 218
Hale, Joanne, 242
Hale, Monte
  and Autry, Gene, 242
  *The Big Bonanza*, 240
  career, 239–42
  and comic books, **241**
  and Elliott, Bill, 240
  and Foy Willing & the Riders
    of the Purple Sage, 240
  *Giant*, 241
  *Home on the Range*, 240
  *Last Frontier Uprising*, 214
  *Man from Rainbow Valley*, 214,
    240
  and Pardner, **240**
  *The Purple Monster Strikes*, 240
  *Steppin' in Society*, 240
  *The Timber Trail*, 240
  *Trail of Robin Hood*, 241
  *The Vanishing Westerner*, 240
  and Whitley, Ray, 159, 241–42
  and Yates, Herbert J., 239
  *Yukon Vengeance*, 241
"Half as Much," 220
Hall, Ewan, 36
Hall, Harry, 76
Hall, Joanie, 287
Hall, Wendell, 32
"Hallelujah, I'm a Bum," 40
Hamblen, Stuart
  and American Record
    Corporation, 46
  and the Beverly Hillbillies, 44
  "By the Sleepy Rio Grande,"
    44
  career, 44–46
  and Carson, Ken, 282
  "It Is No Secret," 46
  "The Johnstown Flood," 44
  and Jones, Buck, **45**
  and KFWB, 293
  and Montana, Patsy, 55
  "Poor Unlucky Cowboy," 46
  "Remember Me (I'm the One
    Who Loves You)," 46
  and Satherley, Arthur E., 46
  and Sons of the Pioneers, 46
  "Texas Plains," 46
  "This Old House," 46

Hamblen, Stuart *(continued)*
  and Tuttle, Wesley, 231
  and yodeling, 44
Hammerstein, Oscar, 4
Hampton, R.W., 269, 322
"The Hanging Tree," 309
Hank Newman & the Georgia
  Crackers, 199, 220
Hank Penny & His Plantation
  Boys, 199, 220
Hanna-Barbera, 268
Hannah, Jack, 322, **324**
Hannah, Joe, 322, **324**
Hannah, Lon, 322, **324**
Hansen, Aleth, 50
Happy Hank, 39
"Happy Trails," 194
*Happy Trails Theater*, 272
"Hard Times Come Again No
  More," 4
Hardin, Ira, 178
Hardin, Tex, 60
Harding, Tex (John Thye), 218–
  19, **219**
Hardy, Oliver, 155
*Harlem on the Prairie*, 178
*Harlem Rides the Range*, 178
Harmonica Bill, 220
*Harmony Trail*, 234
Harper, Heck, 269
Harrell, Scotty, 227, 248, **251**
Harris, Phil, 208
Hart, William S., 8
Hatton, Raymond, 190
"Haunted Hunter," 43
*Haunted Ranch*, 212
*Have Gun, Will Travel*, 245, 311
"Have I Stayed Away Too Long,"
  165
"Have I Told You Lately That I
  Love You?," 139
"Have You Written Mother
  Lately?," 278
*Hawaiian Buckaroo*, 170
"Hawaiian Cowboy," 302
*Hawk Laribee*, 252
Hawks, Howard, 98–99
Hayden, Russell, 168, 209
Hayden, Sterling, 230, 269
Hayes, George "Gabby," 105–6,
  190, 292
*Hayloft Jamboree*, 64
Hays Office, 98
"Headin Back to Texas," 53
*Headin' for the Rio Grande*, 167
*Headin' North*, 99

"Hear Dem Bells," 80
*Heart of the Golden West*, 192
Hedwig Laboratories, 110
*Heldorado*, 214
Henie, Sonja, 112
"Here Comes Santa Claus," 139
Hershey, June, 154
"He's Gone up the Trail," 81
*Hiawatha*, 3
*Hidden Valley Days*, 258
"High Chin Bob," 69
"High Noon," 166, 169
*High Noon*, 168–69, 257
"High Steppin' Mama Blues,"
  127
Higley, Brewster, 6, 15
Hill, Billy (William Joseph Hill),
  71–72
Hill, George, 71
*Hillbilly Heart Throbs*, 61
"The Hills of Old Wyomin'," 165
*His Family Tree*, 175
*Hit the Saddle*, 177
Hoag, Curly, 201
"Hobo Bill's Last Ride," 127
*Hoedown*, 263
Hoeptner, Tex, **202**, 285
Hokum, Andy, 287
"Hold That Critter Down," 80
Holden, William, 81
Holly, Joe, 209
*Hollywood Barn Dance*
  and Andy Parker & the
    Plainsmen, 252
  and Bond, Johnny, 250
  and Cotton, Carolina, 247
  and Cottonseed Clark, 290
  and Curtis, Ken, 291
  and Ford, Mary, 250
  as the Grand Ole Opry of the
    West, 291
  and Grant, Kirby, 250
  and Guthrie, Jack, 301
  and KNX, 23
  and the Sunshine Girls, 250,
    292
  and Tubb, Ernest, 216
*Hollywood Canteen*, 53
Holmes, Floyd "Salty," **55**, 56, 58
Holt, Tim, 157, 159, 214, **237**
"Home in Caroline," 53
*Home in Oklahoma*, 193
"Home in San Antone," 81
*Home in San Antone*, 214
"Home on the Range"
  Beverley Hillbillies, 280